Lecture Notes in Computer Science 4877

Commenced Publication in 1973
Founding and Former Series Editors:
Gerhard Goos, Juris Hartmanis, and Jan van Leeuwen

Costantino Thanos   Francesca Borri
Leonardo Candela (Eds.)

Digital Libraries: Research and Development

First International DELOS Conference
Pisa, Italy, February 13-14, 2007
Revised Selected Papers

 Springer

Volume Editors

Costantino Thanos
Francesca Borri
Leonardo Candela
Consiglio Nazionale delle Richerche
Istituto di Scienza e Tecnologie dell'Informazione
Via Moruzzi, 1, 56124, Pisa, Italy
E-mail: {costantino.thanos,francesca.borri,leonardo.candela}@isti.cnr.it

Library of Congress Control Number: 2007940368

CR Subject Classification (1998): H.2, H.4, H.3, H.2.4, H.5

LNCS Sublibrary: SL 3 – Information Systems and Application, incl. Internet/Web
and HCI

ISSN   0302-9743
ISBN-10   3-540-77087-9 Springer Berlin Heidelberg New York
ISBN-13   978-3-540-77087-9 Springer Berlin Heidelberg New York

Springer is a part of Springer Science+Business Media

springer.com

© Springer-Verlag Berlin Heidelberg 2007

Typesetting: Camera-ready by author, data conversion by Scientific Publishing Services, Chennai, India
Printed on acid-free paper   SPIN: 12199099   06/3180   5 4 3 2 1 0

Preface

Digital libraries represent the meeting point of a large number of technical areas within the field of informatics, i.e., information retrieval, document management, information systems, the Web, image processing, artificial intelligence, human – computer interaction, mass-storage systems, and others. Moreover, digital libraries draw upon other disciplines beyond informatics, such as library sciences, museum sciences, archives, sociology, psychology, etc. However, they constitute a relatively young scientific field, whose life spans roughly the last 15 years. During these years the DELOS Network of Excellence on Digital Libraries (http://www.delos.info) has represented a constant presence aiming to contribute to the consolidation of the field.

The activities of DELOS started many years ago, with the "DELOS Working Group" at the end of the 1990s, and the DELOS Thematic Network, under the Fifth Framework Program, from 2001 to 2003. Since the beginning, the main objective of DELOS has been to advance the state of the art in the field of digital libraries by coordinating the efforts of the major European research teams conducting activities in the major fields of interest.

Every year DELOS organizes the All-Tasks meeting, the annual appointment of the DELOS community where the scientific results achieved during the previous year are presented. Instead of the usual status reports from the various DELOS Tasks, in 2006 it was decided to issue a Call for Papers, soliciting papers reporting the scientific achievements of the DELOS members during 2006, and to organize a conference. The first DELOS conference was held during February 13–14, 2007, at the Grand Hotel Continental in Tirrenia, Pisa, Italy.

The conference represented a good coverage of the 27 research tasks in DELOS, with 38 papers being presented. In addition, two invited papers: "Semantic Digital Libraries" (John Mylopoulos, University of Toronto) and "Digital Libraries: From Proposals to Projects to Systems to Theory to Curricula" (Edward Fox, Virginia Tech) completed the program. The conference was open to the larger digital library community and not just to the DELOS partners. About 120 people attended , half of whom were not from DELOS partners. We believe that this is an indication of the increased interest in digital libraries, and the recognition that the DELOS research activities have played and are playing an important role in the European digital library scene.

This volume includes extended and revised versions of the papers presented at the DELOS Conference. We believe that it should be of interest to a broad audience potentially interested in the digital library research area. It has been structured into 10 sections, corresponding to the different sessions in which the conference was structured, which in turn correspond to the major areas of research where DELOS has focussed its attention recently.

October 2007

Costantino Thanos
Francesca Borri
Leonardo Candela

Organization

General Chair

Costantino Thanos (Chair) Istituto di Scienza e Tecnologie dell'Informazione "A. Faedo" - Consiglio Nazionale delle Ricerche - Pisa, Italy

Scientific Committee

Vittore Casarosa Istituto di Scienza e Tecnologie dell'Informazione "A. Faedo" - Consiglio Nazionale delle Ricerche - Pisa, Italy

Tiziana Catarci Dipartimento di Informatica e Sistemistica "A. Ruberti" - Università di Roma "La Sapienza" - Rome, Italy

Stavros Christodoulakis Laboratory of Distributed Multimedia Information System - Technical University of Crete - Crete, Greece

Alberto del Bimbo Dipartimento di Sistemi e Informatica - Facoltà di Ingegneria University of degli Studi di Firenze - Florence, Italy

Norbert Fuhr Department of Computational and Cognitive Sciences - Faculty of Engineering Sciences of the University of Duisburg-Essen - Duisburg, Germany

Yannis Ioannidis Department of Informatics - National and Kapodistrian University of Athens - Athens, Greece

Bruno Le Dantec The European Research Consortium for Informatics and Mathematics - Sophia Antipolis, France

Liz Lyon UKOLN - University of Bath - Bath, UK

Seamus Ross Humanities Advanced Technology and Information Institute - University of Glasgow - Glasgow, UK

Hans-Jörg Schek Database & Information Systems Group - Universität Konstanz - Konstanz, Germany

Organizing Committee

Francesca Borri Istituto di Scienza e Tecnologie dell'Informazione "A. Faedo" - Consiglio Nazionale delle Ricerche - Pisa, Italy

Alessandro Launaro Istituto di Scienza e Tecnologie dell'Informazione "A. Faedo" - Consiglio Nazionale delle Ricerche - Pisa, Italy

Table of Contents

Similarity Search

Architectures

Personalization

Interoperability

Evaluation

Miscellaneous

Preservation

Video Data Management

3D Objects

Peer to Peer

MESSIF: Metric Similarity Search Implementation Framework*

Michal Batko, David Novak, and Pavel Zezula

Masaryk University, Brno, Czech Republic
{xbatko,xnovak8,zezula}@fi.muni.cz

Abstract. The similarity search has become a fundamental computational task in many applications. One of the mathematical models of the similarity – the metric space – has drawn attention of many researchers resulting in several sophisticated metric-indexing techniques. An important part of a research in this area is typically a prototype implementation and subsequent experimental evaluation of the proposed data structure. This paper describes an implementation framework called MESSIF that eases the task of building such prototypes. It provides a number of modules from basic storage management, over a wide support for distributed processing, to automatic collecting of performance statistics. Due to its open and modular design it is also easy to implement additional modules, if necessary. The MESSIF also offers several ready-to-use generic clients that allow to control and test the index structures.

1 Introduction

The mass usage of computer technology in a wide spectrum of human activities brings the need of effective searching of many novel data types. The traditional strict attribute-based search paradigm is not suitable for some of these types since they exhibit complex relationships and cannot be meaningfully classified and sorted according to simple attributes. A more suitable search model to be used in this case is *similarity search* based directly on the very data content.

This research topic has been recently addressed using various approaches. Some similarity search techniques are tailored to a specific data type and application, others are based on general data models and are applicable to a variety of data types. The *metric space* is a very general model of similarity which seems to be suitable for various data and which is the only model applicable to some important data types, e.g. in multimedia processing. This concept treats the dataset as unstructured objects together with a *distance* (or *dissimilarity*) measure computable for every pair of objects.

Number of researchers have recently focused on indexing and searching using the metric space model of data. The effort resulted in general indexing principles

* This research has been funded by the following projects: Network of Excellence on Digital Libraries (DELOS), national research project 1ET100300419, and Czech Science Foundation grant No. 102/05/H050.

C. Thanos, F. Borri, and L. Candela (Eds.): Digital Libraries: R&D, LNCS 4877, pp. 1–10, 2007.

and fundamental main-memory structures, continued with designs of disk-based structures, and also of distributed data-structures for efficient management of very large data collections. An important part of research in this area is typically a prototype implementation and subsequent experimental evaluation of the proposed data structure. Individual structures are often based on very similar underlying principles or even exploit some existing structures on lower levels. Therefore, the implementation calls for a uniform development platform that would support a straightforward reusability of code. Such a framework would also simplify the experimental evaluation and make the comparison more fair.

This reasoning led us to a development of MESSIF – The Metric Similarity Search Implementation Framework, which brings the above mentioned benefits. It is a purely modular system providing a basic support for indexing of metric spaces, for building both centralized and distributed data structures and for automatic measurement and collecting of various statistics.

The rest of the paper maps individual MESSIF components from basic management of metric data in Sections 2 and 3, over the support for the distributed processing in Section 4, to the user interfaces in Section 5. Description of each area which MESSIF supports is subdivided into three parts – the theoretical background, specific assignment for the framework (MESSIF Specification), and description of the currently available modules which provide the required functionality (MESSIF Modules). The architecture of the framework is completely open – new modules can be integrated into the system in a straightforward way.

2   Metric Space

The metric space is defined as a pair $\mathcal{M} = (\mathcal{D}, d)$, where $\mathcal{D}$ is the domain of objects and d is the total distance function $d : \mathcal{D} \times \mathcal{D} \longrightarrow \mathbb{R}$ satisfying the following conditions for all objects $x, y, z \in \mathcal{D}$: $d(x,y) \geq 0$, $d(x,y) = 0$ iff $x = y$ (*non-negativity*), $d(x,y) = d(y,x)$ (*symmetry*), and $d(x,z) \leq d(x,y) + d(y,z)$ (*triangle inequality*). No additional information about the objects' internal structure or properties are required. For any algorithm, the function d is a black-box that simply measures the (dis)similarity of any two objects and the algorithm can rely only on the four metric postulates above.

MESSIF Specification. Our implementation framework is designed to work with a generic metric space objects. The internal structure of the objects is hidden and not used in any way except for the purposes of evaluation of the metric function. In particular, every class of objects contains an implementation of the metric function applicable to the class data.

For the purposes of quick addressing, every object is automatically assigned a unique identifier *OID*. Since the metric objects are sometimes only simplified representations of real objects (e.g. a color histogram of an image), the objects also contain a URI locator address pointing to the original object – a web address of an image for instance.

MESSIF Modules. Currently, there are two basic data types with different metric functions: **Vectors** with L_p metric function, quadratic form distance and some functions from MPEG7 standard; and **Strings** with (weighted) edit distance and protein distance functions.

2.1 Collections and Queries

Let us have a collection of objects $\mathcal{X} \subseteq \mathcal{D}$ that form the database. This collection is dynamic – it can grow as new objects $o \in \mathcal{D}$ are inserted and it can shrink by deletions. Our task is to evaluate queries over such a database, i.e. select objects from the collection that meet some specified similarity criteria. There are several types of similarity queries, but the two basic ones are the range query **Range**(q, r) and the k-nearest neighbors query **kNN**(q, k).

Given an object $q \in \mathcal{D}$ and a maximal search radius r, *range query* **Range**(q, r) selects a set $S_A \subseteq \mathcal{X}$ of indexed objects: $S_A = \{x \in \mathcal{X} \mid d(q, x) \leq r\}$.

Given an object $q \in \mathcal{D}$ and an integer $k \geq 1$, *k-nearest neighbors query* **kNN**(q, k) retrieves a set $S_A \subseteq \mathcal{X} : |S_A| = k, \forall x \in S_A, \forall y \in \mathcal{X} \setminus S_A : d(q, x) \leq d(q, y)$.

MESSIF Specification. In MESSIF, we introduce concept of *operations* to encapsulate manipulations with a collection. An operation can either modify the collection – insert or delete objects – or retrieve particular objects from it. Every operation carries the necessary information for its execution (e.g. an object to be inserted) and after its successful evaluation on the collection it provides the results (e.g. a list of objects matching a range query). If the operation is a query, it also provides an implementation of its basic evaluation algorithm – the *sequential scan*. It is a straightforward application of the particular query definition: given a collection of objects, the operation inspect them one by one updating the result according to that particular query instance.

MESSIF Modules. At present time, MESSIF supports **insert** and **delete operations** that allow addition or removal of objects from collections. To retrieve similar objects, the basic metric-space **range**, **kNN** and **incremental kNN query operations** are available.

3 Metric Data Management

We have explained the concept of the metric-based similarity search. In this section, we will focus on efficient management and searching of metric data collections. So far, we can use the aforementioned framework modules to design a primitive data structure – it would execute the sequential scan implementation of a query on the whole collection of generic metric space objects. This works for small and static data sets, but when the data is dynamic and its volume can grow, more sophisticated effectiveness-aimed structures are needed. The framework offers additional modules to simplify the task of implementing such structures – namely the data management support, reference objects choosing (including partitioning) and the encapsulation envelope for algorithms that provides support for operation execution.

A vital part of every implementation is its performance assessment. Without any additional effort required, the framework automatically gathers many statistic values from the summarizing information about the whole structure to the details about local operation execution. In addition, every structure can define its own statistics, which can take advantage of other framework modules.

3.1 Storing the Collections

Above, we have defined the collection as the finite subset of the metric domain $\mathcal{X} \subseteq \mathcal{D}$. Practically, the collection is any list of objects of arbitrary length, which is stored somewhere, e.g. the result of any query is a collection too. Moreover, a union of two collections is also a collection and also its subset is a collection.

MESSIF Specification. The collections of objects can be stored in data areas called *buckets*. A bucket represents a metric space partition or it is used just as a generic object storage. The bucket provides methods for inserting one or more objects, deleting them, retrieving all objects or just a particular one (providing its *OID*). It also has a method for evaluating queries, which pushes all objects from the bucket to the sequential scan implementation of the respective query. Every bucket is also automatically assigned a unique identifier *BID* used for addressing the bucket. An example of a bucket is shown in Figure 1b. The buckets have

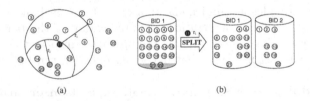

Fig. 1. Ball partitioning (a) and a bucket split (b)

usually limited capacity and MESSIF offers methods for splitting them if they overflow as depicted by the figure.

MESSIF Modules. To physically store objects, MESSIF offers **main memory** and **disk storage buckets**. The former is implemented as a linked list of objects while the latter uses block organization with a cached directory.

3.2 Partitioning the Collections

As the data volume grows, the time needed to go through all objects becomes unacceptable. Thus, we need to partition the data and access only the relevant partitions at query time. To do this in a generic metric space, we need to select some objects – we call them *pivots* – and using the distance between the pivots and the objects, we divide the collection. The two basic partitioning principles are called the *ball partitioning* and the *generalized hyperplane partitioning* [1] and they can divide a set of objects into two parts – see an example of ball partitioning in Figure 1a. Since the resulting partitions can be still too large, the partitioning can be applied recursively until all the partitions are small enough.

At query time, the metric's triangular inequality property is exploited to avoid accessing some partitions completely. All the remaining partitions are searched by the sequential scan. Even then, some distance-function evaluations can be avoided provided we have stored some distances computed during object insertion. We usually refer to this technique as the *pivot filtering* [2].

MESSIF Specification. One of the issues in the metric-space partitioning is the selection of pivots, since it strongly affects the performance of the query evaluation. There are several techniques [1] that suggests how to do the job and the framework provides a generic interface allowing to choose an arbitrary number of pivots from a particular collection (usually a bucket or a set of buckets). These pivots are usually selected so that effectiveness of a specific partitioning or filtering is maximized.

MESSIF Modules. Automatic selection of reference objects can be currently done by **random, incremental** or **on-fly pivot choosers**. The first select pivots randomly while the second uses a sophisticated and good but time-consuming method. The third is a low-cost chooser with slightly worse results.

3.3   Metric Index Structures

The previous sections provide the background necessary for building an efficient metric index structure. We have the metric space objects with the distance function abstraction, we can process and store dynamic collections of objects using operations and we have tools for partitioning the space into smaller parts. Thus, to implement a working metric index structure we only need to put all these things together. Practically all algorithms proposed in the literature, see for example surveys [3,1], can be easily built using MESSIF.

MESSIF Specification. The building of an index technique in MESSIF means to implement the necessary internal structures (e.g. the navigation tree) and create the operation evaluation algorithms. Since the buckets can evaluate operations themselves, the index must only pick the correct buckets according to the technique used and the actual internal state of the index. A MESSIF internal mechanism also automatically detect the operations implemented by an algorithm (the algorithms do not necessarily implement available operations) and also supports their parallel processing in threads.

To demonstrate the simplicity of the implementation, we provide an example of a basic Vantage Point Tree (VPT) algorithm [1]. The structure builds a binary

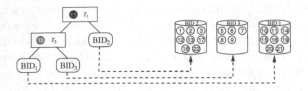

Fig. 2. Example of Vantage Point Tree structure

tree (see Figure 2), where every internal node of the tree divides the indexed data into two partitions – specifically, the ball-partitioning depicted in Figure 1a is used – and objects are stored in leaves. In MESSIF, we need to implement the inner nodes, i.e. a data structure holding a pivot and a radius. Leaf nodes are the MESSIF buckets, so no additional implementation effort is needed. Then, the insert and range query operations are implemented, but this only involves a simple condition-based traversal of the inner tree nodes. Once we reach the leaf nodes, the MESSIF bucket's processing takes over and provides the results.

MESSIF Modules. Several centralized metric indexing algorithms are implemented using MESSIF: **M-Tree** [4], **D-Index** [5], **aD-Index** and **VPT**, that can serve as an implementation tutorial.

3.4 Performance Measurement and Statistics

We have described the potential and the building blocks provided by the framework for creating index structures. However, essential part of every index is the performance statistics gathering. Statistics allow either automatic or manual tuning of the index and that can also serve during the operation-cost estimation (e.g. for a query optimizer). In the metric space, computation of the distances can be quite time demanding. Therefore, the time necessary to complete a query can vary significantly and it is also not comparable between different metric spaces. Thus, not only the time statistics should be gathered, but also the distance computations of various operations should be counted.

MESSIF Specification. Framework provides an automatic collecting of various statistics during the lifetime of an index structure – no additional implementation effort is needed. Any other statistics required by a particular index structure can be easily added. However, their querying interface is the same as for the automatic ones and they are accessible in the same way.

Specifically, every MESSIF module contains several global statistical measures. These are usually counters that are incremented whenever a certain condition occurs. For example, the *distance computations* counter is incremented when a metric function is evaluated. Moreover, other statistics can be based on the already defined ones – they can bind to an existing measure and then they will be updated every time the parent statistic is modified.

Another very important issue is the statistics gathering during evaluation of operations, e.g. queries. Even though they can be executed simultaneously, MESSIF separates the respective statistics correctly – the concept of binding is used again, but the statistics are updated only locally within an operation.

MESSIF Modules. The MESSIF automatically gathers **query operation statistics** (e.g. response time, number of distance computations, buckets accessed) **bucket statistics** (e.g. numbers of inserts/deletions in a bucket and a sum of query statistics) and whole **algorithm statistics**.

4   Distributed Data Structures

The huge amounts of digital data produced nowadays make heavy demands on scalability of data-oriented applications. The similarity search is inherently expensive and even though sophisticated dynamic disk-oriented index structures can reduce both computational and I/O costs, the similarity indexing approach requires some radical changes if a swift processing of large datasets is required.

The distributed computing provides not only practically unlimited storage capacity, but also significant augmentation of the computational power with a potential of exploiting parallelism during query processing. The Structured Peer-to-Peer Networks seem to be a suitable paradigm because of its inherent dynamism and ability to exploit arbitrary amounts of resources with respect to the size of the dataset managed by the system.

4.1   Computing Network

The objective of this part of the MESSIF platform is to provide the infrastructure necessary for the distributed data structures. The structured peer-to-peer networks consist of units (peers) equal in functionality. Each peer has a storage capacity and has access to the computational resources and to the communication interface. The concept of this basic infrastructure is depicted in Figure 3a.

The peer is identified by a unique address, and can communicate (using any underlying computer network) directly with any other peer whose address it knows. Peers can pose queries into the system. The request propagate arbitrarily through the system and some peers answer to the originator. The framework should provide support for this behavior.

MESSIF Specification. The MESSIF networking operates over the standard internet or intranet using the family of IP protocols. Individual peers are identified by the IP address plus a port number. The entire communication is based on messages using the TCP and UDP protocols.

Generally, every message originated by a peer is sent to an arbitrary number of target peers. A receiver can either forward it further or reply to the originator (or both). If the sender expects receiving some replies it generally waits for a set of peers not known at the time message emission. To support this general message propagation algorithm, each message carries information about the peers

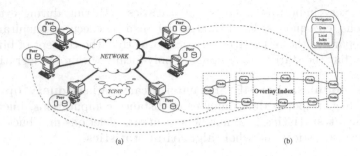

Fig. 3. The computing network (a) provides infrastructure for overlay index (b)

it wandered through. As the reply messages arrive to the sender, it can use the message paths to manage the list of peers to await a reply from. The receiver is also able to recognize when the set of responses is complete. Moreover, the computational statistics (see Section 3.4) of the processing at individual peers are collected automatically by the messages, thus overall statistics are also provided.

MESSIF Modules. The **Message** encapsulates the data and the routing information. It also carries statistics collected from the visited peers. The **Message dispatcher** module provides the message sending service using the TCP and UDP protocols. Among others, it supports pooling of the TCP connections. The management of a correct waiting for all replies to a particular request message is ensured by the **Reply receiver** module.

4.2   Peer-to-Peer Metric Structures

The modules described in the previous section form the infrastructure necessary for building peer-to-peer data structures. These distributed systems are composed of *nodes* which consist of two logical components: (1) data storage – data managed by a local index structure; (2) navigation structure – a set of addresses of nodes in the system together with routing rules. Figure 3b depicts such an overlay index and its utilization of the computing infrastructure. Every node is hosted by a physical computer that provides the CPU, the memory (volatile and persistent) and the network access. They maintain their local collections that together form the overall data volume of the whole distributed structure.

Any node can issue an operation (e.g. to insert an object) that is processed by the distributed index. The navigation mechanism is applied in order to route the operation to the nodes responsible for the respective data (e.g. a node holding the object's space partition). In these nodes, the operation is executed locally (e.g. the object is stored in the local data storage).

MESSIF Specification. The realization of the node concept in MESSIF follows its logical structure. The node's data storage can employ buckets or any centralized indexes available as MESSIF modules as defined in Section 3.1 or

3.3, respectively. Therefore, the task of processing the operations locally is inherently available within the MESSIF functionality. The core of the distributed index is thus the navigation logic. It is responsible for determining the addresses of the nodes that should be reached by a specific operation. Once known, the MESSIF communication interface is used to contact the nodes and to wait for all the responses. The navigation needs not to be direct – several rerouting steps can occur at the contacted nodes. However, the essence of every distributed navigation algorithm is its ability to determine the correct address of the requested data. Generally, the distributed structures built using MESSIF are aimed developing metric-based similarity search, but also classical distributed hash table algorithms can be implemented.

MESSIF Modules. The following peer-to-peer structures for metric data management have been implemented using MESSIF: *GHT**, *VPT**, *MCAN*, *M-Chord* [6]. Also, implementations of two distributed hash tables are available: *Chord* and *Skip Graphs* [7,8].

5   MESSIF User Interfaces

Finally, let us briefly mention the interfaces that can be used by the user to control the index structures built using MESSIF. Since all structures use the same application interface, we can control them uniformly. The designer can annotate the published parts of a newly implemented structure to provide a unified description and help texts for the structure, its parameters, operations, etc. The MESSIF can also automatically detect all operations that are supported by a specific algorithm and offer them to be used by the user. All statistics gathered by MESSIF are available to the users as well.

The MESSIF provides several user interfaces, capabilities of which vary from the most simple ones allowing the user to write commands to a simple prompt to a sophisticated graphical client, which offers comfortable manipulation with the running structure along with an easy-to-read statistics presented by graphs. In a distributed environment, the user interface (client) can connect to the peers to control them. The MESSIF also includes a special monitoring interface for distributed environment, allowing to show status of the running peers.

MESSIF Modules. The following user interfaces are currently available for MESSIF: **batch-run interface** that can execute predefined batches of operations, **telnet user interface** offering a simple command prompt, **web user interface** is a graphical applet that can connect to a running index structure, and **window user interface** which is a full-featured client with wizards and graphs for MESSIF statistics. Additionally, the **web peer monitor** allows monitoring a distributed peer-to-peer network.

6 Conclusions

The similarity search based on the metric space data-model has recently become a standalone research stream, which arouses greater and greater interest.Since we concern ourselves with this research area, we felt the need for a development platform that would make the implementation easier.We have developed a framework called MESSIF, which encapsulates the concept of the metric space in a very general way. Further, it introduces the concept of an atomic metric storage and supplies several implementations of these buckets. It provides a wide support for distributed data structures, especially for those based on the peer-to-peer paradigm. Various statistics are automatically collected and are available for evaluation of the structures performance. The usability of our library was confirmed by several data structures that have been successfully implemented using the MESSIF.

References

1. Zezula, P., Amato, G., Dohnal, V., Batko, M.: Similarity Search: The Metric Space Approach. Advances in Database Systems, vol. 32. Springer, Heidelberg (2006)
2. Dohnal, V.: Indexing Structures fro Searching in Metric Spaces. PhD thesis, Faculty of Informatics, Masaryk University in Brno, Czech Republic (May 2004)
3. Hjaltason, G.R., Samet, H.: Index-driven similarity search in metric spaces. In: TODS 2003. ACM Transactions on Database Systems, vol. 28(4), pp. 517–580 (2003)
4. Ciaccia, P., Patella, M., Zezula, P.: M-tree: An efficient access method for similarity search in metric spaces. In: Proceedings of VLDB 1997, August 25-29, 1997, pp. 426–435. Morgan Kaufmann, Athens, Greece (1997)
5. Dohnal, V., Gennaro, C., Savino, P., Zezula, P.: D-Index: Distance searching index for metric data sets. Multimedia Tools and Applications 21(1), 9–33 (2003)
6. Batko, M., Novak, D., Falchi, F., Zezula, P.: On scalability of the similarity search in the world of peers. In: Proceedings of INFOSCALE 2006, May 30–June 1, 2006, pp. 1–12. ACM Press, New York (2006)
7. Stoica, I., Morris, R., Karger, D., Kaashoek, M.F., Balakrishnan, H.: Chord: A scalable peer-to-peer lookup service for internet applications. In: Proceedings of ACM SIGCOMM, pp. 149–160. ACM Press, San Diego, CA, USA (2001)
8. Aspnes, J., Shah, G.: Skip graphs. In: Fourteenth Annual ACM-SIAM Symposium on Discrete Algorithms, pp. 384–393 (January 2003)

Image Indexing and Retrieval Using Visual Terms and Text-Like Weighting*

Giuseppe Amato, Pasquale Savino, and Vanessa Magionami

ISTI-CNR, Pisa, Italy
`firstname.lastname@isti.cnr.it`

Abstract. Image similarity is typically evaluated by using low level features such as color histograms, textures, and shapes. Image similarity search algorithms require computing similarity between low level features of the query image and those of the images in the database. Even if state of the art access methods for similarity search reduce the set of features to be accessed and compared to the query, similarity search has still an high cost.

In this paper we present a novel approach which processes image similarity search queries by using a technique that takes inspiration from text retrieval. We propose an approach that automatically indexes images by using visual terms chosen from a visual lexicon.

Each visual term represents a typology of visual regions, according to various criteria. The visual lexicon is obtained by analyzing a training set of images, to infer which are the relevant typology of visual regions. We have defined a weighting and matching schema that are able respectively to associate visual terms with images and to compare images by means of the associated terms.

We show that the proposed approach do not lose performance, in terms of effectiveness, with respect to other methods existing in literature, and at the same time offers higher performance, in terms of efficiency, given the possibility of using inverted files to support similarity searching.

1 Introduction

Retrieval of documents in digital libraries is obtained by either searching metadata associated with documents, or by searching the actual content of documents. In the first case, a digital library system matches the query expressed by the user against metadata produced by cataloguers, according to some specific format and schema. In the second case the query of the user is matched against the actual content of documents managed by the digital library system. This second type of search paradigm is typically referred as *content based retrieval*.

In case of textual documents, the content based retrieval paradigm is quite intuitive: words contained in a document are used to judge its pertinence to the user query [10]. On the other hand, image content base retrieval is not so obvious. In this case, image retrieval is typically obtained by comparing low level features extracted from images, such as color histograms, textures, shapes, etc. The assumption here is that if the low

---

* This work was partially supported by the DELOS NoE and the Multimatch project, funded by the European Commission under FP6 (Sixth Framework Programme).

C. Thanos, F. Borri, and L. Candela (Eds.): Digital Libraries: R&D, LNCS 4877, pp. 11–21, 2007.

level features are similar then also the corresponding images are similar [5,8,11]. In this paradigm a query consists of an image and the system is asked to search for other images similar to the query image.

Various approaches were proposed in literature that can be used for efficient image similarity search [4,1,2]. However, efficiency of image similarity techniques is currently not comparable to the efficiency provided by text based retrieval techniques, used for instance in large scale search engines such as web search engines.

In this paper, we present an approach to content based image retrieval that takes inspiration from text retrieval techniques, as in [3,12,6]: images are indexed and retrieved by means of visual terms. In our approach a *visual term* is a prototype representing a class of typical visual region that can be found in an image. Different visual terms represent different classes of regions which contain regions related according to various criteria. For instance, classes might contain (and the corresponding visual term represents) sets of regions containing very similar colors, other might contain similar textures, shapes, etc.

The set of visual terms form the *visual lexicon*. Basically, the visual lexicon is a set of prototypes of visual regions, that is a set of typical regions, which can be found in images. Ideally, the visual terms contained in the visual lexicon should be able to represent all regions that can be found in images.

An image is indexed by associating it with the set of visual terms that are judged to be contained in it. In other words, a visual terms is associated with an image if the image contains a region that can be represented by the visual term. This is similar to text indexing, where a document is associated with the set of terms it contains.

In order to realize the proposed approach there are some issues that have to be carefully considered and addressed.

1. *Visual lexicon generation*: how the set of visual terms is built and how are terms represented?
2. *Image indexing*: which visual terms are associated with an image and how we discriminate the importance of terms in an image?
3. *Image retrieval*: how image queries are matched against indexed images?

In the following, Sections 2, 3, and 4 discuss these aspects. Section 5 evaluates the proposed approach.

2   Visual Lexicon Generation

In our approach we index images by using visual terms, which in our proposal are prototypes of visual regions. We perform image retrieval by checking the co-occurrence of visual terms in the query and in the images of the database.

In order this approach to be realistic, the set of visual terms (prototypes of regions) contained in the visual lexicon should be finite and well defined. However, by applying a segmentation algorithm to a data set of images, the number of regions that will be obtained is large and the probability to have "exactly" the same region extracted in different images i close to zero. This would imply that direct use of the extracted regions as terms of the visual lexicon, would not be helpful, since the probability of finding regions co-occurring in the query and in images of the database is negligible.

Note, on the other hand, that very similar regions might play the same role and might carry the same descriptive meaning, even if they are not identical. Accordingly, we propose to group together similar regions and to represent them by representatives.

Here the approach is again similar to text indexing, where variations of the same word are represented by a word-stem (consider for instance "print", "print*ers*", "print*ing*"). In text retrieval systems there are well defined morphological rules to decide which are the terms of the lexicon. However, in our context it is not obvious what is the nature of a visual term. Intuitively, regions that play the same role have to be represented by the same visual term. Thus, we assume that visual similarity is an indication of equivalence of descriptive meaning of visual regions.

We build the visual lexicon by choosing a training set of images and by using segmentation to extract regions. We use a clustering algorithm to group together visually similar regions. The representative of each obtained cluster is a visual term.

Let us describe this process more precisely. Visual similarity of regions is judged by extracting low level features and by comparing the extracted features by means of a similarity (or dissimilarity) function. There are several low lever features that can be extracted from regions, which consider various aspects to judge the visual similarity. Choosing different features may lead to different results of the clustering algorithms. For instance, the use of color histograms groups together regions having similar colors, while the use of shape descriptors groups together regions having the same shape.

We propose to group together regions according to various features so that we obtain a *multi-feature visual lexicon* containing visual terms obtained by considering different features. The multi-feature lexicon is the union of a number of *mono-feature visual lexicons*. For instance, there will be visual terms that represent group of regions having similar shapes and terms that represent regions having similar colors. Specifically, the clustering algorithm is applied multiple times to the training set. In each application a different visual descriptor is used. Each application returns a mono-feature visual lexicon consisting of a set of prototypes representing regions that are judged to be similar, according to one visual descriptor.

In our experiments, we have used the ITI Segmentation algorithm [7] to segment the images. We used the five MPEG-7 visual descriptors [9] to represent the features extracted from regions. Finally we have used the simple k-means algorithm to cluster regions.

3   Image Indexing

Once we have a visual lexicon, we have to define how visual terms are associated with images. In principle, a visual term should be associated with an image when the image contains a region represented by the visual term.

To do that, every image is first segmented into regions and the low level features, the same used for building the visual lexicon, are extracted from them. The terms are chosen by selecting, for each extracted region, the n most similar visual terms in each mono-feature visual lexicon, where n is a parameter that can be tuned to optimize the performance of the approach. Suppose the multi-feature visual lexicon is composed of f mono-feature lexicons, each region is associated with $n \cdot f$ visual terms. The set of terms corresponding to a region can be considered as different *senses* of the region.

To consider the relevance of a visual term in an image we also give a weight to the selected visual terms. The weighting strategy that we use is again inspired to text retrieval systems and specifically to the $TF * IDF$ technique [10]. The TF factor gives the importance of a terms in the document (its frequency in text retrieval systems). The IDF factor represents the importance of a term with respect to the entire dataset (the inverse of the frequency in the dataset).

We use the same terminology used in text retrieval systems and we re-define TF and IDF according to our context. The weight (relevance) w_t^I of term t in image I is

$$w_t^I = TF_t^I * IDF_t.$$

Intuitively, the TF_t^I of term t in image I should be directly proportional to similarity between a region and the visual term, and to the size of the region in the image. In addition, it should be directly proportional to the number of regions, in the image, represented by t. This can be expressed as

$$TF_t^I = \sum_{r \in Regions(I,t)} sim(r,t) * cover(r,I),$$

where $Regions(I,t)$ is the set of regions of I that are represented by t, $sim(r,t)$ gives the similarity of region r to the visual term t, according to the low level feature of the lexicon of t, and $cover(r,I)$ is the percentage of the area covered by r in I.

The IDF_t is defined as in traditional text retrieval systems. It is the logarithm of the ratio between the dataset size N and the number n_t of images, which t is associated with:

$$IDF_t = \log_e \frac{N}{n_t}.$$

Note that this indexing schema has the property to determine the most relevant terms for an image in a given collection. Given that terms are obtained by using different low level features (color histograms, textures, shapes, etc.), an implicit outcome of this approach is that we are also able to automatically select and combine the most relevant features for a given image in a given collection.

4   Image Retrieval

As previously discussed, we suppose that a query consist of a query image I_q. The task of the search algorithm is to find the the k most similar images to the query image. In our proposal we obtain this by appositively matching the visual terms associated with the query image and those associated with the images in the database.

In order to realize this retrieval schema, the image I_q is first indexed as described in previous section. The similarity between an image I of the dataset and the query image I_q is then obtained by matching the terms respectively associated.

More specifically, we use the vector space model [10] for doing that. In the vector space mode, every indexed document is associated with a vector of weights W. The vector contains an element for each term of the lexicon. Each element of the vector contains the weight (relevance) of the term for the document. The weight of a term is 0 if the term is not associated with the document.

In our case, documents are images, terms are visual terms, and the weights in the vectors are determined as discussed in previous section. Similarity between two images I_1, I_2 is computed as the cosine of the angle α_{I_1,I_2} between the two vectors of weights W_{I_1} and W_{I_2}. This can be obtained as:

$$cos(\alpha_{I_1,I_2}) = \frac{W_{I_1} \cdot W_{I_2}}{\|W_{I_1}\| \cdot \|W_{I_2}\|}$$

This indexing schema allows using inverted files, which are widely used for efficient text retrieval, to perform image retrieval.

In our case the inverted file can be built by associating each visual term t, with a list of pairs $(I_i, w_t^{I_i})$. When the pair $(I_i, w_t^{I_i})$ occurs in the list associated with t, it means that image I_i contains the term t, and that term t has relevance $w_t^{I_i}$ in image I_i.

Various techniques are available for efficiently retrieving the k best documents using inverted files and the cosine similarity.

This, in addition to obvious efficiency advantage with respect to other access structures [4,1], has also the advantage to save memory space. In fact, with traditional techniques all features extracted by all images have to be stored somewhere to be matched against the query. In this case just the representation of the visual terms in the lexicon should be stored, along with the weights of the regions in the images with a significant reduction of required storage space.

5 Experiments

We have carried-out experiments to investigate the performance of our approach. Here we briefly report the comparisons against the use of pure MPEG-7 [9], the SIMPLIcity system [12], and KeyBlock [6]. For the comparison with the Simplicity system we have re-implemented its indexing and retrieval schema using the segmentation and feature extraction tools we have used. For the comparison with KeyBlock we have adopted their segmentation and feature extraction techniques in our system.

5.1 Comparison with MPEG-7

In this test we compared our approach, according to various settings, with the direct use of the MPEG-7 descriptors [9]. MPEG-7 offers five descriptors which take into considerations different visual aspects in an image. Each descriptor is associated with a similarity function which can be used to judge the similarity between two images according to a specific descriptor. Image retrieval can be performed by extracting a descriptor from a query image and by searching the k most similar images according to the chosen descriptor. Our objective here is to compare our proposal with the direct use of the specific MPEG-7 descriptors.

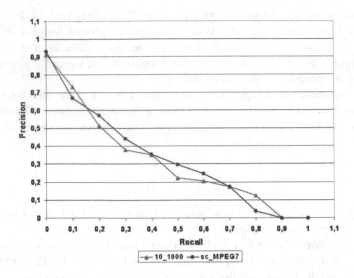

Fig. 1. Comparing our technique with use of pure MPEG-7. In our method we used a lexicon of size 1000 and each region was associated with 10 visual terms. For the MPEG-7 method we used the Scalable Color descriptor, which resulted to be the best among all descriptor, in the dataset that we used. Performance of our approach is comparable to the best MPEG-7 descriptor.

Description of the experiments. For this test we used a collection of 10000 images (a subset of the Department of Water Resources in California Collection) stored in JPEG format with size 384X256 or 256X384 containing scenes of various types. Our approach was tested using various configurations according to various sizes of the lexicon, number of senses assigned to each region (see Section 3), and descriptors used. We tested separately the various descriptors, and we also combined all descriptors together, having our indexer determine the importance of the various descriptors.

The direct use of MPEG-7 was tested using all MPEG-7 descriptors independently. Different descriptor might give different results according to different queries.

We used a TREC-like approach for executing the tests. Union of results obtained by the various configurations of our approach and by the direct use of MPEG-7 were ranked by a user and used to judge the performance of the various systems.

Experiment settings. The entire dataset was segmented using the ITI segmentation algorithm [7]. The ITI algorithm was set to extract about 10 regions from each image. From each region we extracted the five MPEG-7 visual descriptors (Scalable Color, Edge Histogram, Dominant Color, Region Shape, Homogenous Texture), by using the MPEG-7 reference software.

The regions belonging to a subset of 1000 images were used as the training set for the clustering algorithm for the generation of the visual lexicon (see section 2). Two different visual lexicons were generated. The first visual lexicon contains 100 visual terms, the second one contains 1000 visual terms. Both lexicons were separately used to index the entire dataset. More specifically, each lexicon was used to index the entire

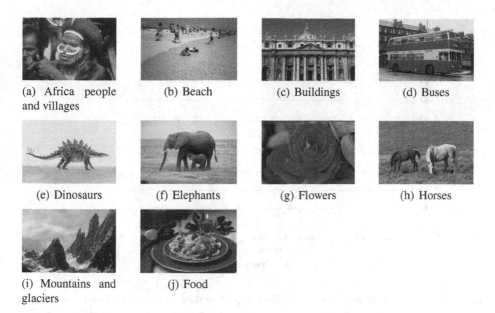

(a) Africa people and villages

(b) Beach

(c) Buildings

(d) Buses

(e) Dinosaurs

(f) Elephants

(g) Flowers

(h) Horses

(i) Mountains and glaciers

(j) Food

Fig. 2. Examples of images for each category

dataset multiple times according to different indexing parameters. The visual lexicon of size 100 was used to independently index the dataset using 1, 5, and 10 senses (see section 3) for each region. The visual lexicon of size 1000 was used to independently index the dataset using 1, 5, 50 , and 100 senses for each region. Our approach was tested by individually using the mono-feature visual lexicons and by combining the mono-feature visual lexicons in a single multi-feature lexicon (combined method). We used 15 different queries to perform the experiments. For each query, the union of the first 40 retrieved images returned by each configuration and by the pure MPEG-7 retrieval techniques is considered to be the candidate set of relevant documents. This set of documents is ranked by a user according to the relevance to the query. The obtained ranking is used to compare the various configurations of our approach and the different MPEG-7 based techniques. Precision and recall was used as a performance measure.

Results. We have observed that the combined method (the use of a multi-feature lexicon) offered better performance both in case of lexicons of size 100 and 1000. In case of lexicon of size 100 the best performance was obtained using 5 senses per regions. In case of lexicons of size 1000, the best performance was obtained with 10 senses per region. For what concerns the direct use of the MPEG-7 descriptors the best performance was obtained with the scalable color descriptor. Figure 1 shows the comparison between our combined method and the direct use of the scalable color MPEG-7 descriptor. Our method results to be almost equivalent to it. The advantage in our case is that we do not have to chose in advance the correct descriptor (scalable color in this case is the best), given that our indexing method automatically adapts the weight of the various components. In fact, the direct use of the other MPEG-7 descriptor present a performance that is much worse than the scalable color descriptor.

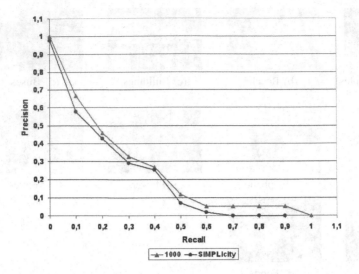

Fig. 3. Comparing our technique with Simplicity. In our method we used a lexicon of size 1000 and each region was associated with 10 visual terms. In Simplicity we used the MPEG-7 Scalable Color descriptor, which was the best among the MPEG-7 descriptors. Performance of our approach is better than SIMPLIcity applied to the best MPEG-7 descriptor.

5.2 Comparison with Simplicity

Simplicity [12] is a system that also uses region based retrieval. Our objective here is to compare Simplicity and our approach in terms of the pure indexing and retrieval functionality.

Description of the experiments. We have performed two different tests. The first is very similar to the comparison with the direct use of MPEG-7 descriptors. We have used also in this case a TREC like approach to compare the two systems. In this case the database that we have used is the COREL database.

The second test is exactly the same test executed in the Simplicity paper [12]. In this test a subset of the COREL collection with images classified in different classes was used. We measured how the two systems were able to retrieve images of specific classes.

Experiment settings. In order to perform an objective comparison we have re-implemented the Simplicity indexing and retrieval algorithms, however differently from the original Simplicity system, we have used also in our Simplicity implementation the ITI[7] segmentation tool and the MPEG-7 reference software to respectively extract region and describe them in terms of visual features.

For the first experiment we have used the entire COREL collection, consisting of about 60000 images. All images were segmented in at most 10 regions, and we used a lexicon of 1000 visual terms obtained by clustering the regions extracted from a subset of 1000 images. Indexing was performed by giving 10 senses to every visual term.

For the second experiment we used the same subset of COREL used in the Simplicity paper [12]. It consists of 1000 images classified into 10 classes. Each class contains 100 images. An example of images from each class is shown in Figure 2. Every image of the dataset was used as a query and retrieval rank of all remaining imeges was recorded. A retrieved image was considered a correct match if and only if it was in the same class of the query. The two systems were compared by computing the precision within the first 100 retrieved images. The total number of semantically related images for each query was fixed to 100, that is the size of each class. For this test we have used two different settings for segmentation. We used a fine grained segmentation that returned about 30 regions per images, and a coarse grained segmentation that returned about 10 regions per image. We have also generated two different lexicons containing respectively 100 and 1000 visual terms. In the Figure we just report the results with 1000 visual terms, which returned the best results. We used 5 senses per region with the small lexicon and 10 senses per region with the large lexicon. The Simplicity system was tested with all 5 MPEG-7 descriptor separately.

Results. Simplicity obtained the best performance by using the Scalable Color MPEG-7 visual descriptor. The result of the first test are reported in Figure 3. Here we report the comparison of our approach using the combined (multi-feature lexicon) method and Simplicity with the use of the Scalable Color. As it can be seen, our approach always outperforms Simplicity.

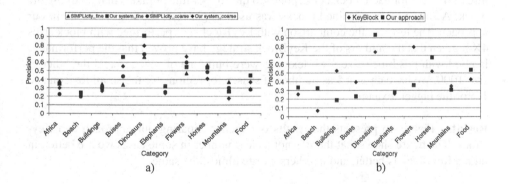

Fig. 4. Comparing our technique of weighting with SIMPLIcity and KeyBlock

The results of the second test are shown in Figure 4a. Here we compare our system and Simplicity, with the use of the Scalable Color, under various configurations.

It is evident that the result varies in correspondence of different classes. The use of a finer segmentation improves the performances in the both systems but especially in our system, with the exception of Flowers categories for which the results with coarse segmentation are better for both systems. Globally we can see that there is not a clear winner between the two systems. In some cases our approach performs better, in some cases Simplicity performs better, in others they almost overlap. However a clear advantage of our approach is that it requires much less storage memory. In fact, Simplicity in order to obtain the score of an image with respect to a query has to compute the similarity among their regions. This means that the descriptors of all regions in the database have to be maintained. In our case, given that images are described in terms of visual terms, and given that just a few visual terms are used in our tests, just the visual descriptors of such visual terms should be stored.

5.3   Comparison with Keyblock

Here we compare our approach with that used by the KeyBlock system [6]. In KeyBlock images are segmented by dividing them in blocks of the same size. RGB values of pixels that compose a block are used as features of the block itself.

Description of the experiments. In order to compare our system with keyblock we have again used the 1000 images from the COREL collection as described in previous section and we have performed the test that checks the ability to retrieve images belonging to the same collection, as discussed in previous section.

Experiment settings. Given that the KeyBlock approach strongly depends on the segmentation strategy and feature extraction, we have adopted their proposals also in our system. Thus the images were partitioned into smaller blocks of fixed size. The features extracted for each block corresponds to the RGB value of pixels that compose the block. A subset of the obtained blocks was used to generate the lexicons used in our approach. The tests for the comparison with KeyBlock was performed with block sizes 4X4, given that the authors of the KeyBlock strategy have proved that the performance is good with this block size. Two lexicons were built one of size 256 and the other of size 1000. We have chosen 5 as number of senses for regions for the small lexicon and 10 for the bigger lexicon.

Results. Figure 4b presents the results obtained comparing our approach and Key-Block. The figure shows that there is not a clear winner in some cases we are better, in others KeyBlock is better, and in others we are almost the same.

6   Conclusions

We have discussed a proposal for performing image similarity retrieval by means of techniques inspired to text retrieval. The approach is promising given the reduced space required for maintaining necessary data structures and for the possibility of using efficient techniques that have been tested in text retrieval systems. We have performed some effectiveness tests and the results seems to be comparable and sometime better than that obtained by other techniques, where much more storage space is required and less efficiency can be obtained.

References

1. Amato, G., Rabitti, F., Savino, P., Zezula, P.: Region proximity in metric spaces and its use for approximate similarity search. ACM Transactions on Information Systems (TOIS) 21(2), 192–227 (2003)
2. Ciaccia, P., Patella, M., Zezula, P.: M-tree: An efficient access method for similarity search in metric spaces. In: Jarke, M., Carey, M.J., Dittrich, K.R., Lochovsky, F.H., Loucopoulos, P., Jeusfeld, M.A. (eds.) VLDB 1997. Proceedings of 23rd International Conference on Very Large Data Bases, Athens, Greece, August 25-29, 1997, pp. 426–435. Morgan Kaufmann, San Francisco (1997)
3. Fauqueur, J., Boujemaa, N.: Mental image search by boolean composition of region categories. Multimedia Tools and Applications 31(1), 95–117 (2004)
4. Guttman, A.: R-trees: A dynamic index structure for spatial searching. In: Proceedings of the 1984 ACM SIGMOD International Conference on Management of Data, Boston, MA, pp. 47–57. ACM Press, New York (1984)
5. Hafner, J.L., Sawhney, H.S., Equitz, W., Flickner a, M., Niblack, W.: Efficient color histogram indexing for quadratic form distance functions. IEEE Transactions on Pattern Analysis and Machine Intelligence 17(7), 729–736 (1995)
6. Lei Zhu, A.Z.: Theory of keyblock-based image retrieval. ACM Trans. Inf. Syst. 20(2), 224–257 (2002)
7. Mezaris, V., Kompatsiaris, I., Strintzis, M.G.: Still image segmentation tools for object-based multimedia applications. International Journal of Pattern Recognition and Artificial Intelligence 18(4), 701–725 (2004)
8. Niblack, W., Barber, R., Equitz, W., Flickner, M., Glasman, E.H., Petkovic, D., Yanker, P., Faloutsos, C., Taubin, G.: The qbic project: Querying images by content, using color, texture, and shape. In: SPIE 1993. Proceedings of Storage and Retrieval for Image and Video Databases, pp. 173–187 (1993)
9. Salembier, P., Sikora, T., Manjunath, B.: Introduction to MPEG-7: Multimedia Content Description Interface. John Wiley & Sons, Inc., New York, NY, USA (2002)
10. Salton, G., McGill, M.J.: Introduction to Modern Information Retrieval. McGraw-Hill Book Company, New York (1983)
11. Smith, J.R.: Integrated Spatial and Feature Image Systems: Retrieval, Analysis, and compression. PhD thesis, Graduate School of Arts and Sciences, Columbia University (1997)
12. Wang, J.Z., Li, J., Wiederhold, G.: SIMPLIcity. IEEE Transactions on Pattern Analysis and Machine Intelligence 23(9), 947–963 (2001)

A Reference Architecture for Digital Library Systems: Principles and Applications

Leonardo Candela, Donatella Castelli, and Pasquale Pagano

Istituto di Scienza e Tecnologie dell'Informazione "Alessandro Faedo"
Consiglio Nazionale delle Ricerche
Via G. Moruzzi, 1 – 56124 Pisa – Italy
{candela,castelli,pagano}@isti.cnr.it

Abstract. A reference architecture for a given domain provides an architectural template which can be used as a starting point for designing the software architecture of a system in that domain. Despite the popularity of tools and systems commonly termed "Digital Library", very few attempts exist to set the foundation governing their development thus making integration and reuse of third party assets and results very difficult. This paper presents a reference architecture for the Digital Library domain characterised by many, multidisciplinary and distributed players, both resource providers and consumers, whose requirements evolve along the time. The paper validates this reference architecture by describing the structure of two current systems, DILIGENT and DRIVER, facing the problem to deliver large-scale digital libraries in two different contexts and with diverse technologies.

1 Introduction

Digital Library is a complex area where a large number of heterogeneous disciplines and fields converge. This highly multidisciplinary nature has created several conceptions of what a Digital Library is, each one influenced by the perspective of the primary discipline of the conceiver(s) [1,2,3,4,5,6]. One of the consequences of this heterogeneity is that during the last fifteen years a lot of Digital Library Systems have been pragmatically developed by specialized methodologies obtained by adapting techniques borrowed from other disciplines. This kind of approach produced very many heterogeneous entities and systems, thus rendering the interoperability, reuse, sharing, and cooperative development of digital libraries extremely difficult.

The Digital Library community recognizes these drawbacks and expresses the needs to invest in Architectures for Digital Library Systems (DLSs) and to implement generic Digital Library Management Systems (DLMSs) having all the key features that appear fundamental in supporting the entire spectrum of digital library functionality as it arises in several possible contexts [3,4]. In particular, a DLMS should incorporate functionality that is related to all generic issues as well as the generic components of all mixed issues. Moreover, its design should allow for easy integration of sub-systems supporting the specialized functionality required by each particular environment.

To speculate on this understanding, the DELOS Network of Excellence on Digital Libraries promotes an activity aiming at setting the foundations for and identifying the

C. Thanos, F. Borri, and L. Candela (Eds.): Digital Libraries: R&D, LNCS 4877, pp. 22–35, 2007.

cornerstone concepts within the Digital Library universe in order to facilitate the integration of research results and propose better ways of developing appropriate systems. The first outcome of this activity is *The Digital Library Manifesto* [7,8]. This document offers a new vision of this universe by presenting it as populated by three different "systems" and by carefully establishing the roles of these constituent "systems" and the relationships among them. The three systems are the Digital Library (DL), the Digital Library System (DLS), and the Digital Library Management System (DLMS), as depicted in Figure 1. In particular, the DL is the abstract system as perceived by end-users, the DLS emerges as the software system providing all the functionality that is required by a particular DL, while the DLMS is the software system that provides the infrastructure for producing and administering a DLS and integrates additional software offering extra functionality.

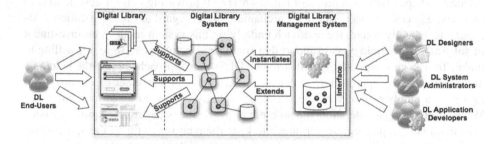

Fig. 1. DL, DLS, and DLMS: A Three-Tier Framework

To realise this idea, the Manifesto proposes to implement a series of frameworks that collectively concur to meet the initial goal, i.e. facilitate the implementation of digital library "systems". These frameworks are: (*i*) a *Reference Model*, consisting of "a minimal set of unifying concepts, axioms and relationships within a particular problem domain. It is independent of specific standards, technologies, implementations, or other concrete details" [9]; (*ii*) one or more *Reference Architectures*, containing an architectural design pattern indicating an abstract solution in implementing the concepts and relationships identified in the Reference Model; and (*iii*) one or more *Concrete Architectures*, containing additional elements that make the reference architecture more concrete; e.g. it replaces the mechanisms envisaged in the Reference Architecture with concrete standards and specifications.

This paper presents a first step toward the definition of a fully-fledged Reference Architecture for a Digital Library domain characterised by many, multidisciplinary and distributed players, both providing and consuming resources, whose requirements evolve along the time. Essentially, such first attempt of reference architecture identifies a consistent and comprehensive set of software components necessary for a DLS and the interactions between them. It acts as a blueprint for the creation and management of a DLS.

The remainder of this paper is organised as follows. Section 2 contextualises the work by providing a survey of current and past effort spent in similar tasks. Section 3 presents the reference architecture. Section 4 validates the reference architecture by describing the structure of two existing systems, namely DILIGENT and DRIVER, that rely on the reference architecture. Finally, Section 5 presents the conclusion of this work and the future research issues.

2   Related Work

In addition to the attempt presented in this paper, few other initiatives exist to tackle the definition of Digital Library architectures especially in the framework of large-scale DLSs, i.e. DLSs characterised by a huge number of distributed resources aiming at serving one or more distributed communities. One of the first attempt is represented by Dienst [10] in 1995. This DLS, developed at Cornell University, proposes tasks clearly divided and specified by a protocol based on HTTP providing helpful abstractions to its users, e.g. collections uniformly searchable without regard to objects locations. Although technically sound, the approach underlying this system requires an investment in software, methodology and support that some prospective users were not willing to make. To reach interoperability in distributed DLSs two approaches exist: the federated and the harvesting approaches. In the federated approach a number of organizations agree on a number of service specifications, usually expressed as formal standards. When establishing a federation, the problem to overcome is the effort required by each organization to implement the services and keep them current with all the agreements. For instance, many libraries have standardized on the Z39.50 protocol [11] to meet the needs for record sharing and distributed search. On the other hand, the Open Archive Initiative [12] promotes the harvesting model as the mechanism for building digital library services over archives making their metadata available through a simple and lightweight protocol. Suleman [13] proposes to extend the work of the OAI to support the inter-component interaction within a componentized DLS built by connecting small software components that communicate through a family of lightweight protocols. Gonçalves, Fox, Watson, and Kipp [14] introduced a formal framework based on five fundamental abstractions, i.e. Streams, Structures, Spaces, Scenarios, and Societies, to define digital libraries rigorously and usefully. In such a framework the architecture of DLSs is expressed in terms of services by focusing on their behavioural description (scenarios) and on the possibility to model co-operating services (structures). An exploitation of such a framework to implement DLSs is described in [15]. The JISC Information Environment (JISC IE) technical architecture[1] [16] specifies a set of standards and protocols that support the development and delivery of an integrated set of networked services that allow the end-user to discover, access, use and publish resources as part of their learning and research activities.

In parallel with the above initiatives, three systems architecture paradigms have emerged in the last years: Service Oriented Architectures, Peer-to-Peer Architectures, and Grid Infrastructures. In [17], a survey of these architectural paradigms and their exploitation in current DLSs is reported. This study aims at identifying the similarities

---

[1] JISC Information Environment Architecture
http://www.ukoln.ac.uk/distributed-systems/jisc-ie/arch/

among these paradigms as well as their distinguishing peculiarities in fulfilling the various requirements arising in the Digital Library arena. The major outcome of this study consists in the recognition of the complementary nature of these architectures and of the needs to combine them in order to fruitfully exploit the available resources in different contexts.

3   The Digital Library System Organization

The concept map presented in Figure 2 (extracted from the Reference Model [18]) shows the main entities and their relationships in modelling DLS architectures. In particular, this map captures the fact that the architecture of a software system is defined as the organization or structure of the system's significant components (*Architectural Component*) interacting with each other through their interfaces. These components may be in turn composed of smaller and smaller components and interfaces; however, different Architectural Components may result incompatible each other, i.e. cannot coexist in the context of the same system. The term "component" is used to mean an encapsulated part of a system, ideally a non-trivial, nearly independent, and replaceable part of a system that fulfils a clear function in the context of a well-defined architecture.

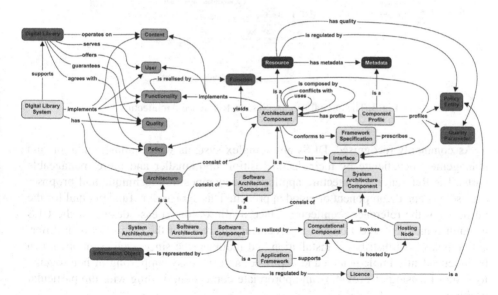

Fig. 2. The Digital Library System Concept Map

Architectural Components are classified in Software Architecture Components and System Architecture Components. The former are realised by Software Components, i.e. components encapsulating the implementation of a portion of a software system. The latter, i.e. System Architecture Components, are realised by Hosting Nodes and Computational Components. A Hosting Node encapsulates the implementation of the environment needed to host and run software components. A Computational Component represents the running instances of a Software Component active on a Hosting Node.

Moreover, the Reference Model identifies the concept of *Application Framework*, i.e. the software component available at the hosting nodes and providing the run-time environment for the computational components.

Based on this conceptualization, Figure 3 shows the Digital Library System Reference Architecture that we propose in order to fulfil the needs of large-scale digital libraries, i.e. digital libraries characterised by a large amount of resources and serving one or more communities world-wide spanned, multidisciplinary and whose requirements evolve along the time.

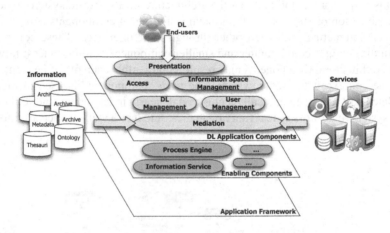

Fig. 3. The Digital Library System Reference Architecture

As commonly recognised, DLSs are complex systems whose implementation and management beneficiate by their decomposition into smaller and more manageable parts. The Reference Architecture applies the decomposition technique and proposes a loosely coupled component oriented approach. This approach is fundamental for the purposes of the reference architecture since it allows for (*i*) easy design of the DLS through component selection and replacement, (*ii*) reuse of the components in different contexts, (*iii*) distributed installation and maintenance since each component can be independently implemented and deployed, and (*iv*) easy supporting of heterogeneity issues by using or providing an appropriate component dealing with the particular problem.

In addition to the component-oriented approach, this Reference Architecture adopts a layered approach. This approach organizes components on three tiers: (*i*) the *Application Framework* layer, i.e. the set of software libraries and subsystems supporting the operation of the other DLS components; (*ii*) the *Enabling Components* layer, i.e. the DLS components providing the functionality required to support the communication and co-operation among the components implementing the DL application; (*iii*) the *DL*

Application Components layer, i.e. the DL system components providing the end-user specific DL functionality.

In the context of the Reference Model, a set of functionalities have been identified and grouped in functional areas. DL Application Components are thus described and organized through these functional areas: (*i*) the *Mediation* area dealing with and providing access to third party information sources varying in their structure, format, media, and physical representation as well as third party services; (*ii*) the *Information Space Management* area implementing and managing the digital library information objects by providing storage and preservation facilities; the (*iii*) *Access* area supporting discovery of the DL information objects via search and browse facilities; the (*iv*) *User Space*

Table 1. The Digital Library System Reference Architecture: Mandatory Components

Mediation area	User Space Management area

– Document Conformer
– Collection Virtualizer
– Ontology Aligner
– Metadata Schema Mapper
– Content Transformer
– Content Translator
– Service Wrapper
	– User Registry
	  • User Manager, Tracer, Registration, User Profile Config Manager
	– Group Registry
	  • Group Manager, Subscription, Group Profile Config Manager
	– Profile Repository
	  • Role Manager, Role Enforce, Role Config Manager, Checker
	– Policy Manager

Information Space Management area	
– Storage Component – Repository Component • Preservation Support Manager, Information Object Management, Ingest, Policy Enforce, Error Recovery, IO Registry, Configuration Manager, Metadata Generator, Storage Manager, Validation – Collection Manager – Annotation Manager	**DL Management area** – User Administration – Publication Process Manager – DL Monitoring – Recommender – Preservation Manager
Access area	**Presentation area**

– Search
  • Query Parser, Query Optimizer, Query Execution, Query Adapter, Collection Selection, Collection Description, Personalization
– Index
  • Feature Extractor, Trigger
– Data Fusion
	– User Interface
	– OAI-PMH Publisher
	– API Interface
	
	Enabling Components area
	
	– Information Service
	– Authentication, Authorization, and Auditing (AAA)
	– Broker
	– Process Engine

Management area providing support for registration and other activities concerning administration of the users; (*v*) the *DL Management* area implementing the functionality for the administration of the DL in terms of librarian activities, e.g. review processes, policies management, preservation activities; and (*vi*) the *Presentation* area providing users with friendly access to the DL information and services, namely the graphical user interface.

By relying on the concepts identified in the Reference Model, the components reported in Table 1 have been envisaged as the minimal pool needed to deliver the expected functionality. Openness, i.e. the possibility to add a new component or replace an existing one with a new one, is one of the most important characteristics to ensure the sustainability of the system. This characteristic is guaranteed by the presence of the Enabling Components taking care of the management activity, aimed at ensuring the desired quality of service. This is not a trivial task and the pool of services needed to reach it may vary a lot dependently on the concrete application scenario. It involves many functions such as: security, e.g. authorization of the request, encryption and decryption as required, validation, etc.; deployment, e.g. dynamically redeployment (movement) around the network of the services for achieving a better performance, a greater level of redundancy, improving availability, etc.; logging for auditing, metering, etc.; dynamic rerouting for fail over or load balancing and maintenance, i.e. management of new versions of a service or new services to satisfy new users needs.

The component-oriented approach of the DLS Reference Architecture makes it possible to design and implement DLMSs equipped with a DL Generator. This component is in charge of automatically creating a DLS by appropriately selecting, aggregating (and potentially deploying) a set of available components in order to fulfil the requirements of a certain community. This kind of DLMS allows delivering DLs according to the Business on Demand Model (BoDM), a model created around the Internet rush that became the de facto business model of the 21st century. The goal of this model is to efficiently manage and synchronize resources to match fluctuating requirements and to release the optimal service at an affordable cost via controlled resource sharing.

In the next section, the components and principles envisaged in the Reference Architecture are validated by describing the structure of two current systems, namely DILIGENT and DRIVER.

4   Applying the Reference Architecture

The Reference Architecture proposes an abstract architectural design pattern that can have multiple instances once implemented in a concrete scenario. This section describes two existing large-scale digital library systems using the reference architecture in different application contexts. Another exploitation of the Reference Architecture is represented by the DelosDLMS [19]. The goal of this system is to to deliver a prototype of next-generation system by integrating various specialised DL functions provided by partners of the DELOS Network of Excellence. For further details about this system please refer to [20].

4.1   DILIGENT A Digital Library Infrastructure on Grid ENabled Technologies

DILIGENT [21,22] is an ongoing EU IST project combining Digital Library and Grid technologies in order to deliver an infrastructure servicing scientists in the definition and operation of the supporting environment they are looking for, i.e. an integrated working environment giving access to the data and the facilities needed to perform their daily tasks. In this system the emphasis is on the exploitation of Grid facilities to gather both computing and storage power on demand as well as on the dynamic organization of the resources needed to operate a Digital Library on demand.

The DILIGENT architecture is depicted in Figure 4.

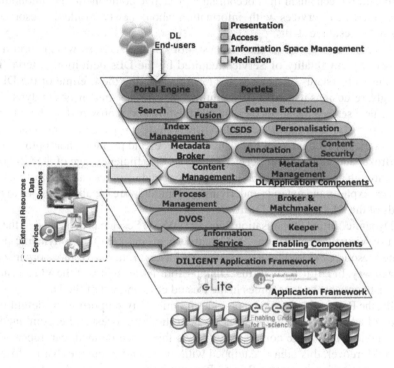

Fig. 4. The DILIGENT Architecture

The DILIGENT Application Framework layer is in charge of providing other components with the hosting environment they needed to operate, thus it must provide Grid facilities in the DILIGENT scenario. To this aim it hosts the gLite components [23] needed to interact with the Grid infrastructure released by the EGEE project [24]. Moreover, all the services constituting the system are designed by relying on the facilities provided by the WSRF specifications [25] in terms of dynamic service creation, lifetime management, notification, manageability, naming and discovering of service instances. As a consequence, the DILIGENT application framework layer hosts the container implementing these functionalities realised by the Globus project [26]. Moreover, the DILIGENT application framework layer hosts a pool of software libraries easing the interaction of the DILIGENT partaking services with the services forming the Enabling Components layer.

Many services form the DILIGENT Enabling Components layer. These services are in charge of providing the functionality for (*i*) ensuring that the other DILIGENT services work together securely and correctly, (*ii*) enabling the definition and creation of DLs by dynamically deploying and aggregating the needed resources, and (*iii*) enabling the creation of advanced functionality by combining resources via processes.

The Information Service supports the discovery and real-time monitoring of DILIGENT resources. In particular it (*i*) provides an interface enabling the other services to query for resources having certain characteristics and (*ii*) supports the subscription/notification mechanism thus becoming a proactive component that autonomously provides interested services with information about newly available resources or changes in the resource status.

The Keeper Service acts as the "orchestrator" of the services which form a DLS whilst assuring the Quality of Service required by the DLs definition criteria. To do so, it monitors the status of services and resources during the lifetime of the DL and, accordingly, re-designs its topology at runtime. This re-design consists in dynamically deploying new service instances on available hosting nodes provided by the infrastructure. By relying on such facilities, the DILIGENT system is capable to maintain up and running a series of DLs on a pool of shared resources and promote their optimal use.

The Broker and Matchmaker Service facilitates the efficient usage of the Grid infrastructure through an optimal distribution of services and resources across hosting nodes. The service exploits and extends underlying grid middleware capabilities so as to match the needs of the DLs hosted by DILIGENT.

The Dynamic Virtual Organisation Support (DVOS) Service is dedicated to the management of Virtual Organizations. A Virtual Organisation (VO) is a dynamic pool of distributed resources shared by a dynamic set of users from one or more organizations in a trusted way. In DILIGENT, Virtual Digital Libraries make use of the VO mechanism to glue together users and resources in the trusted environment of the DL.

Finally, the Process Management provides functionality supporting the definition and execution of advanced functionality via the definition of processes, i.e. combination of existing services into more complex workflows that, once defined, can repeatedly be executed. Moreover, this area is equipped with an execution engine that performs the steps defined in each process in a Peer-to-Peer modality in order to take advantage from the presence of distributed and replicated resources.

On top of these infrastructural services there resides the pool of those services devoted to deliver the functionality expected by end-users. According to the Reference Architecture they are organised in the Information Space Management, Access, and Presentation areas.

The Information Space Management area provides all the functionality required for storing information objects and their associated metadata, organizing such information objects into collections, and dealing with annotations. In order to take advantage from the presence of the potentially huge storage capacity deriving from the Grid, this area is also equipped with replication management facilities. These facilities automatically create and distribute replicas of information objects, thereby significantly increasing their availability. Finally, a service taking care of applying watermark and encryption techniques in order to protect the information objects from unauthorized accesses completes this area. The latter aspect is particularly relevant since the storage facilities provided by the Content Management service make use of Grid storage facilities, therefore it might occurs that physical files are stored on third party devices that are not under the direct control of the DILIGENT infrastructure.

The Access provides the functionality required to discover the DL information objects . The whole task is orchestrated by the Search service that exploits the capabilities provided by (*i*) the Index Management, that builds and maintains various types of indexes of the DL content; (*ii*) the Feature Extraction, that extracts different types of features from different kinds of media; (*iii*) the Content Source Description & Selection, that supports the discovery of the collections where to search in for a given cross collection query by comparing collection content description with the query; (*iv*) the Data Fusion, that supports the merging of the result sets resulting from querying the involved collections; and (*v*) the Personalization, that enriches the query with user characteristics for customizing the search results. All of them have been designed to co-operate by relying on the Process Management facilities. Further details are reported in [27].

Finally, the Presentation provides the graphical user interface needed to make DILIGENT resources and functionality available in an intuitive and easy to use environment. From a technological point of view, the required functionality is implemented via Portal and Portlets technologies, where portlets are pluggable user interfaces that can be managed and hosted in a portal via appropriate standards. In particular, the DILIGENT infrastructure is equipped with a set of portlets, one for each service having a user interface, and the WebSphere portal engine has been used to host them.

The principles and guidelines proposed in the context of the Reference Architecture proved to be very useful in the context of a complex system like DILIGENT. The layered approach together with the component oriented one as well as the functional areas proposed fitted very well the organization of DILIGENT.

4.2 DRIVER Digital Repository Vision for European Research

DRIVER [28] is an IST project co-funded by the European Commission under the Framework 6 "Research Infrastructure" program. It officially started in June 2006 and has a planned duration spanning across eighteen months. The goal of this project is to develop an organization and a system as the first step towards a pan-European Digital Repository Infrastructure, i.e. an European production-quality infrastructure integrating existing national, regional and thematic repositories in order to provide a virtually centralized view over their distributed content. The project emphasis is therefore on providing cross-repository services in a large-scale scenario. Despite previous attempts have been implemented with a similar goal, e.g. the National Science Digital Library in US [29] and the Dutch network of Digital Academic Repositories (DARE) [30], they potentially suffer of the sustainability problem because in their context, like in the DRIVER one, consumers are world-wide, heterogeneous, multidisciplinary and evolving. To overcome this problem the DRIVER architecture has taken advantage from the Reference Architecture and, in particular, by the loosely coupled component oriented

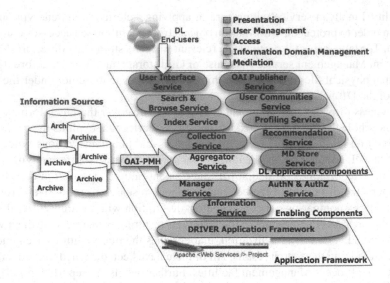

Fig. 5. The DRIVER Architecture

approach giving the possibility to easily replace one piece of the system and thus to adapt it to novel requirements.

The DRIVER architecture is depicted in Figure 5. All the components are realized as Web services. These services represent classes of services that co-exist and interact in multiple running instances in the DRIVER infrastructure. As a consequence the DRIVER Application Framework is equipped with a hosting environment implementing the Web Service standards. Moreover, it is provided with a pool of software libraries supporting hosted services in accessing the rest of the services forming the system.

In accordance with the Reference Architecture, the DRIVER Enabling Components layer offers the functionalities required to support the co-operation among the service running instances. These functionalities are: (*i*) controlled access to the pool of DRIVER resources, (*ii*) discovering of the pool of the dynamic pool of DRIVER resources, and (*iii*) orchestration of family of services to deliver complex functionality.

The Authentication and Authorization Service addresses *security*, i.e. the service guarantees that access to services occurs according to the established policies and that only recognized and authorized consumers "consume" them; the service adopts the eXtensible Access Control Markup Language (XACML) standard;

The Information Service addresses *discoverability*, i.e. the service acts as the registry of the service oriented architecture providing functions to register new resources, to find the services that respect specific capabilities or properties, and to notify the appropriate services when specific events affect the lifetime of the registered services;

Finally, the Manager Service addresses *orchestration*, i.e. the service automatically (*i*) orchestrates the interaction of services, by instructing them on the specific tasks they should accomplish, and (*ii*) monitors the status of all services running in the infrastructure. This activity is performed to safeguard the infrastructure Quality-of-Service by taking corrective actions any time faults, errors or malicious accesses threaten the proper infrastructural behavior.

On top of these infrastructural services there resides the pool of services devoted to deliver the functionality expected by end-users. According to the Reference Architecture they are organised in the Mediation, Information Domain Management, Access, User Management, and Presentation areas.

The Mediation area implements the functionality needed to collect content from external information sources and populate the DRIVER information space. In particular, the Aggregator Service gathers content from external sources and makes it available to the other services [31].

The Information Domain Management area implements the DRIVER information space. In particular, the MD Store stores collected metadata while the Collection Service supports the organization of the gathered content into dynamic collections.

The Access area offers functionality to discover objects forming the Information Space. Index Service provides appropriate data structures supporting content retrieval while Search & Browse Service provides facilities enabling content discovery.

The User Management area implements facilities for dealing with end-users. In particular, User Communities Service supports the management of users and groups; Profiling Service collects information about registered users that are employed to customize the system behaviour; Recommendation Service notifies registered users each time an event the user is interested in occurs.

Finally, the Presentation area offers the interfaces needed to interact with the system. In particular, the User Interface Service implements the graphical user interface providing users with access to the system functionality while the OAI-Publisher Service implements the OAI-PMH making DRIVER an open archive data provider [12,31].

The approaches proposed by the Reference Architecture have proved their usefulness in a distributed and large-scale system like DRIVER. The component oriented approach as well as the identification of the three layers and the functional areas is demonstrated in a context characterised by many, multidisciplinary and distributed players, both providing and consuming resources, whose requirements evolve along the time.

5   Conclusion and Future Trends

Many Digital Library Systems are still poorly designed and implemented from scratch by focusing on the specific problems and requirements the system have to deal with. We argue for a development process based on general purpose DLMSs capable to deliver classes of DLSs fulfilling end-user requirements. To support such a view we presented a first step toward a Reference Architecture for Digital Library Systems adopting a component oriented approach and establishing the organization of such components in functional areas. Such reference architecture promotes component reuse as well as plug-ability of novel and specialized components to fulfil specific requirements. This development process complies with the Business on Demand Model supporting an efficient management of available resources.

Despites the proposed guidelines and principles proved to be very useful and appropriate to the context they are envisaged for, i.e. Digital Library Systems serving communities whose requirements evolve along the time and characterised by many, multidisciplinary and distributed players, both providing and consuming resources, further effort must be invested in providing additional details and abstract solutions having a fine-grained granularity. As a consequence, the until now envisaged components can be split in minor components as to promote component sharing and reuse in a fine grained scenario. We are well aware of the "distance" between the current Reference Architecture and the form that it should have to be easily used to realise Concrete Architectures. However, the until now proposed guidelines and approaches have proven to be appropriate for organising and describing concrete and complex systems as DILIGENT, DRIVER and the DelosDLMS. This suggest to continue in this direction and to propose additional patterns and solution to be included in the next versions of the framework.

Acknowledgments. This work is partially funded by DELOS the Network of Excellence on Digital Libraries (IST-507618). Special thanks go to Maria Bruna Baldacci for her valuable help in improving the readability of the paper.

References

1. Fox, E.A., Akscyn, R.M., Furuta, R., Leggett, J.J.: Digital Libraries. Communications of the ACM 38, 23–28 (1995)
2. Ioannidis, Y.: Digital Libraries: Future Directions for a European Research Programme. Brainstorming report, DELOS, San Cassiano, Italy (2001)
3. Ioannidis, Y.: Digital libraries at a crossroads. International Journal on Digital Libraries 5, 255–265 (2005)
4. Ioannidis, Y., Maier, D., Abiteboul, S., Buneman, P., Davidson, S., Fox, E., Halevy, A., Knoblock, C., Rabitti, F., Schek, H., Weikum, G.: Digital library information-technology infrastructures. International Journal on Digital Libraries 5, 266–274 (2005)
5. Soergel, D.: A Framework for Digital Library Research: Broadening the Vision. DLib Magazine 8 (2002)
6. Borgman, C.L.: What are digital libraries? Competing visions. Information Processing and Management 35, 227–243 (1999)
7. Candela, L., Castelli, D., Ioannidis, Y., Koutrika, Y., Meghini, C., Pagano, P., Ross, S., Schek, H.J., Schuldt, H.: The Digital Library Manifesto. Technical report, DELOS (2006)
8. Candela, L., Castelli, D., Ioannidis, Y., Koutrika, G., Pagano, P., Ross, S., Schek, H.J., Schuldt, H., Thanos, C.: Setting the Foundations of Digital Libraries The DELOS Manifesto. D-Lib Magazine 13 (2007)
9. MacKenzie, C.M., Laskey, K., McCabe, F., Brown, P., Metz, R.: Reference Model for Service Oriented Architecture 1.0. Technical report, OASIS, Public Review Draft 1.0 (2006)
10. Lagoze, C., Davis, J.R.: Dienst - An Architecture for Distributed Document Libraries. Communication of the ACM 38, 47 (1995)
11. ANSI/NISO Z39.50 Information retrieval: Application Service Definition & Protocol Specification. NISO Press, National Information Standards Organization (2003)
12. Lagoze, C.: Van de Sompel, H.: The open archives initiative: building a low-barrier interoperability framework. In: Proceedings of the first ACM/IEEE-CS Joint Conference on Digital Libraries, ACM Press, pp. 54–62 (2001)
13. Suleman, H.: Open Digital Libraries. PhD thesis, Virginia Polytechnic Institute and State University (2002)

14. Gonçalves, M.A., Fox, E.A., Watson, L.T., Kipp, N.A.: Streams, Structures, Spaces, Scenarios, Societies (5S): A Formal Model for Digital Libraries. ACM Transactions on Information Systems (TOIS) 22, 270–312 (2004)

15. Gonçalves, M.A.: Streams, Structures, Spaces, Scenarios, and Societies (5S): A Formal Digital Library Framework and Its Applications. PhD thesis, Virginia Polytechnic Institute and State University (2004)

16. Powell, A.: A 'service oriented' view of the JISC Information Environment (2005), http://www.ukoln.ac.uk/distributed-systems/jisc-ie/arch/soa/

17. Agosti, M., Bischofs, L., Candela, L., Castelli, D., Ferro, N., Hasselbring, W., Moumoutzis, N., Schuldt, H., Weikum, G., Wurz, M., Zezula, P.: Evaluation and Comparison of the Service Architecture, P2P, and Grid Approaches for DLs. Deliverable D1.1.1, DELOS Network of Excellence on Digital Libraries (2006)

18. Agosti, M., Candela, L., Castelli, D., Dobreva, M., Ferro, N., Ioannidis, Y., Koutrika, G., Meghini, C., Pagano, P., Ross, S., Schuldt, H.: The digital library reference model. Technical report, DELOS (Forthcoming)

19. Schek, H.J., Schuldt, H.: DelosDLMS - Infrastructure for the Next Generation of Digital Library Management Systems. ERCIM News, Special Issue on European Digital Library, 21–22 (2006)

20. Agosti, M., Berretti, S., Brettlecker, G., del Bimbo, A., Ferro, N., Fuhr, N., Keim, D., Klas, C.P., Lidy, T., Norrie, M., Ranaldi, P., Rauber, A., Schek, H.J., Schreck, T., Schuldt, H., Signer, B., Springmann, M.: DelosDLMS - the Integrated DELOS Digital Library Management System. In: Digital Libraries: Research and Development Selected and Revised Papers from the First DELOS Conference, Pisa, Italy, 13-14 February, 2007 (2007)

21. DILIGENT: A DIgital Library Infrastructure on Grid ENabled Technology. IST No. 004260, http://www.diligentproject.org/

22. Candela, L., Akal, F., Avancini, H., Castelli, D., Fusco, L., Guidetti, V., Langguth, C., Manzi, A., Pagano, P., Schuldt, H., Simi, M., Springmann, M., Voicu, L.: DILIGENT: integrating Digital Library and Grid Technologies for a new Earth Observation Research Infrastructure. International Journal on Digital Libraries (2007)

23. EGEE: gLite: Lightweight Middleware for Grid Computing (accessed August 2007), http://glite.web.cern.ch/glite/

24. EGEE: Enabling Grids for E-sciencE. INFSO 508833, http://public.eu-egee.org/

25. Banks, T.: Web Services Resource Framework (WSRF) - Primer. Committee draft 01, OASIS (2005), http://docs.oasis-open.org/wsrf/wsrf-primer-1.2-primer-cd-01.pdf

26. Globus Alliance: The Globus Alliance Website, http://www.globus.org/

27. Simeoni, F., Candela, L., Kakaletris, G., Sibeko, M., Pagano, P., Papanikos, G., Polydoras, P., Ioannidis, Y.E., Aarvaag, D., Crestani, F.: A grid-based infrastructure for distributed retrieval. In: Kovács, L., Fuhr, N., Meghini, C. (eds.) ECDL 2007. Research and Advanced Technology for Digital Libraries, 11th European Conference, Budapest, Hungary, September 16-21, 2007. LNCS, vol. 4675, pp. 161–173. Springer-Verlag, Heidelberg (2007)

28. DRIVER: Digital Repository Infrastructure Vision for European Research. IST No. 034047, http://www.driver-repository.eu/

29. NSDL: The National Science Digital Library. http://nsdl.org/

30. van der Kuil, A., Feijen, M.: The Dawning of the Dutch Network of Digital Academic REpositories (DARE): A Shared Experience. Ariadne 41 (2004)

31. Candela, L., Castelli, D., Manghi, P., Pagano, P.: Item-Oriented Aggregator Services. In: Third Italian Research Conference on Digital Library Systems, Padova, Italy (2007)

DelosDLMS - The Integrated DELOS Digital Library Management System

Maristella Agosti[1], Stefano Berretti[2], Gert Brettlecker[3], Alberto del Bimbo[2],
Nicola Ferro[1], Norbert Fuhr[4], Daniel Keim[5], Claus-Peter Klas[4],
Thomas Lidy[6], Diego Milano[3,8], Moira Norrie[7], Paola Ranaldi[3,8],
Andreas Rauber[6], Hans-Jörg Schek[8], Tobias Schreck[5], Heiko Schuldt[3],
Beat Signer[7], and Michael Springmann[3]

[1] Information Management Systems Research Group, University of Padua (IT)
[2] Visual Information Processing Laboratory, University of Florence (IT)
[3] Database and Information Systems Group, University of Basel (CH)
[4] Information Systems Group, University of Duisburg-Essen (DE)
[5] Databases, Data Mining and Visualization Group, University of Constance (DE)
[6] Information & Software Engineering Group, Technical University of Vienna (AT)
[7] Institute for Information Systems, ETH Zürich (CH)
[8] Database and Information Systems Group, University of Constance (DE)

Abstract. DelosDLMS is a prototype of a next-generation Digital Library (DL) management system. It is realized by combining various specialized DL functionalities provided by partners of the DELOS network of excellence. Currently, DelosDLMS combines text and audio-visual searching, offers new information visualization and relevance feedback tools, provides novel interfaces, allows retrieved information to be annotated and processed, integrates and processes sensor data streams, and finally, from a systems engineering point of view, is easily configured and adapted while being reliable and scalable. The prototype is based on the OSIRIS/ISIS platform, a middleware environment developed by ETH Zürich and now being extended at the University of Basel.

Keywords: Digital Library Management System, SOA.

1 Introduction

The overall goal of the DelosDLMS is the implementation of a prototype of a next-generation Digital Library management system [1]. This system combines text and audio-visual searching, offers personalized browsing using new information visualization and relevance feedback tools, provides novel interfaces, allows retrieved information to be annotated and processed, integrates and processes sensor data streams, and finally, from a systems engineering point of view, is easily configured and adapted while being reliable and scalable.

Previous work in the DELOS network has mainly focused on improving Digital Libraries (DLs) by developing independent, powerful and highly sophisticated prototype systems in cooperation of few partners. In addition, a dedicated

C. Thanos, F. Borri, and L. Candela (Eds.): Digital Libraries: R&D, LNCS 4877, pp. 36–45, 2007.
© Springer-Verlag Berlin Heidelberg 2007

DELOS activity is the definition of a Reference Model for Digital Libraries [2]. The goal of the DELOS integration activities is twofold. First, it aims at integrating these prototype systems as building blocks into OSIRIS/ISIS, an existing middleware environment that was developed at ETH Zurich. The result of the integration – that is, the middleware infrastructure together with all the advanced DL functionality – constitutes the DelosDLMS prototype. Second, DelosDLMS will serve as a partial implementation of the DELOS Reference Model.

This paper reports on the integration of DL functionality which includes audio (TU Vienna) and 3D features (Univ. Florence), a new paper-based interface (iPaper from ETH Zürich), a SOM visualization of the feature space (Univ. Konstanz), and an annotation service (FAST, Univ. Padua) which have been added to DelosDLMS and the integration of DelosDLMS into the Daffodil interface.

The paper is organized as follows. Section 2 introduces the ISIS/OSIRIS middleware which is the basis for DelosDLMS. Section 3 presents in detail the services and DL functionality that has been added. Section 4 concludes.

2 OSIRIS/ISIS Middleware

OSIRIS (Open Service Infrastructure for Reliable and Integrated process Support) is a platform that allows for combining different distributed services into processes [3]. The OSIRIS platform itself does not provide any application functionality but, by combining specialized application services, supports the definition and reliable execution of dedicated processes (also known as "programming-in-the-large"). When different specialized DL application services are made available to the OSIRIS platform, users can define and run powerful Digital Library processes by making use of these services. This is realized by a set of generic (application-independent) services that include the registration of services and processes, interfaces for application development, an engine for decentralized execution of processes, and services for load balancing. OSIRIS processes themselves are wrapped by a service interface. Therefore, a process can be invoked just like any other service (and used in other processes as well).

OSIRIS distinguishes between system services and application services. System services are used internally for coordinating the execution of processes in a distributed way, without relying on a central execution engine/scheduler. For application services, OSIRIS further distinguishes between loosely coupled and tightly coupled services. Usually, a part of the distributed OSIRIS middleware (called OSIRIS layer) runs on each host providing application services. This is the case for tightly coupled services. Loosely coupled application services are those that have to be called remotely, without a local ORISIS layer available. The integration/invocation is done via WSDL for service description and SOAP for invocation. The system architecture of OSIRIS is depicted in Figure 1. Another focus of OSIRIS is scalability of process execution. OSIRIS' decentralized peer-to-peer approach for process execution, which is realized by sophisticated replication mechanisms for control flow dependencies, avoids any single point of failure during process execution and provides a high degree of scalability.

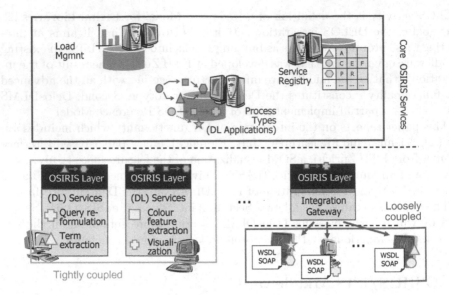

Fig. 1. The OSIRIS Middleware at a Glance

Peer-to-peer process execution also incorporates sophisticated load balancing in order to distribute process load among available, suitable peers.

Finally, OSIRIS is equipped with the O'GRAPE (Osiris GRAphical Process Editor) user interface for process definition. In addition, O'GRAPE supports the integration of existing application services via existing Web service standards (SOAP and WSDL).

The core of OSIRIS has been developed at ETH Zürich and is currently being extended at the University of Basel. There are two versions of OSIRIS: one is implemented in C++ and runs on Microsoft platforms, the other version is implemented in Java.

ISIS (Interactive SImilarity Search) is a prototype application for information retrieval in multimedia collections [4]. It supports content-based retrieval of images, audio and video content, and the combination of any of these media types with text retrieval. Basically, ISIS consists of a set of pre-defined processes and several application services (like feature extraction, index management, index access, relevance feedback, etc.) that have been developed on the basis of the OSIRIS middleware. ISIS includes a sophisticated index structure (VA-file) for similarity search, which is particularly well suited for high-dimensional vector spaces. It also provides basic support for relevance feedback and visualization.

With the DelosDLMS, existing ISIS services are significantly enriched by other specialized DL services that have been developed within the DELOS network. This is achieved by integrating these services into the OSIRIS infrastructure, thereby combining them with other ISIS and non-ISIS services into advanced, process-based DL applications.

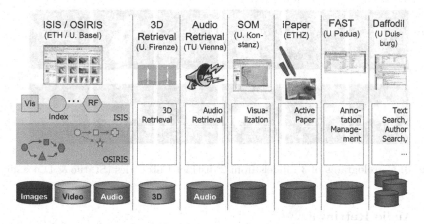

Fig. 2. Overview of Systems which have been integrated into DelosDLMS

3   Integration Activities

The starting point for the DelosDLMS integration activities is illustrated in Figure 2. In what follows, all these components are presented in more detail.

3.1   Content-Based 3D Retrieval

Histograms of surface curvature have been used to support global description and retrieval of 3D objects. However, since histograms do not include any spatial information, they are liable to false positives. To overcome such problems, we used curvature correlograms as a model for representation and retrieval of 3D objects [5,6]. Correlograms have been previously used with success for retrieval of images based on colour content [7]. In particular, with respect to description based on histograms of local features, correlograms enable also encoding of information about the relative position of local features. Correlograms are used to encode information about curvature values and their localization on the object surface. For this peculiarity, description of 3D objects based on correlograms of curvature proves to be effective for the purpose of content based retrieval of 3D objects. In order to compute curvature correlograms of a 3D object, the principal curvatures are computed for every vertices of the mesh. Values of the mean curvature are then derived from principal curvature, and quantized into N classes of discrete values. For this purpose, the mean curvature value is processed through a stair-step function so that many neighbouring values are mapped to one output value.

The proposed retrieval approach has been applied to the models included in the Princeton Shape Benchmark database [8]. This archive includes 1814 models categorized in a hierarchy of classes. In DelosDLMS, the curvature correlograms of the Princeton 3D-collection have been extracted and indexed with ISIS' VA-file and a Web service offering online feature extraction by Delos DLMS has been developed.

Fig. 3. Correlograms of 3 Models from 2 distinct Categories (Statue & Dinosaur)

3.2 Audio Retrieval

TU Vienna has developed three different feature sets for content-based music retrieval. These feature sets for musical content description – Rhythm Patterns, Statistical Spectrum Descriptors and Rhythm Histograms – are integrated into DelosDLMS. The feature extraction algorithm is as follows:

In a pre-processing step the audio signal is converted to a mono signal and segmented into chunks of approximately 6 seconds. Typically, the first and last one or two segments are skipped and from the remaining segments every third one is processed.

For each segment the spectrogram of the audio is computed using the short time Fast Fourier Transform (STFT). The Bark scale, a perceptual scale which groups frequencies to critical bands according to perceptive pitch regions, is applied to the spectrogram, aggregating it to 24 frequency bands.

From this representation of perceived loudness statistical measures (mean, median, variance, skewness, kurtosis, min and max) are computed per critical band, in order to describe fluctuations within the bands extensively. The se result is a Statistical Spectrum Descriptor.

In a further step, the varying energy on the critical bands of the Bark scale Sonogram is regarded as a modulation of the amplitude over time. Using a Fourier Transform, the spectrum of this modulation signal is retrieved. The result is a time-invariant signal that contains magnitudes of modulation per modulation frequency per critical band. This matrix represents a Rhythm Pattern, indicating occurrence of rhythm as vertical bars, but also describing smaller fluctuations on all frequency bands of the human auditory range. Subsequent to the Fourier Transform, modulation amplitudes are weighted according to a function of human sensation of modulation frequency, accentuating values around 4 Hz. The application of a gradient filter and Gaussian smoothing potentially improves similarity of Rhythm Patterns which is useful in classification and retrieval tasks.

A Rhythm Histogram is constructed by aggregating the critical bands of the Rhythm Pattern (before weighting and smoothing), resulting in a histogram of rhythmic energy for 60 modulation frequencies. The feature vectors are computed for a piece of audio by taking the median of the descriptors of its segments.

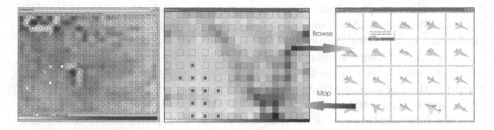

Fig. 4. Left: SOM for DelosDLMS Database Content; Right: SOM-Based Database Browsing and Exploration Concept

3.3 SOM-Based Retrieval Support

A standard method to visualize the result set of a user query in a DL is to display a sorted list of answer objects. Visualizing multiple object sets at once, as well as their structure and interrelationships between each other, possibly in different feature spaces, is feasible with projections from high-dimensional feature space to low-dimensional (2D) display space. Among other algorithms such as Principal Component Analysis and Multidimensional Scaling, the Self-Organizing Map (SOM) algorithm is a projection and vector quantization algorithm with interesting theoretical and practical properties, which is also highly suited for visualization. Previous work done at the University of Constance has focused on the application of the SOM algorithm for effective retrieval and visual analysis in multimedia databases. For DELOS, this work was leveraged in computing SOM projections for an image database described in different feature spaces. A web service was developed, which, based on the offline calculated maps, is able to render two basic SOM views. Query and result objects are marked on the map. The overall goal of this visualization is to support the user in analyzing and comparing the relationships between query and result sets, possibly under different feature representations. Furthermore, the visualization allows the user to effectively explore the contents and structure of a previously unknown data repository (visual analysis and scatter browsing).

3.4 Daffodil

The DL system Daffodil is a front-end system for Digital Libraries, targeted at strategic support of users during the information search process. For searching, exploring, and managing DL objects it provides user-customisable information seeking patterns over a federation of heterogeneous DLs. Searching with Daffodil makes a broad range of information sources easily accessible and enables quick access to a rich information space. Daffodil already provides a broad range of tools to help the user in query formulation, e.g. a thesaurus, a spell-checker, a classification browser, and a related-term service. For the user interface design, Daffodil implements a tool-based design paradigm, where objects resulting from the interaction with one tool can be dragged to other tools for further processing.

Based on this metaphor, Daffodil implements the user-oriented integration of DL tools in the DelosDLMS, thus complementing the system-oriented integration performed by the OSIRIS middleware.

As a first reference implementation, the Daffodil system was extended by an image search tool connecting to the ISIS system described above. For this purpose, the Daffodil system was extended by two special functions: (i.) Query by Example: Given any picture link from the Web, similar pictures are searched. The similarity feature can be chosen, e.g. colour histograms. A set of answers pictures is returned. The pictures can then be used for further searching. (ii.) Query by Keyword: Given a specific keyword, the system is able to search for pictures, which are indexed with this keyword.

A feedback list is implemented in both functions. The user is able to specify relevant or non-relevant pictures in order to refine the answer set of searched pictures. The communication between OSIRIS and Daffodil is handled by HTTP and based on the processes given by the ISIS picture search. Through the integration within the Daffodil system, users can also apply other tools on queries and retrieved images, like maintaining a search history, storing queries and images within their personal libraries, sharing them with other users or adding annotations (see Section 3.6).

3.5   iPaper

Information managed by the DelosDLMS can be accessed by a variety of digital user interfaces. The goal of the iPaper extension for the DelosDLMS was to enhance existing paper documents with functionality offered by DelosDLMS thereby bridging the gap between paper documents and services offered by Digital Library management systems.

We developed an interactive printed museum guide as a physical user interface to the DelosDLMS. The system is based on a Bluetooth-enabled digital pen that can track user interactions within paper documents or any other surface covered with a special printed Anoto pattern consisting of tiny, almost invisible dots. Active paper areas can be defined within paper documents and linked to digital information or services. In the case of the interactive museum guide shown in Figure 5, existing printed text components and images, as well as some new interface components in the form of blue "paper buttons" have been associated with specific ISIS queries.

A first query that can be formulated based on the paper interface is retrieving images based on a set of given keywords. A user can either select specific underlined words within the text, which is similar to selecting hyperlinks on the Web, or they can enter specific words in a special keyword input area. Any keywords entered in the keyword area are transformed to a text string by an Intelligent Character Recognition (ICR) process. As soon as the user selects the 'Search' button with the digital pen, a query consisting of the set of keywords is sent to ISIS and a list of images matching these keywords is returned. Another type of query is based on finding image similarities. By touching images in the museum guide with the digital pen, a user can add them to the set of images to be used

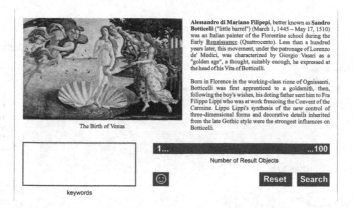

Fig. 5. Paper-based DelosDLMS Query Interface

in a similarity search. After selecting the 'Search' button, a query with the set of selected images as parameter is sent to ISIS and a list of best matching images is returned. Note that the keyword and image-based searches may be combined and queries containing keywords as well as images can be formulated. Finally, there are some paper buttons to configure specific query parameters such as the preferred size of the result set (from 1 up to 100 images).

The iPaper infrastructure [9,10] used to implement the paper-based interface for DelosDLMS was developed by the Global Information Systems (GlobIS) research group at ETH Zürich. It is based on a general cross-media information management server (iServer) [11] enabling the integration of arbitrary digital and physical resources.

3.6 FAST Annotation

FAST [12] is a flexible system designed to support both various architectural paradigms and a wide range of different DLMSs. In order to achieve the desired flexibility: (i.) FAST is a stand-alone system, i.e., it is not part of any particular DLMS; (ii.) the core functionalities of the annotation service are separated from the functionalities needed to integrate it into different DLMSs. The flexibility of FAST and its independence from any particular DLMS are key features to provide users with a uniform way of interaction with annotation functionalities. In this way, users do not need to change their annotative practices only because they work with different DLMSs.

Within FAST, annotations are composite multimedia objects, which can annotate multiple part of a given digital object and can relate this annotated digital object to various other digital objects, if needed. Furthermore, once it has been created, an annotation is considered as a first class digital object, so that it can be annotated too. In this way, users can create not only sets of annotations concerning a digital object, but also threads of annotations, i.e., annotations which reply to one another. These threads of annotations are the basis for actively involving users with the system and for enabling collaboration.

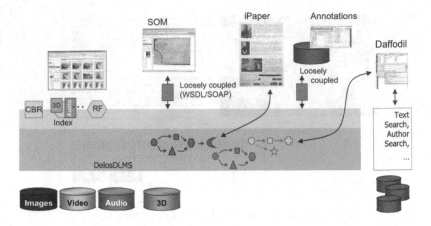

Fig. 6. Summary of the First Phase of DelosDLMS Service Integration

From a functional point of view, FAST offers annotation management functionalities, such as creation, access, and so on. Furthermore it supports collaboration among user by introducing scopes of annotation and groups of users: annotations can be private, shared or public; public; if an annotation is shared, different groups of users can share it with different permissions, e.g., one group can only read the annotation while another can also modify it. Finally, FAST offers advanced search functionalities based on annotations by exploiting annotations as a useful context in order to search and retrieve relevant documents for a user query [13,14]. The aim is to retrieve more documents that are relevant and to have them ranked in a way which is better than a system that does not makes use of annotations.

3.7 Summary of Integration Activities

All integration activities of the first phase are summarized in Figure 6. Audio and 3D features have been added to the VA-file index of DelosDLMS. The FAST annotation management and the SOM visualization are available as web services and have been loosely integrated into DelosDLMS. For this, OSIRIS processes have been extended accordingly in order to make use of these new services. The iPaper front-end creates a query which is sent and executed in DelosDLMS. Similarly, the Daffodil client generates a query which is sent to DelosDLMS.

4 Summary and Outlook

The DelosDLMS prototype development will first continue with a tight integration of services already coupled in a loosely way. Second, functionality (espacially for feature extraction) which has been integrated off-line will be made online as dedicated Web service. It will then be possible to create OSIRIS processes that allow for the upload and indexing of new objects and/or for searching with objects that are not yet indexed. Third, new functionality will be added. This includes personalisation, term extraction, query support for XML documents, semantic video services, video annotation, and video retrieval, P2P search, natural language and speech interfaces and further visualizations.

References

1. Schek, H.J., Schuldt, H.: DelosDLMS - Infrastructure for the Next Generation of Digital Library Management Systems. ERCIM, Special Issue on European Digital Library 66 (July 2006)
2. Candela, L., Castelli, D., Pagano, P., Thanos, C., Ioannidis, Y., Koutrika, G., Ross, S., Schek, H.J., Schuldt, H.: Setting the Foundations of Digital Libraries: The DELOS Manifesto. D-Lib Magazine 13 (2007)
3. Schuler, C., Türker, C., Schek, H.J., Weber, R., Schuldt, H.: Scalable Peer-to-Peer Process Management. International Journal of Business Process Integration and Management (IJBPIM) 1(2), 129–142 (2006)
4. Mlivoncic, M., Schuler, C., Türker, C.: Hyperdatabase Infrastructure for Management and Search of Multimedia Collections. In: Proc. DELOS Workshop (2004)
5. Antini, G., Berretti, S., Bimbo, A.D., Pala, P.: Curvature Correlograms for Content Based Retrieval of 3D Objects. In: Roli, F., Vitulano, S. (eds.) ICIAP 2005. LNCS, vol. 3617, Springer, Heidelberg (2005)
6. Antini, G., Berretti, S., Bimbo, A.D., Pala, P.: Retrieval of 3D Objects using Curvature Correlograms. In: Proc. ICME 2005, Amsterdam, The Netherlands (2005)
7. Huang, J., Kumar, R., Mitra, M., Zhu, W.J., Zabils, R.: Spatial Color Indexing and Application. International Journal of Computer Vision 35, 245–268 (1999)
8. Shilane, P., Kazhdan, M., Min, P., Funkhouser, T.: The Princeton Shape Benchmark, Shape Modeling International, Genova, Italy (2004)
9. Norrie, M., Signer, B., Weibel, N.: General Framework for the Rapid Development of Interactive Paper Applications. In: Proc. CoPADD 2006, Banff, Canada (2006)
10. Norrie, M.C., Palinginis, A., Signer, B.: Content publishing framework for interactive paper documents. In: ACM Symp. on Document Engineering (2005)
11. Norrie, M.C., Signer, B.: Information Server for highly-connected cross-media Publishing. Inf. Syst. 30(7), 526–542 (2005)
12. Agosti, M., Ferro, N.: A System Architecture as a Support to a Flexible Annotation Service. In: Proc. of the 6th Thematic DELOS Workshop, pp. 147–166 (2005)
13. Agosti, M., Ferro, N.: Annotations as Context for Searching Documents. In: Crestani, F., Ruthven, I. (eds.) CoLIS 2005. LNCS, vol. 3507, Springer, Heidelberg (2005)
14. Agosti, M., Ferro, N.: Search Strategies for Finding Annotations and Annotated Documents: The FAST Service. In: Larsen, H.L., Pasi, G., Ortiz-Arroyo, D., Andreasen, T., Christiansen, H. (eds.) FQAS 2006. LNCS (LNAI), vol. 4027, Springer, Heidelberg (2006)

ISIS and OSIRIS: A Process-Based Digital Library Application on Top of a Distributed Process Support Middleware

Gert Brettlecker[1], Diego Milano[1,2], Paola Ranaldi[1,2], Hans-Jörg Schek[2],
Heiko Schuldt[1], and Michael Springmann[1]

[1] Database and Information Systems Group, University of Basel, Switzerland
[2] Database and Information Systems Group, University of Constance, Germany

Abstract. Future information spaces such as Digital Libraries require new infrastructures that allow to use and to combine various kinds of functions in a unified and reliable way. The paradigm of service-oriented architectures (SoA) allows providing application functionality in a modular, self-contained way and to individually combine this functionality. The paper presents the ISIS/OSIRIS system which consists of a generic infrastructure for the reliable execution of distributed service-based applications (OSIRIS) and a set of dedicated Digital Library application services (ISIS) that provide, among others, content-based search in multimedia collections.

Keywords: Distributed Process Management, Content-based Multimedia Retrieval, Service-oriented Architecture.

1 Introduction

Seven years ago the Database Group at ETH Zürich developed a vision [1,2] for future research in information systems (taken from [2]):

"In the past, we talked about single information systems. In the future, we expect an ever increasing number of information systems and data sources, reaching from traditional databases and large document collections, information sources contained in web pages, down to information systems in mobile devices as they will occur in a pervasive computing environment. Therefore not only the immense amount of information demands new thoughts but also the number of different information sources. Essentially, their coordination poses a great challenge for the development of future tools that will be suitable to access, process, and maintain information. We talk about the continuous, 'infinite' information, shortly called the 'information space'. Information in this space is distributed, heterogeneous and undergoes continuous changes. So, the infrastructure for information spaces must provide convenient tools for accessing information, for developing applications for analyzing, mining, classifying, and processing information, and for transactional processes that ensure consistent propagation of information changes and simultaneous invocations of several (web) services within

C. Thanos, F. Borri, and L. Candela (Eds.): Digital Libraries: R&D, LNCS 4877, pp. 46–55, 2007.
© Springer-Verlag Berlin Heidelberg 2007

a transactional workflow. As far as possible, the infrastructure should avoid global components. Rather, a peer-to-peer decentralized coordination middleware must be provided that has some self-configuration and adaptation features".

Under the label "hyperdatabase" research, we started developing OSIRIS and ISIS as a concrete implementation of parts of this vision. Meanwhile the paradigm of service-oriented architectures (SoA) helped in further pursuing these ideas on a much broader scale. SoA supports the provision of application functionality in a modular, self-contained way and their individual combination and is thus increasingly becoming important for the design and development of DLs.

ISIS (*Interactive SImilarity Search*) is a set of Digital Library services (like feature extraction, index management, index access, relevance feedback, etc.). In addition, it encompasses a set of specialized processes in which some of these services are combined for the definition of complex DL applications.

The latter functionality, i.e., the definition and execution of DL processes based on existing services is provided by the OSIRIS *middleware* (*Open Service Infrastructure for Reliable and Integrated process Support*). In OSIRIS, we distinguish between system services and application services. System services are used internally for coordinating the execution of processes in a distributed way, without relying on a central execution engine. In addition, the distributed architecture of OSIRIS allows for reliable peer-to-peer process management and sophisticated failure handling and is able to balance the load among several providers of the same service. For application services, we distinguish between loosely coupled and tightly coupled services. Usually, a part of the distributed OSIRIS middleware (called *OSIRIS layer*) runs on each host providing application services. These application services are considered as tightly coupled since, in case information on their transactional properties like compensation or re-invocation (retriability) is available, dedicated transactional guarantees for processes can be provided. Loosely-coupled application services are those that have to be called remotely, without a local ORISIS layer available. The integration/invocation is done via WSDL for service description and SOAP for invocation.

The core of OSIRIS and ISIS has been developed at ETH Zürich. Currently, both systems are being extended at the University of Basel. There are two versions of OSIRIS: one is implemented in C++ and runs on Microsoft platforms, the other version is implemented in Java. Both systems also built the backbone of DelosDLMS, the integrated DELOS prototype of a next-generation Digital Library (DL) management system [3].

The paper is organized as follows. Section 2 introduces the OSIRIS middleware that supports the execution of composite services in a reliable way. Section 3 presents the ISIS DL services which are deployed and used on top of the OSIRIS platform. Section 4 concludes.

2   OSIRIS: Distributed Infrastructure for Processes

OSIRIS [4,5] is a platform that allows combining different distributed services into processes. The OSIRIS platform itself does not provide any application functionality but, by combining specialized application services, supports the definition and reliable execution of dedicated processes (this is also known as "programming-in-the-large"). OSIRIS processes themselves are wrapped by a service interface. Therefore, a process can be invoked just like any other service (and used in other processes as well).

Following the model of transactional processes [6], processes in OSIRIS contain two orders on their constituent services: a (partial) precedence order specifies regular execution while the precedence order is defined for failure handling purposes (alternative executions). Data flow between services of a process can be defined independently of control flow. Activities in a process are invocations of application services. Ideally, the transactional behaviour of each application service is known. This transactional behaviour includes information on compensation (how can the effects of a service execution be semantically undone in case of a failure) and on whether a failed service can be re-invoked (retriability).

In addition to transactional guarantees and reliability, OSIRIS focuses on scalability of process execution. The decentralized peer-to-peer approach for process execution in OSIRIS, which is realized by sophisticated replication mechanisms for control flow dependencies, avoids any single point of failure during process execution and provides a high degree of scalability. Peer-to-peer process execution also incorporates sophisticated load balancing in order to distribute process load among available, suitable peers.

Finally, OSIRIS is equipped with the O'GRAPE (OSIRIS GRAphical Process Editor) user interface for process definition which also supports the integration of existing application services via existing Web service standards (SOAP, WSDL).

2.1   System Services and Their Functionality

Among the system services, the global repositories are important since they store all necessary information for process execution. The OSIRIS layer of each node offers a replication service with is in charge of replicating sufficient information in order to allow for decentralized and decoupled process execution. Additional system services support tasks like process management, replication, messaging, routing, and load balancing.

Global Repository Services. The *Process Repository* holds the global definitions of all processes types (DL applications). Process definitions are decomposed into pairs of subsequent activities within the control flow, called execution units. Execution units are tuples containing process ID, ID of current activity, ID of subsequent activity/activities in control flow, and event type. On termination of the current activity, the OSIRIS layer produces an event to indicate the status of current activity execution. For example, if the current activity has not terminated gracefully, an error event is produced. The event type allows for different control flows for regular execution and for failure handling. In addition, an activity may have multiple direct successors in the control flow for the same event type, which corresponds to a split in the process execution. Therefore, in OSIRIS only execution units are replicated from the process repository where the first activity corresponds to a service available at the local provider.

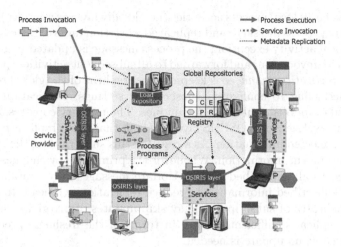

Fig. 1. OSIRIS Architecture & Distributed Execution of OSIRIS Processes

The *Service Registry* keeps a list of all available (tightly coupled) services, offered by all providers in the OSIRIS network.

The *Load Repository* stores information on the current load situation of providers in the OSIRIS network. Additionally, freshness parameters on subscriptions are used to avoid unnecessary propagation of minor load updates.

The *UDDI Registry* is in charge of keeping a registry of loosely coupled services together with their WSDL descriptions, since loosely coupled services do not register themselves at the service repository. This registry is necessary to keep the OSIRIS infrastructure informed about available loosely coupled services.

All these repositories do not require a centralized service implementation. If the number of nodes in the OSIRIS network is increasing, additional repositories of same kind can reduce the load (i.e., by applying horizontal partitioning). Figure 1 illustrates the OSIRIS architecture. It shows the upload of a sample process to the process repository. After the upload, the process description is divided into execution units. These execution units are replicated to the local OSIRIS layers of nodes providing participating tightly coupled services. Also necessary load and available service information is replicated from load and subscription repositories. Finally, after replication, sufficient process and service meta information is locally available to allow for peer-to-peer process execution.

Functionality of the Local OSIRIS Layer. The local OSIRIS layer allows for a reliable exchange of messages between all nodes of the OSIRIS network.

The *Horus component* is responsible for activation and deactivation of local services. External communication is done via two pipelines for incoming and outgoing messages, respectively. Pluggable handlers are applied to the pipeline and offer specific processing support for messages.

Process execution is done by exchanging process messages, which are processed by a dedicated *process handler*. It is plugged in the incoming message pipeline of the

Horus and executes local process activities (i.e., locally invokes a service) based on information in process messages and replicated execution units of the current process. After local activity execution, the process message is updated (e.g., with results of a service invocation) and forwarded to all subsequent activities (providers).

The local *replication manager* is keeping local replicas of the global repository consistent according to configured subscription settings. Replication management is based on publish/subscribe techniques. The primary copy resides at the global repository. Each local OSIRIS layer as client that needs replicas has to subscribe for the selected information. As a result of this subscription, the repository publishes the current information. Whenever the primary copy changes, updates are published to all subscribed clients. Update messages only contain changed parts of the subscribed information to reduce replication overhead. In addition, freshness predicates of subscriptions may skip updates of marginal changes. As long as the replica is sufficiently close (in terms of the freshness predicate) to the primary copy, no update is needed.

The *routing handler* is a handler in the outgoing message pipeline of the Horus and responsible for selection of an appropriate provider as destination of outgoing messages. If multiple providers are able to process the corresponding message, the best suitable according to current load (the locally replicated approximation) is selected (load balancing).

The *SOAP component* is an OSIRIS system service managed by the Horus, which is in charge of the invocation of SOAP calls for the interaction with loosely coupled services. This component wraps an OSIRIS service call into a standardized Web service invocation.

The *Web component* is a local system service managed by the Horus, which is in charge of making OSIRIS functionality accessible by standard Internet protocols like HTTP/HTML and offers an HTML interface for user interaction.

Finally, the *process component* is a local OSIRIS system service managed by the Horus, which is in charge of starting the execution of a process within the OSIRIS network.

2.2 Application Services and Their Integration

Based on the system services presented in the previous section, a Digital Library architect needs to integrate user-defined application-specific services within Digital Library processes. These application-specific services are called application services. There are two possibilities to integrate application services into the OSIRIS infrastructure. Firstly, they can be integrated as tightly coupled services, which offer more functionality for process management. Secondly, they can be integrated as loosely coupled services which do not require a local OSIRIS layer at the provider's host.

Tightly Coupled Services. follow a proprietary OSIRIS service specification and offer additional interfaces to allow controlling the life-cycle of service instances and to retrieve information about the current state of the service instance (e.g., load situation, reliability and correctness of service invocations) which is needed for load balancing and failure handling of processes. Currently evolving Web standards like WSRF address these additional service specification demands, e.g. life-cycle and resource management. Future versions of OSIRIS will consider these standards as replacement for proprietary formats. Tightly coupled application services behave in the same way as system services and can be directly called as activities within OSIRIS processes.

Loosely Coupled Services. provide the fastest and easiest way to integrate application-specific services into OSIRIS-based processes via OSIRIS' SOAP component. Loosely coupled services are built upon the existing Web service standards, i.e., SOAP and WSDL. However, due to the loose coupling, these services cannot benefit from load balancing, and advanced failure handling.

3   ISIS: Services for Content-Based Multimedia Retrieval

ISIS (Interactice SImilarity Search) is a prototype application for information retrieval in multimedia collections [7]. It supports content-based retrieval of images, audio and video content, and the combination of any of these media types with sophisticated text retrieval [8]. The screenshots in Figure 2 show a combined search for flowers. Starting point is the query front-end, depicted in Figure 2(a), where keyword and reference image can be specified. Figure 2(b) then shows the query results for this combined query.

One of the main considerations in designing ISIS was to ensure high scalability and flexibility. Therefore, instead of implementing one monolithic application, ISIS consists of a set of specialized application services for similarity search which are combined by the OSIRIS middleware. The ISIS services can be easily distributed among several nodes in a network [9]. The query presented in Figure 2 is therefore implemented as a process. It is important to note that the process specification just contains the details of all application services it encompasses (WSDL description) and their order of invocation. The actual service providers are determined at run-time. Therefore, information on the location of these providers is not part of the process description. Hence, each step of the process can be executed by any node providing the required service. After issuing the query a first time, a user can refine and re-issue her query. The query process (including user feedback) consists of the steps Query Reformulation (based on relevance feedback the user has issued), Query Execution (index access), and Result Filtering (which may again take user feedback into account). In Figure 3, this process is shown in the design view of the O'GRAPE tool.

In order to process complex content-based similarity queries effectively and efficiently, ISIS makes use of the VA-file index structure [10]. In addition, indexes are replicated on several nodes to serve more requests in parallel and to balance the load between these nodes. While replication helps to cope with query load, it increases complexity of modifying a collection by inserting, deleting, or updating objects since the updates of all indexes have to be coordinated to ensure consistency. In ISIS, this is done by appropriate system processes, i.e., processes that

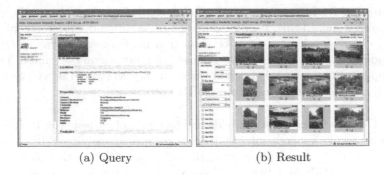

(a) Query　　　　　　　　　　(b) Result

Fig. 2. Combined Text and Images Similarity Search

have been designed by system administrator and which run automatically to guarantee consistency over several replicas of the index. ISIS attempts to divide the insertion of multimedia objects in several sub-tasks which are executed on different nodes while relying on OSIRIS to ensure correctness of the distributed execution [11]. The process used in ISIS to insert new objects is depicted in Figure 4. ISIS comprises a collection of more than 600'000 images.

3.1　Collection Management

Each object contained in the Digital Library is assigned a unique identifer (OID) within the collection. The *Meta Database component* maintains the association of an OID and the object. In addition, each object has an object type (OType), which can be image, audio, video, video sequence, or text and can be associated with several locations, e.g., the original URL from which the object has been downloaded, the filename of the local copy, or the address of a thumbnail image. Further meta data like size in bytes of the file or whether the object is copyrighted is stored.

Storage service is able to deliver the file content of the object and monitor changes in a directory of the file system. In case a change is detected, an OSIRIS process is started. The storage service heavily uses the underlying OSIRIS middleware also for other tasks, e.g., to transfer objects from one node to another.

The *Web Crawler* service periodically monitors websites for modifications. For fast access, a local copy is stored and updated in case of modifications. If a new link is found and this link is qualified for inclusion, the crawler follows this link and inserts the new object. Similar to the Storage service, processes are triggered according to modification events. The only difference is that here it is also necessary to specify at what time and in which intervals the crawler should visit the websites, inclusion and exclusion patterns need to be defined, etc.

3.2　Search Interface and Query Processing

ISIS provides a web interface to the user to issue searches. The design is stored in HTML template files extended by a tag library using XSLT. The OSIRIS

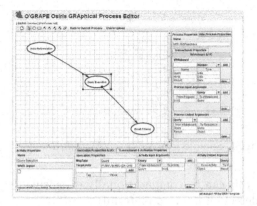

Fig. 3. Design View of an ISIS Search Process in O'GRAPE

Web component automatically applies those templates to visualize the results or error messages. This makes the customization of a Digital Library an easy task.

The *Session Management* service provides the basic handling of the user interactions. Each query issued by the user is executed as a new process as displayed in Figure 4. The result of the process is handed over to the Web component, which will layout the result based on the templates.

The *Relevance Feedback* component evaluates the feedback that a user can issue for previously executed queries. As identified in the search process, this may take place in two execution steps: (i.) before the query is executed, it can be re-formulated, e.g., by adding more reference objects to the query or modifying their weights, (ii.) after the query has been executed, it can filter out some unwanted objects or rearrange the position within the result.

The *Indexing service* is used to answer queries efficiently. A sample query process is depicted in Figure 3. Several types of indexes are supported. The first two, attribute and set indexes, use relational databases. The difference between the two is that attribute indexes are build on one particular value, e.g., the size of an object in number of bytes. This can be handled easily by the functionality that common RDBMS provide. Set indexes, in contrast, can contain multiple values, e.g., used to provide text retrieval in vector space model, for which term frequencies and document frequencies are needed to measure relevance. Query processing of these two indexes is optimized by the used database. For high-dimensional feature spaces, e.g., if colour histograms of images are used, additional indexes are stored outside the RDBMS. The Indexing component optimizes and executes queries on these index types. When complex queries are used, it is also necessary to aggregate the results delivered by the individual indexes [7].

3.3   Feature Extraction

Content-based information retrieval for multimedia data employs features that have been extracted from the objects prior to search. Depending on the type of

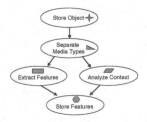

Fig. 4. Sample Process *InsertMultimediaObject*

features to extract, this can be computationally expensive (e.g., the analysis of audio files or shot detection in video material).

There are many different features supported in ISIS, which are offered by a couple of different services. To ease the handling, feature extractors that are implemented as tightly coupled services share a common interface for extraction and for registering to the ISIS system. In order to support several types of features, an administration tool exists in ISIS that automatically generates a sub-process within the activity "Extract Features" for the process in Figure 3, where the administrator simply has to select which features should be extracted and indexed. At registration time of a service, it is possible to specify the storage format, dependencies on other features, and a preferred distance measure for similarity evaluation.

The general *Feature Extractor component* provides the following features: (i.) Colour histogram in RGB color space, (ii.) color moments in HCL and Lab colour space, and (iii.) Gabor texture moments on luminance. All of these can be applied on the image as a whole, on overlapping rectangles, or on "5 fuzzy regions", which basically is one region starting in each corner and a ellipse in the image centre where a membership function defines for each pixel of the image its influence on the feature of the region.

The *Face Detector* offers several algorithms to analyze images to identify regions that contain a face. It returns the number of face found and a bounding box for each. The *Audio Feature Extractor* uses the MARSYAS library to extract the features "beat" and "pitch", which are again feature vectors. The *Hypertext Feature Extractor* analyzes HTML documents for embedded links. It also identifies images and assigns the surrounding text to it.

The *Term Frequency Extractor* is applied to plain text, in particular to the output of the Hypertext Feature Extractor. It returns a list of all found terms and the number of their occurrences. This feature is stored as a set index and used for Boolean and vector space retrieval. The sample ISIS process illustrated in Figure 4 shows all necessary activities for inserting a new multimedia object into the ISIS Digital Library. Activities, like Extract Features, may itself be complex processes again using a composition of services, e.g., a colour histogram service, a face detector service, and a segmentation service. Activities may be system services, e.g., storing some meta-data tuples in a database, or storing an image in a file system, but also application specific services like a face detector.

4 Summary and Outlook

Service-oriented architectures have a very strong influence on DLs and Digital Library Management Systems (DLMS). In particular, they significantly change the way future DL applications will be built. Instead of having complex monolithic applications, DL functionality is made available by means of services and can be combined in an application-specific way by using processes. This paper has presented ISIS and OSIRIS, a prototype implementation of a DLMS that combines dedicated DL services (ISIS) with a flexible and reliable platform for service composition (OSIRIS). ISIS and OSIRIS build the core part of Delos-DLMS, the integrated DELOS prototype of a next-generation DLMS.

References

1. Schek, H.J., Schuldt, H., Weber, R.: Hyperdatabases: Infrastructure for the Information Space. In: Proc. VDB 2007, Bisbane, Australia (2002)
2. Schek, H.J., Schuldt, H., Schuler, C., Weber, R.: Infrastructure for Information Spaces. In: Manolopoulos, Y., Návrat, P. (eds.) ADBIS 2002. LNCS, vol. 2435, Springer, Heidelberg (2002)
3. Schek, H.J., Schuldt, H.: DelosDLMS - Infrastructure for the Next Generation of Digital Library Management Systems. ERCIM, Special Issue on European Digital Library 66, 22–24 (2006)
4. Schuler, C., Türker, C., Schek, H.J., Weber, R., Schuldt, H.: Scalable Peer-to-Peer Process Management. International Journal of Business Process Integration and Management (IJBPIM) 1(2), 129–142 (2006)
5. Schuler, C., Schuldt, H., Türker, C., Weber, R., Schek, H.J.: Peer-to-peer Execution of (transactional) Processes. Int. Journal of Cooperative Information Systems 14(4), 377–406 (2005)
6. Schuldt, H., Alonso, G., Beeri, C., Schek, H.J.: Atomicity and Isolation for Transactional Processes. ACM Transactions Database Systems 27(1), 63–116 (2002)
7. Böhm, K., Mlivoncic, M., Schek, H.-J., Weber, R.: Fast Evaluation Techniques for Complex Similarity Queries. In: Proc. VLDB 2001, San Francisco, USA (2001)
8. Springmann, M.: A Novel Approach for Compound Document Matching. Bulletin of the IEEE Technical Committee on Digital Libraries (TCDL) 2(2) (2006)
9. Weber, R., Bolliger, J., Gross, T.R., Schek, H.-J.: Architecture of a Networked Image Search and Retrieval System. In: Proc. CIKM 1999, Kansas City, USA (1999)
10. Weber, R., Schek, H.-J., Blott, S.: A Quantitative Analysis and Performance Study for Similarity-Search Methods in High-Dimensional Spaces. In: Proceedings VLDB 1998, New York City, USA, pp. 194–205 (1998)
11. Weber, R., Schek, H.-J.: A Distributed Image-Database Architecture for Efficient Insertion and Retrieval. In: Proc. MIS 1999, Indian Wells, California, pp. 48–55 (1999)

An Architecture for Sharing Metadata Among Geographically Distributed Archives

Maristella Agosti, Nicola Ferro, and Gianmaria Silvello

Department of Information Engineering, University of Padua, Italy
{agosti,ferro,silvello}@dei.unipd.it

Abstract. We present a solution to the problem of sharing metadata between different archives spread across a geographic region. In particular we consider the Italian Veneto Region archives. Initially we analyze the Veneto Region information system based on a domain gateway system called "SIRV-INTEROP project" and we propose a solution to provide advanced services against the regional archives. We deal with these issues in the context of the SIAR – Regional Archival Information System – project.

The aim of this work is to integrate different archive realities in order to provide unique public access to archival information. Moreover we propose a non-intrusive, flexible and scalable solution that preserves archives identity and autonomy.

1 Introduction

The experience gained in the context of the DELOS cooperative activities on service architectures for *Digital Library Systems (DLSs)* has enabled the launch and participation in a new project of interest to the Italian Veneto Region for the management of metadata on public archives distributed throughout the region. The project has been named *Sistema Informativo Archivistico Regionale (SIAR)* and is a project for the design and development of a prototype able to manage metadata of interest for the building of a "Regional Archival Information System". In fact the aim of SIAR is to offer access to archival information which is maintained in several repositories spread across the Veneto Region.

In this study, we discuss how to address the problem of sharing archival metadata stored in different repositories geographically distant from each other.

The Veneto Region archives belong to different kinds of institutions, such as Municipalities; they are managed by different *Information Management Systems (IMSs)*. In this context, we have to satisfy a strong requirement for cooperation and inter-operability, while at the same time preserving not only the autonomy of all these institutions, but also their way of managing and organizing their archives. As a consequence, the different IMSs have to be considered as legacy systems and cannot be modified or changed in order to be integrated together.

Moreover, a central service has to be provided to give external users the possibility of accessing and obtaining archival metadata stored in the regional

C. Thanos, F. Borri, and L. Candela (Eds.): Digital Libraries: R&D, LNCS 4877, pp. 56–65, 2007.

archives. This service should save a coherent way of accessing the archival information and should preserve users from having to physically visit an archive.

Finally, the system proposed has to be integrated into the national telematic infrastructure for the Public Administration, which is being developed in order to provide the inter-operation between different applications of the public administrations.

The paper is organized as follows: Section 2 reports on the Italian National telematic infrastructure for the public administrations which is based on domain gateways, it explains also how SIRV-INTEROP works; this is a project developed by the Veneto Region. Section 3 addresses the design of the SIAR infrastructure and presents a conceptual system architecture which involves the Veneto Region and the regional territory archive keepers. Section 4 presents SIRV-PMH architecture. Section 5 draws some conclusions.

2   The National Telematic Infrastructure for the Public Administration

The Veneto Region participates in the creation of the Italian National Net of services which enables an infrastructure for the interconnection of public administrations. The Veneto Region participates to the National Net by means of its SIRV-INTEROP project. SIRV-INTEROP project implements a Domain Gateway System based on Applicatory Cooperation principles [3]. Through this system the Veneto Region is able to participate in the Italian National Net of services. The Italian National Net improves cooperation and integration between the various administrations and provides various services to external users.

The main goal of the domain gateway system is to integrate the service of different administrations. A highly important issue for this system is to maintain the independence of each cooperative information system. In this way any system that wants to fulfill a service to the Net community could maintain its internal structure unchanged. We define as **domain** a particular organization set of resources and policies. The domain is also considered the organization *responsibility boundary*. The National Net is conceived as a domains federation. Communication takes place through uniform entities (domains) and the main goal of the cooperative architecture is to enable the integration of policies of the informative objects (e.g. data and procedures) and the different domains.

The fundamental element of this system is represented by the modalities through which a server domain exports its services for the clients domains. The technological element for realizing this system is a **Domain gateway**; it has a resources access proxy function. A domain gateway represents the summa of all things necessary for accessing the domain resources, as shown in figure 1(a).

From an architectural point of view, domain gateways are seen as adaptors which enable cooperation between the National Net and many different information systems, as shown in figure 1(b). Domain gateways are divided into two main classes:

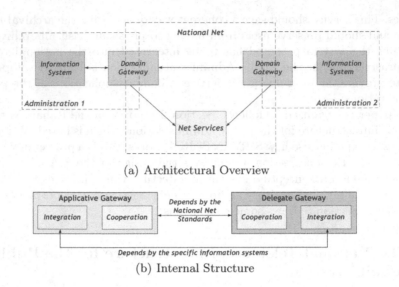

(a) Architectural Overview

(b) Internal Structure

Fig. 1. Domain Gateway System

- **Applicative Gateway:** This is the domain gateway which grants services; every domain which can distribute services carries out this function through this gateway. Information systems are connected by applicative gateway through a particular module called *Wrapper*;
- **Delegate Gateway:** Is the domain gateway that requests services to application gateways. Delegate gateway is realized by the information systems that use *net services* to realize the collaboration.

From a logical point of view, every domain gateway is composed of two main components:

- **Cooperation:** Realizes data communications generical functions;
- **Integration:** Realizes the adaptation towards the information systems and guarantees that the applicatory content respects formats and coding policies.

Cooperation components depend on the National Net standards; in contrast integration components depend both on the National Net standards and the characteristics of the information system they have to integrate.

Communication and data exchanges between Applicative and Delegate gateways take place by means of *Simple Object Access Protocol (SOAP)*, protocol which use *eXtensible Markup Language (XML)* technologies to define an extensible messaging framework [4].

Through SIRV-INTEROP project the Veneto Region is able to share services and information between many public administrations. The SIRV-INTEROP project guarantees interoperability, in this way different public administrations can use different information systems.

3   The SIAR Infrastructure

The SIAR project backdrop is characterized by the presence of different institutional needs. To design the SIAR system we have to consider each of these needs. On the one hand we have to guarantee that the local bodies maintain the management autonomy of their archives. On the other hand, however, we have to build-up regional coordination so that we can have an integrated global vision of the local archives participating in SIAR; for this reason the Veneto Region has to define a set of useful rules for the coordination and integration of local archival bodies present in the Region.

We need to guarantee the different juridical subjects autonomy with regard to the archival and information system choices; a possible solution could be a net of autonomous archives which share regional authority lists together with a protocol for metadata exchange. With this kind of solution local archives would exchange with SIAR only the metadata describing their archival resources, SIAR would store the harvested metadata in a central repository. This central repository would constitute the basis of unique access portal to the regional archives. This system would enable a user to identify a particular archival resource and SIAR would provide the information enabling the user to physically or virtually reach the archive containing the resource.

3.1   Integration Requirements

SIAR is constituted by a federation of autonomous archives characterized by unique access point. It will supply advanced research and integration services granting a common starting point; these services could also be implemented at a later date. However, it is important to identify some basic pre-requisites which are fundamental to the integration process:

Authority lists are the first requirement. It is mandatory for local archive coordination and integration. The definition of authority lists is a necessary tool to enable data exchange and integration between two or more subjects. An authority list enable the unique identification of the particular entity it describes. Moreover, authority lists supply an entity shared description; in this way identification and description are common to all the users using the same authority list.

The first step towards integrated access to the resources distributed across the Region is the utilization of a set of authority lists created and defined by the archival conservation subjects (archive keepers) with the coordination of the Veneto Region. SIAR will supply a common access point to the different archival resources distributed through the Veneto Region. It will be a portal which enables an integrated view of the Veneto Region's archival resources and it will be a unique public access point.

Protocol for metadata exchange is another essential requirement. In general, a protocol for data exchange is a protocol that defines a rules set which fixes the data format, the channel and the means of communication. A part of this requirement is the data format choice, which is useful for the metadata exchange between archive keepers and the Veneto Region.

Collaboration of local bodies. Different archive keepers could obtain a benefit from the common authority lists defined by the Veneto Region. Moreover, they should form metadata following the rules defined by the common protocol chosen by the Veneto Region.

3.2 Conceptual Architecture

We have to consider that SIAR is an institutional project and that there has been a recent digital administration legal framework. Also for these reasons, we think it is important to propose an architecture based on standards and on open source softwares. Standards enable the development of interoperable systems which are also based on a methodological study which guarantees a long lifetime to the project itself. The use of open source tools is desirable both because it is consistent with the most recent legal dispositions about digital administration and because it is supported by a community of developers and users which guarantee its development and analysis in a continuous way.

As we have just mentioned, the international initiative called *Open Archives Initiative (OAI)* is very important in an archival context. The main goal of OAI is to develop and promote interoperability standards to facilitate the dissemination of content, in this case the archival contents. The SIAR project is an occasion to promote local archives to disseminate their contents. In this context OAI could be the right choice for setting up the methodological and technological equipment useful for designing a system which manages and shares archival contents.

Open Archives Initiative Protocol for Metadata Harvesting (OAI-PMH) [2] allows us to achieve a technological integration of the information systems participating in the SIAR project. OAI-PMH is based on the distinction between the roles of the participants; they can be a *Data Provider* or a *Service Provider*. In our case study the Veneto Region is the Service Provider, because it is the subject which gives advanced services such as data and public access to them. Archive keepers are seen as Data Providers because they supply archive metadata. These metadata will be harvested, stored and probably indexed by the Veneto Region in order to provide services.

As we can see in Figure 2 the Veneto Region has to get harvester software, instead archive keepers have to get repository software which answers the harvester requests. Repository software has to prepare and send metadata in a specific and agreed format.

As we have just seen, archive keepers autonomy is very important, in this way there could be the presence and the co-existence of many different archive management information systems. There will be the need to propose an automatic or manual procedure to import metadata from the different keepers systems inside repositories which will be harvested by the Veneto Region harvester software.

Moreover, archival integration between the different archive keepers will be fundamental; this is possible by means of the Veneto Region guidelines which have to be shared between them. The Veneto region has to define the standards

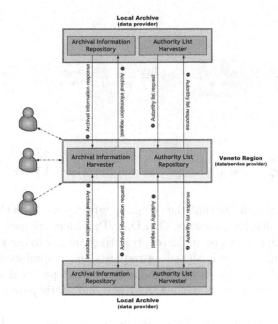

Fig. 2. Conceptual Architecture of SIAR

for the archival descriptions and it has to produce and keep the authority lists. Authority list sharing assures a first degree of integration, this could be used not only for metadata aggregation but also for constituting a common public access point to the Veneto Region archive information. In this context archive keepers need a mechanism enabling them to obtain the authority lists. OAI-PMH could be used on this occasion too; archive keepers would have harvester software whereas the Veneto Region would have repository software for managing the authority files. In this system the Veneto Region would be a Service Provider when it offers advanced services on metadata and a Data Provider when it keeps and delivers authority files to the archive keepers. We can see these peculiarities in the conceptual architecture design in Figure 2.

4   Integration of OAI-PMH into the National Telematic Infrastructure

In this section we propose a solution capable of adapting OAI-PMH functionalities to the domain gateway system. We perform OAI Data and Service Provider as domain gateways, in this way the two systems can be adapted to each other without any particular modification.

The main idea is that the Service Provider works as a delegate gateway which takes user requests and requires services to the various applicative gateways. Users require archive metadata by means of a portal system and so the delegate gateway harvests metadata records from the various repositories using the six

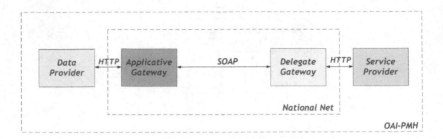

Fig. 3. OAI-PMH over National Net: General View

OAI-PMH verbs. We can say that the delegate gateway harvests the repositories which look like applicative gateways. OAI Data Providers are seen as applicative gateways which supply services; in this context they answer to the six verbs of the metadata harvesting protocol. Metadata requests and responses occur between applicative and delegate gateways through the SOAP protocol [4]. From this point of view, archives are open to the OAI-PMH and participate in the National Net of services.

In Figure 3 we can see how the National Net, which is based on the exchange of XML messages, could be used to harvest metadata by means of OAI-PMH. Service/data providers and domain gateway communication takes place by HTTP post/get method. In contrast data communication between domain gateways takes place by means of a SOAP protocol. This consideration shows that the two systems do not change their internal functioning, indeed they always use their default transport protocols.

We have to make a few additions to the Veneto Region system: we have to add a delegate gateway for the service provider and an applicative gateway for each repository participating in the system. We utilize an applicative gateway for each repository because different repositories constitute different domains and different domains implicate different domain gateways. In this way, repositories participating in the National Net can offer other services besides those provided by OAI-PMH. In addition, the service provider maintains its OAI-PMH functions and the delegate gateway works as an *"adaptor"* between OAI-PMH requests and the National Net. The delegate gateway harvests metadata; it crowns OAI-PMH requests inside XML SOAP messages. The applicative gateway is connected to the data provider and offers services to the National Net by means of wrappers around the information systems which are the base of a specific service; in this context applicative gateways interface data providers.

4.1   A Conceptual Architecture

The biggest issue for integrating OAI-PMH inside the National Net is to carry OAI-PMH requests by SOAP protocol and to do the same with the responses.

In this case the principal role of domain gateways is to encapsulate the requests or the responses into SOAP envelopes. On the other hand, domain gateways have

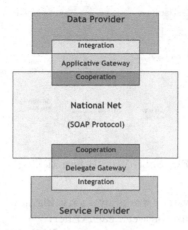

Fig. 4. The Role of Integration and Cooperation Components

to extract OAI-PMH requests and responses from their SOAP envelope. Domain gateways are composed of two main components: *cooperation* and *integration*. These two parts are helpful for addressing our problem; Figure 4 is a visual representation of how they act and shows how cooperation and integration components work as interfaces between the National Net and OAI Data/Service providers.

Now we have to consider how to implement solutions to integrate OAI-PMH with the National Net without making any substantial modifications to the two systems; the fundamental idea is to use OAI-PMH as a layer over SOAP [1].

4.2 SIRV-PMH Design

SIRV-PMH represents the joining of the SIRV-INTEROP project and OAI-PMH. Integration is a logical component which on the one hand acts as OAI Data Provider and on the other hand acts as an OAI Service Provider. In particular, the Integration component in the Delegate Gateway is composed of:

- **OAI Data Provider:** Receives OAI requests and answers with the required metadata;
- **OAI-SIRV Wrapper:** Encapsulates the OAI request inside a SOAP message consistent with the National Net.

Instead the Integration component in Applicative Gateways is composed of:

- **OAI-SIRV Wrapper:** Extracts the OAI request from the SOAP envelopment;
- **OAI Service Provider:** Sends OAI requests to the OAI Data Provider and receives the required metadata.

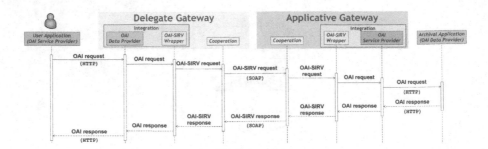

Fig. 5. SIRV-PMH Functioning

We can see how this system works by analyzing how OAI Service and Data Provider exchange metadata between each other.

The Applicative Gateway has to receive an XML SOAP message using the *cooperation component*; by the use of the *OAI-SIRV wrapper* it has to remove SOAP tags from the message and extract the OAI-PMH request. The extracted request is sent by means of the *OAI Service Provider Integration component* to the OAI Data Provider which has to process the OAI-PMH request and query the repository to obtain the required information. Afterwards, it has to build up an OAI-PMH response. When the response is ready, it has passed again to the Applicative Gateway which has to receive the response, add SOAP tags and send the XML SOAP message through the National Net.

The delegate Gateway and Service Provider have a similar role and more or less work in the same manner. In fact the Service Provider has to formalize an OAI-PMH request and pass it to the Delegate Gateway. The Delegate Gateway has to receive the OAI request, encapsulate the OAI-PMH request inside an XML SOAP message and send it to the Applicative Gateway by means of the National Net. Moreover, the Delegate Gateway has to receive the answer message by the Applicative Gateway, remove SOAP tags, extract the OAI-PMH response and send it to the OAI Service Provider.

If we consider a typical OAI-PMH request, for example a ListIdentifier [2] which harvests records headers from a repository, we can see how this request goes from the OAI Service Provider to the OAI Data Provider: an OAI Service Provider builds up a ListIdentifier request and sends it to the Delegate Gateway. The Delegate Gateway receives the request by means of its integration component. The OAI-SIRV Wrapper adds SOAP tags to the request so that it can be sent to the correct Applicative Gateway through the National Net. When the Applicative Gateway receives the request, it can extract the OAI-PMH request which can then be sent to the specificated Data Provider by means of a Service Provider. The Data Provider processes the request and builds up the response which follows the inverse procedure to reach the Service Provider. We can see SIRV-PMH functioning in Figure 5.

In this way the metadata contained in Data Providers can also be harvested by the Service Providers which do not participate in the National Net of services.

5   Conclusions

In this work we have presented an information system which addresses the problem of sharing archive metadata between different repositories geographically distant from each other. With this system, we can both preserve the autonomy of archive systems and provide a unique central public access point to the information they contain. We proposed a solution which integrates the Veneto Region system with an advanced, flexible and widely adopted protocol which is OAI-PMH. Moreover, we have seen how OAI-PMH can be adopted to work within SOAP and with different information systems. This system is called SIRV-PMH and would enable broad access to archive information which otherwise could only be reached by physically visiting the archives. SIRV-PMH does not modify the internal functioning of OAI-PMH and the SIRV-INTEROP project; it integrates these systems to provide advanced services on archives.

Now we have to implement the OAI-SIRV wrapper module and experimentally verify the efficiency of the SIRV-PMH system. The Data and Service Provider softwares also need to be taken into account, and we are evaluating *Online Computer Library Center (OCLC)* OAICat[1] and OCLC Harvester2[2] open source software tools. We have to verify if these software tools are truly effective for our purposes and if there is the need to adapt, add or change some of their functionalities.

Acknowledgements

The necessary background work of the study reported in this paper has been partially supported by the DELOS Network of Excellence on Digital Libraries, as part of the Information Society Technologies (IST) Program of the European Commission (Contract G038-507618).

The study is partially supported by a grant from the Italian Veneto Region.

References

1. Congia, S., Gaylord, M., Merchant, B., Suleman, H.: Applying SOAP to OAI-PMH. In: ECDL, pp. 411–420 (2004)
2. Van de Sompel, H., Lagoze, C., Nelson, M., Warner, S.: The Open Archives Initiative Protocol for Metadata Harvesting. Technical report (2004)
3. Gazzetta Ufficiale N. 78 del 3 Aprile 2002 ALLEGATO n. 2: Rete Nazionale: caratteristiche e principi di cooperazione applicativa
4. Gudgin, M., Hadley, M., Mendelsohn, N., Moreau, J., Nielson, H.F.: SOAP Version 1.2 Part 1: Messaging Framework and Part 2: Adjuncts. Technical report (2003)

---

[1] http://www.oclc.org/research/software/oai/cat.htm
[2] http://www.oclc.org/research/software/oai/harvester2.htm

Integration of Reliable Sensor Data Stream Management into Digital Libraries

Gert Brettlecker[1], Heiko Schuldt[1], Peter Fischer[2], and Hans-Jörg Schek[3]

[1] University of Basel
[2] ETH Zürich
[3] University of Konstanz

Abstract. Data Stream Management (DSM) addresses the continuous processing of sensor data. DSM requires the combination of stream operators, which may run on different distributed devices, into stream processes. Due to the recent advantages in sensor technologies and wireless communication, the amount of information generated by DSM will increase significantly. In order to efficiently deal with this streaming information, Digital Library (DL) systems have to merge with DSM systems. Especially in healthcare, the continuous monitoring of patients at home (telemonitoring) will generate a significant amount of information stored in an e-health digital library (electronic patient record). In order to stream-enable DL systems, we present an integrated data stream management and Digital Library infrastructure in this work. A vital requirement for healthcare applications is however that this infrastructure provides a high degree of reliability. In this paper, we present novel approaches to reliable DSM within a DL infrastructure. In particular, we propose information filtering operators, a declarative query engine called MXQuery, and efficient operator checkpointing to maintain high result quality of DSM. Furthermore, we present a demonstrator implementation of the integrated DSM and DL infrastructure, called OSIRIS-SE. OSIRIS-SE supports flexible and efficient failure handling to ensures complete and consistent continuous data stream processing and execution of DL processes even in the case of multiple failures.

1 Introduction

Recent trends in pervasive computing, together with new (wearable) sensor technologies, powerful mobile devices, and wearable computers strongly support novel types of applications. In the healthcare domain, for instance, applications make use of this new technology in order to improve the quality of treatment and care for patients and the elderly. Continuous data streams generated by (wearable/mobile) sensors have to be processed online in order to detect critical situations. For this purpose, usually different streams (generated by different types of sensors) have to be combined. This is done by making use of specialized operators. An infrastructure for data stream management (DSM) has to be able to reliably combine these operators in an application-specific way. In general, the area of DSM is very challenging for several reasons. First, the number of

C. Thanos, F. Borri, and L. Candela (Eds.): Digital Libraries: R&D, LNCS 4877, pp. 66–76, 2007.

(hardware and/or software) sensors for continuous data generation is continuously increasing. These sensors produce vast amounts of data which needs to be processed, analyzed and managed online and in a reliable way. Generally, sensor data streams are feeding and constantly modifying data kept in Digital Libraries. Thus, having an appropriate infrastructure for both digital library management and data stream management [1] is crucial. This integrated infrastructure allows for data generated by sensor information (e.g., after aggregating data over a certain time window or outliers with special semantics which have been detected in a stream) to be added to a DL. In the healthcare example, this means to store aggregated stream data and critical health states detected in the sensor signals in an eHealth Digital Library [2] (electronic health record). Therefore, the infrastructure for data stream management has to consider i.) operators which deal with continuous streams of data and ii.) discrete operators/services which allow for the interaction between DSM and Digital Libraries. Additionally, Digital Libraries affect also DSM, e.g., automatic adaptation of data stream processing when new laboratory results are arriving in the patients electronic health record.

Example applications are monitoring and managing road traffic. Most of the existing systems only cover specific "hot-spot" areas with a lot of traffic due to the high cost of deploying fixed sensors, the necessary communications systems and the complex control and indicator systems. Additionally, new mobile and embedded street and vehicle sensors can built up a distributed sensor network which depends on a reliable DSM infrastructure.

Another important field of application is eHealth. In particular telemonitoring applications enable healthcare institutions to take care of their patients while they are out of hospital, which is especially useful for managing various chronic diseases as well as for measuring the effects of treatments under real-life conditions. In addition, they serve as instrument for performing research and for accomplishing medical studies with incorporation of information from medical Digital Libraries. As a consequence, the patient's disease will be better managed with less hospitalization (which usually has physical and emotional impact) and higher quality of life. In the EU, 23 million adults are suffering from diabetes [3]. As a vision for the future, caregiver are able to equip their patients with wearable telemonitoring systems (e.g., consisting of a smart shirt [4] and a glucose measuring watch [5]). This setup will allow for unobtrusive monitoring As Figure 1 illustrates, the body sensors will wirelessly communicate with his home automation system in order to exchange data. Beside that, the telemonitoring infrastructure also aggregate additional context measurements received from the patient's smart-home infrastructure. Roughly estimated all data acquired about a single patient will likely exceed one GByte per day. Typically a caregiver will have to monitor thousands of patients. Therefore an efficient and reliable Digital Library infrastructure is needed, which will provide the services to analyze the data accumulated, to extract, filter, and to forward relevant information to the patient and the care provider in charge and additionally offer storing and analysis of information within an e-Health DL.

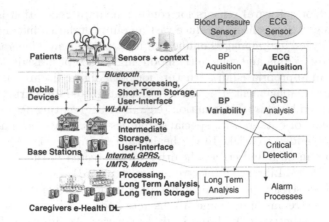

Fig. 1. Example of Distributed Data Stream Processing for Telemonitoring

This document is organized as follows: Sect. 2 presents a core data stream service of the infrastructure, called Information Filter System, developed at ETH. Sect. 3 introduces OSIRIS-SE, a reliable, stream-enabled Digital Library management infrastructure [1]. Sect. 4 discusses related work and Sect. 5 concludes.

2 Overview on the Context-Aware Information Filter System

Information Filters play an important role in processing streams of events, both for filtering as well as routing events based on their content. An information filter connects sources and sinks of information using profiles. Parties interested in receiving information (sinks) submit a profile of their interest to the information filter, while parties interested in disseminating information (sources) send messages to the information filter. Sources are often sensors or data derived from sensors. A context-aware information filter has two input streams: (a) a stream of messages (e.g., blood pressure readings) that need to be routed and (b) a stream of context updates such as the position or activity of a person.

2.1 Information Filters in Data Streams

Information Filters allow loose coupling of data producers and consumers via content-based profiles, which is particularly useful in the medical and traffic scenarios in this document:

- Support for personalized information delivery by profiles, e.g. delivering news about medical progress to patients and doctors based on the illnesses of the patients.
- Forwarding/retaining of sensor data from a patient to other systems depending on the context: a heart rate above 130 is OK for a young person doing sports, but indicates problems otherwise.

– Routing of medical events to the nearest/best fitting medical supplier/ treatment institution, based on the location of patients, ambulances and also the preliminary medical analysis.

To support these functionalities, information filters should be integrated at the various stages of the architecture: mobile devices, home PCs/gateways, healthcare and service providers.

A demonstrator is targeted towards large number of profiles, high message rates and high context update rates [6], also supporting batched handling of messages to increase message throughput [7]. In addition, the information filter system has support for high availability and reliability. On the basis of this information filter system, a QoS study has been performed, focusing on the impact of processing strategies [8].

A significant amount of streaming data is already in XML format. Therefore, MXQuery [9] is an open-source, lightweight implementation of an XML information filter based on the web-service enabled XQueryP [10] and the streaming extensions developed at ETH. MXQuery has been implemented very efficiently, giving comparable performance to specialized relational implementations like Aurora [11]. Efficient and reliable Information Filters are core data stream services of the integrated stream-enabled Digital Library management infrastructure OSIRIS-SE.

3   Data Stream Processing and Failure Handling with OSIRIS-SE

DSM is done by combining dedicated data stream operators into stream processes. These operators might run on different distributed devices (e.g., sensor signal filtering at a PDA while sophisticated analysis and correlation operators are hosted by a more powerful server). Especially in healthcare, the continuous telemonitoring of patients and integrating this information in an e-Health DL (electronic patient record) is becoming more and more important. A vital requirement in telemonitoring is that the infrastructure for distributed DSM provides a high degree of reliability and availability, since it can potentially be life-saving (e.g., a patient is equipped with a wearable telemonitoring system as described in Figure 1). A telemonitoring infrastructure offers distributed DSM, supports the analysis of the sensory data accumulated, and allows to extract and forward relevant information to the healthcare provider in charge and offers integration into Digital Libraries for long term storage and analysis. No data stream elements are allowed to be omitted from processing since the infrastructure is in charge of detecting critical situations or even anticipating them. In this work, we focus on the reliability of an integrated data stream management and Digital Library infrastructure. In particular, we investigate algorithms for the reliable execution of data stream operators within a stream process based on coordinated and efficient checkpointing of operator states.

3.1 OSIRIS-SE

OSIRIS (Open Service Infrastructure for Reliable and Integrated process Support) [12,13,14,15] is a prototype Digital Library infrastructure developed at ETH Zurich and the basis of the Delos Digital Library Management infrastructure (DelosDLMS) [1]. OSIRIS controls the execution of traditional processes as needed for DL applications. We refer to traditional processes as partially ordered sets of well defined activities which correspond to the invocation of services in a request/reply style. Furthermore, OSIRIS allows for reliable and distributed process execution in a peer-to-peer style without centralized control in a shared-nothing network. According to this, a node of the OSIRIS network works off its part of a process based on locally replicated meta-data about the process definition and then directly migrates the process instance data to a node offering a suitable service for the next activity in the process. For this reason, the OSIRIS architecture consists of two parts (see Fig. 2): i.) a software layer on each node (OSIRIS layer), and ii.) core services offering repositories for meta-data. Due to the invocation of discrete services, these processes are not able to perform data stream processing.

We have extended OSIRIS to OSIRIS-SE (Stream Edition) [16,17,18,19], which supports DSM. Similar to process execution in OSIRIS, the execution of DSM processes, called stream processes, is based on locally replicated meta-data. Additional information in core repositories is needed for stream processing, like available operators and providers, and stream process definitions. Also the reliable FIFO-transfer of stream elements and duplicate elimination is added for DSM.

3.2 Data Stream Model and Failure Handling

The basis of the proposed reliable data stream management is the operator and failure model, we present in this section. All definitions are based on data

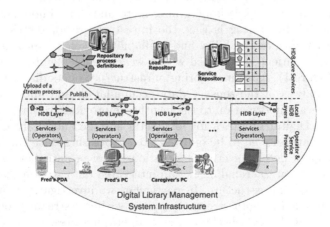

Fig. 2. OSIRIS-SE Architecture

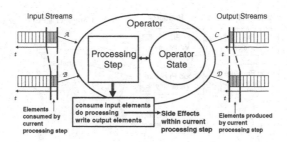

Fig. 3. Operator Model

streams, which are defined as a continuous transmission of sequentially ordered data elements. Each data element contains several data items as payload information and has discrete time context, e.g., a sequence number.

Operators (Fig.3) are the basic building blocks of data stream management. Running operator instances consume input elements from one ore more input streams and/or produce output elements (marked in grey color in Fig. 3) for one or more output streams during the execution of an atomic processing step, while performing a state transition. Produced output elements are stored in output queues for downstream operators. A node in the DSM infrastructure hosting a running operator is also called provider. With respect to the investigated application scenario, we consider operators as stateful and deterministic machines, for example considering an operator calculating an average value over heart rate measurement readings of the last hour. Essentially, every operator produces the same output stream and result into the same operator state when provided with the same input stream starting from the same operator state. Optionally, the processing step may produce a *side effect*, e.g., performing a backup of the current operator state. A *stream process* is a well defined set of logically linked operators continuously processing the selected input data streams, thereby producing results and having side effects. Figure 5 illustrates a stream process which continuously monitors ECG and blood pressure of a patient. Each box in Figure 4 contains a full-fledged operator of Fig. 3.

Failure Handling for Reliable Data Stream Management. In general, reliable and fault-tolerant DSM implies that stream processes have to be executed in a way that the process specification is met, even in case of failures, i.e., to correctly execute all operators in proper order without generating gaps, duplicates, or wrong elements in the result stream. The definition based on our deterministic operator model reads as follows: Reliable DSM produces a result stream and side effects, which are equal to the result stream and side effects produced by an ideal, faultless DSM system. In this work, our approach supports the following failure scenarios for reliable DSM: single or multiple fail-stop failures of operator instances or their providers and single or multiple network failures. Multiple failures are a sequence of single failures within the recovery time. With respect to failure handling, we apply the following failure classification:

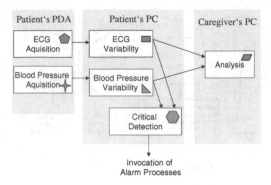

Fig. 4. Example Stream Process

Temporary failures, e.g., a temporary network disconnection (loss of messages) or a temporary failure of a provider which is able to recover within the maximum allowed delay time *dmax*, are compensated by the output buffers of the upstream provider. For recovery, the upstream provider resends the data stream elements and receives an acknowledge message. Failures exceeding *dmax* become permanent failures. *Permanent failures*, e.g., a permanent network disconnection or failure of a provider, require to migrate the operator instance with its aggregated operator state from the affected provider to another suitable provider. Operator migration implies the continuation of an operator instance from a recent checkpoint on a new provider in order to allow for seamless continuation of DSM, and eventually the stopping of an old running operator instance. Further details on failure detection in OSIRIS-SE can be found in [16,17,18,19].

Whereas for temporary failures no further failure handling by the OSIRIS-SE infrastructure is needed, the infrastructure has different possibilities to deal with permanent failures: Firstly, we have *transparent failure handling*, which is done by OSIRIS-SE without any application-specific behavior. Transparent failure handling is automatically applied by the infrastructure if a permanent failure occurs. Failure handling is done by operator migration based on recent and consistent operator state backups. Permanent failures cause the unavailability of one or more operator instances of a running stream process. In order to replace the unavailable (failed) operators and seamlessly continue stream processing, the infrastructure creates new operator instances running on still available providers and initializes the newly created operators with recent operator state backups. The efficient and coordinated checkpointing (ECOC) algorithm applied by OSIRIS-SE guarantees the availability of a recent and consistent operator state backup even in the case of multiple failures occurring at the same time [17,18,19]. Furthermore, if transparent failure handling is not applicable, there are two more *application-specific failure* handling mechanisms available in OSIRIS-SE. Firstly, the application designer, which is graphically creating the stream process, is able to define *alternative execution branches*. In case of failure, the infrastructure is able to move to an alternative execution branch, which is using a different set of operators, in order to continue stream processing. For example, for patient Fred it could be sufficient to derive only the heart rate from the ECG and do no further ECG signal analysis in case of limited available computing resources. Secondly, if also alternative execution branches are not applicable, the OSIRIS-SE infrastructure is able to generate application specific *alarm processes*. These alarm processes are traditional discrete processes as used for DL application and can generate information for the e-Health DL or inform physicians, emergency services, and patients. For example, if the patient is leaving the house and therefore continuous telemonitoring is unavailable, the OSIRIS-SE infrastructure will feed this information into the e-Health DL in order to maintain unmonitored periods for the analysis of the physician and may additionally inform Fred, that he is currently unmonitored.

The OSIRIS-SE prototype is programmed in Java and runs on various platforms, including also PDAs with MS Windows Mobile 2003. The demonstration scenario includes mobile devices (PDA), a smart ECG sensor and blood pressure senors in order to demonstrate the usability for telemonitoring. Additional context information is produced by a webcam and motion sensor. Fig. 5 illustrates the demo setup and the process editor O'Grape [15].

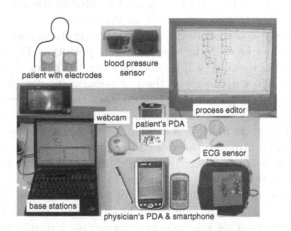

Fig. 5. The Data Stream Demonstrator Setup

4 Related Work

Data Stream Management has received quite some attention recently. Although only few work is focusing on aspects of availability and reliability.

Aurora [11] is one of the major DSM project that also focus on high availability of stream processing [20]. In contrast to our work, this work addresses reliability at the level of the whole stream processing engine running on the affected node whereas we focus on reliability at the level of operator execution. Further work [21] presented in the context of Borealis, an extension of Aurora, allows for reduced result quality which is not applicable considering our indented healthcare application scenario.

TelegraphCQ [22] is another major DSM project with focus on load balancing and fault tolerance. Flux [23] is providing adaptive partitioning of operator execution over multiple network nodes. This is realized by placing Flux between producer/consumer pairs. Therefore, contrarily to our approach, Flux describes an active-standby approach, where parts of stream processing are partitioned to be reliably executed in parallel. This active approach is not applicable to our intended healthcare monitoring scenario, where hardware resources at the patient homes are limited.

5   Conclusion and Outlook

In this paper, we have reported on the prototype system for integrated data stream processing and process management into Digital Libraries that has been jointly developed. Starting with an evaluation of use cases for managing and processing continuous streams of data, two core parts of the stream-enabled Digital Library infrastructure have been developed. First, information filtering operators allow for analysis of data streams and extracting relevant information. Second, it contains a reliable infrastructure for combining data stream operators and (traditional) discrete web services. This document has described in details the concepts of these demonstrators, their implementation, and also how these demonstrators can be used. In future work, this prototype DL system will be refined and more functionality will be added. From the point of view of the DL infrastructure, we will emphasize on the performance of complex stream processes with intra-process parallelism, i.e., on data stream processes containing join and split operators, and stream processes with cyclic data stream processing flows. From a user's point of view, it is planned to add the support for personalizing operators and stream processes. This means that based on individual profiles, different sensor measurements should be interpreted differently for different users (e.g., in the eHealth applications: high blood pressure for an athlete while engaging in strenuous training does not need to raise an alarm, whereas for a patient that has already suffered a heart attack, such a reading might indicate hypertension). This also affects information filtering in that queries, filters, and alarm triggers need to be personalized. Finally, support for using historic data from Digital Libraries for data stream processing will be added. Various telemonitoring applications require the comparison of current stream data to historic data. This is, for instance, important when changes to the diurnal biorhythm have to be detected (e.g., as it is required for monitoring patients with cognitive disabilities).

References

1. Agosti, M., Beretti, S., Brettlecker, G., Bimbo, A., Ferro, N., Fuhr, N., Keim, D., Klas, C., Lidy, T., Norrie, M., Ranaldi, P., Rauber, A., Schek, H., Schreck, T., Schuldt, H., Signer, B., Springman, M.: DelosDLMS - the Integrated DELOS Digital Library Management System. In: Post-proceedings of Delos Conference on Digital Libraries (2007)

2. Schuldt, H.: Service-oriented Advanced Digital Libraries in Healthcare and their Application to Virtual Electronic Health Records and Telemonitoring. In: HDL 2005. Proc. of the Healthcare Digital Libraries Workshop (2005)
3. Petersen, S., Peto, V., Rayner, M., Leal, J., Luengo-Fernandez, R., Gray, A.: The European Cardiovascular Disease Statistics. In: European Heart Network (2005)
4. Park, S., Mackenzie, K., Jayaraman, S.: The wearable motherboard: a framework for personalized mobile information processing (PMIP). In: Proc. of the 39th Conf. on Design Automation, pp. 170–174 (2002)
5. Animas Technologies: The Glucowatch G2 Biographer (2007), http://www.glucowatch.com
6. Dittrich, J.P., Fischer, P.M., Kossmann, D.: Agile: adaptive indexing for context-aware information filters. In: Proc. of the SIGMOD Conference, pp. 215–226 (2005)
7. Fischer, P.M., Kossmann, D.: Batched processing for information filters. In: ICDE 2005. Proc. of International Conference on Data Engineering, pp. 902–913 (2005)
8. Fischer, P.M., Kossmann, D.: Quality of Service in Stateful Information Filters. In: Proc. of International Workshop Data Management in Sensor Networks (DMSN), pp. 41–46 (2006)
9. Fischer, P.M., et al.: MXQuery (2007), http://mxquery.org
10. Carey, M., Chamberlin, D., Fernandez, M., Florescu, D., Ghelli, G., Kossmann, D., Robie, J., Simeon, J.: XQueryP: An XML Application Development Language. In: Proc. of XML Conference (December 2006)
11. Abadi, D., Carney, D., Çetintemel, U., Cherniack, M., Convey, C., Lee, S., Stonebraker, M., Tatbul, N., Zdonik, S.: Aurora: A New Model and Architecture for Data Stream Management. VLDB Journal Special Issue on Best Papers of VLDB 2002 12(2) (2003)
12. Schuler, C., Schuldt, H., Türker, C., Weber, R., Schek, H.-J.: Peer-to-Peer Execution of (Transactional) Processes. International Journal of Cooperative Information Systems (IJCIS) 14(4), 377–405 (2005)
13. Schuler, C., Weber, R., Schuldt, H., Schek, H.J.: Peer–to–Peer Process Execution with OSIRIS. In: Proc. of ICSOC Conf., Trento, Italy, pp. 483–498 (2003)
14. Schuler, C., Weber, R., Schuldt, H., Schek, H.J.: Scalable Peer–to–Peer Process Management – The OSIRIS Approach. In: Proc. of ICWS Conf., San Diego, CA, USA, pp. 26–34 (2004)
15. Weber, R., Schuler, C., Neukomm, P., Schuldt, H., Schek, H.J.: Web Service Composition with O'Grape and OSIRIS. In: Proc. of VLDB Conf., Berlin, Germany (2003)
16. Brettlecker, G., Schuldt, H., Schatz, R.: Hyperdatabases for Peer–to–Peer Data Stream Processing. In: Proc. of ICWS Conf., San Diego, CA, USA, pp. 358–366 (2004)
17. Brettlecker, G., Schuldt, H., Schek, H.J.: Towards Reliable Data Stream Processing with OSIRIS-SE. In: Proc. of BTW Conf., Karlsruhe, Germany, pp. 405–414 (March 2005)
18. Brettlecker, G., Schek, H.J., Schuldt, H.: Eine Pervasive-Healthcare-Infrastruktur für die verlässliche Informationsverwaltung und -verarbeitung im Gesundheitswesen. Datenbank-Spektrum 6(17), 33–41 (2006)
19. Brettlecker, G., Schuldt, H., Schek, H.J.: Efficient and Coordinated Checkpointing for Reliable Distributed Data Stream Management. In: Manolopoulos, Y., Pokorný, J., Sellis, T. (eds.) ADBIS 2006. LNCS, vol. 4152, pp. 296–312. Springer, Heidelberg (2006)

20. Hwang, J., Balazinska, M., Rasin, A., Cetintemel, U., Stonebraker, M., Zdonik, S.: High Availability Algorithms for Distributed Stream Processing. In: Proc. of ICDE Conference, Tokyo, Japan, pp. 779–790 (April 2005)
21. Balazinska, M., Balakrishnan, H., Madden, S., Stonebraker, M.: Fault-Tolerance in the Borealis Distributed Stream Processing System. In: Proc. of ACM SIGMOD Conf., Baltimore, MD, USA, June 2005, pp. 13–24. ACM Press, New York (2005)
22. Chandrasekaran, S., et al.: TelegraphCQ: Continuous Dataflow Processing for an Uncertain World. In: Proc. of CIDR Conf., Asilomar, USA (2003)
23. Shah, M.A., Hellerstein, J.M., Brewer, E.: High Available, Fault-Tolerant, Parallel Dataflows. In: Proc. of ACM SIGMOD Conf., Paris, France, pp. 827–838. ACM Press, New York (2004)

Content-Based Recommendation Services for Personalized Digital Libraries

G. Semeraro, P. Basile, M. de Gemmis, and P. Lops

Dipartimento di Informatica
Università di Bari
Via E. Orabona, 4 - 70125 Bari - Italia
{semeraro,basilepp,degemmis,lops}@di.uniba.it

Abstract. This paper describes the possible use of advanced *content-based* recommendation methods in the area of Digital Libraries. Content-based recommenders analyze documents previously rated by a target user, and build a profile exploited to recommend new interesting documents. One of the main limitations of traditional keyword-based approaches is that they are unable to capture the semantics of the user interests, due to the natural language ambiguity. We developed a semantic recommender system, called ITem Recommender, able to disambiguate documents before using them to learn the user profile. The Conference Participant Advisor service relies on the profiles learned by ITem Recommender to build a personalized conference program, in which relevant talks are highlighted according to the participant's interests.

Keywords: H.3 [Information Storage and Retrieval]: H.3.1 Content Analysis and Indexing, H.3.3 Information Search and Retrieval, H.3.7 Digital Libraries.

1 Introduction

Personalization has become an important topic for Digital Libraries to take a more active role in dynamically tailoring its information and service offer to individuals in order to better meet their needs [2]. Most of the work on personalized information access focuses on the use of machine learning algorithms for the automated induction of a structured model of a users interests, referred to as user profile, from labeled text documents [9]. Keyword-based user profiles suffer from problems of polysemy and synonymy. The result is that, due to synonymy, relevant information can be missed if the profile does not contain the exact keywords occurring in the documents and, due to polysemy, wrong documents could be deemed as relevant. This work explores a possible solution for this kind of issues: the adoption of semantic user profiles that capture key concepts representing users' interests from relevant documents. Semantic profiles will contain references to concepts defined in lexicons like WordNet [8] or ontologies. The solution is implemented in the ITem Recommender (ITR) system which induces semantic user profiles from documents represented by using WordNet [4]. An example of intelligent personalized recommendation service based on ITR will be shown.

C. Thanos, F. Borri, and L. Candela (Eds.): Digital Libraries: R&D, LNCS 4877, pp. 77–86, 2007.

2 Related Work

Our research was mainly inspired by the following works. Syskill & Webert [11] is an agent that learns a user profile exploited to identify interesting Web pages. The learning process is performed by first converting HTML source into positive and negative examples, represented as keyword vectors, and then using learning algorithms like Bayesian classifiers, a nearest neighbor algorithm and a decision tree learner. Personal WebWatcher [9] is a Web browsing recommendation service that generates a user profile based on the content analysis of the requested pages. Learning is done by a naïve Bayes classifier where documents are represented as weighted keyword vectors, and classes are interesting and not interesting. Mooney & Roy [10] adopt a text categorization method in their Libra system that performs content-based book recommendations by exploiting product descriptions obtained from the Web pages of the Amazon online digital store. Also in this case, documents are represented by using keywords and a naïve Bayes text classifier is adopted. The main limitation of these approaches is that they represent items by using keywords. The objective of our research is to create accurate semantic user profiles. Among the state-of-the-art systems that produce semantic user profiles, SiteIF [6] is a personal agent for a multilingual news web site that exploits a sense-based representation to build a user profile as a semantic network, whose nodes represent senses of the words in documents requested by the user. The role of linguistic ontologies in knowledge-retrieval systems is explored in OntoSeek [5], a system designed for content-based information retrieval from online yellow pages and product catalogs. OntoSeek combines an ontology-driven content-matching mechanism based on WordNet with a moderately expressive representation formalism. The approach has shown that structured content representations coupled with linguistic ontologies can increase both recall and precision of content-based retrieval. We adopted a content-based method able to learn user profiles from documents represented by using senses of words obtained by a word sense disambiguation strategy that exploits the WordNet IS-A hierarchy.

3 ITem Recommender: A framework for the Design of Services for Intelligent Information Access

The framework is bases on the idea that the problem of learning user profiles can be cast as a binary text categorization task: Each document has to be classified as interesting or not on the ground of the user preferences. The set of categories is $C = \{c_+, c_-\}$, where c_+ is the positive class (*user-likes*) and c_- the negative one (*user-dislikes*). In our approach, a naïve Bayes algorithm learns *sense-based* user profiles as binary text classifiers (*user-likes* and *user-dislikes*) from documents disambiguated by means of a *semantic indexing* procedure. The idea of learning user profiles from disambiguated documents was successfully introduced in [4].

The conceptual architecture of ITR is depicted in Figure 1. The *Content Analyzer* allows introducing semantics in the recommendation process by analyzing documents in order to identify relevant concepts representing the content. The core of the *Content Analyzer* is a procedure for assigning senses to words. Here, *sense* is used as a synonym of *meaning*. This task is known as Word Sense Disambiguation (WSD) and consists in determining , among all the possible meanings (senses) of an ambiguous word, the correct one according to the context in which the word appears. [7].

In this way, documents are represented using concepts instead of keywords, in an attempt to overcome the problems of the natural language ambiguity. The final outcome of the preprocessing step is a repository of disambiguated documents. This semantic indexing is strongly based on natural language processing techniques, such as Word Sense Disambiguation, and heavily relies on linguistic knowledge stored in the WordNet lexical ontology.

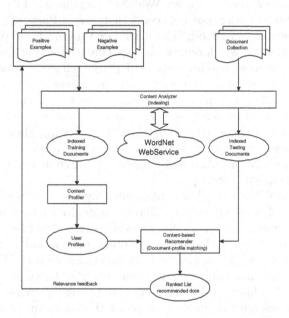

Fig. 1. The conceptual architecture of ITR

The *Profile Learner* implements a supervised learning technique for inferring a probabilistic model of the interests of a (target) user by learning from disambiguated documents rated according to her interests. This model represents the semantic profile, which includes those concepts that turn out to be most indicative of the user's preferences.

The *Recommender* exploits the user profile to suggest relevant documents, by matching concepts contained in the semantic profile against those contained in the documents to be recommended.

In the scientific congress scenario, the participant profile is learned from rated papers in the ISWC 2002 and 2003 paper repository. Then, the profile is matched against all ISWC 2004 accepted papers in order to identify the most relevant ones (which will be highlighted in the participant's personalized conference program).

The remainder of this paper describes the details of the process that leads to build semantic user profiles and the conference programs (properly) personalized for those profiles.

3.1   The Word Sense Disambiguation Algorithm

The goal of a WSD algorithm is to associate the appropriate meaning (or sense) s to a word w_i in document d, by exploiting its *(window of) context C*, that is a set of words that precede and follow w_i. The sense s is selected from a predefined set of possibilities, usually known as *sense inventory*. In our system, the sense inventory is obtained from WordNet (version 1.7.1)[1]. WordNet was designed to establish connections between four types of Parts of Speech (POS): Noun, verb, adjective, and adverb. The basic building block for WordNet is the SYNSET (SYNonym SET), which represents a specific meaning of a word. The specific meaning of one word under one type of POS is called a sense. Synsets are equivalent to senses, which are structures containing sets of words with synonymous meanings. Each synset has a gloss, a short textual description that defines the concept represented by the synset. For example, the words *night, nighttime* and *dark* constitute a single synset that has the following gloss: "the time after sunset and before sunrise while it is dark outside". Synsets are connected through a series of relations: Antonymy (opposites), hyponymy/hypernymy (IS-A), meronymy (PART-OF), etc.

JIGSAW is the WSD algorithm implemented by the *Content Analyzer*. It is based on the idea of combining three different strategies to disambiguate nouns, verbs, adjectives and adverbs. In this section we will describe the main idea behind the proposed approach. A more detailed description of the algorithm can be found in [14]. An adaptation of Lesk's dictionary-based WSD algorithm has been used to disambiguate adjectives and adverbs [1], an adaptation of the Resnik algorithm has been used to disambiguate nouns [12], while the algorithm we developed for disambiguating verbs exploits the nouns in the context of the verb and the nouns both in the glosses and in the phrases that WordNet utilizes to describe the usage of the verb. The algorithm disambiguates only words which belong to at least one synset.

The motivation behind our approach is that the performance of the WSD algorithms change in accordance to the POS tag of the word to be disambiguated. JIGSAW algorithm takes as input a document $d = \{w_1, w_2, \ldots, w_h\}$ and will output a list of WordNet synsets $X = \{s_1, s_2, \ldots, s_k\}$ ($k \leq h$) in which each element s_i is obtained by disambiguating the *target word* w_i based on the information obtained from WordNet about a few immediately surrounding words. We define the *context C* of the target word to be a window of n words to the left and another n words to the right, for a total of $2n$ surrounding words. The algorithm is based on three different procedures for nouns, verbs, adverbs and

---

[1] http://wordnet.princeton.edu

adjectives, called $JIGSAW_{nouns}$, $JIGSAW_{verbs}$, $JIGSAW_{others}$, respectively. The POS tag of each word to be disambiguated is computed by the HMM-based tagger ACOPOST t3[2].

JIGSAW proceeds in several iterations by using the disambiguation results of the previous iteration to reduce the complexity of the next one. First, JIGSAW performs noun disambiguation by executing the $JIGSAW_{nouns}$ procedure. Then, verbs are disambiguated by $JIGSAW_{verbs}$ by exploiting the words already disambiguated by $JIGSAW_{nouns}$. Finally, the $JIGSAW_{others}$ procedure is executed. The WSD procedure is used to obtain a synset-based vector space representation that we called Bag-Of-Synsets (BOS), described in the next section.

3.2 Semantic Document Indexing: Keyword-Based and Synset-Based Document Representation

In the Bag-Of-Synsets model (BOS), each document is represented by the vector of synsets recognized by the JIGSAW algorithm, rather than a vector of words, as in the classical Bag-Of-Words (BOW) model [13]. Another characteristic of the approach is that each document is represented by a set of *slots*. Each slot is a textual field corresponding to a specific feature of the document, in an attempt to take into account its structure. In our application scenario, in which documents are scientific papers, we selected three slots: *title, authors, abstract* (Figure 2). The text in each slot is represented according to the BOS model by counting separately the occurrences of a synset in the slots in which it appears.

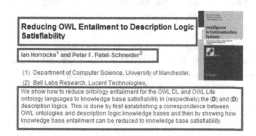

Fig. 2. The description of a paper structured in three slots

An example of BOW-represented document is depicted in Figure 3. The BOS-representation of the same document is presented in Figure 4.

Our hypothesis is that the BOS model helps to obtain profiles able to recommend documents semantically closer to the user interests. The difference with respect to keyword-based profiles is that synset unique identifiers are used instead of words. The next section describes the learning algorithm adopted to build semantic user profiles, starting from the BOS document representation.

---

[2] http://acopost.sourceforge.net/

```
title: {document: 1; categorization: 1; classification: 1}
authors: {sam: 1; scott: 1}
abstract: {categorization: 2; learning: 1; classification: 1; AI: 1;
           artificial: 1; intelligence: 1}
```

Fig. 3. An example of document represented using the Bag-of-Words model. Each slot contains terms and their corresponding occurrences in the original text.

```
title: {06424377 [text file, document] ((computer science) a computer
        file that contains text (and possibly formatting instructions)
        using seven-bit ASCII characters): 1

        00998694} [categorization, categorisation, classification,
        compartmentalization, compartmentalisation, assortment]
        -- (the act of distributing things into classes or categories
        of the same type): 2}

authors: {sam_scott}

abstract: {00998694 [categorization, categorisation, classification,
        compartmentalization, compartmentalisation, assortment]
        (the act of distributing things into classes or categories of
        the same type): 3

        06052624 [artificial intelligence, AI] (the branch of computer science
        that deal with writing computer programs that can solve problems
        creatively; "workers in AI hope to imitate or duplicate intelligence
        in computers and robots"): 2

        00590335 [learn, larn, acquire] (gain knowledge or skills;
        "She learned dancing from her sister"; "I learned Sanskrit";
        "Children acquire language at an amazing rate"): 1}
```

Fig. 4. An example of document represented using the Bag-of-Synsets model. Each slot contains the synsets associated by JIGSAW to the words in the original text. For the sake of readability, the synset descriptions (that are not included in the actual BOS representation) are also reported.

3.3 Profile Learner and Recommender

Services implemented by using the ITR framework are able to recommend items by learning from their textual descriptions and ratings given by users. The Profile Learner implements the naïve Bayes classifier, a popular algorithm in text classification applications. It is able to classify documents as interesting or uninteresting for a particular user by exploiting a probabilistic model, learned from training examples represented according to the BOS model described in the previous section. The final outcome of the learning process is a probabilistic model used to classify a new document as interesting or uninteresting. The model is used as a personal profile including those concepts (synsets) that turn out to be most indicative of the users preferences, according to the value of the parameters of the model. The Recommender performs the matching between profiles and testing documents and assigns a score representing the degree of interest of the user on those documents by using the Bayes classification formula. As a proof of concepts, we integrated the ITR functionalities to develop a service for supporting users to plan the participation to a scientific congress.

4   An Intelligent Service for Digital Libraries

The Conference Participant Advisor service is based on ITR and provides personalized support for conference participation planning. The semantic profile of each test user registered to the service is exploited to suggest the most interesting talks to be attended at the conference by producing a one-to-one personalized conference program. The prototype has been realized for the International Semantic Web Conference 2004, by adding to the conference homepage (a copy of the official web site) a login/registration form to access the service.

The registered user can browse the whole document repository or search for papers presented during 2002 and 2003 ISWC events, in order to provide ratings. The search engine used to select the training examples relies on the BOS model in order to allow users to perform a *semantic* search and to reduce the overload in providing the system with appropriate training examples. Let us suppose that the user now submits the query categorization to the paper retrieval system. The search engine analyzes the query and shows the sense inventory corresponding to the keyword. Among all the possible senses listed, the user can choose one or more of them according to her wishes. In the proposed scenario, the user is interested in papers about text categorization, which is the task of assigning documents to a list of predefined categories. Therefore, the most appropriate sense for the query is the third one in the sense inventory (Figure 5).

Notice that the word matching against the query, highlighted by the search engine, is different from the one in the query issued by the user. This is due to the fact that the two words are in the same synset, thus the system was able to realize a *semantic* matching by exploiting the synonymy relation in WordNet. This semantic search allows for a more accurate selection of training examples: the document retrieved in the aforementioned example would not have been retrieved by using a traditional keyword search.

Given a sufficient number of ratings (at present the minimum number of training documents is set to 20), the system learns the semantic profile of the participant. In the profile, concepts representing the participants research interests are stored. ISWC 2004 accepted papers are classified using the learned profile to obtain a personalized list of recommended papers and talks, which is sent by email to the participant. Recommended talks are highlighted in the personalized electronic program (Figure 7).

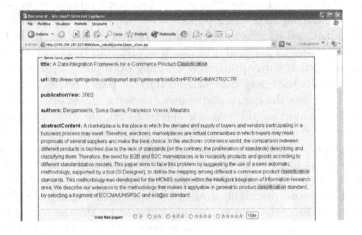

Type of search:	not personalized
Selected slotS:	title abstractContent
Selected category:	all
KeywordS:	categorization
	Search

Search with Term Sense

Maybe you are looking for "categorization" with sense:

Noun:

☐ *classification, categorization, categorisation -- (a group of people or things arranged by class or category)], [6636222]*

☐ *classification, categorization, categorisation, sorting -- (the basic cognitive process of arranging into classes or categories)], [4916095]*

☑ *categorization, categorisation, classification, compartmentalization, compartmentalisation, assortment -- (the act of distributing things into classes or categories of the same type)], [769615]*

| Search with these senses! |

Fig. 5. The user selects the most appropriate sense for the keyword "categorization"

title: A Data Integration Framework for e Commerce Product Classification

url: http://www.springerlink.com/openurl.asp?genre=article&id=HPEXMG4MW2?02C7R

publicationYear: 2002

authors: Bergamaschi, Sonia Guerra, Francesco Vincini, Maurizio

abstractContent: A marketplace is the place in which the demand and supply of buyers and vendors participating in a business process may meet. Therefore, electronic marketplaces are virtual communities in which buyers may meet proposals of several suppliers and make the best choice. In the electronic commerce world, the comparison between different products is blocked due to the lack of standards (on the contrary, the proliferation of standards) describing and classifying them. Therefore, the need for B2B and B2C marketplaces is to reclassify products and goods according to different standardization models. This paper aims to face this problem by suggesting the use of a semi automatic methodology, supported by a tool (SI Designer), to define the mapping among different e commerce product classification standards. This methodology was developed for the MOMIS system within the Intelligent Integration of Information research area. We describe our extension to the methodology that makes it applyable in general to product classification standard, by selecting a fragment of ECCMA/UNSPSC and ecl@ss standard.

Vote this paper: ○ ☆   ○ ☆☆   ○ ☆☆☆   ○ ☆☆☆☆   ○ ☆☆☆☆☆   Vote

Fig. 6. A paper retrieved by the semantic search provided by ITR and the rating scale for collecting the user feedback

An experimental evaluation of semantic profiles was carried out on ISWC papers in order to estimate if the BOS version of ITR improves the performance with respect to the BOW one. Experiments were carried out on a collection of 100 papers rated by 11 real users. Classification effectiveness was evaluated in terms of precision and recall [Sebastiani02]. We obtained an improvement both in precision (+1%) and recall (+2%) of the BOS-generated profiles with respect to the BOW-generated ones [3].

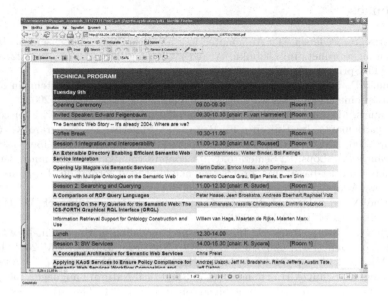

Fig. 7. The personalized program sent to the user

5 Conclusions and Future Work

We presented the ITR framework exploiting a bayesian learning method to induce semantic user profiles from documents represented using WordNet synsets. Our hypothesis is that replacing words with synsets in the indexing phase produces a more accurate document representation to infer more accurate profiles. This is confirmed by the experiments carried out to evaluate the effectiveness of the "Conference Participant Advisor" service and can be explained by the fact that synset-based classification allows to select documents within a Digital Library with a high degree of semantic coherence, not guaranteed by word-based classification. As a future work, we plan to also exploit domain ontologies to realize a more powerful document indexing.

Acknowledgments

This research was partially funded by the European Commission under the 6th Framework Programme IST Integrated Project VIKEF No. 507173, Priority 2.3.1.7 Semantic Based Knowledge Systems, http://www.vikef.net, and under the DELOS Network of Excellence on Digital Libraries, Priority: Technology-enhanced Learning and Access to Cultural Heritage - Contract n. G038-507618, http://www.delos.info.

References

1. Banerjee, S., Pedersen, T.: An adapted lesk algorithm for word sense disambiguation using wordnet. In: Gelbukh, A. (ed.) CICLing 2002. LNCS, vol. 2276, pp. 136–145. Springer, Heidelberg (2002)
2. Callan, J.P., Smeaton, A.F.: Personalization and recommender systems in digital libraries joint nsf-eu delos working group report. Technical report (2003)
3. Degemmis, M., Lops, P., Basile, P.: An intelligent personalized service for conference participants. In: Esposito, F., Raś, Z.W., Malerba, D., Semeraro, G. (eds.) ISMIS 2006. LNCS (LNAI), vol. 4203, pp. 707–712. Springer, Heidelberg (2006)
4. Degemmis, M., Lops, P., Semeraro, G.: A content-collaborative recommender that exploits wordnet-based user profiles for neighborhood formation. User Modeling and User-Adapted Interaction, 217–255 (2007)
5. Guarino, N., Masolo, C., Vetere, G.: Content-based access to the web. IEEE Intelligent Systems 14(3), 70–80 (1999)
6. Magnini, B., Strapparava, C.: Improving user modelling with content-based techniques. In: Bauer, M., Gmytrasiewicz, P.J., Vassileva, J. (eds.) UM 2001. LNCS (LNAI), vol. 2109, pp. 74–83. Springer, Heidelberg (2001)
7. Manning, C., Schütze, H.: Foundations of Statistical Natural Language Processing. In: chapter 7: Word Sense Disambiguation, pp. 229–264. The MIT Press, Cambridge, US (1999)
8. Miller, G.: Wordnet: An on-line lexical database (Special Issue). International Journal of Lexicography 3(4) (1990)
9. Mladenic, D.: Text-learning and related intelligent agents: a survey. IEEE Intelligent Systems 14(4), 44–54 (1999)
10. Mooney, R.J., Roy, L.: Content-based book recommending using learning for text categorization. In: Proc. of the 5th ACM Conference on Digital Libraries, San Antonio, US, pp. 195–204. ACM Press, New York (2000)
11. Pazzani, M., Billsus, D.: Learning and revising user profiles: The identification of interesting web sites. Machine Learning 27(3), 313–331 (1997)
12. Resnik, P.: Disambiguating noun groupings with respect to WordNet senses. In: Proceedings of the Third Workshop on Very Large Corpora, pp. 54–68. Association for Computational Linguistics (1995)
13. Sebastiani, F.: Machine learning in automated text categorization. ACM Computing Surveys 34(1) (2002)
14. Semeraro, G., Degemmis, M., Lops, P., Basile, P.: Combining Learning and Word Sense Disambiguation for Intelligent User Profiling. In: IJCAI. Proceedings of the Twentieth International Joint Conference on Artificial Intelligence, January 6-12, 2007, pp. 2856–2861. Morgan Kaufmann, San Francisco (2007)

Integrated Authoring, Annotation, Retrieval, Adaptation, Personalization, and Delivery for Multimedia*

Horst Eidenberger[1], Susanne Boll[2], Stavros Christodoulakis[3], Doris Divotkey[1], Klaus Leopold[4], Alessandro Martin[5], Andrea Perego[6], Ansgar Scherp[7], and Chrisa Tsinaraki[3]

[1] Vienna University of Technology, Austria
eidenberger@ims.tuwien.ac.at, doris.divotkey@ims.tuwien.ac.at
[2] University of Oldenburg, Germany
susanne.boll@informatik.uni-oldenburg.de
[3] Technical University of Crete
stavros@ced.tuc.gr, chrisa@ced.tuc.gr
[4] University of Klagenfurt, Austria
klaus.leopold@itec.uni-klu.ac.at
[5] University of Milan, Italy
martin@dico.unimi.it
[6] University of Insubria at Varese, Italy
andrea.perego@uninsubria.it
[7] OFFIS Institute for Information Technology, Germany
scherp@offis.de

Abstract. In this paper we present CoCoMA, an integrated platform, developed in the framework of the DELOS II European Network of Excellence on Digital Libraries, aiming at the unification of the most important aspects of multimedia management and multimedia presentation. The paramount goal of CoCoMA is to maximize the added value from task and data integration by the identification and exploitation of connection points and inherent workflow similarities. The paper provides a brief description of the involved research fields, suggests an architecture for integrated multimedia consumption and presentation, and discusses the most prominent connection points. Problems and solutions are discussed jointly, and illustrated by the components of the application prototype developed for the DELOS project.

1   Introduction

Multimedia presentations containing interactive media content go through a number of processing steps before they arrive at the user interface. Media streams are captured and manually or (semi-)automatically annotated on various levels

---

* This research was supported by the European Network of Excellence on Digital Libraries (DELOS) and by the Austrian Scientific Research Fund under grant number P16111.

C. Thanos, F. Borri, and L. Candela (Eds.): Digital Libraries: R&D, LNCS 4877, pp. 87–103, 2007.

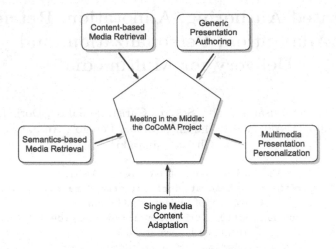

Fig. 1. The CoCoMA project for integrated multimedia presentation design

of semantics. Single media items are spatio-temporally organized and authored to interactive presentations. During delivery, the content of media streams is adapted to technical requirements and personalized to user requirements.

In this paper we describe an approach to integrate these processing steps. We present the CoCoMA task of the DELOS II European Network of Excellence on Digital Libraries (www.delos.info). CoCoMA aims at a solution for the provision of content- and context-aware rich interactive multimedia presentations by controlling data fusion and metadata reuse.

Figure 1 sketches the basic idea. We focus on four major functions: generic presentation authoring, content-based and semantics-based annotation and retrieval, content adaptation and media personalization. For the sake of simplicity, the latter two areas are distinguished in this paper by the following attribution. Content adaptation summarizes all single and multi-media manipulation operations that are targeted towards technical requirements (e.g. network bandwidth). Media personalization denotes all manipulation operations targeted towards user requirements (e.g. special interests).

We believe that each of the four considered functions can benefit significantly from data collected and generated by the other functions. Content-based metadata (features like color histograms, camera motion, and cepstral audio features) may provide valuable control data for the content adaptation function (especially, in mobile environments). For example, such metadata can be employed to skip irrelevant information during encoding, or to select less restrictive quantization schemes for sensitive content (content with high motion activity). Semantically represented annotations (based on ontologies) and content-based metadata can jointly be used for interactive media querying in multimedia presentations. A common foundation could, e.g., be provided by the MPEG-7 standard [1]. The integration of the media annotation function with presentation authoring and presentation personalization allows for the seamless integration of the search functions. This way, personal experiences by non-linear movement through multimedia presentations become possible. Furthermore, search functions can be employed to provide novel means of presentation authoring and personalization. For example, we propose a novel presentation item that describes media objects bycontent-based queries instead of links to media files. Queries are executed at run-time (enriched with user knowledge) and the results are integrated with static presentation elements. This flexible way of personalization decides the presentation contents at view-time hand in hand with the user. Eventually, the application of constraint-based presentation authoring methods allows for flexible presentation personalization. The spatio-temporal relationships of CoCoMA presentations are not defined statically but by space and time operators. This paradigm reduces the burden of a layout on the presentation personalization to a minimum. Media objects can be added, exchanged and removed easily, if appropriate spatial and/or temporal rules for these operations are provided.

The CoCoMA project comprises of three steps. First, the exploitation of the fundamental idea and the identification of chances for integration. Second, the closer investigation of promising starting points and the design of solutions. In the second step, a complicating factor is that CoCoMA should possibly be based on earlier work by the involved research groups. Hence, the design process must consider architectural requirements and constraints of existing solutions. The last step is the implementation of the proposed design in a proof of concept prototype, and the construction of an application demonstrator. Suitable applications can, e.g., be identified in the sports domain such as summary presentations of soccer transmissions and various cultural domains like virtual tourist applications, preservation and cultural heritage applications. In summary, the CoCoMA activity aims at meeting in the middle, the integration of related functions of multimedia presentation design where promising starting points can be identified. The project addresses different research areas such as semantic multimedia retrieval, personalized multimedia authoring and presentations, which are integrated in the the CoCoMA activity.

The paper is organized as follows. Section 2 gives background information on the involved research areas and illuminates starting points for integration. In Sect. 3 we present the architecture and building blocks of the proof of concept prototype. Section 4 focuses on challenging research questions. Solutions are illustrated by samples from the CoCoMA prototype. Due to the limitation of space we focus on presenting the integrated architecture and the related challenges for multimedia research. For details on the related work and own previous work in the different fields we would like to point the interested reader to [2].

2   Research Areas and Starting Points for Integration

2.1   Content-Based Retrieval

Content-based Retrieval means retrieval of media objects by their perceivable content: in case of image or video this means visual cues such as colors or shapes and in case of audio, retrieval is done by audible cues like sound or loudness.

Multi-modal retrieval combines various media types such as text, image, audio and video. State-of-the-art in content-based retrieval bases on the representation of audio and video by features. Meaningful features are extracted from the media objects and the actual retrieval step is performed by similarity measurement among media objects according to the extracted features. The difficulty to express high-level concepts with low-level features is called the semantic gap [3]. There exist various audio-visual features, similarity measures and retrieval models. Probabilistic models employ user relevance feedback information for retrieval (e.g., Binary Independence Retrieval). On the other hand, the most commonly applied approach is the Vector Space Model whereby media objects are represented by their feature vector and similarity is given as a distance measure (e.g., Euclidean distance) in the feature space [4].

2.2   Semantics-Based Retrieval

Semantics-based retrieval for multimedia content relies on the metadata describing the content semantics, and it is often based on MPEG-7 [1], which is the dominant standard in multimedia content description. Although MPEG-7 allows, in the MPEG-7 MDS, the semantic description of the multimedia content using both keywords and structured semantic metadata, several systems follow the keyword-based approach [5,6,7], which is limiting, as it results in reduced precision of the multimedia content retrieval. This problem may be solved, at least at some extent, if the structured semantic description capabilities provided by MPEG-7 are exploited. Domain knowledge, captured in domain ontologies expressed using MPEG-7 constructs, is systematically integrated in semantic MPEG-7 descriptions in [8]. In addition, a methodology for the integration of OWL domain ontologies in MPEG-7 has been developed in [9,10], in order to allow the utilization of existing OWL domain ontologies, which make interoperability support within user communities easier. However, structured semantic content descriptions cannot be fully exploited by keyword-based user preferences. In order to address this issue, a semantic user preference model for MPEG-7/21 has been proposed in [11], for expressing preferences about every aspect of an MPEG-7 multimedia content description. Finally, another limitation is due to the lack of a transparent and unified multimedia content retrieval framework that allows exploiting all the aspects of the MPEG-7 multimedia content descriptions. A proposal for solving this problem is made in [11], where a powerful query language for querying MPEG-7 descriptions, called MP7QL, is presented. The MP7QL queries may utilize the user preferences as context, thus allowing for personalized multimedia content retrieval.

2.3   Presentation Modeling

A multimedia presentation may be considered as a graph, where each node corresponds to a set of heterogeneous multimedia objects (e.g., text, images, audio and video files), grouped depending on their content relationships and organized according to a given spatial and temporal disposition. By contrast, the edges connecting the nodes denote the execution flow of the presentationi.e., the sequence according to which the objects in each node are displayed to the user. Multimedia presentation modeling then concerns two main issues: representing the presentation structure (i.e., the presentation graph) and representing the spatial and temporal disposition of objects in each node. The available approaches can be grouped into two main classes, operational and constraint-based, depending on how the spatial and temporal disposition of objects is represented. In operational approaches, a presentation is specified by describing its final form; thus, they have the advantage of being easy to implement, but they are not user-friendly. In constraint-based approaches the final presentation is generated starting from a specification where constraints are used to represent the spatial and temporal relations existing among objects. As a consequence, constraint-based systems are more flexible and user-friendly than operational ones, although they are more complex, due to the fact that they must carry out the presentation generation task. Independently from their differences, both operational and constraint-based approaches are designed for building presentations using a fixed structure (usually modeled as a tree with one or more branches) and a fixed set of objects. In order to address this issue, a multimedia presentation authoring model has been developed, described in [12], where content relationships among objects are used to identify the objects associated with each node of the presentation and to build automatically different execution flows of the same presentation.

2.4 Content Adaptation

In [13] the architecture of an adaptive proxy for MPEG-4 visual streams is described which adapts MPEG-4 resources according to device capabilities and network characteristics. To this end, an adaptor chain concept has been introduced enabling the concatenation of several adaptation steps. The information of when an adaptor has to be invoked is hard coded in the proxy. Thus, this approach lacks extensibility in the sense that new adaptors can only be integrated into the existing system by re-compilation of the whole adaptation engine. The MPEG-21 framework also supports tools for multimedia adaptation. This work is based on Bitstream Syntax Descriptions (BSD) [14,15], i.e., an additional metadata layer which describes the high-level structure of a media bitstream. The main limitation of this approach is that one can only perform editing-style adaptation operations like removing, inserting, or updating parts of the bitstream. Another adaptation tool defined in the MPEG-21 framework is Adaptation QoS (AQoS) [15,16] which enables users to describe the device and network quality of service (QoS). AQoS specifies the relationship between environmental constraints, media quality, and feasible adaptation operations. Adaptation engines can then perform look-ups in the AQoS table to ascertain adaptation operations for the multimedia content. Therefore, AQoS can provide hints for an adaptation decision taking engine. Only few projects are known at the moment that try to exploit the extended metadata annotation possibilities available with the new MPEG standards; examples are the ViTooKi Video Tool Kit project (`vitooki.sourceforge.net`) [17,13] or the work described in [18].

2.5 Presentation Personalization

Personalization of multimedia presentations can be understood as the creation of multimedia content reflecting the specific preferences, interests, background and situational context of a user—captured in a user profile. Even though one could prepare different presentations for each targeted user, this would quickly become too laborious for many different user profiles. Hence, a dynamic creation of personalized content lies near at hand. Here, we find different approaches in the field. A research approach towards the dynamic generation of multimedia presentations based on constraints and logic programming is the Cuypers system [19]. Within the Opéra project, a generic architecture for the automated construction of multimedia presentations based on transformation sheets and constraints is developed [20]. This work is continued within the WAM project with the focus on a negotiation and adaptation architecture for mobile multimedia services [21]. As shown, these and other existing research solutions typically use declarative descriptions like rules, constraints, style sheets and the like to express the dynamic multimedia content creation. However, only those presentation adaptation problems can be solved that can be covered by such a declarative specification. Whenever a complex and application-specific personalization task is required, the systems find their limit and need additional programming. Approaches that base on XSLT would generally allow for a computationally complete transformation process. However, they find their limitations in the manageability of large personalization applications. Consequently, we find with the MM4U framework a software engineering approach for the multimedia content adaptation and presentation [22,23]. This framework provides application developers with a general, domain independent support for the creation of personalized multimedia content by exploiting the different approaches for multimedia content adaptation. In order to be able to create multimedia content that is personalized for a certain user one needs multimedia content that can be used for the different users. Hence, retrieval of media content based on semantics, access to user profiles and the availability of adaptive content are prerequisites for building an integrated multimedia information system.

3 System Design and Building Blocks

In this section, we present the component architecture of CoCoMA. The design falls in the two groups *presentation creation* and *presentation consumption*. Section 3.1 provides an overview of the project. The detailed discussions of design issues of presentation consumption and creation in Sect. 3.2 and 3.3 are structured by the involved components, mostly stemming from our earlier work.

3.1   The Component-Based Architecture of CoCoMA

Above we have sketched the overall goal of the CoCoMA activity, the integration of major aspects of multimedia presentation design. In detail, we endeavor to answer to the following major research questions:

1. How can the authoring process be enhanced by semantics-based and content-based media descriptions?
2. How can media metadata—in particular, content-based descriptions—be employed to achieve sophisticated content adaptation?
3. How can personalization and querying based on media metadata be integrated seamlessly? Is it possible to exploit the knowledge enveloped in the metadata for on-demand personalization?
4. How can semantics-based (e.g., ontology-based) and content-based metadata be merged and queried together?
5. Can we identify a constraint-based authoring process and presentation description scheme that simplifies personalization by offering the required degrees of freedom?

Obviously, all questions are targeted towards efficient metadata unification and reuse. Hence, design of metadata management is the central topic of the CoCoMA activity.

The building blocks that produce and consume the metadata are the same as named in the introduction: authoring, content-based annotation, semantics based annotation, content adaptation and personalization. Figure 2 structures their relationships and their interfaces to the outside world. The presentation author and media annotator interacts with the authoring building block and the semantic annotation interface. A knowledge base of ontologies supports the annotation process. The presentation consumer interacts exclusively with the personalization and delivery component. Content-based annotation and content adaptation have no external interfaces. Content-based annotation is controlled by the authoring process. Content adaptation is triggered by the presentation engine.

Media data and media metadata are organized in two major databases. The media database holds the temporal (e.g., audio, video) and non-temporal (e.g., text, image) media content specific to the presentation context. The metadata database stores a variety of media-related metadata, user knowledge and system parameters. Metadata includes non-temporal data (e.g., textual media segment descriptions, domain ontologies, presentation constraints) and temporal data (e.g., motion descriptions, spectral audio descriptions). The metadata database is mostly filled by the two annotation building blocks and by the authoring process. Metadata is consumed by the content adaptation function (e.g., low-level color models, high-level relevance estimations) and by the personalization building block (e.g., merged with user knowledge for content-based media selection).

Apart from the research issues listed above, the integration process constitutes some engineering problems that have to be solved properly. An important prerequisite is that the CoCoMA design should—as far as possible—be based on existing solutions provided by the project participants. Hence, the integration process should—similarly to enterprise application integration—focus on

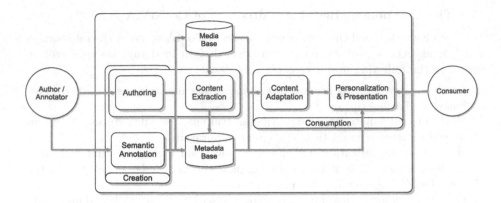

Fig. 2. CoCoMA building blocks and workflow

appropriate metadata formats. In this context, a prominent role is played by the MPEG-7 standard for multimedia content description [1]. MPEG-7 provides structures for textual annotation and content-based annotation. These structures are employed for single media and multimedia descriptions. In addition, extensions are implemented where necessary (e.g., for ontology integration, MPEG-21-based media stream description, etc.). See Sect. 4 for details.

The remainder of this section discusses the building blocks of the CoCoMA design.

3.2   Presentation Consumption

MM4U for Personalized Multimedia Presentations. The overall goal of the MM4U framework [22,23] is to simplify and to improve the development process of personalized multimedia applications. For this, the framework provides application developers with an extensive support for creating personalized multimedia content. This support comprises assistance for the access to media elements and associated metadata as well as user profile information and contextual information.

The framework provides for the selection, composition, and transformation of media elements into a coherent multimedia presentation. For supporting the different tasks of the general multimedia personalization process, we developed a layered architecture. Each layer provides modular support for the different tasks of the multimedia personalization process such as access to user profile information and media elements, composition of the multimedia presentation in an internal multimedia content representation model, its later transformation into the concrete presentation output formats, and the rendering of the multimedia presentation on the end device. To be most flexible in regard of the different requirements of concrete personalized multimedia applications, the framework's layer allow for extending and adapting the functionality of the MM4U framework towards particular requirements that can occur in the development of personalized multimedia applications.

KoMMA for Multimedia Content Adaptation. Intelligent adaptation of multimedia resources is becoming increasingly important and challenging for two reasons. First, the market continuously brings up new mobile end-user devices to which the content has to be adapted as these devices support different display formats and operate on various types of networks. On the other hand, with the help of metadata annotations, which are now available in the MPEG-7 and MPEG-21 standard, advanced forms of resource adaptations on the content level become possible. As none of the existing multimedia transformation tools and libraries can support all these different forms of basic and advanced adaptation operations, an intelligent multimedia adaptation node has to integrate such external tools and algorithms and perform an adequate sequence of adaptation operations on the original resource before sending it to the client [24].

In order to compute an adequate sequence of adaptation operations, we utilize a knowledge-based planning approach [25]. In general, a planner computes a plan by applying actions on an initial state to reach a goal state. In the context of multimedia adaptation, the initial state corresponds to the original multimedia resource, which can be described by means of MPEG-7 descriptions. The goal state is the adapted multimedia content according to the usage context which is, e.g., terminal capabilities or usage environment. The usage context can be expressed by means of MPEG-21 descriptions. Finally, actions are adaptation operations that have to be applied on the original multimedia content in order to meet the usage context.

In the implementation of the multimedia adaptation node, the described planner—referred to as the adaptation decision-taking engine—acts as preprocessing module for the adaptation engine. Upon a client request, the adaptation decision-taking engine computes an adaptation plan which is later executed by the adaptation engine [26].

3.3   Presentation Creation

VizIR for Content-based Media Annotation and Retrieval. VizIR is an open framework providing common ground functionalities and strategies for the development of multimedia applications that benefit from multimedia retrieval techniques [27]. The framework provides a comprehensive collection of classes for all major multimedia retrieval tasks, such as storage and management of media and annotated metadata [28], and it allows for the textual annotation of semantic information about the content as well as content-based metadata directly extracted from the media content. The core item of the VizIR system is the strong and flexible querying and retrieval component. It comprises algorithms for automatic feature extraction and similarity measurement among media objects based on the derived media descriptions. Furthermore, the VizIR framework contains a set of user interfaces for browsing the media databases, query formulation (by example or sketch) and query refinement and a couple visualization tools. The framework provides implementations of various content-based descriptors for image, audio and video data, and it incorporates a set of state-of-the-art audio descriptors from various application domains [29].

VizIR allows for the usage of arbitrary features and querying models, by using a generic querying language developed for this purpose [30]. Depending on the underlying querying model that is used the formulation of queries happens on different levels of abstraction. This means that it is either possible to state queries on a very low-level by defining explicitly the low-level features and the used querying scheme or to define queries on a semantically high level. Thereby, the querying component uses models to break down the high-level query and translates it to a lower level that can be solved. Moreover, the combination of features of different type (audio, video, text) is possible, which lays the foundation for multi-modal retrieval. The retrieval component in general and the querying language in particular may as well be adapted to take semantics-based annotations into account. For this purpose, the VizIR framework contains an implementation of the full MPEG-7 Multimedia Description Schemes to describe and annotate multimedia data [31].

DS-MIRF for Semantics-based Media Annotation and Retrieval. The DS-MIRF (Domain-Specific Multimedia Indexing, Retrieval and Filtering) Framework [9,8,10] aims to facilitate the development of knowledge-based multimedia applications (including multimedia information retrieval, information filtering, user behavior description, multimedia content segmentation, multimedia information extraction and multimedia browsing and interaction) utilizing and extending the MPEG-7 and MPEG-21 standards. The major components of the DS-MIRF framework are the following. The first component is the *DS-MIRF Metadata Repository*, where domain ontologies and multimedia content descriptions are stored in MPEG-7 format. In addition to the current MPEG-7/21 metadata, the DS-MIRF Metadata Repository allows the management of semantic user preferences as described in [11]. Semantic queries are supported on top of the DS-MIRF metadata repository. The repository is accessed by the end-users through appropriate application interfaces that utilize the expressive power of the MP7QL query language [11]. The second component is the *DS-MIRF Ontological Infrastructure* [9,10], which includes: (1) An OWL Upper Ontology that fully captures the MPEG-7 MDS and the MPEG-21 DIA Architecture (the latter has been developed in the context of CoCoMA). (2) OWL Application Ontologies that provide additional functionality in OWL that either makes easier the use of the MPEG-7 MDS from the users (like a typed relationship ontology based on the MPEG-7 MDS textual description) or allows the provision of advanced multimedia content services (like a semantic user preference ontology that facilitates semantics-based filtering and retrieval). (3) OWL Domain Ontologies that extend both the Upper Ontology and the Application Ontologies with domain knowledge (e.g. sports ontologies, educational ontologies etc.). The third major component is *GraphOnto* [32], an ontology-based semantic annotation tool. GraphOnto facilitates both OWL ontology editing and OWL/RDF metadata definition and allows transforming both domain ontologies and metadata to MPEG-7 metadata descriptions. The MPEG-7 metadata may be stored in files or in the DS-MIRF Metadata Repository.

SyMPA for Content-based Multimedia Presentation Authoring and Generation. The presentation specification and generation component of the CoCoMA architecture, referred to as SyMPA, is based on the multimedia presentation model described in [12], which allows authors to group semantically related objects into independent sets representing each one a *topic*. This is obtained by using a new class of constraints, called content constraints, that allow the author to define high-level, content-related semantic relations among objects, in order to build different presentation topics and the interconnections among them. In SyMPA, content constraints are not explicitly specified by the presentation author, but inferred from the annotations possibly associated with multimedia objects. Authors annotate objects using multiple metadata vocabularies (which may be plain sets of descriptors, conceptual hierarchies, and ontologies), concerning both high- and low-level features. Then they make use of content metadata in order to define the main topic of a presentation. Based on this, SyMPA retrieves the objects satisfying the query, and it groups them into nested subsets, determining both the nodes of the presentation and its structure. The author may then revise the presentation by modifying the presentation structure, the contents of each node of the presentation, and/or the spatio-temporal disposition of objects. This approach has two main advantages. First, it can be easily applied to large repositories of multimedia objects (such as digital libraries), where multiple authors can annotate objects in a collaborative way and objects can be added and removed dynamically. Second, the content-based clustering of objects outlined above automatically returns all the possible execution flows of a presentation, which can be selected by end-users depending on their preferences. Besides presentation specification and generation, SyMPA is designed also as a system for the management and annotation of multimedia objects stored in distributed repositories.

4   Integration Challenges and Solutions

This section describes how the individual CoCoMA components are merged and how the components are employed for the benefit of others. Figure 3 sketches the components and the neuralgic connection points (mostly characterized by usage relationships). Sections 4.1 to 4.5 explicate the five major points of integration.

4.1   Integration of Content-Based and Semantics-Based Retrieval

An important issue is the integration of CBR (Content-based Retrieval—based on low-level features) with SBR (Semantics-based Retrieval). A lot of independent research exists for both the approaches, but there are several real-life situations where none of the approaches can work by itself at a satisfactory level. Consider, as an example, a user interested in art who wants to get a drawing containing a girl who wears a hat. The user also remembers that the black colour dominates in the drawing. In this case, if the user uses SBR only, he will receive all the drawings containing a girl who wears a hat and the user has to browse

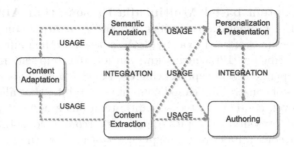

Fig. 3. CoCoMA integration challenges

the results in order to locate the one he has in mind. Using CBR only, the user would request the drawings where black dominates and the user has to browse the results in order to locate the one he has in mind. A more convenient approach would be to allow the user to pose queries having both semantic components and visual feature components and use one technique (e.g., SBR) for pre-filtering and the other (e.g., CBR) for refinement.

In order to support the above approach, we are working on the support of *Semantic and Content Based Retrieval* (SCBR), which allows for providing *Semantic and Content Based Queries* (SCBQs). These queries allow the specification of preference values (in the range $[-100, 100]$) for their constituents and may contain boolean operators, and they can be expressed using the MP7QL syntax [11].

4.2   Content-Based and Semantics-Based Metadata for Content Adaptation

The knowledge-based multimedia adaptation node within the CoCOMA architecture is designed as a proxy server, which forwards incoming client requests to the multimedia server. The server transfers the requested content together with the MPEG-7 description to the adaptation proxy which then adapts the content based on the client's usage context which is described by means of MPEG-21 metadata. Finally, the adapted content is streamed to the client together with the adapted MPEG-7 descriptions.

The main concept of the adaptation decision-taking engine is to describe multimedia adaptation operations semantically by their inputs, outputs, preconditions, and effects (IOPE). The operation's preconditions express the conditions that must hold before an operation can be applied. Typical preconditions for an image grey scale operation are, e.g., "the multimedia content is a JPEG image" and "the image is colored." Effects express the changes after applying an adaptation operation. The effect of a grey scale operation might be "the output image is grey." The semantics of an adaptation operation like, for instance, "JPEG image" is introduced by referencing MPEG-7 and MPEG-21 metadata which enables content-aware media adaptation.

The content-aware approach offers a wide range of possibilities for media adaptation, starting with general adaptation to meet the client's usage context and up to new sophisticated CBR-based content adaptation. Content adaptation based on CBR means that content-based features (as extracted for retrieval) are employed in the adaptation process. For example, it would be thinkable to use motion features to judge the visual complexity of scenes and adapt the encoding accordingly. On a semantically higher level, content-based features could be used to summarize scenes, skip irrelevant scenes and save bandwidth. Audio features could be employed to estimate the type of content (speech, music, etc.) and choose the encoding appropriately.

4.3   Authoring Based on Content-Based and Semantics-Based Metadata

The availability of content-based and semantic metadata, associated with multimedia objects, can be used by SyMPA to automatically carry out the presentation specification task. In particular, such metadata can be used in our authoring model to infer the content relationships existing among objects, which will then determine the set of objects associated with each node of the presentation and the presentation structure itself. Author's intervention is required for carrying out two main tasks: (a) determining the spatial and temporal disposition of objects in each node of the presentation, and (b) selecting the objects to be actually used, based on their relevance. The presentation specification process consists of the following steps. First, an author specifies a presentation by defining a set of topics in terms of the semantic metadata available in the system. Based on this, the system returns the set of objects belonging to each node; then the author decides which objects will be used, and their spatial and temporal disposition. Finally, the possible execution flows of the presentation are obtained evaluating the semantic relationships existing among the selected objects. In order to integrate this authoring approach into CoCoMA, SyMPA has been extended with an interface allowing the exploitation of the features provided by the DS-MIRF framework. More precisely, the MPEG-7/21 metadata stored in the DS-MIRF Metadata Repository, which are associated with multimedia objects, are utilized to automatically carry out the presentation specification task in SyMPA. In addition, the DS-MIRF Metadata Repository is used (a) for storing multimedia presentations and object annotations defined using SyMPA, (b) for locating multimedia objects that will be utilized in the presentations (using the semantic retrieval capabilities of the DS-MIRF framework), and (c) for retrieving the metadata associated with the multimedia objects, which are used by the authoring model to infer the content relationships that exist among objects. The user preferences stored in the DS-MIRF Metadata Repository will be utilized systematically in order to allow presentation personalization. Finally, the DS-MIRF ontological infrastructure is utilized by SyMPA as a set of metadata vocabularies for the selection of knowledge domain and topic of interest, and will be extended with an ontology about 'art'. The integration actvities involving SyMPA end the DS-MIRF framework are described in detail in [33].

4.4   Adaptive Streaming in Personalized Multimedia Presentations

The MM4U framework for the dynamic creation of personalized multimedia presentations has been integrated with the KoMMA framework for adaptive streaming of video content. During the presentation of a personalized multimedia document the adaptive streaming framework delivers the continuous media stream that best meets the current presentation situation. During the composition phase of the multimedia document, the media access layer of the MM4U framework searches the underlying media store and includes a reference to the content into the document. The profile that drives the composition of the personalized presentation provides the parameters that apply to the adaptive video streaming. During the personalized composition of the multimedia document, those parameters from the user profile that affect the presentation such as device configuration, bandwidth, etc., are included as an MPEG-21 description into the document. For the later access to the media content the media locator also includes the location of the KoMMA proxy that finally creates and delivers the adapted stream. Hence, the parameters relevant for the adaptation are selected during the composition process of the MM4U framework and inserted in the presentation. After the composition of the multimedia content, a transformation into the final presentation format such as SMIL, SVG, or Flash is executed. When the presentation is delivered to the user and is rendered the player actually accesses the media content. Here, the reference to the media content is resolved and the player accesses the KoMMA adaptation proxy to receive the adapted media content. This request includes the presentation context parameters which are used by the KoMMA framework to dynamically adapt the streaming media content to the client's presentation requirements.

4.5   Personalized Presentation Composition Based on Content-Based Retrieval

Besides the integration with adaptive streaming framework for video content, the MM4U framework has also been integrated with the visual information retrieval framework VizIR. The VizIR framework provides a generic querying language and allows for different query models. For the integration of the MM4U and VizIR frameworks, the k-nearest neighbor model is used. The interfaces between the frameworks are kept generic such that they allow for future adaptation and extension to different models. A new media connector for the MM4U framework has been developed using a generic query object that provides for content-based retrieval queries to the VizIR framework. The querying object is passed from the MM4U framework to the VizIR framework. The VizIR framework determines a ranked list of the most suitable media elements and returns the query result back to the media connector. The retrieved query result is then converted within the media connector of the VizIR framework to a MM4U compliant representation of the media elements for multimedia composition and personalization. The MM4U framework can use the content-based retrieval functionality of the VizIR framework in different usage scenarios. However, no knowledge about content-based querying is required from the user; especially no feature-selection needs to be conducted by the user. The MM4U framework uses a set of predefined or default values for the querying parameter, e.g., by appropriate descriptors identifying the type of the query like "sunset" or "landscape". Here, the MM4U framework exploits the users profile information to optimize the content-based querying.

5   Conclusions and Future Work

The CoCoMA task of the DELOS II European Network of Excellence on Digital Libraries endeavors to integrate traditionally independent components of multimedia systems. The integration of content-based retrieval and semantics-based retrieval results in more precise retrieval results. Employing content-based and semantics-based retrieval methods for multimedia authoring, content adaptation, and personalization provides additional degrees of freedom for the media designer and leads to richer multimedia applications with higher flexibility. Eventually, the consideration of personalization issues in the multimedia authoring process refines it to a user-centered activity expressed in presentation-specific constraints. In this paper, we described the vision of CoCoMA, briefly sketch the involved research areas, state the major integration problems, and illustrate novel paths to solve them. CoCoMA is work in progress with a clear focus on methodological integration. Currently, we are designing a service-oriented architecture where the individual components act as services and are integrated by a workflow management system. Following this scheme, our future work will be the implementation and user-based evaluation of a full-featured CoCoMA infrastructure.

Acknowledgements. The authors would like to thank Christian Breiteneder and Hermann Hellwagner for their support and valuable suggestions for improvement.

References

1. Manjunath, B.S., Salembier, P., Sikora, T. (eds.): Introduction to MPEG-7: Multimedia Content Description Interface. Wiley, Chichester (2002)
2. Eidenberger, H., Boll, S., Christodoulakis, S., Divotkey, D., Leopold, K., Martin, A., Perego, A., Scherp, A., Tsinaraki, C.: Towards integrated authoring, annotation, retrieval, adaptation, personalization and delivery of multimedia content. In: DELOS 2007 (2007)
3. Del Bimbo, A.: Visual Information Retrieval. Morgan Kaufmann, San Francisco (1999)
4. Fuhr, N.: Information retrieval methods for multimedia objects. In: Veltkamp, R.C., Burkhardt, H., Kriegel, H.P. (eds.) State-of-the-Art in Content-based Image and Video Retrieval, pp. 191–212. Kluwer Academic Publishers, Dordrecht (2001)
5. Graves, A., Lalmas, M.: Video retrieval using an MPEG-7 based inference network. In: SIGIR 2002, pp. 339–346 (2002)

6. Tseng, B.L., Lin, C.Y., Smith, J.: Using MPEG-7 and MPEG-21 for personalizing videos. IEEE Multimedia 11(1), 42–52 (2004)
7. Wang, Q., Balke, W.T., Kießling, W., Huhn, A.: P-News: Deeply personalized news dissemination for MPEG-7 based digital libraries. In: Heery, R., Lyon, L. (eds.) ECDL 2004. LNCS, vol. 3232, pp. 256–268. Springer, Heidelberg (2004)
8. Tsinaraki, C., Polydoros, P., Kazasis, F., Christodoulakis, S.: Ontology-based semantic indexing for MPEG-7 and TV-Anytime audiovisual content. Multimedia Tools and Application Journal 26, 299–325 (2005)
9. Tsinaraki, C., Polydoros, P., Christodoulakis, S.: Interoperability support for ontology-based video retrieval applications. In: Enser, P.G.B., Kompatsiaris, Y., O'Connor, N.E., Smeaton, A.F., Smeulders, A.W.M. (eds.) CIVR 2004. LNCS, vol. 3115, pp. 582–591. Springer, Heidelberg (2004)
10. Tsinaraki, C., Polydoros, P., Christodoulakis, S.: Interoperability support between MPEG-7/21 and OWL in DS-MIRF. IEEE Trans. on Knowledge and Data Engineering 19(2), 219–232 (2007)
11. Tsinaraki, C., Christodoulakis, S.: A user preference model and a query language that allow semantic retrieval and filtering of multimedia content. In: SMAP 2006 Workshop, pp. 121–128 (2006)
12. Bertino, E., Ferrari, E., Perego, A., Santi, D.: A constraint-based approach for the authoring of multi-topic multimedia presentations. In: ICME 2005, pp. 578–581 (2005)
13. Schojer, P., Böszörményi, L., Hellwagner, H.: QBIX-G – A transcoding multimedia proxy. In: MMCN 2006 (2006)
14. Devillers, S., Timmerer, C., Heuer, J., Hellwagner, H.: Bitstream syntax description-based adaptation in streaming and constrained environments. IEEE Trans. on Multimedia 7(3), 463–470 (2005)
15. Vetro, A., Timmerer, C.: Digital item adaptation: Overview of standardization and research activities. IEEE Trans. on Multimedia 7(3), 418–426 (2005)
16. Mukherjee, D., Delfosse, E., Kim, J.G., Wang, Y.: Optimal adaptation decision-taking for terminal and network quality-of-service. IEEE Trans. on Multimedia 7(3), 454–462 (2005)
17. Böszörményi, L., Hellwagner, H., Kosch, H., Libsie, M., Podlipnig, S.: Metadata driven adaptation in the ADMITS project. EURASIP Signal Processing and Image Communication Journal 18, 749–766 (2003)
18. Steiger, O., Sanjuan, D.M., Ebrahimi, T.: MPEG-based personalized content delivery. In: IEEE ICIP 2003, pp. 14–16. IEEE Computer Society Press, Los Alamitos (2003)
19. Geurts, J., van Ossenbruggen, J., Hardman, L.: Application-specific constraints for multimedia presentation generation. In: MMM 2001, pp. 339–346 (2001)
20. Bes, F., Jourdan, M., Khantache, F.: A generic architecture for automated construction of multimedia presentations. In: MMM 2001, pp. 229–246 (2001)
21. Lemlouma, T., Layaïda, N.: Context-aware adaptation for mobile devices. In: IEEE MDM 2004, pp. 106–111. IEEE Computer Society Press, Los Alamitos (2004)
22. Scherp, A., Boll, S.: MM4U: A framework for creating personalized multimedia content. In: Srinivasan, U., Nepal, S. (eds.) Managing Multimedia Semantics, pp. 246–287. IRM Press (2005)
23. Scherp, A., Boll, S.: Paving the last mile for multi-channel multimedia presentation generation. In: MMM 2005, pp. 190–197 (2005)
24. Leopold, K., Jannach, D., Hellwagner, H.: A knowledge and component based multimedia adaptation framework. In: IEEE MSE 2004, pp. 10–17. IEEE Computer Society Press, Los Alamitos (2004)

25. Jannach, D., Leopold, K., Timmerer, C., Hellwagner, H.: A knowledge-based framework for multimedia adaptation. Applied Intelligence 24(2) (2006)
26. Jannach, D., Leopold, K.: Knowledge-based multimedia adaptation for ubiquitous multimedia consumption. Journal of Network and Computer Applications 30(3), 958–982 (2007)
27. Eidenberger, H., Breiteneder, C.: VizIR – A framework for visual information retrieval. Journal of Visual Languages and Computing 14(5), 443–469 (2003)
28. Eidenberger, H., Divotkey, R.: A data management layer for visual information retrieval. In: ACM MDM Workshop, ACM Press, New York (2004)
29. Mitrovic, D., Zeppelzauer, M., Eidenberger, H.: Analysis of the data quality of audio descriptors of environmental sounds. In: WMS 2006, pp. 70–79 (2006)
30. Divotkey, D., Eidenberger, H., Divotkey, R.: Artificial intelligence and query execution methods in the VizIR framework. Journal of the Austrian Artificial Intelligence Society 24(2), 17–27 (2005)
31. Salembier, P.: MPEG-7 multimedia description schemes. IEEE Trans. on Circuits and Systems for Video Technology 11(6), 748–759 (2001)
32. Polydoros, P., Tsinaraki, C., Christodoulakis, S.: GraphOnto: OWL-based ontology management and multimedia annotation in the DS-MIRF framework. In: WMS 2006 (2006)
33. Tsinaraki, C., Perego, A., Polydoros, P., Syntzanaki, A., Martin, A., Christodoulakis, S.: Semantic, constraint & preference based multimedia presentation authoring. Journal of Digital Information Management 4(4), 207–213 (2006)

Gathering and Mining Information from Web Log Files

Maristella Agosti and Giorgio Maria Di Nunzio

Department of Information Engineering, University of Padua, Italy
{agosti,dinunzio}@dei.unipd.it

Abstract. In this paper, a general methodology for gathering and mining information from Web log files is proposed. A series of tools to retrieve, store, and analyze the data extracted from log files have been designed and implemented. The aim is to form general methods by abstracting from the analysis of logs which use a well-defined standard format, such as the Extended Log File Format proposed by W3C. The methodology has been experimented on the Web log files of The European Library portal; the experimental analyses led to personal, technical, geographical and temporal findings about the usage and traffic load. Considerations about a more accurate tracking of users and users profiles, and a better management of crawler accesses using authentication are presented.

1 Introduction

From the point of view of users, the Web is a growing collection of a large amount of information, and usually a great amount of time is needed to look for and find the appropriate information. Personalization is a possibility for the successful evolution of a Web infrastructure. For this reason, Web sites are created and adapted to make contents more easily accessible, using profiles to make recommendations or to target users with ad hoc advertising. An ideal environment would have at its disposal the exact history and information about a user, thus informing us about his tastes and needs. This goal may be achieved using user authentication, or cookie files with an identifier. But this is not always possible: privacy issues step in, and this kind of information may not be available, considering that some users are not willing to subscribe to a site to use its services.

Web log file analysis began with the purpose of offering to Web site administrators a way to ensure adequate bandwidth and server capacity to their organization. This field of analysis made great advances with the passing of time, and now e-companies seek ways to use Web log files to obtain information about visitor profiles and buyer activities. The analysis of Web logs may offer advice about a better way to improve the offer, information about problems occurring to the users, and even about problems for the security of the site. Traces about hacker attacks or heavy use in particular intervals of time may be really useful for configuring the server and adjusting the Web site.

C. Thanos, F. Borri, and L. Candela (Eds.): Digital Libraries: R&D, LNCS 4877, pp. 104–113, 2007.
© Springer-Verlag Berlin Heidelberg 2007

The collaboration with The European Library[1], the organization which has designed and manages the portal created to offer access to the digital and/or bibliographical resources of many European National libraries, gave us the possibility to access the data contained in the logs of their Web servers. The aim of this work is to propose a methodology for acquiring and managing data from Web log files by abstracting from the analysis of the Web logs of The European Library. A series of tools to retrieve, store, and analyze the data extracted from these Web logs have been designed and implemented, in order to give advice on the development of the portal from the point of view of both the security and the improvement of personalization.

In Sect. 2 we introduce this methodology, giving an overview on the parser and on the database designed and developed; in particular, the conceptual level of the database design process is presented. In Sect. 3 we show some of the results, with some observations regarding them, with particular reference to the trends discovered about visits. In Sect. 4 we draw conclusions, giving some advice for the future continuation of the work.

2 A Methodology for Acquiring and Managing Data from Web Log Files

The term log is used today in the context of a systematic and chronological collection of events. Different types of logs are currently used: user logs, system logs, and server logs. This last type of log is the one we are interested in for this research. A server log file is a file which stores information on an application server activity. A typical example may be a Web server log that stores the chronology of the Web pages requested. In this paper we use the name "Web server log" for the log file that contains the *HyperText Transfer Protocol (HTTP)* requests made from clients to the Web server of a Web site.

Several formats are available for servers to build their log files, but the most used is the World Wide Web Consortium Extended Log File Format[2]. As the name says it extends the Common Log File Format[3], overthrowing its main limitation, which was the fixed amount of information about each transaction. The Extended Log File Format permits the control of recorded data and the customization of the choice of the fields of the record of a log to be stored.

Therefore, we have at our disposal a great source of information in the log files, but the format is not optimized for search and retrieval: usually log files come in a text file format. In the methodology for acquiring data from Web log files we propose, two problems have been identified:

– gathering the information;
– storing the information.

---

[1] http://www.theeuropeanlibrary.org/
[2] http://www.w3.org/TR/WD-logfile
[3] http://www.w3.org/Daemon/User/Config/Logging.html#common-logfile-format

A possible solution for the problem of gathering information from a log file is the creation of a parser. The use of a parser requires a well-defined standard format in order to recognize each single field of a record of a log, such as the Extended Log File Format. A solution for the problem of storing the information contained in a log file is the use of a database application. With a database application it is possible to better organize and structure log fields in order to perform queries and to obtain statistical information useful for the development of the site.

The proposed methodology is general and can be applied in any situation where the W3C Extended Log File Format [1] is used to format Web server log files. The logs of The European Library are compliant with this format, so the methodology can be successfully applied.

In Sect. 2.1, we present the methodology for gathering information from a Web log file, and also some important considerations on how to parse log files. In Sect. 2.2, we present the design of the database that manages the data extracted from log files.

2.1   Gathering Data from Web Logs

The Extended Log File Format defines the structure of a record of a log, which contains a specific request performed by a client in a particular instant of time. Nevertheless, this format allows the possibility both to set a specific order of the fields of the record and to decide whether to include optional fields. Therefore, the building of a parser to read data from Web logs requires particular attention, including the study of the sequences of fields that may be different depending on the choices of Web administrators.

Table 1 presents the choice of fields included in the Web log files we have studied, and the presentation order is the same which appears in the files. Table 2 shows the initial part of some records of the current logs of The European Library we inspected.

In the following sections, we analyze in detail three particular fields of the logs that needed specific attention for the scope of our research: date-time and the user agent fields.

Date and Time: Building Timestamps. The first thing to observe is that in the log files there are several entries with the same *date* and *time* (see for example the second and third line of the extract of the log shown in Tab. 2). This is because the precision is limited to seconds, and therefore it is not possible to discriminate between requests made with a smaller temporal gap. In general, a Timestamp structure is of the following type: YYYY-MM-DD hh:mm:ss.lll, with l as digit for milliseconds. In the logs, we have only the date with structure YYYY-MM-DD and the time with structure hh:mm:ss. But if we observe that the log entries are chronologically ordered (the last log record is inserted as the last record of the text file), we can obtain the chronological chain of events, even with small temporal gaps. The problem regarding the sensibility limited to seconds on the time field can be overcome by adding an incremental value for the milliseconds field.

Table 1. Fields used in the Web log files of The European Library

date:	Date, in the form of yyyy-mm-dd
time:	Time, in the form of hh:mm:ss
s-ip:	The IP of the server
cs-method:	The requested action. Usually GET for common users
cs-uri-stem:	The URI-Stem of the request
cs-uri-query:	The URI-Query, where requested
s-port:	The port of the server for the transaction
cs-username:	The username for identification of the user
c-ip:	The IP address of the client
cs(User-Agent):	The User-Agent of the Client
cs(Referer):	The site where the link followed by the user was located
sc-status:	HTTP status of the request, i.e. the response of the server
sc-substatus:	The substatus error code
sc-win32-status:	The Windows status code

Table 2. Initial part of some records of the Web log file under study. Client IP addresses are obscured for privacy reasons.

```
2005-11-30 23:00:37 192.87.31.35 GET /index.htm - 80 - 152.xxx.xxx.xxx Mozilla/4.0+(comp...
2005-11-30 23:00:38 192.87.31.35 GET /portal/index.htm - 80 - 152.xxx.xxx.xxx Mozilla/4.0+...
2005-11-30 23:00:38 192.87.31.35 GET /portal/scripts/Hashtable.js - 80 - 152.xxx.xxx.xxx...
2005-11-30 23:00:44 192.87.31.35 GET /portal/scripts/Session.js - 80 - 152.xxx.xxx.xxx...
2005-11-30 23:00:46 192.87.31.35 GET /portal/scripts/Query.js - 80 - 152.xxx.xxx.xxx...
2005-11-30 23:00:47 192.87.31.35 GET /portal/scripts/Search.js - 80 - 152.xxx.xxx.xxx...
```

User Agent Field. The user agent string may offer a great amount of information useful for optimizing and personalizing Web sites. It is a valuable source that gives hints about browsers, operating systems used by users, and even analyzes the activity of crawlers. The user agent provides all these kinds of information, but there are no standards that define it. Indeed, it is a string of characters, which may even be empty, and which requires a specific parser to extract the data contained in it. A user agent parser should therefore extract: information like the browser, the operating system and their respective versions, when a standard definition is found; identify a crawler with its name, or its owner, when a non-standard sequence of characters is found. A more detailed report on the possible use of the user agent string is reported in [2].

2.2 Storing Web Log Information

The extraction of the data from Web logs gives access to information that has to be managed efficiently in order to be able to exploit it for analyses. The solution we propose for storing the information contained in a Web log file is based on database methods and technology. With a database approach the fields of a log file can be organized in such a way that it is possible to perform queries that emerge during the working out of the research, for example to obtain statistical

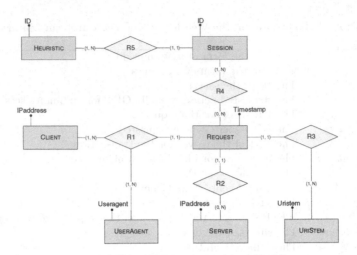

Fig. 1. Conceptual Level. Only the attributes that identify each entity are shown.

information useful for the development of the site and to allow subsequent mining of the managed data.

The design of the database application began with the analysis of the raw log files and followed with the identification of each entity with a top-down approach. The name of each entity is written in small capital letters to highlight it. The analysis has identified the entity REQUEST as a central one from which to start the design of the conceptual schema of the application. Relevant entities identified during the analysis are: CLIENT, USERAGENT, REQUEST, URISTEM, and SERVER. Please consider that a URI stem represents the local address of the resource requested to the server (for example **/portal/images/grey_arrow.gif**), and that the notion of user agent includes both browsers and crawlers. Moreover, we added two more entities to model the results of the analysis on the identification of sessions according to different heuristics: SESSION, HEURISTIC. A detailed description of sessions and heuristics is given in Sect. 3.

Figure 1 presents the conceptual schema that was designed at the end of the conceptual design step, the Entity-Relationship model was used to design the schema [3]. The CLIENT, identified by its IP address, is in relation with USERAGENT and REQUEST. This relation (named R1 in Fig. 1) expresses the fact that the same user can make different requests with different browsers.

A REQUEST is identified by the Timestamp. A request participates in all the relations involved with it – with the exception of R4 – with cardinality (1, 1) since there can only be one client, with its user agent, one server and one URI stem involved in a single request.

A USERAGENT is identified by the user agent string, a SERVER by its IP address, and the URISTEM by the string that localizes the resource.

Now, we consider the entities that are not physically present in the log files but that have been introduced during the analysis of the data in order to perform a deep study on the available data.

A SESSION is identified by a unique code, such as the HEURISTIC. It is worth noticing that the cardinality between the entity REQUEST and the association R4 is (0, N) because a request may be contained in different sessions according to what heuristic has been chosen. For example, request-1 may be included in session-1 for the heuristic-1 and also in session-5 for the heuristic-3. On the other hand, a specific session may be created by only one heuristic.

3   Analysis of Experimental Data

In this Section, we present the most relevant results on the log files of The European Library which were carried out. More details can be found in [4], [5], and [6].

The analysis was performed on the Web log files, and correspond to seven months of The European Library Web log files, starting from October 1st 2006 to April 30th 2007. As mentioned above, the structure of the log file record conforms to the W3C Extended Log File Format.

The analyses presented in the following subsections cover the following aspects: accesses, operating systems and browsers used by clients; sessions; temporal and geographical analyses.

3.1   Accesses, Operating Systems and Browsers

A total of 22,458,350 HTTP requests were recorded during the analyzed period with:

- a monthly average of 3,208,336 HTTP requests,
- a daily average of 105,936 requests,
- and an hourly average of 4,414 requests.

Figures 2a and 2b show the distribution of the operating systems and the browsers used by visitors respectively on the basis of the number of recorded HTTP requests.

It is possible to see how the products of Microsoft are by far the most used by visitors of The European Library portal: Windows alone is used by about 74% of the users; this tendency also affects the situation found in Figure 2b, with Internet Explorer as the most used browser, since it is used by 60% of users. However, we noticed an increase in the use of Mozilla Firefox, compared to the findings of a preliminary analysis of a sample of the initial months of the logs (from November 2005 to January 2006) as reported in [2]; in the reported period Mozilla Firefox was used by 13% of users.

3.2   Sessions

A session refers to a set of HTTP requests that are performed by a single user during the browsing activity. Since a user is supposed to access the portal more then once during the analysed period, a time-out is applied to distinguish different sessions of the same user.

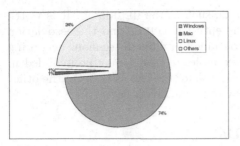

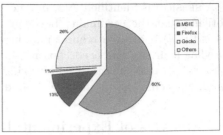

(a) Operating systems used by clients.   (b) Browsers used by clients.

Fig. 2. Web log general results based on HTTP requests

Table 3. Number of sessions per groups of HTTP requests, October 2006 - April 2007

HTTP requests per session	number of sessions	% of number sessions
<= 25	535,035	77.44%
> 25, <= 50	54,363	7.87%
> 50, <= 75	29,510	4.27%
> 75, <= 100	17,418	2.52%
> 100	54,553	7.90%
Total	690,879	100.00%

The reconstruction of sessions is an important process that allows the identification of single users (either human or software-agent), their tracking during the portal navigation and eventually their grouping on the basis of similar behaviors. In order to reconstruct a session, we used a heuristic that identifies a single user with the pair IP address and user-agent, and permits only a fixed gap of time between two consecutive requests. In particular, a new request is put in an existing session if two conditions are valid:

- the IP address and the user-agent are the same as the requests already inserted in the session [7],
- the request is made less than fifteen minutes after the last request inserted [8].

The reason for the choice of the couple of IP addresses and user-agent as identifiers is to distinguish different users coming from the same proxy. Different people using the same proxy appear in requests made by the same IP, despite the real identity of the clients. Taking into consideration the user-agent also enables the source of requests to be more clearly differentiated.

During the reported period, according to the heuristic we chose, 690,879 sessions were reconstructed. Table 3 presents the distribution of absolute number and percentage number of sessions per number of HTTP requests.

There is a sizeable number of sessions which last more than 60 seconds regardless of the number of requests per session. Therefore, an analysis of the sessions with more than 100 requests has been computed separately, since we believe that

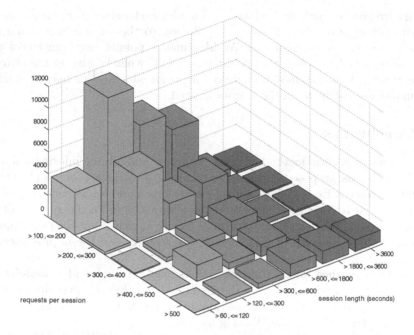

Fig. 3. Sessions (heuristic) which last more than 60 seconds with a number of requests per session > 100

these sessions are valuable for the analysis of users for personalization purposes. The results are shown in Figure 3.

3.3 Temporal and Geographical Analyses

In relation to the data reported in Sect. 3.1, since The European Library service is a 7 days and 24 hour service, it can be considered a busy service that answers an average of 74 requests per second, 7 days/24 hours.

An analysis of the distribution of requests per hour of day[2] shows that this distribution follows the one expected for European countries, considering that the time recorded by the server refers to the Central European Time: a higher activity during the day compared to the one during the night.

With the available data, it is possible to focus on the geographic location of the accesses and to study the amount of traffic performed by either human users or automatic crawlers. For this kind of analysis, it is possible to use freely available databases containing the associations between IP ranges and nations[4] to map an IP address to a country.

It is important to remember that in order to have valuable data for user profiling we need to discriminate between human users and crawlers for the analysis of the distributions of the accesses per country. In one of the analyses, we compared the geographical origin of the requests with the pattern of the

---

[4] See for example: http://software77.net/cgi-bin/ip-country/geo-ip.pl

network traffic per time unit, and we found a mismatch between the large number of visits coming from IP addresses that belong to the United States and the time distribution of the requests. We identified a possible explanation of this behavior in the IP addresses that result as a ".com" when looking at the Domain Name System, but that may be indeed European addresses or may be part of Multinationals operating in the European area.

4   Conclusions

In this paper, a general methodology for gathering and mining information from Web log files was proposed and a series of tools to retrieve, store, and analyze the data extracted from Web logs has been designed and implemented.

The aim was to form general methods by abstracting from the analysis of the Web logs of The European Library in order to give advice about the development of a portal from the point of view of both the security and the improvement of personalization.

In order to gather information from a log file a parser and a well-defined standard format for logs, such as the Extended Log File Format proposed by W3C, are required. With a database application it is possible to manage and mine data extracted from the Web log files.

With the initial experimental analysis carried out on the Web log files of The European Library, important findings and future directions can be drawn about:

 - the number of users and accesses to the Web site;
 - the browsers and operating systems used by visitors;
 - the pattern of the network traffic per time unit;
 - the geographical origin of the requests.

The heuristics used to identify users and sessions suggested that authentication would be required since it would allow Web servers to identify users, track their requests, and more importantly create profiles to tailor specific needs. This would be particularly important for the portal of The European Library since it deals with resources of different cultures and languages that may require specific attentions for each class of users.

Moreover, authentication would also help to resolve the problem concerning crawler accesses, granting access to some sections of the Web site only to registered users, and blocking crawlers using faked user agents. In fact, we identified more than three hundred different crawlers visiting The European Library for a total of a 50% of sessions.

Acknowledgements

The work reported in this paper has been conducted in the context of a joint effort of the DELOS Network of Excellence on Digital Libraries and The European Library.

The authors wish to thank all the staff of The European Library for their continuing support and cooperation.

References

1. Hallam-Baker, P., Behlendorf, B.: Extended Log File Format, W3C Working Draft WD-logfile-960323, [last visited 2007, July 4] (1996), URL: http://www.w3.org/TR/WD-logfile.html
2. Agosti, M., Di Nunzio, G, Niero, A.: From Web Log Analysis to Web User Profiling. In: Thanos, C., Borri, F. (eds.) DELOS Conference 2007. Working Notes, Pisa, Italy, pp. 121–132 (February 2007)
3. Chen, P.: The Entity–Relationship Model – Towards a Unified View of Data. ACM Transactions on Database Systems (TODS) 1, 9–36 (1976)
4. Agosti, M., Di Nunzio, G.M.: Web Log Mining: A study of user sessions. In: PersDL 2007. Proc. 10th DELOS Thematic Workshop on Personalized Access, Profile Management, and Context Awareness in Digital Libraries, Corfu, Greece, pp. 70–74 (2007)
5. Agosti, M., Coppotelli, T., Di Nunzio, G.M., Ferro, N., van der Meulen, E.: Log and multilingual information analysis to personalize access to the european library. In: Workshop on Cross-Media and Personalized Learning Applications on top of Digital Libraries, Budapest, Hungary, pp. 70–74 (2007)
6. Agosti, M., Coppotelli, T., Di Nunzio, G., Angelaki, G.: Analysing HTTP Logs of an European DL Initiative to Maximize Usage and Usability. In: Proc. 10th International Conference on Asian Digital Libraries, Special Track on European Digital Library Initiatives, Hanoi, Vietnam (2007)
7. Nicholas, D., Huntington, P., Watkinson, A.: Scholarly journal usage: the results of deep log analysis. Journal of Documentation 61 (2005)
8. Berendt, B., Mobasher, B., Nakagawa, M., Spiliopoulou, M.: The impact of site structure and user environment on session reconstruction in web usage analysis. In: Zaïane, O.R., Srivastava, J., Spiliopoulou, M., Masand, B. (eds.) WEBKDD 2002 - Mining Web Data for Discovering Usage Patterns and Profiles. LNCS (LNAI), vol. 2703, Springer, Heidelberg (2003)

Modelling Intellectual Processes: The FRBR - CRM Harmonization

Martin Doerr[1] and Patrick LeBoeuf[2]

[1] ICS-FORTH
martin@ics.forth.gr
[2] Bibliotheque National de France
PATRICK.LE-BOEUF@bnf.fr

Abstract. Even though the Dublin Core Metadata Element Set is well accepted as a general solution, it fails to describe more complex information assets and their cross-correlation. These include data from political history, history of arts and sciences, archaeology or observational data from natural history or geosciences. Therefore IFLA and ICOM are merging their core ontologies, an important step towards semantic interoperability of metadata schemata across all archives, libraries and museums. It opens new prospects for advanced global information integration services. The first draft of the combined model was published in June 2006.

1   Introduction

Semantic interoperability of Digital Libraries, Library- and Collection Management Systems requires compatibility of both the employed Knowledge Organization Systems (KOS; eg classification systems, terminologies, authority files, gazetteers) and of the employed data and metadata schemata. Currently, the notion and scope of Digital Libraries covers not only traditional publications, but also scientific and cultural heritage data. The difference between traditional publication in text form and structured data in form of databases is more and more blurring, with databases containing texts in XML form, texts and multimedia data being described by structured metadata records, and Natural Language Processing techniques extracting structured information from free texts. The grand vision is to see all these data integrated so that users are effectively supported in searching for and analyzing data across all domains. Even though the Dublin Core Metadata Element Set is well accepted as a general solution, it fails to describe more complex information assets and their cross-correlation. These include data from political history, history of arts and sciences, archaeology or observational data from natural history or geosciences etc.

Core ontologies describing the semantics of metadata schemata are the most effective tool to drive global schema and information integration [1], and provide a more robust, scalable solution than tailored 'cross-walks' between individual schemata. Information and queries are mapped to and from the core ontology,

C. Thanos, F. Borri, and L. Candela (Eds.): Digital Libraries: R&D, LNCS 4877, pp. 114–123, 2007.

which serves as a virtual global schema and has the capability to integrate complementary information from more restricted schemata. This is an important step beyond metadata serving just as finding aids for objects that share some common characteristics. Many scientists question the feasibility of such a global ontology across domains. On the other side, schemata like Dublin Core reveal the existence of overarching concepts. Ideally, the envisaged European Digital Library would be based on one sufficiently expressive core ontology, not by selecting arbitrarily one out of a set of alternatives, but by harmonization and integration of all relevant alternatives. The challenge is to practically explore the limits of harmonizing conceptualizations from coming from different domains which maintain data that support relevant cross-domain search scenarios.

2 The CIDOC Conceptual Reference Model

The CIDOC Conceptual Reference Model (CRM) has been developed since 1996 under the auspices of the International Committee on Documentation (CIDOC) of the International Council for Museums (ICOM) Documentation Standards Working Group. ICS-FORTH, Heraklion plays a leading role in this activity. The CRM has been accepted as ISO standard (ISO 21127:2006) in September 2006. It is a core ontology aiming to integrate cultural heritage information [2]cid. It already generalizes over most data structures used by highly diverse museum disciplines, archives, and site and monument records. Even the common library format MARC ('MAchine Readable Cataloguing') can be adequately mapped to it [9]. Four ideas are central to the CRM (see fig 1)

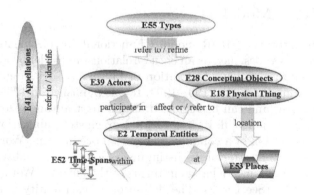

Fig. 1. Top-level Entities of the CIDOC CRM

1. The possible ambiguity of the relationship between entities and the identifiers ("Appellations") that are used to refer to the entities are a part of the historical reality to be described by the ontology rather than a problem to be resolved in advance. Therefore, the CRM distinguishes the nodes representing a real item from the nodes representing only the names of an item.

2. "Types" and classification systems are not only a means to structure information about reality from an external point of view, but also part of the historical reality in their nature as *human inventions*. As such they fall under "Conceptual Objects", inheriting properties of creation, use etc. Similarly, all documentation is seen as part of the reality, and may be described together with the documented content itself.

3. The normal human way to analyze the past is to split up the evolution of matters into discrete events in space and time. Thus the documented past can be formulated as series of events involving "Persistent Items" (also called endurants, see [2]) like "E18 Physical Things" and Persons. The involvement can be of different nature, but it implies at least the presence of the respective items. The linking of items, places and time through events creates a notion of history as "world-lines" of things meeting in space and time (see fig 2). Events, seen as processes of arbitrary scale, are generalized as "Periods" and further as "E2 Temporal Entities" (also called perdurants [2]). Only the latter two classes are directly connected to space and time in the ontology. The Temporal Entities have fuzzy spatiotemporal boundaries which can be approximated by outer and inner bounds. E18 Physical Things may be found on a E53 Place as result of an event such as a move or its creation.

4. Immaterial objects ("E28 Conceptual Objects") are items that can be created but can reside on more than one physical carrier at the same time, including human brains. Immaterial items can be present in events through the respective physical information carriers. (see fig 3) Immaterial items cannot be destroyed, but they disappear when the last carrier is lost.

3   The FRBR Model

Quite independently, the FRBR model ('Functional Requirements for Bibliographic Records') was designed as an entity-relationship model by a study group appointed by the International Federation of Library Associations and Institutions (IFLA) during the period 1991-1997. It was published in 1998. Its focus is domain-independent and can be regarded as the most advanced formulation of library conceptualization [3]ifl. Its innovation is to cluster publications and other items around the notion of a common conceptual origin - the 'Work' - in order to support information retrieval. It distinguishes four levels of abstraction from conception to the book in my hands in terms of the entities: Work, Expression, Manifestation, Item (See fig 2). The definition of each entity is an elaborate explanation of meaning and intended use. Here an extract [8]:

1. Work is "a distinct intellectual or artistic creation. A *work* is an abstract entity; there is no single material object one can point to as the *work*. We recognize the *work* through individual realizations or *expressions* of the *work*, but the *work* itself exists only in the commonality of content between and among the various *expressions* of the *work*.

2. Expression is "the intellectual or artistic realization of a *work* in the form of alpha-numeric, musical, or choreographic notation, sound, image, object,

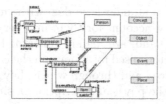

Fig. 2. Top-level Entities of FRBR

movement, etc., or any combination of such forms. An *expression* is the specific intellectual or artistic form that a *work* takes each time it is 'realized'.".

3. Manifestation is "the physical embodiment of an *expression* of a *work*. The entity defined as *manifestation* encompasses a wide range of materials, including manuscripts, books, periodicals, maps, posters, sound recordings, films, video recordings, CD-ROMs, multimedia kits, etc. As an entity, *manifestation* represents all the physical objects that bear the same characteristics, in respect to both intellectual content and physical form".

4. Item is "a single exemplar of a *manifestation*. The entity defined as *item* is a concrete entity. (e.g., a copy of a one-volume monograph, a single audio cassette, a monograph issued as two separately bound volumes, a recording issued on three separate compact discs, etc.).

Besides that, FRBR describes a rich set of attributes for those entities to capture all relevant bibliographic information for cataloguing and finding literature. It defines in particular the construction of identifiers needed for the entities Work and Expression that are newly required for the bibliographic practice.

4   The Harmonization Project

Initial contacts in 2000 between the two communities eventually led to the formation in 2003 of the International Working Group on FRBR/CIDOC CRM Harmonisation. The common goals were to express the IFLA FRBR model with the concepts, ontological methodology and notation conventions provided by the CIDOC CRM, and to merge the two object-oriented models thus obtained. Although both communities have to deal with collections pertaining to cultural heritage, those collections are of course very different in nature, and that difference is reflected in significant variations in focus between the two models. Most of library holdings are non-unique copies of "publications," i.e., non-unique exemplars of products obtained as the result of more or less industrialised processes. FRBR focuses therefore on the "abstract" characteristics that all copies of a single publication should typically display in order to be recognised as a copy of that publication. The cultural context in which either those physical copies or their immaterial content came into being is not regarded as particularly relevant in library catalogues and is therefore widely ignored in the FRBR model. Of course, libraries do also hold unique items, such as manuscripts; but there are no internationally agreed standards to deal with such materials, and FRBR mentions them but does not account for them in a very detailed way.

Museums, on the other hand, are mainly concerned with unique items - the uniqueness of which is counterpoised by a focus on the cultural circumstances under which they were produced and through which they are interrelated. CIDOC CRM highlights therefore the physical description of singular items, the context in which they were produced, and the multiple ways in which they can be related to other singular items, categories of items, or even just ideological systems or cultural trends. Of course, museums may also have to deal with exemplars of industrially produced series of artefacts, but CIDOC CRM covers that notion just with the multi-purpose E55 Type class. Most interesting are the relations between museum and library objects that are not automatically covered by a set of homogenous metadata elements for both: Museum objects may be referred to in literature kept in libraries. Museum objects may illustrate subjects described in literature. Literature and objects may be created by the same persons or in the same wider activities.

The Working Group has published the first complete draft of FRBRoo, ie the object-oriented version of FRBR, harmonized with CIDOC CRM, in June 2006. This formal ontology is intended to capture and represent the underlying semantics of bibliographic information and to facilitate the integration, mediation and interchange of bibliographic and museum information. The intellectual rigour of the methodology of the CIDOC CRM demanded clarification and explication of many notions more vaguely specified in FRBR. After that, FRBRoo could completely be formulated as a specialization of the CRM, some smaller, upwards-compatible modifications of the CRM not withstanding. In its draft version summer 2007 [10], the object-oriented definition of FRBR amounts to 39 classes and 55 properties, and re-uses 44 classes and 45 properties from CIDOC CRM. This version will undergo a final internal review Dec. 2007 and then be submitted to IFLA and CIDOC for approval.

5   Selected Results

The process of developing this model turned out to be very demanding. The combined model on one side enriches the CIDOC CRM with notions of the stages of intellection creation and refines the model of the CRM of identifiers and the associated discourse. On the other side, it makes available to FRBR the general model of historical events and context of creation contained in the CRM. FRBR is not event-aware. As a consequence, many attributes are attached to entities they do not causally belong to, and the precise semantics remain unclear. E.g., it was a surprise that in reality the date and place of publication is not necessarily related to the event of printing a book.

But at the heart of the work, the major innovation is a realistic, explicit model of the intellectual creation process (see fig 3), which should still be developed further in the future for the benefit of librarians and scholars from the various museum disciplines. FRBRoo makes the following distinctions:

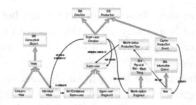

Fig. 3. Partial model of the intellectual creation process

- The substance of *Work* is the concepts or internal representations of our mind. The unity of a Work is given by the intellectual coherence of its concepts. *Work* can be created by multiple people together, and be understood and continued by other people, such as by translation, derivation, completion. A stage or part of a *Work* is regarded as an *Individual Work*, if it is complete from its elaboration and logical coherence of its content, or regarded as a complete unit by its author. Otherwise it is a *Complex Work*, which may consist of a set or sequence of self-contained versions or components in no particular temporal order.
- The substance of *Expression* is signs or symbols. It is only representation. It has no direct intellectual qualities, but humans can interpret the signs and recognize the Work behind. Consequently, an Expression cannot be translated, but only be used as a basis for the translator to access or "grasp" the ideational content of the Work it represents, and render that ideational content in a different language (similarly, music notation embodied in a score serves as a basis for the performer to study what the sonic features of the musical Work represented by the notation were presumably meant to be, and elaborate a performance on that basis). Expressions can be complete in the sense, that they represent an Individual Work. Then they are regarded as *Self-Contained Expressions*. Else they are *Expression Fragments*.
- "Manifestation" as defined in FRBR can be interpreted as covering two completely different things: Either it is a *Manifestation Product Type*, an industrial product, i.e., a class of things, such as a particular car model, or it is a *Manifestation Singleton*, a Physical Man-Made Thing in terms of the CRM, that was produced as a unique carrier of an *Expression*. Industrially printed books belong to the first category, and are indirectly related to the main author's original creations.

The idea is that products of our mind, as long as they stay in one person's mind only, are relatively volatile and not evident, but may already exist as parts of a Work. Even though a person may claim having conceived a Work at a certain date, it is not before the Work is "externalized" for the first time that its creation becomes evident. Further, we all have experienced how thought takes shape during communicating it to others, or even during the very process of writing it down. Therefore we basically tie the intellectual creation with the event of "first externalization", the *Expression Creation*, which comes after the *Work Conception*, if there is any evidence for the latter. In practical terms, externalization means that the expression must be transferred to another physical carrier. This can be just another person's memory, as in the case of oral tradition (the CRM regards persons as physical objects), or more usually a paper manuscript or, in these days, a computer disc.

The transfer to another carrier is a physical process, which leaves more or less material traces. In terms of documentation, we would normally regard that a manuscript is produced as a new object. However, if we do not use raw writing material, but scribble a text on a wall, the object is rather modified than produced. In the CRM, E11 Modification is a generalization of E12 Production. Therefore we model the FRBRoo concept *Expression Creation* as a specialization of the CRM classes E65 Creation for immaterial items (such as Expressions) and E11 Modification for the modification or production of a physical carrier. To our knowledge, this is the first time that the material and immaterial aspects of intellectual creation are modelled explicitly. The CRM has no particular construct how both aspects relate. Also, explicitly modelling oral tradition may be worthwhile doing.

Another important part of the discussion had to do with works consisting of other, pre-existing works, such as anthologies. In the course of discussion however it was recognized that virtually any book is composed of multiple, distinct works: the text, the illustrations, the editors work on lay-out, type phase etc. The latter was widely ignored in FRBR (just like in library practice, which tends traditionally to reduce publishers' role to a minimum and does not acknowledge publishers' and producers' actual interference in the processes of intellectual and artistic creation), and discussions tend to confuse the question of which contribution and work is the most relevant part with how to make the necessary distinctions in a model. This situation demanded a general model explicating both the individual contribution and the unity of the integrated product. The FRBRoo solution considers that the Work itself does not contain any other work. Rather, the containment happens at the Expression level, the signs. In other terms, in a collection of poems, the final overall Expression is a representation of the collector's work, and contains expressions of the collected works. This does not imply that the concepts represented in each of the collected expressions are "part" of the concepts of the collection itself as a Work (e.g., an editor who selects for an anthology of poems the sonnet that begins with the famous line "Tired with all these, for restful death I cry" does not express his or her own suicidal tendencies; the concepts expressed in Shakespeare's sonnet are not endorsed by the anthology itself, the purpose of which is entirely distinct from Shakespeare's purpose when he wrote the sonnet). The overall Expression is not separable into the different contributions: If all poems are cut out, the collection is not properly expressed by the - potentially empty - rest (i.e., although the concepts conveyed by the words "Tired with all these, for restful death I cry" are not a component part of the concepts conveyed by the anthology, those words themselves are an indispensable part of the text of the anthology). In the further elaboration of the model we found that Work incorporating expressions of other Works are a very fundamental intellectual process - different from derivation - that takes many shapes. For instance, a graphics designer incorporates the text of a manuscript in a publication; a movie text book may incorporate texts of a theatre play, the actors' speech incorporates the movie text book, the recording incorporates the actors' speech.

Finally, library practice has a lot to do with complex identifiers with meaningful parts. Librarians work from bottom to top: They draw from the item at hand conclusions about the Manifestation, Expression, and Work. This implies detailed rules for the creation of unique associated identifiers. The CRM will benefit from an explicit model of constructing identifiers from parts, so far ignored by the CRM.

The harmonization work covered a complete reinterpretation of the FRBR entities, attributes and relationships in terms of a formal ontology extending the CRM. FRBR promoters claim that the model is applicable to any intellectual production process, including performing arts. The Working Group separated the issues. The argumentation was first deliberately restricted to written material - notions well understood in the typical library context - in order to avoid over-generalizing from the very beginning. Then, a convincing equivalence of material publishing to electronic publishing could be established, the basic idea being that the individual copy of a file on a particular machine corresponds to the creation of an Item, such as "the book in my hands".

The equivalences to performing arts appeared to be more demanding, since a performance is basically an event, which leaves material traces and memories but cannot be stored. What libraries strive to preserve can only be those physical traces left by performances and rehearsals (such as: promptbooks, costumes, sketches, stage set models, etc.), and elaborations based on those performances (such as: accounts for memories, critical appraisals, studies, photographs, recordings, etc.); library documentation about performances themselves cannot be compared with library documentation about physical holdings, it can only serve to identify what unites those physical traces and elaborations, what makes them interrelated. The Working Group is now finalizing in FRBRoo a model of *performance*, the *Expressions* they employ and *recording* to capture these aspects in a way relevant to cultural documentation. The current draft contains this model, a complete mapping of FRBR constructs to FRBRoo concepts and the subset of concepts employed from the CRM.

6   Conclusions and Future Work

The potential impact of the combined models can be very high. The domains explicitly covered by the models are already immense. Further, they seem to be applicable to the experimental and observational scientific record for e-science applications and documentation for Digital Preservation. From a methodological perspective, the endeavour of core ontology harmonization experimentally proves the feasibility of finding viable common conceptual grounds even if the initial conceptualizations seem incompatible [3]doe:hun:lag. Characteristically, a number of experts from both sides questioned in the beginning the feasibility of this harmonization process. Even though this process is intellectually demanding and time-consuming, we hope the tremendous benefits of nearly global models will encourage more integration work on the core-ontology level. A recent practical application of these models is the derivation of the CRM Core Metadata schema [5]crm, which is compatible and similar in coverage and complexity to Dublin Core, but much more powerful. It allows for a minimal description of complex processes, scientific and archaeological data, and is widely extensible in a consistent way by the CRM-FRBR concepts. CRM Core can be easily used by Digital Libraries. The FRBRoo Working Group intends now to develop a similar FRBR core model to capture the fundamental relationships between intellectual products as identified by FRBRoo, since the current form is not easy to digest and too detailed for light-weighted systems.

The Working Group intends to promote the standardization process further: FRBRoo will be submitted to IFLA for review and approval by the end of 2007. We hope that IFLA will take up this work in appropriate form to inform their standardization efforts. CIDOC will propose an amendment for the CIDOC CRM to ISO to incorporate the improvements motivated by the analysis of FRBR concepts and required for complete compatibility of FRBRoo. Then the way will be open to standardize a common library and museum model. In contrast to the CRM, which describes current museum documentation, FRBR does not completely reflect current library practice, but the intended future library practice. Therefore some time will be needed for developing proof-of-concept systems and testing the new concepts before a real standard based on FRBR / FRBRoo is proposed. We further intend a similar collaboration with ICA, the International Council of Archives, on a common conceptual model.

References

1. Patel, M., Koch, T., Doerr, M., Tsinaraki, C., Gioldasis, N., Golub, K., Tudhope, D.: Semantic Interoperability in Digital Library Systems. DELOS Network of Excellence on Digital Libraries - deliverable 5.3.1 (2005)
2. Doerr, M.: The CIDOC CRM - An Ontological Approach to Semantic Interoperability of Metadata. AI Magazine 4(1) (2003)
3. LeBoeuf, P. (ed.): Functional Requirements for Bibliographic Records (Frbr): Hype or Cure-All? Haworth Press, Inc. (January 2005) ISBN:0789027984
4. Doerr, M., Hunter, J., Lagoze, C.: Towards a Core Ontology for Information Integration. Journal of Digital information 4(1) (2003)
5. Sinclair, P., Addis, M., Choi, F., Doerr, M., Lewis, P., Martinez, K.: The use of CRM Core in Multimedia Annotation. In: SWAMM 2006. Proceedings of First International Workshop on Semantic Web Annotations for Multimedia, part of the 15th World Wide Web Conference, Edinburgh, Scotland, May 22-26, 2006 (2006)
6. Definition of the CIDOC CRM: http://cidoc.ics.forth.gr

7. Definition of CRM Core:
   http://cidoc.ics.forth.gr/working-editions-cidoc.html
8. IFLA Study Group on the functional requirements for bibliographic records: Functional requirements for bibliographic records. Final report. Volume 19 of UBCIM Publications. New Series. K. G. Saur,Munich (1998)
9. Le Boeuf, P., Lahanier, C., Aitken, G., Sinclair, P., Lewis, P., Martinez, K.: Integrating Museum & Bibliographic Information: The SCULPTEUR Project. In: Proc. ICHIM 2005 Conference, Paris (2005)
10. Successive drafts of the model and minutes of the Harmonisation Group's meetings are available from both the CIDOC CRM Web site at http://cidoc.ics.forth.gr/frbr_inro.html and the FRBR Review Group's Web site at http://www.ifla.org/VII/s13/wgfrbr/FRBR-CRMdialogue_wg.htm

XS2OWL: A Formal Model and a System for Enabling XML Schema Applications to Interoperate with OWL-DL Domain Knowledge and Semantic Web Tools

Chrisa Tsinaraki and Stavros Christodoulakis

TUC/MUSIC, Technical University of Crete Campus, 73100 Kounoupidiana, Crete, Greece
{chrisa,stavros}@ced.tuc.gr

Abstract. The domination of XML in the Internet for data exchange has led to the development of standards with XML Schema syntax for several application domains. Advanced semantic support, provided by domain ontologies and semantic Web tools like logic-based reasoners, is still very useful for many applications. In order to provide it, interoperability between XML Schema and OWL is necessary so that XML schemas can be converted to OWL. This way, the semantics of the standards can be enriched with domain knowledge encoded in OWL domain ontologies and further semantic processing may take place. In order to achieve interoperability between XML Schema and OWL, we have developed XS2OWL, a model and a system that are presented in this paper and enable the automatic transformation of XML Schemas in OWL-DL. XS2OWL also enables the consistent transformation of the derived knowledge (individuals) from OWL-DL to XML constructs that obey the original XML Schemas.

Keywords: Interoperability, Standards, XML Schema, OWL, Ontologies.

1 Introduction

Web applications and services have formed an open environment, where the applications developed by different vendors interoperate on the basis of the emergent standards. The dominant data exchange standard in the Internet today is the *eXtensible Markup Language (XML)* [2]. The XML documents are usually structured according to schemas expressed in *XML Schema Language* [5] syntax. XML Schema uses XML syntax, supports very rich structures and datatypes for XML documents and plays a central role in the data exchange in the Internet. As a consequence, important standards in different application domains have been specified in XML Schema such as the MPEG-7 [4] and the MPEG-21 [14] for multimedia, the IEEE LOM [10] and SCORM [1] in e-learning, the METS [9] for Digital Libraries etc.

Advanced semantic support, though, would be very useful for several standard-based applications that need to integrate domain knowledge expressed in domain ontologies and perform semantic processing (including reasoning) within the constructs of the standards. As an example, consider the MPEG-7 based multimedia applications. MPEG-7 provides rich multimedia content description capabilities and has been specified using XML Schema syntax, like many other standards. MPEG-7 based

C. Thanos, F. Borri, and L. Candela (Eds.): Digital Libraries: R&D, LNCS 4877, pp. 124–136, 2007.

services (e.g. retrieval, filtering etc.) would benefit from domain knowledge integration. MPEG-7 provides general-purpose constructs that could be used for domain knowledge description [18], but the developers that are going to integrate domain knowledge in MPEG-7 are likely to be more familiar with the *Web Ontology Language (OWL)* [13] than with the domain knowledge description mechanisms of MPEG-7. In addition, some applications of MPEG-7, like the (semi-)automatic multimedia content annotation may greatly benefit from using logic-based reasoners for OWL. As a consequence, the capability to work with the semantics of MPEG-7 expressed in OWL and integrated with OWL domain ontologies is beneficial for such applications. Since other MPEG-7 applications may work with the XML Schema version of MPEG-7, the derived knowledge should be converted back to standard MPEG-7/XML constructs.

We present in this paper the XS2OWL transformation model that allows to transform the XML Schema constructs in OWL, so that applications using XML Schema based standards will be able to use the Semantic Web methodologies and tools. XS2OWL also supports the conversion of the OWL-based constructs back to the XML Schema based constructs in order to maintain the compatibility with the XML schema versions of the standards. XS2OWL has been implemented as an *XML Stylesheet Transformation Language (XSLT)* [7] stylesheet and transforms every XML Schema based standard in an OWL-DL *Main Ontology*. This way, the constructs of the standard become first class Semantic Web objects and may be integrated with domain knowledge expressed as OWL domain ontologies. In addition, all the OWL-based Semantic Web tools, including reasoners, can be used with the standard-based descriptions. In addition, a *Mapping Ontology* is generated for each XML Schema, which allows encoding all the knowledge needed to transform the individuals generated or added later on to the main ontology back to XML syntax valid according to the original XML Schema.

The research conducted in the support of interoperability between XML Schema and OWL is limited. We had observed the need for such support for the MPEG-7 standard in the context of the DS-MIRF framework [16, 17, 18]. In order to achieve it, we first defined manually an Upper OWL-DL ontology capturing the *MPEG-7 Multimedia Description Schemes (MDS)* [12] and the *MPEG-21 Digital Item Adaptation (DIA) Architecture* [11]. This way, domain knowledge expressed in OWL domain ontologies could be integrated with the semantics of the standards captured in the Upper ontology, as was done with ontologies for soccer and Formula 1. Finally, we developed a set of transformation rules for transforming the OWL individuals that describe the multimedia content and have been defined using the Upper ontology and the domain ontologies back to the original MPEG-7/21 constructs. The transformation rules rely on a mapping ontology that systematically captures the semantics of MPEG-7/21 that cannot be captured in the Upper ontology. This work is an important motivating example for the need of the general-purpose mechanism described here.

The automatic transformation of XML Schema constructs to OWL constructs has been proposed in [6]. According to this methodology, an XML Schema is transformed to an OWL-Full ontology that partially captures the XML Schema semantics. This way, information is lost during the transformation from XML Schema to OWL, and no support is provided in order to transform OWL individuals obeying the ontologies produced back to XML syntax valid according to the original XML Schemas. Finally some XML Schema construct transformations of to OWL in [6] do not follow closely the XML Schema semantics. The XS2OWL model presented in this paper allows automatically transforming XML Schema constructs to OWL-DL constructs (not OWL-Full) without loosing any information. This way, computational completeness and decidability of reasoning are guaranteed in the OWL ontologies produced and back transformations are supported.

The rest of the paper is structured as follows: In section 2 we provide background information. The proposed model for transforming XML Schema constructs in OWL-DL is presented in section 3. The mapping ontologies that represent the XML Schema semantics that cannot be directly transformed in OWL-DL are described in section 4. In section 5 we present the realization of the XS2OWL model, so that the transformations are carried out automatically. The paper conclusions are presented in section 6.

2 Background

In this section we present the background information needed in other parts of the paper. In particular, we present in brief the *XML Schema Language* and the *Web Ontology Language (OWL)*.

The XML Schema Language. The *XML Schema Language* [5] allows the definition of classes of XML documents using XML syntax and provides datatypes and rich structuring capabilities. An XML document is composed of *elements*, with the root element delimiting the beginning and the end of the document. Reuse of the element definitions is supported by the *substitutionGroup* attribute, which states that the current element is a specialization of another element. The elements may either have a predefined order (forming XML Schema *sequences*) or be unordered (forming XML Schema *choices*). Both sequences and choices may be nested. The minimum and maximum number of occurrences of the elements, choices and sequences are specified, respectively, in the *minOccurs* and *maxOccurs* attributes (absent "minOccurs" and/or "maxOccurs" attributes correspond to values of 1). Reusable complex structures, combining sequences and choices, may be defined as *model groups*.

The XML Schema language allows for the definition of both complex and simple elements. Complex elements belong to *complex types*, which may include other elements and carry *attributes* that describe their features. Simple elements belong to *simple types*, which are usually defined as restrictions of the basic datatypes provided by XML Schema (i.e. strings, integers, floats, tokens etc.). Simple types can neither contain other elements nor carry attributes. Inheritance and constraints are supported for both simple and complex types. Sets of attributes that should be used simultaneously may form *attribute groups*. Default and fixed values may be specified for XML Schema attributes and simple type elements.

The top-level XML Schema constructs (attributes, elements, simple and complex types, attribute and model groups) have unique *names* (specified in their "name" attribute), while the nested types and groups are unnamed. All the XML Schema constructs may have unique identifiers (specified in their "id" attribute). The top-level constructs may be referenced by other constructs using the "ref" attribute.

The Web Ontology Language (OWL). The *Web Ontology Language (OWL)* [13] is the dominant standard in ontology definition. OWL has followed the description logics paradigm and uses *RDF (Resource Description Framework)/RDFS (Resource Description Framework Schema)* [8, 3] syntax. Three OWL species of increasing descriptive power have been specified: *OWL-Lite*, which is intended for lightweight reasoning but has limited expressive power, *OWL-DL*, which provides description logics expressivity and guarantees computational completeness and decidability of reasoning, and *OWL-Full*, which has more flexible syntax than OWL-DL, but does not guarantee computational completeness and decidability of reasoning.

The basic functionality provided by OWL is: *(a) Import of XML Schema Datatypes*, that represent *simple types* extending or restricting the basic datatypes (e.g. ranges etc.). The imported datatypes have to be declared, as *RDFS datatypes*, in the ontologies they are used; *(b) Definition of OWL Classes*, organized in subclass hierarchies, for the representation of sets of individuals sharing some properties. Complex OWL classes can be defined via *set operators* (intersection, union or complement of other classes) or via *direct enumeration* of their members; *(c) Definition of OWL Individuals*, essentially instances of the OWL classes, following the restrictions imposed on the class in which they belong; and *(d) Definition of OWL Properties*, which may form property hierarchies, for the representation of the features of the OWL class individuals. Two kinds of properties are provided by OWL: *(i) Object Properties*, which relate individuals of one OWL class (the property domain) with individuals of another OWL class (the property range); and *(ii) Datatype Properties*, which relate individuals belonging to one OWL class (the property domain) with values of a given datatype (the property range). Restrictions may be defined on OWL class properties, including type, cardinality and value restrictions. OWL classes, properties and individuals are identified by unique identifiers specified in their "rdf:ID" attributes.

3 Transformation of XML Schema Constructs to OWL-DL

We present in this section a model for the direct transformation of the XML Schema constructs in OWL-DL. The result of the transformation of a source XML Schema is a *main ontology*, an OWL-DL ontology that captures the semantics of the XML Schema constructs. The transformations of the individuals XML Schema constructs are presented in the next paragraphs.

Simple XML Schema Datatypes. OWL does not directly support the definition of simple datatypes; it only allows importing simple datatypes. Existing XML Schema datatypes may be used in OWL ontologies if they have been declared in them. XS2OWL organizes all the simple XML Schema datatype definitions in the "datatypes" XML Schema and for each of them it generates an OWL datatype declaration. Let *st(name, id, body)* be an XML Schema simple datatype, where *body* is the body of the definition of *st*, *id* is the (optional) identifier of *st* and *name* is the name of *st*. *st* is transformed into: (a) The *st'(name', id, body)* simple datatype, which is stored in the "datatypes" XML Schema; and (b) the *dd(about, is_defined_by, label)* datatype declaration in the main ontology.

The *st'* simple type has the same *body* and *id* with *st*, while *name'* is formed as follows: If *st* is a top-level simple type, *name'* has the *name* value. If *st* is a simple type nested in the *ae* XML Schema construct (that may be an attribute or an element), *name'* has the value (a) *id* if *st* has a non-null identifier; and (b) the result of *concatenate(ct_name, '_', ae_name, '_UNType')* if *st* has a null identifier, where: (i) The *concatenate(...)* algorithm takes as input an arbitrary number of strings and returns their concatenation; and (ii) *ct_name* is the name of the complex type containing *ae*. If *ae* is a top-level attribute or element, *ct_name* has the 'NS' string as value.; and (iii) *ae_name* is the name of the property that represents *ae*.

The *dd* datatype declaration carries the following semantics: (a) *about* is the identifier referenced by the datatype declaration and is of the form *concatenate(url,name')*, where *url* is the URL of the "datatypes" XML Schema; (b) *is_defined_by* specifies where the datatype definition is located and has the *url* value; and (c) *label* is the label of *dd* and has *name'* as value.

As an example, consider the nested simple datatype of Fig. 1, which is defined in the "a1" attribute of the "ct1" complex type. It is transformed to the top-level simple datatype shown in Fig. 2, and the OWL datatype declaration shown in Fig. 3.

```
<xs:complexType name="ct1">
 <xs:simpleContent>
  <xs:extension base="xs:integer">
   <xs:attribute name="a1">
    <xs:simpleType>
     <xs:restriction base="xs:string"/>
    </xs:simpleType>
   </xs:attribute>
  </xs:extension>
 </xs:simpleContent>
</xs:complexType>
```

Fig. 1. Definition of a nested simple datatype

```
<simpleType name="ct1_a1_UNType">
 <restriction base="xs:string"/>
</simpleType>
```

Fig. 2. Top-level simple datatype representing the nested datatype of Fig. 1

```
<rdfs:Datatype rdf:about="&datatypes;ct1_a1_UNType">
 <rdfs:isDefinedBy rdf:resource="&datatypes;"/>
 <rdfs:label>ct1_a1_UNType</rdfs:label>
</rdfs:Datatype>
```

Fig. 3. OWL Declaration of the simple datatype of Fig. 2

Attributes. XML Schema attributes describe features with values of simple type. The OWL construct that can represent such features is the datatype property. Thus, XS2OWL transforms the XML Schema attributes into OWL datatype properties.

Let *a(name, aid, type, annot, ct_name, fixed, default)* be an XML Schema attribute, where *name* is the name of *a*, *aid* is the identifier of *a*, *type* is the type of *a*, *annot* is an (optional) annotation element of *a*, *ct_name* is the name of the complex XML Schema type *c_type* in the context of which *a* is defined (if *a* is a top-level attribute, *ct_name* has the null value), *fixed* is the (optional) fixed value of *a* and *default* is the (optional) default value of *a*. XS2OWL, transforms *a* into the OWL datatype property *dp(id, range, domain, label, comment)*, where: (a) *id* is the unique rdf:ID of *dp* and has *concatenate(name, '__', type)* as value; (b) *range* is the range of *dp* and has *type* as value; (c) *domain* is the domain of *dp* and has *ct_name* as value; (d) *label* is the label of *dp* and has *name* as value; and (e) *comment* is the textual description of *dp* and has *annot* as value. If any of the features of *a* is absent, the corresponding feature of *dp* is also absent. Note that: (a) If a fixed value of *a* is specified, it is represented as a value restriction in the definition of the OWL class *c* that represents *c_type*; and (b) If a default value of *a* is specified, it cannot be represented in the main ontology.

As an example, consider the "a1" attribute, shown in Fig. 1, which is transformed to the OWL datatype property shown in Fig. 4.

```
<owl:DatatypeProperty rdf:ID="a1__ct1_a1_UNType">
 <rdfs:domain rdf:resource="#ct1"/>
 <rdfs:range rdf:resource="&datatypes;ct1_a1_UNType"/>
 <rdfs:label>a1</rdfs:label>
</owl:DatatypeProperty>
```

Fig. 4. The OWL datatype property representing the "a1" attribute of Fig. 1

Elements. XML Schema elements represent features of complex XML Schema types and are transformed into OWL properties: The simple type elements are represented as OWL datatype properties and the complex type elements are represented as OWL object properties. Let *e(name, type, eid, annot, ct_name, substitution_group)* be an XML Schema element, where *name* is the name of *e*, *eid* is the identifier of *e*, *type* is the type of *e*, *annot* is an annotation element of *e*, *ct_name* is the name of the complex XML Schema type *c_type* in the context of which *e* is defined (if *e* is a top-level attribute, *ct_name* has the null value) and *substitution_group* is an (optional) element being extended by *e*. We represent *e* in OWL as a (datatype or object) property *p(id, range, domain, label, comment, super_property)*, where: (a) *id* is the unique rdf:ID of *p* and has *concatenate(name, '__', type)* as value; (b) *range* is the range of *p* and has *type* as value; (c) *domain* is the domain of *p* and has *ct_name* as value; (d) *label* is the label of *p* and has *name* as value; (e) *comment* is the textual description of *p* and has *annot* as value; and (f) *super_property* is the specification of the property specialized by *p* and has *substitution_group* as value.

As an example, consider the "e" element, shown in Fig. 5, of type "c_t2", defined in the context of the complex type "c_t1". The "e" element is transformed to the OWL object property shown in Fig. 6.

```
<xs:element name="e" type="c_t2"/>
```

Fig. 5. Definition of the "e" element, nested in the complex type "c_t1"

```
<owl:ObjectProperty rdf:ID="e__c_t2">
 <rdfs:domain rdf:resource="#c_t1"/>
 <rdfs:range rdf:resource="#c_t2"/>
 <rdfs:label>e</rdfs:label>
</owl:ObjectProperty>
```

Fig. 6. The OWL object property representing the "e" element of Fig. 5

Complex Types. The XML Schema complex types represent classes of XML instances that have common features, just as the OWL classes represent sets of individuals with common properties. Thus XS2OWL transforms the XML Schema complex types into OWL classes. Let *ct(name, cid, base, annot, attributes, sequences, choices)* be an XML Schema complex type, where: (a) *name* is the name of *ct*; (b) *aid* is the identifier of *ct*; (c) *base* is the (simple or complex) type extended by *ct*; (d) *annot* is an annotation element of *ct*; (e) *attributes* is the list of the attributes of *ct*; (f) *sequences* is the list of the *ct* sequences; and (g) *choices* is the list of the *ct* choices.

If *ct* extends a complex type, XS2OWL transforms it to the OWL class *c(id, super_class, label, comment, value_restrictions, cardinality_restrictions)*, where: (a) *id* is the unique rdf:ID of *c* and has *name* as value if *ct* is a top-level complex type. If *ct* is a complex type nested within the definition of an element *e*, *name* is a unique, automatically generated name of the form *concatenate(ct_name, '_', element_name, '_UNType')*, where *ct_name* is the name of the complex type containing *e* and *element_name* is the name of *e*. If *e* is a top-level element, *ct_name* has the 'NS' value; (b) *super_class* states which class is extended by *ct* and has *base* as value; (c) *label* is the label of *ct* and has *name* as value; (d) *comment* is the textual description of *ct* and has *annot* as value; (e) *value_restrictions* is the set of the value restrictions holding for the properties of *c*; and (f) *cardinality_restrictions* is the set of the cardinality restrictions assigned to the properties representing the *ct* attributes and the *ct* sequence/choice elements.

```
<owl:Class rdf:ID="ct1">
 <rdfs:subClassOf>
  <owl:Restriction>
   <owl:onProperty rdf:resource="#a1__ct1_a1_UNType"/>
   <owl:maxCardinality rdf:datatype="&xsd;integer">1</owl:maxCardinality>
  </owl:Restriction>
 </rdfs:subClassOf>
 <rdfs:subClassOf>
  <owl:Restriction>
   <owl:onProperty rdf:resource="#content__xs_integer"/>
   <owl:cardinality rdf:datatype="&xsd;integer">1</owl:cardinality>
  </owl:Restriction>
 </rdfs:subClassOf>
 <rdfs:label>ct1</rdfs:label>
</owl:Class>
<owl:DatatypeProperty rdf:ID="content__xs_integer">
 <rdfs:domain rdf:resource="#ct1"/>
 <rdfs:range rdf:resource="&xs;integer"/>
</owl:DatatypeProperty>
```

Fig. 7. OWL class representing the "ct1" complex type of Fig. 1

If *ct* extends a simple type, XS2OWL transforms it to the OWL class *c(id, label, comment, value_restrictions, cardinality_restrictions)*, with the same semantics with the classes representing complex types that extend complex types on the corresponding items. The extension of the simple type is represented by the datatype property *ep(eid, erange, edomain)* of cardinality 1, where: (a) *eid* is the unique rdf:ID of *ep* and has *concatenate(base, '_content')* as value; (b) *range* is the range of *ep* and has *base* as value; and (c) *domain* is the domain of *ep* and takes as value the *id* of *c*.

The attributes and the elements that are defined or referenced in *ct* are transformed to the corresponding OWL-DL constructs.

As an example, consider the complex type "ct1", shown in Fig. 1. The "ct1" complex type is represented by the "ct" OWL class, shown in Fig. 7, together with the "content__xs_integer" datatype property, which states that "ct1" is an extension of xs:integer.

Sequences and Choices. The XML Schema sequences and choices essentially are XML element containers, defined in the context of complex types and model groups. The main difference between sequences and choices is that the sequences are ordered, while the choices are unordered. XS2OWL transforms both the sequences and the choices to unnamed OWL-DL classes featuring complex cardinality restrictions on the sequence/choice items (elements, sequences and choices) and places them in the definition of the classes that represent the complex types where the sequences/choices are referenced or defined.

The lower bound of the minimum cardinality of the construct that represents a sequence/choice item has the value $i\_min\_occurs*s\_min\_occurs$ and the upper bound of the construct maximum cardinality has the value $i\_max\_occurs*s\_max\_occurs$, where: (a) i_min_occurs is the value of the "minOccurs" attribute of the item; (b) s_min_occurs is the value of the "minOccurs" attribute of the sequence; (c) i_max_occurs is the value of the "maxOccurs" attribute of the item; and (d) s_max_occurs is the value of the "maxOccurs" attribute of the sequence. In addition, the cardinality of the sequence/choice items must always be a multiple in the range $[i\_min\_occurs - i\_max\_occurs]$.

Sequence items must appear in their order. Thus, the sequences are transformed to unnamed classes, formed as the intersection of the cardinality restrictions of their items. Notice that the exact sequence cardinalities cannot be computed when a sequence item is contained in a sequence with unbounded maximum number of occurrences and the item has no maximum cardinality restriction. In addition, information regarding the sequence element ordering cannot be represented in OWL.

```
<xs:sequence minOccurs="2" maxOccurs="2">
 <xs:element name="e1" type="xs:string"/>
 <xs:element name="e2" type="xs:string" maxOccurs="3"/>
</xs:sequence>
```

Fig. 8. Sequence defined in the context of the Complex Type "c_type1"

```
<owl:Class>
 <owl:intersectionOf rdf:parseType="Collection">
  <owl:Restriction>
   <owl:onProperty rdf:resource="#e1__xs_string"/>
   <owl:cardinality rdf:datatype="&xsd;integer">2</owl:cardinality>
  </owl:Restriction>
  <owl:Restriction>
   <owl:onProperty rdf:resource="#e2__xs_string"/>
   <owl:minCardinality
rdf:datatype="&xsd;integer">2</owl:minCardinality>
  </owl:Restriction>
  <owl:Restriction>
   <owl:onProperty rdf:resource="#e2__xs_string"/>
   <owl:maxCardinality
rdf:datatype="&xsd;integer">6</owl:maxCardinality>
  </owl:Restriction>
 </owl:intersectionOf>
</owl:Class>
```

Fig. 9. OWL Representation of the sequence shown in Fig. 8

As an example, consider the sequence shown in Fig. 8, which is defined in the context of the complex type "c_t1". The sequence is represented, in the "c_t1" class definition, by the unnamed class shown in Fig. 9.

The choice items may appear at any order. Thus, the choices are transformed to unnamed classes, formed as the union of the allowed combinations of the cardinality restrictions of the choice elements. Notice that the exact choice cardinalities cannot be computed when a choice item is contained in a choice with unbounded maximum number of occurrences.

The unnamed classes that represent XML Schema sequences and choices are produced using the algorithms outlined above, that are available at [15]. It must be noted that, if the maximum number of occurrences of a sequence/choice has a large value (but is not unbounded), the manual generation of the restrictions is tedious and time-consuming and thus becomes error-prone and practically impossible.

References. XML Schema attributes, attribute groups, elements and model groups that are referenced in complex type definitions are transformed into OWL-DL datatype (if they are or contain attributes or simple type elements) or object (if they contain complex type elements) properties. Let *ref(ae)* be a reference, in a complex type *ct*, to the *ae* XML attribute or element. The reference is represented by the (datatype or object) property *rp(id, domain)*, where *id* is the rdf:ID of *rp* and has as value the value of the rdf:ID of the property that represents *ae*, and *domain* is the domain of *rp* and has the rdf:ID of the OWL class *c* that represents *ct* as value.

4 Mapping Ontologies

In section 0 we mentioned that some XML Schema semantics cannot be represented in OWL during the XML Schema to OWL transformation. These semantics do not affect the domain ontologies that may extend the main ontology and they are not used by the OWL reasoners; however, they are important when the individuals defined according to the main ontology have to be transformed back to valid XML descriptions compliant with the source XML Schema. In order to support this functionality, we have defined a model that allows transforming the OWL constructs back to XML Schema constructs. This model captures the XML Schema semantics that cannot be represented in OWL and is expressed as an OWL-DL ontology, the *OWL2XMLRules Ontology* (available at http://elikonas.ced.tuc.gr/ontologies/OWL2XMLRules/ OWL2XMLRules). For a particular XML Schema that is transformed to OWL-DL, XS2OWL generates a *Mapping Ontology* that extends the OWL2XMLRules ontology with individuals and represents the semantics of the schema that are lost during the transformation to OWL.

In the following paragraphs, we present the classes of the OWL2XMLRules ontology as well as the model for the generation of individuals of the classes of the OWL2XMLRules ontology during the transformation of specific XML Schemas.

DatatypePropertyInfoType Class. It captures information about the datatype properties lost during the XML Schema to OWL transformation. This information includes the names of the XML constructs (elements, attributes) transformed to the datatype properties, the default values and the origins of the datatype properties, since an OWL datatype property may be the result of the transformation of an attribute, an element or it may state that a complex type extends a simple type.

Let *ae(name, ae_id, c_type, default)* be an attribute or a simple type element, where *name* is the name of *ae*, *ae_id* is the identifier of *ae*, *c_type* is the complex type in which *ae* has been defined and *default* is the default value of *ae*. *ae* is transformed into the *DatatypePropertyInfoType* individual *dpi(id, did, xml_name, dpi_type, def_val)*, where: (a) *id* is the unique rdf:ID of *dpi* and has *concatenate(ct_name, '_', name, '__', type)* as value, where *ct_name* is the name of the class that represents *c_type* in the main ontology; (b) *did* is the rdf:ID of the *dp* datatype property that represents *ae* in the main ontology; (c) *xml_name* is the name of *ae* and has *name* as value; (d) *dpi_type* represents the construct which has been mapped to *dp* and has the value *'Attribute'* if *ae* is an attribute and the value and *'Element'* if *ae* is an element; and (e) *def_val* represents the default value of *ae* and has *default* as value.

If a datatype property *dp* states that a complex type extends a simple type, a *DatatypePropertyInfoType* individual *dpi(id, did, dpi_type)* is generated for *dp*, where *id* and *did* have the semantics defined above and *dpi_type* has the 'Extension' value.

ElementInfoType Class. It captures information about the XML Schema elements that is lost during the XML Schema to OWL transformation. This information includes the names of the elements and, if they are parts of sequences, their ordering.

Let *e(eid, name, c_type, default, min, max, pos)* be an element, where *name* is the name of *e*, *eid* is the identifier of *e*, *c_type* is the complex type in which *e* has been defined, *default* is the default value of *e*, *min* is the minimum number of occurrences of *e*, *max* is the maximum number of occurrences of *e* and *pos* is the position of *e* if *e* is a sequence element. *e* is represented in the mapping ontology by the *ElementInfoType* individual *ei(id, pid, xml_name, def_val, min_occ, max_occ, position)*, where: (a) *id* is the unique rdf:ID of *ei* and has *concatenate(ct_name, '_', name, '__', type)* as value, where *ct_name* is the name of the class that represents *c_type* in the main ontology; (b) *pid* is the rdf:ID of the *p* property that represents *e* in the main ontology; (c) *xml_name* is the name of *e* and has *name* as value; (d) *dpi_type* represents the construct which has been transformed to *p* and has the *'Element'* value; (e) *def_val* represents the default value of *e* and has *default* as value; (f) *min_occ* represents the minimum number of occurrences of *e* and has *min* as value; (g) *max_occ* represents the maximum number of occurrences of *e* and has *max* as value; and (h) *position* represents the position of *e* if *e* is a sequence element.

ComplexTypeInfoType Class. It captures information lost during the XML Schema to OWL transformation about a complex type that has *name* as name. This information includes information about the datatype properties associated with the corresponding OWL class in the main ontology and the cardinality and ordering of the elements contained in the complex type.

Let *ct(name, ct_id, att_list, seq_list, cho_list)* be a complex type, where *name* is the name of *ct*, *ct_id* is the identifier of *ct*, *att_list* is the list of the *ct* attributes, *seq_list* is the list of the *ct* sequences and *cho_list* is the list of the *ct* choices. *ct* is represented in the mapping ontology by the *ComplexTypeInfoType* individual *ct(id, type_id, dpi_list, container_list)*, where: (a) *id* is the unique rdf:ID of *ct* and has *name* as value; (b) *type_id* represents the identifier of the OWL class *c* that represents *ct* in the main ontology; (c) *dpi_list* is the list of the representations of the datatype properties of *c*; and (d) *container_list* is the list of the representations of the *sc* containers.

ChoiceType and SequenceType Classes. They capture, respectively, information about the exact cardinalities and the structure of XML Schema choices and sequences that is lost during the XML Schema to OWL transformation.

Let *sc(sc_id, c_type, min, max, elements)* be a sequence or choice, where *sc_id* is the identifier of *sc*, *c_type* is the complex type in which *sc* has been defined, *min* is the minimum number of occurrences of *sc*, *max* is the maximum number of occurrences of *sc* and *elements* is the list of the elements of *sc*. We represent *sc* in the mapping ontology by the (*SequenceType* if *sc* is a sequence, *ChoiceType* if *sc* is a choice) individual *st(id, min_occ, max_occ, e_rep)*, where: (a) *id* is the unique rdf:ID of *st* and has *concatenate(ct_name, '__', i)* as value, where *ct_name* is the name of the class that represents *c_type* in the main ontology and *i* is the index of *sc* in *c_type*; (b) *min_occ* represents the minimum number of occurrences of *sc* and has *min* as value; (c) *max_occ* represents the maximum number of occurrences of *sc* and has *max* as value; and (d) *e_rep* is the list of the representations of the *elements* of *sc*.

As an example, consider the complex type "ct1", shown in Fig. 1. *ct1* is represented in the mapping ontology as shown in Fig. 10.

```
<ox:XSDComplexTypeInfoType rdf:ID="ct1">
 <ox:typeID>ct1</ox:typeID>
 <ox:DatatypePropertyInfo>
  <ox:DatatypePropertyInfoType rdf:ID="ct1_a1__ct1_a1_UNType">
   <ox:datatypePropertyID>a1__ct1_a1_UNType</ox:datatypePropertyID>
   <ox:XMLConstructID>a1</ox:XMLConstructID>
   <ox:datatypePropertyType>Attribute</ox:datatypePropertyType>
  </ox:DatatypePropertyInfoType>
 </ox:DatatypePropertyInfo>
 <ox:DatatypePropertyInfoType rdf:ID="ct1_content__xs_integer">
  <ox:datatypePropertyID>content__xs_integer</ox:datatypePropertyID>
  <ox:datatypePropertyType>Extension</ox:datatypePropertyType>
 </ox:DatatypePropertyInfoType>
</ox:XSDComplexTypeInfoType>
```

Fig. 10. Representation of the complex type "ct" of Fig. 1 in the mapping ontology

5   Realization and Evaluation of the XS2OWL Model

We present in this section the design and implementation of the XS2OWL system, which transforms automatically XML Schemas into OWL-DL ontologies and generates their mapping ontologies. According to the XS2OWL model, an XML Schema is transformed into: (a) A *main* OWL-DL ontology that directly captures the XML Schema semantics using OWL-DL constructs; (b) A *mapping* OWL-DL ontology that systematically captures the semantics of the XML Schema constructs that cannot be captured in the main ontology; and (c) A *datatypes* XML Schema containing the simple XML Schema datatypes defined in the source XML Schema, which are imported in the main ontology.

The XS2OWL transformation model has been implemented as an XSLT stylesheet. The information flow during the transformation is shown in Fig. 11. As shown in Fig. 11, the source XML Schema and the XS2OWL stylesheet are given as input to an

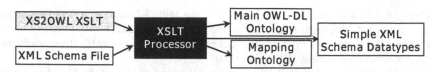

Fig. 11. The Information Flow in XS2OWL

XSLT processor, and the output comprises of the main ontology, the mapping ontology and the datatypes XML Schema.

In order to acquire extensive empirical evidence, we applied XS2OWL to several very large and well-accepted standards expressed in XML Schema: The MPEG-7 Multimedia Description Schemes (MDS) and the MPEG-21 Digital Item Adaptation (DIA) Architecture in the multimedia domain, the IEEE LOM and the SCORM in the e-learning domain and the METS standard for Digital Libraries. The XML Schema constructs of these standards have been automatically converted to OWL for each of those standards. We then produced individuals following the ontologies. Finally, we converted the individuals to XML syntax, valid with respect to the source XML Schemas. The transformations were successful for these standards and we found that in all cases the semantics of the standards were fully captured in the main and mapping ontologies generated by the XS2OWL system.

6 Conclusions

We have presented in this paper the XS2OWL formal model that allows to automatically transform XML Schemas into OWL-DL ontologies. This transformation allows domain ontologies in OWL to be integrated and logic-based reasoners to be used for various applications, as for example for knowledge extraction from multimedia data. XS2OWL allows the conversion of the generated OWL information back to XML. We have presented also the XS2OWL system that implements the XS2OWL model. We have used the implemented system to validate our approach with a number of well-accepted and extensive standards expressed in XML Schema. The automatically created ontologies have been found to accurately capture the semantics of the source XML Schemas.

Acknowledgments. The work presented here was partially funded in the scope of the DELOS II Network of Excellence in Digital Libraries (IST – Project Record #26059).

References

1. ADL Technical Team: Sharable Content Object Reference Model (SCORM) (2004)
2. Bray, T., Paoli, J., Sperberg-McQueen, C.M., Maler, E., Yergeau, F., Cowan, J(ed.): Extensible Markup Language (XML) 1.1. W3C Recommendation (2006),
   http://www.w3.org/TR/xml11/
3. Brickley, D., Guha, R.V(ed.): RDF Vocabulary Description Language 1.0: RDF Schema. W3C Recommendation (2004), http://www.w3.org/TR/rdf-schema

4. Chang, S.F., Sikora, T., Puri, A.: Overview of the MPEG-7 standard. IEEE Transactions on Circuits and Systems for Video Technology 11, 688–695 (2001)
5. Fallside, D., Walmsley, P(ed.): XML Schema Part 0: Primer. W3C Recommendation (2001), http://www.w3.org/TR/xmlschema-0/
6. García, R., Celma, O.: Semantic Integration and Retrieval of Multimedia Metadata. In: The proceedings of the Semannot 2005 Workshop (2005)
7. Kay, M, (ed.): XSL Transformations (XSLT) Version 2.0. W3C Recommendation (2007), http://www.w3.org/TR/xslt20/
8. Manola, F., Milles, E(ed.): RDF Primer. W3C Recommendation (2004), http://www.w3.org/TR/rdf-primer
9. METS: Metadata Encoding and Transmission Standard (METS) Official Website, http://www.loc.gov/standards/mets/
10. IEEE LTSC 2002: IEEE 1484.12.1-2002 – Learning Object Metadata Standard, http://ltsc.ieee.org/wg12/
11. ISO/IEC: 21000-7:2004 – Information Technology – Multimedia Framework (MPEG-21) – Part 7: Digital Item Adaptation (2004)
12. ISO/IEC: 15938-5:2003 – Information Technology –Multimedia content description interface – Part 5: Multimedia description schemes. First Edition, ISO/MPEG N5845 (2003)
13. McGuinness, D.L., van Harmelen, F(ed.): OWL Web Ontology Language: Overview. W3C Recommendation (2004), http://www.w3.org/TR/owl-features
14. Pereira, F.: The MPEG-21 standard: Why an open multimedia framework? In: Shepherd, D., Finney, J., Mathy, L., Race, N.J.P. (eds.) IDMS 2001. LNCS, vol. 2158, pp. 219–220. Springer, Heidelberg (2001)
15. Tsinaraki, C., Christodoulakis, S.: XS2OWL: A Formal Model and a System for enabling XML Schema Applications to interoperate with OWL-DL Domain Knowledge and Semantic Web Tools. Technical Report (2007), http://www.music.tuc.gr/XS2OWL.pdf
16. Tsinaraki, C., Polydoros, P., Christodoulakis, S.: Interoperability support for Ontology-based Video Retrieval Applications. In: Enser, P.G.B., Kompatsiaris, Y., O'Connor, N.E., Smeaton, A.F., Smeulders, A.W.M. (eds.) CIVR 2004. LNCS, vol. 3115, pp. 582–591. Springer, Heidelberg (2004)
17. Tsinaraki, C., Polydoros, P., Christodoulakis, S.: Integration of OWL ontologies in MPEG-7 and TVAnytime compliant Semantic Indexing. In: Persson, A., Stirna, J. (eds.) CAiSE 2004. LNCS, vol. 3084, pp. 398–413. Springer, Heidelberg (2004)
18. Tsinaraki, C., Polydoros, P., Kazasis, F., Christodoulakis, S.: Ontology-based Semantic Indexing for MPEG-7 and TV-Anytime Audiovisual Content. Multimedia Tools and Application Journal (MTAP) 26, 299–325 (2005)

A Framework and an Architecture for Supporting Interoperability Between Digital Libraries and eLearning Applications

Polyxeni Arapi, Nektarios Moumoutzis, Manolis Mylonakis,
and Stavros Christodoulakis

Laboratory of Distributed Multimedia Information Systems and Applications, Technical
University of Crete (TUC/MUSIC), 73100 Chania, Greece
{xenia,nektar,manolis,stavros}@ced.tuc.gr

Abstract. One of the most important applications of Digital Libraries (DL) is
learning. In order to enable the development of eLearning applications that
easily exploit DL contents it is crucial to bridge the interoperability gap
between DL and eLearning applications. For this purpose, a generic
interoperability framework has been developed that could also be applied to
other types of applications which are built on top of DL, although this paper
focuses on eLearning applications. In this context, a framework for supporting
pedagogy-driven personalization in eLearning applications has been developed
that performs automatic creation of personalized learning experiences using
reusable (audiovisual) learning objects, taking into account the learner profiles
and a set of abstract training scenarios (pedagogical templates). From a
technical point of view, all the framework components have been organized
into a service-oriented Architecture that Supports Interoperability between
Digital Libraries and ELearning Applications (ASIDE). A prototype of the
ASIDE Framework has been implemented.

Keywords: Digital Libraries, eLearning, Interoperability, Personalization.

1 Introduction

Digital Libraries (DL) are an important source for the provision of eLearning
resources [9]. However, digital library metadata standards and eLearning metadata
standards have been developing independently, which has as result the existence of
interoperability problems between digital libraries and eLearning applications. This is
a complex and multi-level problem which is often encountered between digital
libraries and several types of applications that run on top of digital libraries. It can be
seen as coming from the existence of a stack of conceptual layers where each one is
built on top of the previous one (left part of Fig. 1): There are different data
representations, objects, concepts, domains, contexts and metacontexts in the layer
stack that should be efficiently managed in a standardized way. Metadata models are
languages that are used to represent the knowledge in a particular application area.
Each metadata model is shown as a vertical bar on this stack to cover a specific region

C. Thanos, F. Borri, and L. Candela (Eds.): Digital Libraries: R&D, LNCS 4877, pp. 137–146, 2007.

that represents the parts that the model tries to capture and describe in a standard way. If we place different metadata models besides this stack, we may identify gaps and intersection regions so that it becomes apparent where the interoperability problems among these models occur. Interoperability problems exist also in the overlapping areas, but there the problem of interoperability can be easier solved with standard methods (e.g. by means of mappings). The major problems arise in the areas with no overlaps between the two metadata standards. The right part of Fig. 1 shows such a picture in the case of MPEG7 and SCORM, the major metadata standards in the audiovisual and eLearning domains respectively. It is apparent from this graphical presentation that MPEG7 and SCORM are not completely overlapping meaning that we need additional models to provide interoperability mechanisms between them.

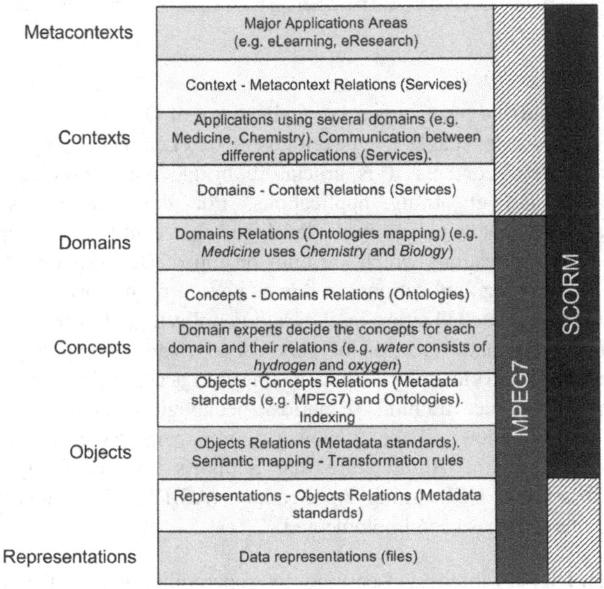

Fig. 1. The multilevel problem of interoperability

For example, SCORM contains an educational part that cannot be mapped, directly or indirectly, completely or partially, to MPEG7 elements. That is because MPEG7 does not include information about possible educational use of audiovisual (A/V) objects because it is not an application-specific context metadata standard. However, educational information is very important in the case that MPEG7 (and generally an A/V digital library) is used for educational purposes. On the other hand, MPEG7 offers a comprehensive set of audiovisual Description Tools to guide the creation of audiovisual content descriptions, which will form the basis for applications that provide the needed effective and efficient access to audiovisual content, which can not be represented in SCORM. Modifying the above standards (e.g. mixing parts of them) is not acceptable, since they have been developed to satisfy the needs of different communities. To overcome them and fill in the gaps between SCORM and MPEG7 we have to use a higher level metadata model that is able to encapsulate both SCORM and MPEG7 in the context of a digital library.

The above considerations lead to a concrete framework and architecture that address the identified interoperability problems and offer a generic framework for the automatic creation of personalized learning experiences using reusable audiovisual learning objects. In the next sections we will firstly propose a methodology for supporting multiple-contexts views of digital objects and its application in the case of A/V learning objects, without loss of important information (educational or A/V) (Section 2), and thereafter a generic architecture that supports interoperability problem between eLearning applications and digital libraries will be presented (Section 3). The implementation of this architecture also offers a generic framework for the automatic creation of personalized learning experiences using reusable A/V learning objects which is also presented. A review of the related literature is presented afterwards (Section 4) and the paper ends with some concluding remarks.

2 Supporting Multiple-Contexts Views of Digital Objects

In general, a digital object can be described in many ways and delivered to many applications (upper part of Fig. 2). Usually, digital objects have a source metadata description that is appropriately transformed to a target metadata description when this object should be delivered to an application. However, performing just a transformation between the source metadata scheme and the target metadata scheme is not always applicable as standards do not always completely overlap.

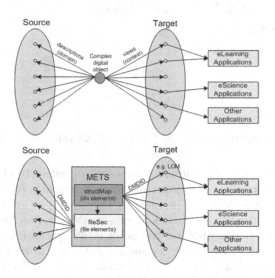

Fig. 2. Supporting multiple-contexts views of a digital object using METS

For example, an audiovisual digital object that resides in a digital library and is described with MPEG7 can be used in eLearning or eScience applications. However, the pure MPEG7 description does not say anything about the educational use (e.g. learning objectives) of the digital object nor contains any information useful for eScience applications. Performing just a transformation between the source metadata scheme and the target metadata scheme does not solve the problem. So, we need a way to incorporate in a digital object description both source metadata (domain) and target metadata (context). We should have multiple descriptions (source metadata (domain), target metadata (context) - pairs) for a digital object showing possible views of the object. Context and domain information should reside in different levels, where context information is above domain information.

A flexible model that satisfies the above needs is the Metadata Encoding and Transmission Standard (METS). METS is a widely-accepted digital library standard that is intended primarily as a flexible, but tightly structured, container for all metadata necessary to describe, navigate and maintain a digital object: descriptive, administrative and structural metadata. Each type of metadata is described in a separate section, which is linked to its counterparts by a comprehensive system of internal identifiers. The metadata (any preferred scheme) itself may be held inline in the METS file or in external files and referenced from within the METS document.

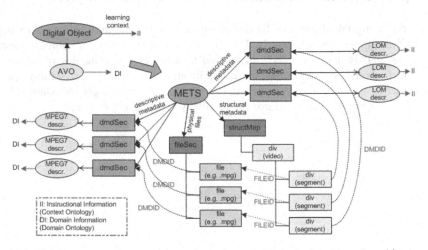

Fig. 3. Combining METS, LOM and MPEG7 to build audiovisual learning objects

Using METS we can create different views of a digital object pointing to both source metadata description and target metadata description (context) in different levels [2]. The methodology is illustrated in the lower part of Fig. 2. Using the DMDID attribute of the <div> elements of the structMap section where the structure of the digital object is described we can point to an appropriate metadata scheme creating a context (view) of this object and its parts (e.g. using LOM). In parallel, using the DMDID attribute of the <file> elements of the fileSec section, where all files comprising this digital object are listed, we can point to a source metadata scheme that describes the lower level features or the semantics of this object (e.g. using MPEG7). This is useful when applications want to further filter the resulted objects according to their multimedia characteristics. Here, we combine METS, MPEG7 and LOM to give to the audiovisual objects and their parts educational characteristics constructing this way audiovisual learning objects (Fig. 3). The DMDID attribute of the <file> element is used to reference the MPEG7 metadata (domain metadata) describing the audiovisual object referenced by FLocat element. In an upper level we put the Context Metadata (in our case educational metadata) using the DMDID attribute of the div element to reference LOM metadata. The video decomposition to segments is described through the METS document (as a complex object) and there is no need to be described in a MPEG7 document using for example the TemporalDecomposition element.

3 The ASIDE Architecture

The previous section presented a framework for the representation and description of digital objects that reside in a digital library in order to support multiple-context views so that these objects can be retrieved from different applications (in this case eLearning applications). This section presents an Architecture for Supporting Interoperability between Digital Libraries and ELearning Applications (ASIDE).

The architecture addresses the identified interoperability problems in a layered manner where eLearning (and other) applications are built on top of digital libraries and utilize their content. ASIDE [2] also offers a generic framework for the automatic creation of pedagogy-driven personalized learning experiences using reusable A/V learning objects. It is service-oriented and conforms to the IMS Digital Repositories Interoperability (IMS DRI) Specification, which provides recommendations for the interoperation of the most common repository functions: search/expose, submit/store, gather/expose and request/deliver.

Fig. 4 illustrates the architecture components, which are the following:

- The *Digital Library*, where digital objects are described using METS integrating LOM (eLearning context), and MPEG7 (A/V descriptions) thus building interoperable A/V learning objects, which can be transformed to SCORM and exploited by eLearning applications. Regarding the MPEG7 descriptions, the methodology described in [11] is used for extending MPEG7 with domain-specific knowledge descriptions expressed in OWL (*domain ontologies*).
- *Learning Designs* are abstract training scenarios (pedagogical templates) in a certain instructional domain built according to an *instructional ontology*, which can be applied to the construction of learning experiences.
- The *Middleware* consists of the following parts:
  - The *METS/SCORM transformation component*, which is responsible for the transformation of the METS integrated descriptions to SCORM Packages [6]. The type of the files is taken into account and, if needed, intermediate html pages are constructed with links to these files (e.g. in case of video files).
  - The *Personalized Learning Experiences Assembler (PALEA)*, which, taking into account the knowledge provided by the Learning Designs (abstract training scenarios) and the Learner Profiles, constructs personalized learning experiences and delivers them in the form of SCORM Packages. The dashed arrow in the left side of PALEA indicates that using this component is optional and that digital library services can be directly accessed (e.g. a teacher wants to find appropriate learning objects to construct manually a learning experience).

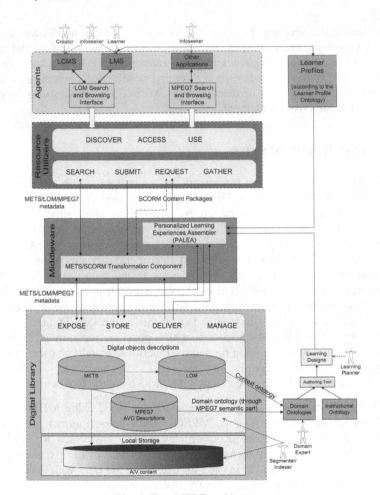

Fig. 4. The ASIDE architecture

- *Applications* (Agents in terms of IMS DRI, like Learning Content Management Systems, Learning Management Systems) that discover, access and use the A/V content of the digital library through appropriate services (resource utilizers).
- The *Learner Profiles* constructed using the vocabulary given in a Learner Profile Ontology.

3.1 Learning Designs and the Instructional Ontology

Learning Designs are abstract training scenarios that are constructed according to an instructional ontology coded in OWL (Fig. 5). This ontology has the important characteristic that learning objects are not bound to the training scenarios at design time, as in current eLearning standards and specifications (e.g. IMS Learning Design and SCORM). Whereas, pedagogy is separated and independent from content achieving this way reusability of Learning Designs or parts of them that can be used

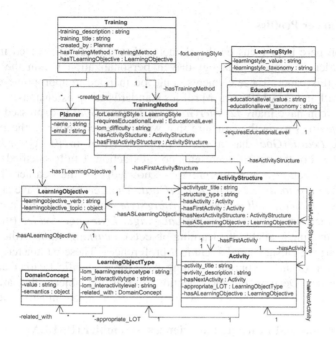

Fig. 5. The instructional ontology

from the systems for the construction of "real" personalized learning experiences, where appropriate learning objects according to the Learner Profile are bound to the learning experience at run-time taking into account several parameters of the Learner Profile. This is possible, since the model makes possible to specify in each Activity the learning objects' requirements, instead of binding the learning objects themselves.

A *Training* is a collection of *TrainingMethods* that refer to the different ways the same subject can be taught depending on the *LearningStyle*, the *EducationalLevel* of the Learner and the preferred *difficulty*. There are several categorizations of Learning Styles and Educational Levels, thus these elements are flexible so that being able to point to values of different taxonomies. A *TrainingMethod* consists of a hierarchy of reusable *ActivityStructures* built from reusable *Activities*. Each *Training*, *ActivityStructure* and *Activity* has a *LearningObjective*. Each *LearningObjective* is defined in a formal way[1] composed of: a) a *learningobjective_verb*, taken from Bloom's Taxonomy [3]) and b) a *learningobjective_topic* that indicates the topic that the Learning Objective is about, referencing a concept or individual of a domain ontology. The *LearningObjectType* is used to describe the desired learning object characteristics without binding specific objects with Activities at design time. Via the *related_with* property we can further restrict the preferred learning objects according to their constituent parts (if they are semantically annotated) connecting them with *DomainConcepts* which refer to concepts or individuals from a domain ontology.

---

[1] In learning objects descriptions expressed in LOM we also incorporate Learning Objectives info this way exploiting its classification element.

3.2 The Learner Profiles

Our intention here is to focus on the elements that should be included in a Learner Model in order to support pedagogy-driven personalization within the framework presented in this paper. These elements could be mapped in appropriate elements of the IEEE PAPI and IMS LIP learner profiles standards using extensions.

A Learner can have many *LearnerGoals*. A *LearnerGoal* is expressed in terms of *LearningObjectives* using the structure that was presented above in the instructional ontology. A *LearnerGoal* has a *status* property (float in [0, 1]) indicating the satisfaction level of the goal (0 represents no satisfaction, 1 fully satisfied). Using this information one can also infer the previous knowledge of the Learner. The Learner can also define a *priority* for each *LearnerGoal*. The Learner can have several types of Preferences: *EducationalLevel* and *LearningStyle* matching with the corresponding elements of the instructional ontology, *Language*, *LearningProvider* (the author or organization making available the learning objects), *LearningPlanner* (the person that develops Learning Designs) and *Technical* preferences. These parameters affect both the construction of an appropriate learning path for a specific Learner according to existing Learning Designs and the selection of learning objects that are thereafter bound at run-time to the learning path to form the resulting learning experience.

3.3 The Personalized Learning Experiences Assembler (PALEA)

The Personalized Learning Experiences Assembler (PALEA) takes into account the knowledge provided by the Learning Designs and the Learner Profiles and constructs personalized learning experiences that are delivered next to eLearning applications in the form of SCORM packages. The goal is to find an appropriate Learning Design that will be used thereafter to construct a learning experience adapted to the Learner's needs. Learning objects are bound to the learning scenario at run-time.

The procedure of constructing an adaptive learning experience is the following:

1. At the beginning, the component tries to find an appropriate Learning Design (Training in terms of the instructional ontology presented) taking into account the Learner's Learning Objectives, Learning Style, Educational Level, preferred Difficulty, and preferred Planner (optional).
2. When an appropriate Learning Design is found its structure is retrieved (Training(T), Activity Structures (AS), Activities(A)) and an appropriate Training Method of this Learning Design is selected, according to the Learner's Learning Style, Educational Level and preferred Difficulty.
3. The structure of this Training Method is further refined, by removing from it Activity Structures and Activities with Learning Objectives that have been satisfied by the Learner (the Learner can define a threshold value t, so that Learning Objectives with satisfaction value>t are considered as satisfied).
4. Finally, appropriate learning objects are retrieved and bound to each node (Activity) of this structure constructing the learning experience. Here, the Learning Object Type describing the characteristics of appropriate learning objects for each Activity is taken into account along with other learner's preferences (e.g. content provider, technical preferences). The resulted learning experience is transformed to SCORM (Transformation Component) and delivered to the Learner.

4 Related Work

Efforts trying to integrate or use in cooperation eLearning standards and A/V standards include the Video Asset Description (VAD) Project [4] the MultImedia Learning Object Server [1] and the Virtual Entrepreneurship Lab (VEL) [8]. Most of these approaches [1, 8] use mappings between standards (e.g. MPEG7 and LOM) or propose adding MPEG7 elements to SCORM elements [4]. As already discussed, using mappings is not enough to solve the interoperability problem between DL and eLearning applications. Extending SCORM is again not acceptable as a general interoperability solution. It results in a model that is not standard and cannot be interoperable with standard SCORM compliant applications and systems. The approach proposed here is more general and provides and interoperable framework of educational and application specific metadata so that eLearning applications can easily use and reuse DL objects in multiple contexts.

Automatic construction of personalized learning experiences is also supported, using and reusing learning designs and learning resources. In [5] a similar approach is followed to represent pedagogy in order to support run-time resource binding. Our approach differs in that it takes into account the learning style, the educational level and learning goals of the learners, supporting the representation of different learning paths (Training Methods) for training in a specific subject. In [10], although the need for supporting different training methods for the same subject is recognized, these methods are not connected as in our approach with the learning styles and educational levels of the learners. Moreover, description of appropriate learning objects characteristics beyond semantics is not supported. An alternative approach is presented in [7] regarding automatic course sequencing, where learning paths are not constructed based on pedagogical models, but are extracted from a directed acyclic graph that is the result of merging the knowledge space (domain model) and the media space (learning objects and their relation) using minimum learning time as an optimization criteria. However, since this approach is highly based on the domain model that does not necessarily imply an instructional model and on the relations of learning objects and their aggregation level, the result of the sequencing process may be not always "pedagogically-right" adapted to the learners' needs.

5 Conclusions

We have presented a framework for the representation and description of digital objects that reside in a DL in order to support multiple-context views so that these objects can be retrieved from different applications (in this case eLearning applications). We have also presented ASIDE, an architecture that supports interoperability between DL and eLearning applications so that eLearning applications can easily use and reuse DL objects in multiple contexts and outlined the various aspects of its implementation. Special emphasis has been placed in the definition and implementation of a software engineering framework for supporting personalization in the ASIDE architecture that performs automatic creation of personalized learning experiences using reusable (audiovisual) learning objects, taking into account the learner profiles and a set of learning designs. This work provides the basis of a generic architectural framework for integrating diverse application classes on top of DL so that DL objects are also reused across application classes that have been built on top of digital libraries.

Acknowledgments. The work presented in this paper is partially funded in the scope of the DELOS II Network of Excellence in Digital Libraries (IST – Project Record Number 507618) JPA2 subproject, named "Interoperability of eLearning applications with digital libraries".

References

1. Amato, G., Gennaro, C., Savino, P., Rabitti, F.: Milos: a Multimedia Content Management System for Digital Library Applications. In: Heery, R., Lyon, L. (eds.) ECDL 2004. LNCS, vol. 3232, pp. 14–25. Springer, Heidelberg (2004)
2. Arapi, P., Moumoutzis, N., Christodoulakis, S.: ASIDE: An Architecture for Supporting Interoperability between Digital Libraries and ELearning Applications. In: ICALT2006. 6th IEEE International Conference on Advanced Learning Technologies, pp. 257–261. IEEE Computer Society Press, Kerkrade, The Netherlands (2006)
3. Bloom, B., Krathwohl, S.: Taxonomy of Educational Objectives: The Classification of Educational Goals. In: Handbook, I. (ed.) Cognitive Domain, Longman, New York (1965)
4. Bush, M., Melby, A., Anderson, T., Browne, J., Hansen, M.: Customized Video Playback: Standards for Content Modeling and Personalization. Educational Technology 44, 5–13 (2004)
5. Capuano, N., Gaeta, M., Lannone, R., Orciuoli, F.: Learning Design and Run-Time Resource Binding in a Distributed E-learning Environment. In: 1st International Kaleidoscope Learning Grid SIG Workshop on Distributed e-Learning Environments, British Computer Society, eWic, Naples, Italy (2005)
6. Christodoulakis, S., Arapi, P., Mylonakis, M., Moumoutzis, N., Patel, M., Kapidakis, S., Vagiati, V., Konsolaki, H.: In: Demonstrator of mapping between the eLearning and AV content description standards, DELOS Deliverable 5.4.2, July 25, 2006 (2006)
7. Karampiperis, P., Sampson, D.: Adaptive Instructional Planning Using Ontologies. In: ICALT2004. 4th IEEE International Conference on Advanced Learning Technologies, pp. 126–130. IEEE Computer Society Press, Joensuu, Finland (2004)
8. Klamma, R., Jarke, M., Wulf, V.: Das Virtual Entrepreneurship Lab (VEL): Eine MPEG7 basierte E-Learning Plattform für potentielle Gründer. In: Informatik 2002, Dortmund, Germany, pp. 359–363 (2002)
9. McLean, N.: The Ecology of Repository Services: A Cosmic View. Keynote Address. In: Heery, R., Lyon, L. (eds.) ECDL 2004. LNCS, vol. 3232, Springer, Heidelberg (2004)
10. Meisel, H., Compatangelo, E., Hörfurter, A.: An ontology-based approach to intelligent Instructional Design support. In: Palade, V., Howlett, R.J., Jain, L. (eds.) KES 2003. LNCS, vol. 2773, pp. 898–905. Springer, Heidelberg (2003)
11. Tsinaraki, C., Polydoros, P., Christodoulakis, S.: Integration of OWL ontologies in MPEG7 and TVAnytime compliant Semantic Indexing. In: Persson, A., Stirna, J. (eds.) CAiSE 2004. LNCS, vol. 3084, pp. 398–413. Springer, Heidelberg (2004)

An Experimental Framework for Interactive Information Retrieval and Digital Libraries Evaluation

Claus-Peter Klas, Sascha Kriewel, and Norbert Fuhr

University of Duisburg-Essen
{klas,kriewel,fuhr}@is.inf.uni-due.de

Abstract. Evaluation of digital libraries assesses their effectiveness, quality and overall impact. In this paper we propose to use the Daffodil system as an experimental framework for the evaluation and research of interactive IR and digital libraries. The system already provides a rich set of working services and available information sources. These services and sources can be used as a foundation for further research going beyond basic functionalities. Besides the services and sources, the system supports a logging scheme for comparison of user behavior. In addition, the system can easily be extended regarding both services and sources. Daffodil's highly flexible and extensible agent-based architecture allows for easy integration of additional components, and access to all existing services. Finally, the system provides a user-friendly graphical interface and facilitating services for log generation and analysis. The experimental framework can serve as a joint theoretical and practical platform for the evaluation of DLs, with the long-term goal of creating a community centered on interactive IR and DL evaluation.

1   Introduction

Evaluation of digital libraries assesses their effectiveness, quality and overall impact. In order to push evaluation and research on evaluation of digital libraries along, community agreements need to be reached. Within the DELOS Network of Excellence we currently work on setting up a complete evaluation framework. It is our goal to provide guidelines, instruments and help for all stakeholders of digital libraries, like content providers, librarians, developers, researcher or end-users.

Such guidelines will be based on current evaluation models, like [10]. For structuring evaluation activities, the use of the Evaluation Computer[1] is recommended. All evaluation data, questionnaires, videos and transaction logs will be shared within the community in an anonymized format for comparison and meta evaluation. As an instrument for implementing and executing these evaluation, we propose the existing Daffodil system as an experimental framework for the evaluation and research of interactive IR and digital libraries. In the following

---

[1] http://www.delos.info/eventlist/wp7_ws_2004/Micsik.pdf

C. Thanos, F. Borri, and L. Candela (Eds.): Digital Libraries: R&D, LNCS 4877, pp. 147–156, 2007.
© Springer-Verlag Berlin Heidelberg 2007

sections we propose Daffodil as a well-suited instrument for evaluation of digital libraries, and give a short overview of current and future evaluation activities using Daffodil. The summary closes this paper.

2   Using Daffodil as an Instrument for Evaluation

2.1   The Graphical User Interface and Existing Services

Daffodil (see [11], [8] and [1]) is a virtual DL targeted at strategic support of users during the information search process. For searching, exploring, and managing DL objects, Daffodil provides information seeking patterns that can be customised by the user for searching over a federation of heterogeneous digital libraries. Searching with Daffodil makes a broad range of information sources easily accessible and enables quick access to a rich information space.

The Daffodil framework consists of two major parts: the graphical user client, depicted in Figure 1, and a set of agent-based services in the back-end.

Graphical user client. The graphical client combines a set of high-level search activities as integrated tools according to the WOB model for user interface design (see [7]). The current Daffodil system for the domain of computer science provides a variaty of tools and functions such as:

- A search tool that allows the user to specify the search domain, set filters and compose queries. The queries are broadcasted to a set of distributed

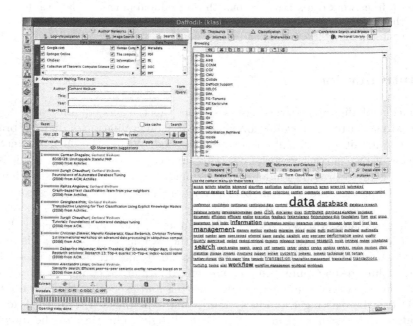

Fig. 1. The Daffodil Desktop

information services via agents and wrappers. Integrated result lists are displayed for navigation and detail inspection by the user.

- A collaborative personal library that stores DL objects in personal or group folders and supports sharing and annotation of stored objects.
- A classification browser that provides hierarchical, topic-driven access to the information space and enables browsing of classification schemes such as the ACM Computing Classification System.
- A thesaurus browser helps in finding broader, narrower or related terms. In addition, subject-specific or web-based thesauri such as WordNet are provided for identifiying related terms.
- A author network browser that supports browsing of social networks based on the co-author relation.
- A journal and conference browser that searches for a journal or conference title by browsing many directories, often with direct access either to the metadata or the full-text of articles.

More functionalities and tools exist or are currently under development, among them tools for inter-user communication, collaboration, pro-active help, or recommendation.

The front-end client is deployed to the user via Java Webstart technology. New tools can be easily integrated into the desktop, as long as they are written or wrapped in the Java programming language.

The back-end services. On the back-end side, each front-end tool is represented by one or more agent-based services, also written in the Java programming language, that provide the actual functionality. Currently, more than 30 services and 15 wrapper agents are used by the Daffodil system. The agent framework itself is modelled very simplistically for high performance and provides parallel threads for each user.

2.2   Logging Facility and Logging Schema

In any actual evaluation the collection of sometimes massive amounts of usage and user data is necessary to validate or invalidate the research hypothesis. This data consists usually of observations, questionnaires and transaction logs. Within Daffodil we provide an integrated questionnaire tool as well as extensive logging facilities to help gathering this data.

The questionnaire is part of the user desktop and can be used by researchers to ask standard questions, allowing for simple yes/no answers, selecting from different options, answers on a Likert scale, or free-form answers. The questions can also be made conditional, depending on previous answers, thus allowing for most of the freedom of paper-based questionnaires. In addition, the questionnaire tool can be used to select appropriate questions dynamically, fitting to the current context of the user or the state of her search. Questions and answers are stored in a database.

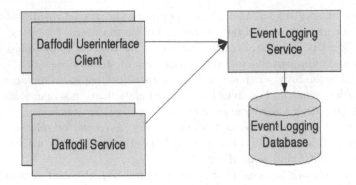

Fig. 2. Logging Service Model

Since Daffodil is a Java application, the framework allows for full access of all input and interaction events by the user, as well as access to system triggered events, thus avoiding the problems often encountered when trying to generate complete transaction logs for web-based DL systems. The logging facility, depicted in Figure 2, is simplistic: the Daffodil user interface client and each Daffodil back-end service can send an event to the event logging service, which handles and stores the event.

Currently, Daffodil handles over 40 different events. The main groups of events are search, navigate and browse events which are generated by users working with the tools provided. Result events are generated by each of the system services (e.g., the thesaurus, the journal and conference browser, or the metadata search tool). The personal library supports events for storing or manipulating data within the folder hierarchy, as well as events involving annotation or authoring of an object.

To facilitate the comparison of different evaluations, to allow the re-use of evaluation data and to support evaluations in general a common logging schema was proposed in [5] and [4] and implemented within Daffodil. When using transaction logs for evaluation, the main participants under survey are the user and the system, as well as the content that is being searched, read, manipulated, or created. The interaction between the system and the user can be examined and captured at various levels of abstraction:

- System parameters
- User-system interaction
  - UI events (keystrokes, mouse movement, etc.)
  - Interface action events (data entry, menu selections, etc.)
  - Service events (use of specific DL services)
  - Conceptual events (generic actions)
- User behaviour

On a very low level, researchers or developers might be interested in getting information about key presses, mouse clicks and movements, and similar concrete interactive events. These can be grouped together into more meaningful interactive events with specific graphical tools or interface elements, several of which in turn might comprise an interaction with a digital library service like a citation search service. For all three of these levels of abstractions a common logging schema will help in comparison, e.g. of the usability of specific interfaces or services between different digital libraries.

An additional level of abstraction, that will be called the conceptual level, can be seen as an abstraction away from the concrete services of specific digital library systems towards generalised actions that users can take in using a DL system. Several generic services that could be captured at this level have been proposed in [3] and [2]. In [5] we suggest a modified and expanded version of this selection.

By separating the log data into user data, system data and different abstraction levels of interaction – all connected by timestamps and identifiers linking a specific user with each event – the transaction logs can be used for following a users actions chronologically along a specific tier of the model. On the other hand, a comprehensive analysis of what exactly happens during a search action of the user across the various tiers is also possible. Of course a digital library system might only capture data on a low level of abstraction to minimise the overhead incured by the logging, and use a mapping of UI events to more abstract events for later analysis.

In order to analyze logged events, we have assumed that different stakeholders need different views of the logging data, requiring a variety of tools for analysis. System owners, content providers, system administration, librarians, developers, scientific researchers, and end-users were identified as stakeholders of a DL. For each of these stakeholders, different questions should be answered by the analytical tool set. A number of tools for facilitating analysis on log data in the new scheme have already been implemented. The example statistics shown in Figures 3a and 3b were produced with the help of these tools.

For visual inspection of individual log sessions, a special log viewer for search histories using the common log schema has been integrated into the Daffodil desktop. It provides visualisations of a single search session, allowing researchers to analyse user behaviour, but also providing end-users with a view of their own search history (see Figures 4 and 5). The tool can be used to retrace the steps of a search, re-issue or store specific queries, or highlight interesting parts of a search, and is to be extended with other functionalities aiding researchers

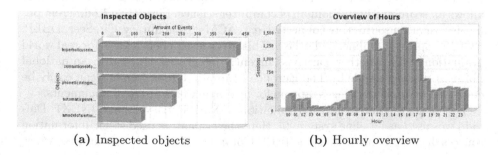

(a) Inspected objects   (b) Hourly overview

Fig. 3. Evaluation graphs

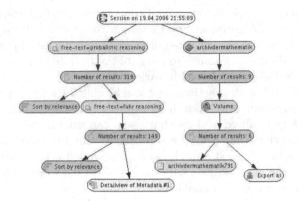

Fig. 4. Graph View

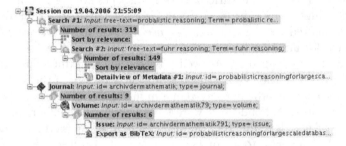

Fig. 5. Tree View

and end-users alike. In case of already existing logs of other DLs help for the conversion of these logs to this logging schema can be provided in order to use these tools.

2.3   Test Collections

Many evaluations suffer from lack of available test collections. Daffodil currently allows for searching in the domain of computer science. More than 12 different online information sources are connected, e.g. ACM digital library, CiteSeer, DBLP, HCIBib, Springer Online, and others. This gives researchers a basis for real world evaluation tasks. Another source is currently integrated, the European national libraries, also accessible by The European Library. Other domains can easily be employed by implementing wrappers for available web sources of documents.

Within the INitiative for the Evaluation of XML Retrieval 2005 (INEX)[2] Daffodil was used as baseline system [9]. Here the evaluators used static information sources drawing on articles of the IEEE Computer Society's publications. A new

---

[2] http://inex.is.informatik.uni-duisburg.de

wrapper was developed and optimized for this corpus. In addition in INEX 2006 the complete XML Wikipedia is added as test collection for searching and evaluating access to Digital Libraries.

2.4 Flexible and Extensible Architecture

By using an agent-based architecture, Daffodil becomes very flexible and easily extensible. In Figure 6 the Daffodil architecture is depicted. The blue frame corresponds with the back-end services. The red frame shows the graphical user client serving as Daffodil's front-end. In the middle (green frame) the connection between internal and external agents is shown; the user clients are one example of external agents. In this middle layer resides the message transfer agent (MTA), which handles communication between the outside (using HTTP messages) and the Daffodil back-end (using CORBA messages).

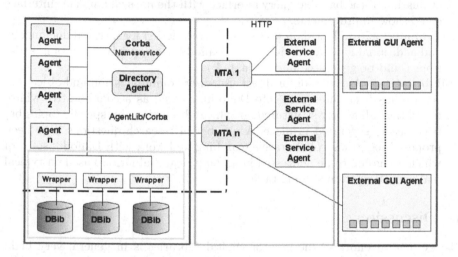

Fig. 6. Daffodil Communictation Architecture

Based on this architecture researchers and evaluators can integrate

- a new service using an agent within the Daffodil back-end, and providing a new tool as part of the GUI; this service can be made stand-alone and will not be reliant on any other Daffodil service;
- an enhanced service, adding value to or replacing an existing service;
- a client service, manipulating data on the client side and presenting it with the help of a new or an existing tool of the Daffodil desktop, providing added value to search results;
- a new analytical tool, using the extensive transaction and interaction log data collected by Daffodil.

3 Possibilities for Evaluations

Currently a number of evaluations using Daffodil are being prepared or under discussion.

The European Library. Currently, wrappers for the European national DL are being developed and integrated into Daffodil in preparation of a comparative evaluation between the TEL1 and the Daffodil user interface. The goal of the analytical evaluation is to assess the functional similarities and differences between the existing TEL search tool and the Daffodil-based search interface. The goal of the empirical evaluation is to evaluate how well each tool supports the users needs.

Natural Language Interface. In the process of research on natural language query interfaces, the intergration of a new tool for the graphical client is being discussed, that would allow entering natural language queries. Those will then transformed into Daffodil queries and processed. A comparative evaluation of the baseline query interface with the natural language interface could show improvements.

Recommendation. Based on user specific transaction logs, stored documents, and additional log information about Daffodil users, profound recommendations could be generated and evaluated.

Collaboration. A chat tool for direct user-user communication and object exchange has been integrated into Daffodil, as well as a collaborative whiteboard that allows for structured, graphical discussions on specific topics between users seperated in place. A number of research questions have been proposed regarding collaborative searching and work with Daffodil, some of which are going to be addressed in an empirical evaluation based on typical real-life information seeking tasks.

4 Discussion

The evaluation effort in the area of Digital Libraries is in general very high, complex and costly. The reasons for this is the need of participants or users who perform the evaluation, a system with the functionality under evaluation, the content to present within the DL and the actual time in preparation, conduction and pre-evaluation by the evaluator.

Within the Daffodil project, master theses, the INEX project and joint-work with the MPI more than seven different evaluations were performed using the Daffodil system as evaluation framework. The main evaluations are described here:

User-interface evaluation. Beside several smaller formative evaluations on the user interface and backend system the first evaluation was conducted in 2002 and presented in Fuhr et alii 2002. Here a heuristic evaluation of the user-interface and a questionare based evaluation of the functionality was performed. The outcome were many improvements on the graphical user-interface and sustainability and performance of the functionality.

Strategic support evaluation. In 2004 are large evaluation on strategic support was accomplished and presented in [6]. The outcome was that the foundation and models used in Daffodil yield a high efficiency and effectiveness in the information retrieval process. Regarding efficiency, only very simple tasks can be solved faster with other systems, whereas Daffodil clearly beats competing systems on more complex tasks. For effectiveness, we could show, that Daffodil's high quality visualisation and the integration of different services provide a useful toolbox and lead to a high user satisfaction.

Deep-Web recommendations. Also in 2004 a joint-work evaluation of Daffodil with the BINGO! focused crawler was conducted and presended in [12]. The information stored in a folder of the personal library is used to search for further information on the WWW. A system-oriented evaluation showed, how flexible and extensible the Daffodil framework is, by integrating the BINGO! crawler into the system.

Active support for query formulation. The investigation on active support during query formulation in [11]. A master student integrated in the graphical user-interface and the backend-system special functions for syntax and semantic checking of user queries.

INEX 2004, 2005 and 2006. Besides the just mentioned evaluation activities in the years 2004, 2005 and 2006 the INEX evaluation on XML retrieval used the Daffodil-system as baseline-system. For each years new interactive trec the user-interface evolved because of the prior evaluation and usualy needed to be extended due to new used XML content. In INEX 2004 the collection consisted of 12,107 articles of the IEEE Computer Society's magazines and transactions, in INEX 2005 the Lonely-Planet collection was added and in INEX 2006 the complete Wikipedia is used for evaluation. For each new content new wrapper were integrated into the system. The INEX-Daffodil-system maintainance, user-interface changes and the integration of new data sources is done by only one person.

The presented evaluations show the variety of possibilities the Daffodil-system can offer researchers to focus on their research instead of re-inventing everything again. From the three major components of a digital library – content, system, and usage – Daffodil allows for easy variation of the first two. Especially, the INEX case shows that new content can be easily integrated in the system.

5 Summary and Outlook

The research of DL is in need of accepted standards, as well as a community that can add value to this field. If the various DL stakeholders can form a community and agree upon models, dimensions, definitions and common sense criteria for the evaluation of DL systems, the process of evaluation will gain impetus among DL researchers.

As an experimental platform for evaluation both within and across DL systems, application of the Daffodil framework can substantially advance this research area, since it currently provides functions and services that are based on a solid theoretical foundation and well known models. Daffodil[3] offers researchers and evaluators a large number of possibilities, and allows to concentrate on new development and evaluation, instead of reinventing the wheel again.

References

1. Fuhr, N., Klas, C.-P., Schaefer, A., Mutschke, P.: Daffodil: An integrated desktop for supporting high-level search activities in federated digital libraries. In: Agosti, M., Thanos, C. (eds.) ECDL 2002. LNCS, vol. 2458, pp. 597–612. Springer, Heidelberg (2002)
2. Goncalves, M.A., Fox, E.A., Cassel, L., Krowne, A., Ravindranathan, U., Panchanathan, G., Jagodzinski, F.: Standards, mark-up, and metadata: The xml log standard for digital libraries: analysis, evolution, and deployment. In: Proceedings of the third ACM/IEEE-CS joint conference on Digital libraries, IEEE Computer Society Press, Los Alamitos (2003)
3. Goncalves, M.A., Shen, R., Fox, E.A., Ali, M.F., Luo, M.: An xml log standard and tool for digital library logging analysis. In: Agosti, M., Thanos, C. (eds.) ECDL 2002. LNCS, vol. 2458, pp. 129–143. Springer, Heidelberg (2002)
4. Klas, C.-P., Albrechtsen, H., Fuhr, N., Hansen, P., Kapidakis, S., Kovács, L., Kriewel, S., Micsik, A., Papatheodorou, C., Tsakonas, G., Jacob, E.: A logging scheme for comparative digital library evaluation. In: Gonzalo, J., Thanos, C., Verdejo, M.F., Carrasco, R.C. (eds.) ECDL 2006. LNCS, vol. 4172, pp. 267–278. Springer, Heidelberg (2006)
5. Klas, C.-P., Fuhr, N., Kriewel, S., Albrechtsen, H., Tsakonas, G., Kapidakis, S., Papatheodorou, C., Hansen, P., Kovacs, L., Micsik, A., Jacob, E.: An experimental framework for comparative digital library evaluation: the logging scheme. In: JCDL 2006. Proceedings of the 6th ACM/IEEE-CS joint conference on Digital libraries, pp. 308–309. ACM Press, New York (2006)
6. Klas, C.-P., Kriewel, S., Schaefer, A.: Daffodil - nutzerorientiertes zugangssystem für heterogene digitale bibliotheken. In: dvs Band (2004)
7. Krause, J.: Visualisation, multimodality and traditional graphical user interfaces. Review of Information Science 2(2) (1997)
8. Kriewel, S., Klas, C.-P., Schaefer, A., Fuhr, N.: Daffodil - strategic support for user-oriented access to heterogeneous digital libraries. D-Lib Magazine 10(6) (2004), http://www.dlib.org/dlib/june04/kriewel/06kriewel.html
9. Malik, S., Klas, C.-P., Fuhr, N., Larsen, B., Tombros, A.: Designing a user interface for interactive retrieval of structured documents — lessons learned from the inex interactive track. In: Gonzalo, J., Thanos, C., Verdejo, M.F., Carrasco, R.C. (eds.) ECDL 2006. LNCS, vol. 4172, Springer, Heidelberg (2006)
10. Saracevic, T., Covi, L.: Challenges for digital library evaluation. Proceedings of the American Society for Information Science 37, 341–350 (2000)
11. Schaefer, A., Jordan, M., Klas, C.-P., Fuhr, N.: Active support for query formulation in virtual digital libraries: A case study with DAFFODIL. In: Rauber, A., Christodoulakis, S., Tjoa, A.M. (eds.) ECDL 2005. LNCS, vol. 3652, Springer, Heidelberg (2005)
12. Theobald, M., Klas, C.-P.: BINGO! and Daffodil: Personalized exploration of digital libraries and web sources. In: In 7th International Conference on Computer-Assisted Information Retrieval (RIAO 2004). Test (2004)

---

[3] The system is open source software, based on the Apache Commons Licence 2.0.

The Importance of Scientific Data Curation for Evaluation Campaigns

Maristella Agosti, Giorgio Maria Di Nunzio, and Nicola Ferro

Department of Information Engineering, University of Padua, Italy
{agosti,dinunzio,ferro}@dei.unipd.it

Abstract. Information Retrieval system evaluation campaigns produce valuable scientific data, which should be preserved carefully so that they can be available for further studies. A complete record should be maintained of all analyses and interpretations in order to ensure that they are reusable in attempts to replicate particular results or in new research and so that they can be referred to or cited at any time.

In this paper, we describe the data curation approach for the scientific data produced by evaluation campaigns. The medium/long-term aim is to create a large-scale *Digital Library System (DLS)* of scientific data which supports services for the creation, interpretation and use of multidisciplinary and multilingual digital content.

1   Introduction

The experimental evaluation of *Information Retrieval (IR)* systems is usually carried out in important international evaluation campaigns, such as *Text REtrieval Conference (TREC)*[1], *Cross-Language Evaluation Forum (CLEF)*[2], and *NII-NACSIS Test Collection for IR Systems (NTCIR)*[3], which bring research groups together, providing them with the means to compare the performances of their systems, and discuss their results. This paper examines the approach traditionally adopted for experimental evaluation in the IR research field in the light of the challenges posed by the recent recognition of the importance of a correct management, preservation and access to scientific data. We discuss how the increasing attention being given to this question impacts on both IR evaluation methodology and on the way in which the data of the evaluation campaigns are organized and maintained over time.

The paper is organized as follows: Section 2 introduces the motivations and the objectives of our research work. Section 3 discusses possible ways of extending the current evaluation methodology both from the point of view of the the conceptual model of the information space involved and a software infrastructure for evaluation campaigns. Section 4 draws some conclusions.

---

[1] http://trec.nist.gov/
[2] http://www.clef-campaign.org/
[3] http://research.nii.ac.jp/ntcir/index-en.html

C. Thanos, F. Borri, and L. Candela (Eds.): Digital Libraries: R&D, LNCS 4877, pp. 157–166, 2007.

2   Evaluation Campaigns and IR Experimental Evaluation

Much IR system evaluation is based on a comparative evaluation approach in which system performances are compared according to the Cranfield methodology, which makes use of test collections [1]. A test collection $\mathcal{C}$ allows the comparison of information access systems according to measurements which quantify their performances. The main goals of a test collection are to provide a common test-bed to be indexed and searched by information access systems and to guarantee the possibility of replicating the experiments.

2.1   Methodology

If we consider the Cranfield evaluation methodology and the achievements and outcomes of the evaluation campaigns in which it is used, it is clear that we are dealing with different kinds of valuable *scientific data*. The test collections and the experiments represent our primary scientific data and the starting point of our investigation. Using the test data, we produce different performance measurements, such as precision and recall, in order to evaluate the performances of IR systems for a given experiment. Starting from these performance measurements, we compute descriptive statistics, such as mean or median, which can be used to summarize the overall performances achieved by an experiment or by a collection of experiments. Finally, we perform hypothesis tests and other statistical analyses in order to conduct in-depth studies and comparisons over a set of experiments.

We can frame the above mentioned scientific data in the context of the *Data, Information, Knowledge, Wisdom (DIKW)* hierarchy [2,3]:

- *data*: the *test collections* and the *experiments* correspond to the "data level" in the hierarchy, since they are the raw, basic elements needed for any further investigation and have little meaning by themselves. An experiment and the results obtained by conducting it are almost useless without knowledge of the test collection used for the experiment; these data constitute the basis for any subsequent computation;
- *information*: the *performance measurements* correspond to the "information level" in the hierarchy, since they are the result of computations and processing on the data; in this way, we can give meaning to the data via certain relations. For example, precision and recall measures are obtained by relating the list of results contained in an experiment with the relevance judgements J;
- *knowledge*: the *descriptive statistics* and the *hypothesis tests* correspond to the "knowledge level" in the hierarchy, since they represent further processing of the information provided by the performance measurements and provide us with some insights about the experiments;
- *wisdom*: *theories*, *models*, *algorithms*, *techniques*, and *observations*, which are usually communicated by means of papers, talks, and seminars, correspond to the "wisdom level" in the hierarchy, since they provide interpretation, explanation, and formalization of the content of the previous levels.

As observed by [3], "while data and information (being components) can be generated per se, i.e. without direct human interpretation, knowledge and wisdom (being relations) cannot: they are human- and context-dependent and cannot be contemplated without involving *human* (not machine) comparison, decision making and judgement". This observation also fits the case of IR system experimental evaluation. In fact, experiments (data) and performance measurements (information) are usually generated automatically by programs, and tools for performance assessment. However, statistical analyses (knowledge) and models and algorithms (wisdom) require a deep involvement of researchers in order to be conducted and developed.

This view of IR system experimental evaluation raises the question of whether the Cranfield methodology is able to support an approach where the whole process from data to wisdom is taken into account. This question is made more compelling by the fact that, when we deal with scientific data, "the lineage (provenance) of the data must be tracked, since a scientist needs to know where the data came from [...] and what cleaning, rescaling, or modelling was done to arrive at the data to be interpreted" [4]. Moreover, as pointed out by [5], provenance is "important in judging the quality and applicability of information for a given use and for determining when changes at sources require revising derived information". Furthermore, when scientific data are maintained for further and future use, they are liable to be enriched and, sometimes, the enrichment of a portion of scientific data implies a *citation* so that useful information can be explicitly mentioned and referenced [6,7]. Finally, [8] highlights that "digital data collections enable analysis at unprecedented levels of accuracy and sophistication and provide novel insights through innovative information integration". Thus, the question is not only to which degree the Cranfield methodology supports passing from data to wisdom, but also whether correct strategies are adopted to ensure the provenance, the enrichment, the citation, and the interpretation of the scientific data.

2.2 Infrastructure

There is a growing interest in the proper management of scientific data by diverse world organizations, among them the European Commission (EC), the US National Scientific Board, and the Australian Working Group on Data for Science. The EC in the i2010 Digital Library Initiative clearly states that "digital repositories of scientific information are essential elements to build European eInfrastructure for knowledge sharing and transfer, feeding the cycles of scientific research and innovation up-take" [9]. The US National Scientific Board points out that "organizations make choices on behalf of the current and future user community on issues such as collection access; collection structure; technical standards and processes for data curation; ontology development; annotation; and peer review". Moreover, those organizations "are uniquely positioned to take leadership roles in developing a comprehensive strategy for long-lived digital data collections" [8]. The Australian Working Group on Data for Science suggests to establishing "a nationally supported long-term strategic framework for scientific data management, including guiding principles, policies, best practices and infrastructure", that "standards and standards-based technologies be adopted and that their use be widely promoted to ensure interoperability between data, metadata, and data management systems", and that "the principle of open equitable access to publicly-funded scientific data be adopted wherever possible [...] As part of this strategy, and to enable current and future data and information resources to be shared, mechanisms to enable the discovery of, and access to, data and information resources must be encouraged" [10].

These observations suggest that considering the IR system experimental evaluation as a source of scientific data entails not only re-thinking the evaluation methodology itself, but also re-considering the way in which this methodology is applied and how the evaluation campaigns are organized. Indeed, changes to IR system evaluation methodology need to be correctly supported by organizational, hardware, and software infrastructure which allow for the management, search, access, curation, enrichment, and citation of the scientific data produced.

Such changes will also impact on the organizations which run the evaluation campaigns, since they have not only to provide the infrastructure but also to participate in the design and development of it. In fact, as highlighted by [8], they should take a leadership role in developing a comprehensive strategy for the preservation of digital data collections and drive the research community through this process in order to improve the way of doing research. As a consequence, the aim and the reach of an evaluation campaign would be widened because, besides bringing research groups together and providing them with the means for discussing and comparing their work, an evaluation campaign should also take care of defining guiding principles, policies, best practices for making use of the scientific data produced during the evaluation campaign itself.

3   Extending the Approach to IR Evaluation

As observed in the previous section, scientific data, their curation, enrichment, and interpretation are essential components of scientific research. These issues are better faced and framed in the wider context of the *curation of scientific data*, which plays an important role in the systematic definition of an appropriate methodology to manage and promote the use of data. The e-Science Data Curation Report gives the following definition of data curation [11]: "the activity of managing and promoting the use of data from its point of creation, to ensure it is fit for contemporary purposes, and available for discovery and re-use. For dynamic datasets this may mean continuous enrichment or updating to keep it fit for purpose". This definition implies that we have to take into consideration the possibility of information enrichment of scientific data; this means that we must archive and preserve scientific data so that experiments, records, and observations will be available for future research, together with information on provenance, curation, and citation of scientific data items. The benefits of this approach include the growing involvement of scientists in international research projects and forums and increased interest in comparative research activities.

There are many reasons why the preservation of the data resulting from an evaluation campaign is important, for example: the re-use of data for new research, including collection-based research to generate new science; retention of unique observational data which is impossible to re-create; retention of expensively generated data which is cheaper to maintain than to re-generate; enhancement of existing data available for research projects; validation of published research results. However, it should be remembered that the Cranfield methodology was developed to create comparable experiments and evaluate the performances of IR systems rather than to model, manage, and curate the scientific data produced during an evaluation campaign.

In the following sections, we discuss some key points to be taken into consideration when extending the current evaluation methodology in order to give evaluation campaigns a leadership role in driving research on IR evaluation methodologies.

3.1   Conceptual Model and Metadata

If we consider the definition of experimental collection, it does not take into consideration any kind of conceptual model, neither the experimental collection as a whole nor its constituent parts. In contrast, the information space implied by an evaluation campaign needs an appropriate conceptual model which takes into consideration and describes all the entities involved by the evaluation campaign. In fact, an appropriate conceptual model is the necessary basis to make the scientific data produced during the evaluation an active part of all those information enrichments, as data provenance and citation. The conceptual model can also be translated into an appropriate logical model in order to manage the information of an evaluation campaign by using a robust data management technology. Finally, from this conceptual model we can also derive appropriate data formats for exchanging information among organizers and participants.

Moreover, [12] points out that "metadata descriptions are as important as the data values in providing meaning to the data, and thereby enabling sharing and potential future useful access". Since there is no conceptual model for an experimental collection, metadata schemes for describing it are also lacking. Consider that there are almost no metadata:

- which describe a collection of documents D; useful metadata would concern, at least, the creator, the creation date, a description, the context the collection refers to, and how the collection has been created;
- about the topics T; useful metadata would regard the creators and the creation date, how the creation process has taken place, if there were any issues, what the documents the creators have found relevant for a given topic are, and so on;
- which describe the relevance judgements J; examples of such metadata concern creators and the creation date, what were the criteria which led the creation of the relevance judgements, what problems have been faced by the assessors when dealing with difficult topics.

The situation is a little bit less problematic when it comes to experiments for which some kind of metadata may be collected, such as which topic fields were used to create the query, whether the query was automatically or manually constructed from the topics and, in some tracks of TREC, some information about the hardware used to run the experiments. Nevertheless, a better description of the experiments could be achieved if we take into consideration what retrieval model was applied, what algorithms and techniques were adopted, what kind of stop word removal and/or stemming was performed, what tunings were carried out.

A good attempt in this direction is the *Reliable Information Access (RIA)* Workshop [13], organized by the US *National Institute of Standards and Technology (NIST)* in 2003, where an in-depth study and failure analysis of the conducted experiments were performed and valuable information about them was collected. However, the existence of a commonly agreed conceptual model and metadata schemas would have helped in defining and gathering the information to be kept.

Similar considerations hold also for the performance measurements, the descriptive statistics, and the statistical analyses which are not explicitly modeled and for which no metadata schema is defined. It would be useful to define at least the metadata that are necessary to describe which software and which version of the software were used to compute a performance measure, which relevance judgements were used to compute a performance measure, and when the performance measure was computed. Similar metadata could be useful also for descriptive statistics and statistical analyses.

3.2   Unique Identification Mechanism

The lack of a conceptual model causes another relevant consequence: there is no common mechanism to uniquely identify the different digital objects involved in an evaluation campaign, i.e. there is no way to uniquely identify and reference collections of documents, topics, relevance judgements, experiments, and statistical analyses.

The absence of a mechanism to uniquely identify and reference the digital objects of an evaluation campaign prevent us from directly citing those digital objects. Indeed, as recognized by [11], the possibility of citing scientific data and their further elaboration is an effective way of making scientists and researchers an active part of the digital curation process. Moreover, this opportunity would strengthen the passing from data to wisdom, discussed in Section 2, because experimental collections and experiments would become citable and accessible just like any other item in the reference list of a paper.

Over the past years, various syntaxes, mechanisms, and systems have been developed to provide unique identifiers for digital objects, among them the following are candidates to be adopted in the unique identification of the different digital objects involved in an evaluation campaign: *Uniform Resource Identifier (URI)* [14], *Digital Object Identifier (DOI)* [15], OpenURL [16], and

Persistent URL (PURL)[4]. An important aspect of all the identification mechanisms described above is that all of them provide facilities for resolving the identifiers. This means that all those mechanisms enable a direct access to each identified digital object starting from its identifier, in this way giving an interested researcher direct access to the referenced digital object together with all the information concerning it.

The DOI constitutes a valuable possibility for identifying and referencing the digital objects of an evaluation campaign, since there have already been successful attempts to apply it to scientific data and it makes possible the association of metadata with the identified digital objects [17,18].

3.3   Statistical Analyses

[19] points out that in order to evaluate retrieval performances, we need not only an experimental collection and measures for quantifying retrieval performances, but also a statistical methodology for judging whether measured differences between retrieval methods can be considered statistically significant.

To address this issue, evaluation campaigns have traditionally supported and carried out statistical analyses, which provide participants with an overview analysis of the submitted experiments. Furthermore, participants may conduct statistical analyses on their own experiments by using either ad-hoc packages, such as IR-STAT-PAK[5], or generally available software tools with statistical analysis capabilities, like R[6], SPSS[7], or MATLAB[8]. However, the choice of whether to perform a statical analysis or not is left up to each participant who may even not have all the skills and resources needed to perform such analyses. Moreover, when participants perform statistical analyses using their own tools, the comparability among these analyses could not be fully granted, in fact, different statistical tests can be employed to analyze the data, or different choices and approximations for the various parameters of the same statistical test can be made.

In developing an infrastructure for improving the support given to participants by an evaluation campaign, it could be advisable to add some form of support and guide to participants for adopting a more uniform way of performing statistical analyses on their own experiments. If this support is added, participants can not only benefit from standard experimental collections which make their experiments comparable, but they can also exploit standard tools for the analysis of the experimental results, which would make the analysis and assessment of their experiments comparable too.

As recalled in Section 2, scientific data, their enrichment and interpretation are essential components of scientific research. The Cranfield methodology traces

---

[4] http://purl.oclc.org/
[5] http://users.cs.dal.ca/~jamie/pubs/IRSP-overview.html
[6] http://www.r-project.org/
[7] http://www.spss.com/
[8] http://www.mathworks.com/

out how these scientific data have to be produced, while the statistical analysis of experiments provides the means for further elaborating and interpreting the experimental results. Nevertheless, the current methodologies do not require any particular coordination or synchronization between the basic scientific data and the analyses on them, which are treated as almost separate items. However, researchers would greatly benefit from an integrated vision of them, where the access to a scientific data item could also offer the possibility of retrieving all the analyses and interpretations on it. Furthermore, it should be possible to enrich the basic scientific data in an incremental way, progressively adding further analyses and interpretations on them.

3.4   IR Evaluation and Digital Library Systems

We consider all the abovementioned key points as requirements that should be taken into account when designing an evaluation campaign which will take on a twofold role. Firstly, an evaluation campaign aims at promoting research in the IR field by highlighting valuable areas which need to be explored and by offering the means for conducting, comparing, and discussing experiments. Secondly, an evaluation campaign has to make the management and the curation of the produced scientific data an integral part of the IR research process. Therefore, an evaluation campaign has to provide guidelines, best practices, conceptual and logical models for data representation and exchange, preservation and curation of the produced scientific data, and support for passing through the whole DIKW hierarchy.

As a consequence, an evaluation campaign has to provide a software infrastructure suitable for carrying out this second new role. In this context, DLSs are the natural choice for managing, making accessible, citing, curating, enriching, and preserving all the information resources produced during an evaluation campaign. Indeed, [5] points out how *information enrichment* should be one of the activities supported by a DLS and, among the different kinds of them, considers provenance as "important in judging the quality and applicability of information for a given use and for determining when changes at sources require revising derived information". In addition, [5] observes that *citation*, intended as the possibility of explicitly mentioning and making references to portions of a given digital object, should also be part of the information enrichment strategies supported by a DLS.

In addition, the evaluation of complex systems, such as a DLS, is a non trivial issue which should analyze different aspects, among which: architecture, information access and extraction capabilities, management of multimedia content, interaction with users, and so on [20]. Since there are so many aspects to take into consideration, a DLS, which is used as an infrastructure for an evaluation campaign, should be constituted by different and cooperating services, each one focused on supporting the evaluation of one of the aspects mentioned above. This approach to the design of such DLSs is coherent with the guidelines proposed in [5], who traces out the service-based design as one of the key points in the scientific development of DLSs.

In conclusion, DLSs can act as the systems of choice to support evaluation campaigns in making a step forward; they are able to both address the key points highlighted above and provide a more mature way of dealing with the scientific data produced during the IR experimental evaluation.

4 Conclusion

This study has addressed the methodology currently adopted for the experimental evaluation in the IR field, and it has proposed extending it to include a proper management, curation, archiving, and enrichment of the scientific data that are produced while conducting an experimental evaluation in the context of evaluation campaigns. We described the approach for maintaining in a DLS the scientific output of an evaluation campaign, in order to ensure long-term preservation, curation of data, and accessibility over time both by humans and automatic systems. The aim is to create a large-scale *Digital Library (DL)* of scientific data which supports services for the creation, interpretation and use of multidisciplinary and multilingual digital content.

Acknowledgements

The work reported in this paper has been partially supported by the DELOS Network of Excellence on Digital Libraries, as part of the Information Society Technologies (IST) Program of the European Commission (Contract G038-507618).

References

1. Cleverdon, C.W.: The Cranfield Tests on Index Languages Devices. In: Readings in Information Retrieval, pp. 47–60. Morgan Kaufmann Publisher, Inc, San Francisco, California, USA (1997)
2. Ackoff, R.L.: From Data to Wisdom. Journal of Applied Systems Analysis 16, 3–9 (1989)
3. Zeleny, M.: Management Support Systems: Towards Integrated Knowledge Management. Human Systems Management 7, 59–70 (1987)
4. Abiteboul, S., et al.: The Lowell Database Research Self-Assessment. Communications of the ACM (CACM) 48, 111–118 (2005)
5. Ioannidis, Y., et al.: Digital library information-technology infrastructures. International Journal on Digital Libraries 5, 266–274 (2005)
6. Agosti, M., Di Nunzio, G.M., Ferro, N.: A Data Curation Approach to Support In-depth Evaluation Studies. In: MLIA 2006. Proc. International Workshop on New Directions in Multilingual Information Access, pp. 65–68, [last visited 2007, March 23] (2006), http://ucdata.berkeley.edu/sigir2006-mlia.htm
7. Agosti, M., Di Nunzio, G.M., Ferro, N.: Scientific Data of an Evaluation Campaign: Do We Properly Deal With Them? In: CLEF 2006. LNCS, vol. 4730, pp. 11–20. Springer, Heidelberg (2007)

8. National Science Board: Long-Lived Digital Data Collections: Enabling Research and Education in the 21st Century (NSB-05-40). National Science Foundation (NSF). [last visited 2007, March 23] (2005), http://www.nsf.gov/pubs/2005/nsb0540/

9. European Commission Information Society and Media: i2010: Digital Libraries. [last visited 2007, March 23] (2006), http://europa.eu.int/information_society/activities/digital_libraries/doc/brochures/dl_brochure_2006.pdf

10. Working Group on Data for Science: FROM DATA TO WISDOM: Pathways to Successful Data Management for Australian Science. Report to Minister's Science, Engineering and Innovation Council (PMSEIC), [last visited 2007, March 23] (2006), http://www.dest.gov.au/sectors/science_innovation/publications_resources/profiles/Presentation_Data_for_Science.htm

11. Lord, P., Macdonald, A.: e-Science Curation Report. Data curation for e-Science in the UK: an audit to establish requirements for future curation and provision. The JISC Committee for the Support of Research (JCSR). [last visited 2007, March 23] (2003), http://www.jisc.ac.uk/uploaded_documents/e-ScienceReportFinal.pdf

12. Anderson, W.L.: Some Challenges and Issues in Managing, and Preserving Access To, Long-Lived Collections of Digital Scientific and Technical Data. Data Science Journal 3, 191–202 (2004)

13. Harman, D., Buckley, C.: The NRRC Reliable Information Access (RIA) Workshop. In: SIGIR 2004. Proc. 27th Annual International ACM SIGIR Conference on Research and Development in Information Retrieval, pp. 528–529. ACM Press, New York (2004)

14. Berners-Lee, T., Fielding, R., Irvine, U.C., Masinter, L.: Uniform Resource Identifiers (URI): Generic Syntax. RFC 2396 (1998)

15. Paskin, N., (ed.): The DOI Handbook – Edition 4.4.1. International DOI Foundation (IDF). [last visited 2007, August 30] (2006), http://dx.doi.org/10.1000/186

16. NISO: ANSI/NISO Z39.88 - 2004 – The OpenURL Framework for Context-Sensitive Services. National Information Standards Organization (NISO). [last visited 2007, March 23] (2005), http://www.niso.org/standards/standard_detail.cfm?std_id=783

17. Brase, J.: Using Digital Library Techniques – Registration of Scientific Primary Data. In: Heery, R., Lyon, L. (eds.) ECDL 2004. LNCS, vol. 3232, pp. 488–494. Springer, Heidelberg (2004)

18. Paskin, N.: Digital Object Identifiers for Scientific Data. Data Science Journal 4, 12–20 (2005)

19. Hull, D.: Using Statistical Testing in the Evaluation of Retrieval Experiments. In: SIGIR 1993. Proc. 16th Annual International ACM SIGIR Conference on Research and Development in Information Retrieval, pp. 329–338. ACM Press, New York (1993)

20. Fuhr, N., Hansen, P., Micsik, A., Sølvberg, I.: Digital Libraries: A Generic Classification Scheme. In: Constantopoulos, P., Sølvberg, I.T. (eds.) ECDL 2001. LNCS, vol. 2163, pp. 187–199. Springer, Heidelberg (2001)

An Approach for the Construction of an Experimental Test Collection to Evaluate Search Systems that Exploit Annotations

Maristella Agosti, Tullio Coppotelli, Nicola Ferro, and Luca Pretto

Department of Information Engineering, University of Padua, Italy
{agosti,coppotel,ferro,pretto}@dei.unipd.it

Abstract. This study addresses the lack of an adequate test collection that can be used to evaluate search systems that exploit annotations to increase the retrieval effectiveness of an information search tool. In particular, a new approach is proposed that enables the automatic creation of multiple test collections without human effort. This approach takes advantage of the human relevance assessments contained in an already existing test collection and it introduces content-level annotations in that collection.

1 Introduction

The topic of annotations is focusing researchers' attention in both the *Digital Library (DL)* and *Information Retrieval (IR)* fields. In DLs, annotations are used to facilitate cooperation between users [1], to enrich the content of documents or to easily describe documents in media different from plain text, like video or audio. In IR, new and better algorithms which aim to improve the system retrieval effectiveness using annotations has been proposed. In fact, annotations offer an interesting opportunity to improve the retrieval performance: the additional information contained in the annotations and the hypertext which connects annotations to documents enable the definition of search strategies which merge multiple sources of evidence in order to increase the system effectiveness. In this perspective, two approaches have been proposed in [2] and [3]. The former presents a theoretical model and discusses how it exploits annotations and the hypertext that documents and annotations constitute in the retrieval process. The latter exploits annotations as a rich source of evidence to augment the content of each document with the content of its attached annotations.

The evaluation of the effectiveness of these approaches is a necessary step that enables not only understanding of their effective performance but also, at a more general level, confirmation that annotations can play an important role in improving system effectiveness. In [2] the authors stressed that an obstacle to the complete evaluation of these kinds of systems was the lack of an experimental test collection. In [3] an effort in this direction has been made with the manual creation of a small test collection that is used to evaluate their own approach.

C. Thanos, F. Borri, and L. Candela (Eds.): Digital Libraries: R&D, LNCS 4877, pp. 167–176, 2007.
© Springer-Verlag Berlin Heidelberg 2007

The greatest difficulty encountered by the author during the creation process was the need to cope with limited resources for the relevance judgement creation.

The creation of an experimental test collection is a consolidated process in IR and an overview of this process and related problems is given in [4]. Despite this, when it comes to the creation of a test collection with annotated documents, the problems which need to be addressed are demanding. To summarize, the creation of a test collection with annotated documents requires the finding of a suitable set of documents that have to satisfy required characteristics, the manual creation of the annotations over these documents, the creation of the topics containing the information that have to be searched and, finally, the evaluation of the document relevance to each topic. Moreover, as we will discuss in greater detail in Section 2, different views of the annotations can lead to the need for different test collections; therefore a different approach to test collections creation would be suitable to cope with this aspect. Instead of using the limited resources to obtain human relevance assessments, an entirely automatic technique can be envisaged. Therefore, the problem of setting an adequate experimental test-bed for search algorithms which exploit annotations was addressed. A flexible strategy to create test collections with annotated documents was identified that, starting from an already existing test collection, brings to the surface the hidden work made by the assessors during the creation of relevance assessments. An interesting feature of this strategy is that it is not limited to the creation of a single test collection, rather by using as a starting point collections with different characteristics, it allows the creation of new collections with the same characteristics as the original one (monolingual or multilingual, general or specialized). An initial proposal was made in [5] and the progress was reported in [6].

The final aim of the research is to establish a framework reusable for the evaluation of different information search tools. This paper reports on the proposed approach and the so called *subtopic view of the graph* that is the starting point for a new algorithm, proposed in [7], which enables the construction of a less sparsely annotated test collection that could be used to evaluate *Information Retrieval Systems(IRSs)* under different testing conditions. This paper and [7] can be considered complementary as they both report on the general approach of constructing a test collection to be used for evaluating search tools that use annotations together with the original documents to solve users information needs. To reach the objective of the study, Section 2 presents an introductory overview on the annotation concepts. Section 3 reports on the adopted approach and Section 4 uses the approach to describe an algorithm that exploits relevance assessments to introduce annotations in the original test collection. Section 5 discusses the obtained test collection. Conclusions and future work are presented in Section 6.

2   Overview on Annotations

The concept of annotation is not limited to the action of a scholar who annotates a text passage writing annotations as it is a rather more complex and multifaceted concept; the concept has been addressed at length and an extensive study is [8].

An intrinsic dualism exists in annotations. Are annotations a *content enrichment* or are they *stand-alone documents*? If they simply enrich the content of the original document, then the annotations can be merged to that document and then annotation and document become an atomic document. The approach to the test collection creation described in [3] adopted this view. As a result, annotations are not autonomous entities, but rely on previously existing information resources to justify their existence. The approach to retrieval adopted in [2] considers the annotations as autonomous objects. Stand-alone annotations can be evaluated relevant to a topic regardless to the document relevance. These two opposite approaches stress how broad the concept of annotation can be and, as a consequence, how hard it can be to build a test collection that enables the evaluation of systems that use annotations.

An important characteristic of annotations is their heterogeneity. Annotations over documents can be created at different times and by different authors each with a different background. The user who annotates a document may know recent information about the topic that the document author did not know. He may disagree with the document content and might like to communicate his different opinion. The author of the document can clarify or modify some text passage. This heterogeneity is a key-point that allows a dynamic improvement in the content of the document and by using this new information it is possible to better estimate the relationship between documents and query, a feature which is so important in document retrieval.

Summing up, the goal of the approach presented in the following Section is to enable the creation of test collections that respect the different aspects of annotations without the need for extensive human effort.

3   The Proposed Approach

3.1   Overview

When building a test collection from scratch finding a suitable set of documents, creating the topics and evaluating the document relevance to each topic are required. All these tasks are not trivial [4] and need an accurate evaluation to avoid the introduction of too many biases in the test collection. The task that we are going to address is even more difficult. The creation of annotations over the selected documents is a very expensive practice. Moreover, it is not possible to use assessors to create the annotations because, to maintain their heterogeneous nature, a wide range of annotations written by different authors in different periods of time would be needed. The pooling method is a consolidated practice that reduces assessor effort during the creation of the relevance judgments. This method requires the assessment of only a reduced number of document for each topic – i.e. 1000. The pooling method relies on a certain number of experiments that are performed with different *Information Retrieval Systems (IRSs)* but the number of systems that use annotations is currently too small to allow the creation of a sufficient number of experiments and this prevents us from using this method. Finally, if we were able to overcome these limitations the standard collection creation process would still be expensive and time consuming.

Our approach avoids all these problems and proposes a different strategy that involves the use of an already existing test collection as a starting point and the automatic construction of a parallel collection of related annotations. This strategy has the following advantages:

1. it reduces the overall effort needed to create the test collection;
2. the results obtained evaluating systems with the new collection are comparable with the previous results obtained on the original test collection; this allows the direct performance comparison between systems that use annotations and systems that do not use them;
3. it exploits the existing pool to deal with a sufficient number of experiments;
4. it allows the creation of multiple collections with different characteristics and the consequent evaluation of the system behavior in different contexts.

The idea is to use as a starting point a test collection that contains documents that are naturally separated in two or more different sets and to use the relevance judgments of the human assessors to link documents that belong to different sets. If document d_i and document $\hat{a}_j$ were both judged relevant to the topic t_z by a human assessor then we know that these documents are put in relation by the content of the topic. We then use the topic as the motivation for the document $\hat{a}_j$ to annotate the document d_i. In this way a set of annotated documents can be created whose relevance to the topics has already been judged in the original test collection.

3.2   The Modelling

The starting test collection can be represented as a triple $C = (D, T, J)$ where D is the set of documents, T is the set of topics and J is the set of relevance assessments defined as $J = D \times T \times \{0, 1\}$ (binary relevance). The documents D of the chosen test collection must be divisible in two disjoint sets, D_1 and $\hat{A}$, where $D = D_1 \cup \hat{A}$ and $D_1 \cap \hat{A} = \varnothing$. We have conducted preliminary experiments where D_1 were newspaper articles and $\hat{A}$ were agency news of the same year [5]. The annotated collection is $C' = (D'_1, T, J)$, where D'_1 contains exactly the same documents as D_1 with the addition of annotations over these documents. Topics and relevance assessments are exactly the same. In C' we use a subset A of $\hat{A}$ to annotate the documents in D_1, thus $\hat{A}$ is the set of candidate annotations and A is the set of actual annotations. The goal is then to find which candidate annotations can be used to correctly annotate documents in D_1 and create the annotation hypertext over these documents. To identify these relationships we take advantage of the fact that in C the topics are made over both D_1 and $\hat{A}$ (thus their relevance to each topic has been judged): if in C both a candidate annotation and a document have been judged relevant to the same topic then we infer that it is possible to annotate that document with that candidate annotation. Referring to Figure 2, these couples (document, annotation) are those connected by a two-edge path in the undirected graph $G_1 = (V_1, E_1)$ where $V_1 = D_1 \cup T \cup \hat{A}$ and $E_1 = (D_1 \cup \hat{A}) \times T$. In G_1 each edge

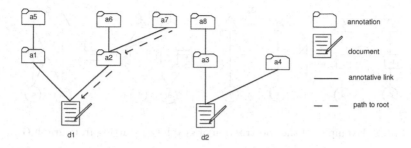

Fig. 1. Annotation constraint

represents a human assessment i.e. a path between annotation $\hat{a}_j$ and document d_i passing through topic t_z means that a person assessed both $\hat{a}_j$ and d_i relevant to t_z. This relevance property creates a path between documents and candidate annotations that is used in Section 4 to introduce annotations in C'. The intuition is that the strength of these paths allows the use of candidate annotations as real annotations for connected documents and that these annotations reflect human annotative behaviour.

The proposed approach respects the so called *annotation constraint*: each annotation can annotate one and only one document or annotation; this means that each annotation is written for exactly one *Digital Object (DO)* but it can still be linked to more DOs [2,8]. This constraint has been introduced to better simulate the annotative behaviour of a user who usually writes an annotation only after the reading of a specific DO. As a consequence of this constraint, the set of documents and annotations become a forest and it is possible, starting from an annotation, to identify the root document of an annotation thread. Consider, for example, Figure 1 where annotation a_7 belongs to the tree rooted in d_1 and note that this would not be possible if a_7 could annotate also a_3. This constraint also has the advantage of allowing the identification for each annotation, independently of its depth, of a single root document.

4   Exploiting the Relevance Assessments to Annotate Documents

Once graph $G_1 = (V_1, E_1)$ is given, the problem of matching a candidate annotation with a suitable document can be addressed. The matches should respect the annotation constraint that one annotation can annotate only one document. This section describes an algorithm which makes use of the positive relevance assessments to match a candidate annotation with a document. The first aim of the algorithm is to match each candidate annotation with the most suitable document. When more than one match is possible, the algorithm heuristically tends to choose matches which maximize the number of annotated documents—indeed, maximizing the number of annotated documents is the second aim of the algorithm.

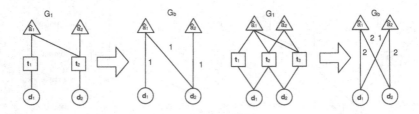

Fig. 2. Examples of the construction of graph G_b, starting from graph G_1

The algorithm works in two phases. In the first phase it constructs a weighted bipartite graph G_b on the basis of G_1, i.e. the graph whose edges represent positive relevance assessments. In the second phase the algorithm works on the weighted bipartite graph G_b to properly match a candidate annotation with a document.

The construction of the weighted bipartite graph $G_b = (V_b, E_b)$ is immediate: the vertices of G_b are all the vertices of G_1 which represent documents or candidate annotations, that is $V_b = D_1 \cup \hat{A}$, and an edge between candidate annotation $\hat{a}$ and document d exists if and only if $\hat{a}$ and d have been judged relevant to at least one common topic, that is $t \in T$ exists such that edges $\hat{a}$-t and t-d are in E_1. Moreover, a weight is assigned to each edge $\hat{a}$-d in E_b, which gives the number of common topics between $\hat{a}$ and d. These weights take account of the fact that when $\hat{a}$ and d are assessed as relevant to more than one common topic at the same time, it is reasonable to suppose that the bond between the candidate annotation $\hat{a}$ and the document d will be strengthened. In Figure 2 simple examples of the construction of G_b, starting from G_1, are given.

Once G_b is constructed, the algorithm works only on G_b to properly match a candidate annotation with a document. It is this second phase of the algorithm that has the two aims described above. The first aim is that of matching the best possible annotation with a document: this is done considering first the edges with the highest weight. The second aim is that of trying to annotate the maximum number of documents, once the best possible annotations have been considered.

The first aim is achieved by first analysing only the edges with the maximum weight and using all of them to match candidate annotations with their suitable documents. After all the edges with the maximum weight have been analysed, only the edges of immediately lower weight are analysed and so on, until all the edges with a positive weight have been analysed. In other words, the algorithm considers each different layer of edge weight separately—the higher the layer, the higher the quality of the matches. When a layer with a certain weight is considered, only edges with that specific weight are analysed.

The second aim, i.e. trying to annotate the maximum number of documents, is achieved by the conceptual application, layer by layer, of two operators, $O_{\text{conflicts}}$ and O_{random}. The first operator is applied to match a candidate annotation with a document, and also has the task of resolving conflicts like those in Figure 3a, where if $\hat{a}_1$ were matched with d_2 it would no longer be possible to annotate document d_1, while the best choice is to match $\hat{a}_1$ with d_1 and $\hat{a}_2$ to d_2.

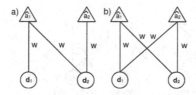

Fig. 3. On the left example of a conflict, on the right example of a deadlock. Note that all edges have the same weight w.

To avoid these conflicts operator $O_{\text{conflicts}}$ first selects all the couples $\hat{a}$-d for which $\hat{a}$ can annotate only one document, like the couple $\hat{a}_2$-d_2 in Figure 3a. Then $O_{\text{conflicts}}$ matches candidate annotations with documents in order to annotate the maximum number of documents: for instance, in the case of Figure 3a, $\hat{a}_1$ will be matched with d_1, since d_2 has already been annotated. Once an edge $\hat{a}$-d is used in a match, it is marked with the negative weight -1, and all the other edges which are incident with the same candidate annotation $\hat{a}$ are deleted from the graph and no longer considered. $O_{\text{conflicts}}$ is iterated until it resolves all possible conflicts. However, in some cases $O_{\text{conflicts}}$ cannot find a match, since no preferable match is suggested by the topology of the graph. This occurs, for instance, when a kind of deadlock exists (see Figure 3b).

In this case an operator O_{random} is applied, which randomly selects one of the possible matches between a candidate annotation and a document. As usual, when a match, that is an edge $\hat{a}$-d, is selected, that edge is marked with the negative weight -1, and all the other edges which are incident with $\hat{a}$ are deleted. The algorithm applies iteratively $O_{\text{conflicts}}$ and O_{random} operators until all the edges with the weight under consideration have been examined. Then a lower weight is examined and so on, until all *positive* weights have been examined.

Finally, edges marked with the negative weight -1 give the desired matches of candidate annotations with documents.

In figure 4 one possible solution of a deadlock problem is proposed. There are four equiprobable edges and if $O_{conflicts}$ cannot match any annotation to document then O_{random} is applied and deletes one edge with probability 0.25. In the example, after the deletion of edge $d_1 - \hat{a}_2$, it is possible to annotate d_2 with annotation $\hat{a}_2$. In the next execution step $O_{conflicts}$ is reapplied that now can match $\hat{a}_1$ with d_1, and not $\hat{a}_1$ with d_2 because d_2 with respect to d_1 is already annotated. Note that by applying O_{random} it is no longer possible to find a unique solution to the matching problem, but this is not relevant with respect to our aim of finding the maximum number of matches.

5   Discussion

The proposed approach is completely automated and allows the creation of a test collection containing a number of documents equal to the cardinality of D and a certain number of annotations over these documents. The number of topics is

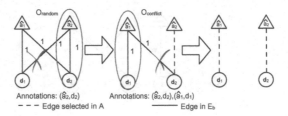

Fig. 4. Example of application of O operators

equal to the cardinality of T while the number of annotations depends on the structure of the graph G_b. Because the graph G_b is build starting from the relevance assessments, it is clear that the number of annotations that this method can introduce strongly depends on the number and distribution of relevance assessments. In this way it is possible to match only the annotations that are assessed relevant to at least one topic. This relationship causes that number to slightly change using different collections and we can state that the test collection obtained with the method presented in Section 4 can be used to simulate a collection with a limited number of annotations with respect to the number of documents. From the point of view of the evaluation, this result is already a good starting point that should enable an initial evaluation of the change in effectiveness of IRSs that use annotations.

The previous algorithm cannot decide anything about candidate annotations that are still in the pool but are not relevant to any topic, because, for construction, in graph G_1 they are not connected to any topic. Despite this, in the original collection there still exists a certain number of candidate annotations that could be correctly used to annotate documents in D. This Section presents a practical justification for their existence. The idea is to build the graph using not only the relevance assessments but also all the information contained in the original test collection, like the information on the documents that entered the pool, the content of both documents and annotations, and, if they exist, metadata about the documents.

We define A_2 as the set of effective annotations identified with the previous algorithm and E_2 as the edges incident to A_2. We define $G_2 = G(V/A_2, E/E_2)$ where G_2 is the graph obtained using the whole pool for each topic in the original collection and removing, due to the annotation constraint, all the candidate annotations already matched. In this new graph we have, for each topic, a set of documents and annotations that are no longer judged relevant to the topic, since those relevant were already assigned by the previous algorithm, but that are still valuable. Consider the graph that represents all documents of G_2 inserted in the pool for a single topic. It is possible to group the vertex of the graph in subsets on the basis of the document contents. For each subset a new topic is ideally created. These new topics are called *subtopic* $S_1, S_2, \ldots, S_k$. The attention is no longer focused on the relevance of documents or annotations to the original topic – since we know by construction that it is not possible – but is focused on finding the couples

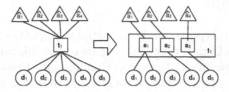

Fig. 5. Subtopic creation

(document, annotation) that are somehow relevant to the same subtopic, like $(d_1, \hat{a}_1)$ and $(d_2, \hat{a}_1)$ in Figure 5.

The following example from a CLEF[1] collection can help to better understand the concept of subtopic. The original topic t is about "Alberto Tomba's skiing victories". The IRSs used to create the pool with the pooling method introduced in the pool for this topic not only relevant documents but also not relevant ones. These not relevant documents can be grouped on the basis of their content in subtopics like "Documents about skiing competitions where Alberto Tomba does not participates" (S_1), "Documents about skiing competitions where Alberto Tomba participates without winning" (S_2) or 'Documents about the social life of Alberto Tomba" (S_3).

It would be useful to find the documents $d_i \in D, \hat{a}_j \in \hat{A}$ where both d_i and $\hat{a}_j$ are incident to the same subtopic S_k. Then the candidate annotations $\hat{a}_j$ could be used to correctly annotate documents d_i. It is important to stress that the goal is not to identify these subtopics, but to find documents that belong to the same cluster. The existence of these subtopics can be used as a practical justification for the algorithm proposed in [7]. Clearly, it is not trivial to find documents and annotations relevant to the same subtopic without knowing these subtopics and to this aim the previous algorithm cannot be used because it relies on human assessments that simply do not exist for subtopics.

6   Conclusions and Future Work

In this paper we pointed out the lack of adequate test collections as the main cause for the incomplete evaluation of IRSs that use annotations to increase system effectiveness. A new and completely automated approach to the creation of necessary test collections has been proposed. The approach is based on an already existing test collection, without annotations, and automatically adds annotations to the collection documents. The reliability of the created test collection is based on the reliability of relevance assessments made by human assessors and hence it has the same quality as the original test collection. The approach is not confined to the creation of a single test collection, but it can be used to create different test collections with different characteristics. The natural continuation of this work is the evaluation of existing systems with the final aim of understanding whether or not the annotations can play an important role in increasing the IRSs effectiveness.

---

[1] http://www.clef-campaign.org/

Acknowledgements

The work reported in this paper has been partially supported by the DELOS Network of Excellence on Digital Libraries, as part of the Information Society Technologies (IST) Program of the European Commission (Contract G038-507618). The work of Tullio Coppotelli was partially supported by a grant of MicroWave Network S.p.A., Padua, Italy.

References

1. Ioannidis, Y., Maier, D., Abiteboul, S., Buneman, P., Davidson, S., Fox, E.A., Halevy, A., Knoblock, C., Rabitti, F., Schek, H.J., Weikum, G.: Digital library information-technology infrastructures. International Journal on Digital Libraries 5, 266–274 (2005)
2. Agosti, M., Ferro, N.: Annotations as Context for Searching Documents. In: Crestani, F., Ruthven, I. (eds.) CoLIS 2005. LNCS, vol. 3507, pp. 155–170. Springer, Heidelberg (2005)
3. Frommholz, I.: Annotation-based document retrieval with probabilistic logics. In: Fuhr, N., Kovacs, L., Meghini, C. (eds.) ECDL 2007. Proc. 11th European Conference on Research and Advanced Technology for Digital Libraries. LNCS, vol. 4675, pp. 321–332. Springer, Heidelberg (2007)
4. Voorhees, E.M., Harman, D.K. (eds.): TREC: Experiment and Evaluation in Information Retrieval. MIT Press, Cambridge (2005)
5. Coppotelli, T.: Creazione di una collezione sperimentale per la valutazione di sistemi di reperimento dell'informazione che utilizzino le annotazioni (in Italian). Master's thesis, Department of Information Engineering, University of Padua (2006)
6. Agosti, M., Coppotelli, T., Ferro, N., Pretto, L.: Exploiting relevance assessments for the creation of an experimental test collection to evaluate systems that use annotations. In: DELOS Conference, Pisa, Italy, pp. 195–202 (2007)
7. Agosti, M., Coppotelli, T., Ferro, N., Pretto, L.: Annotations and digital libraries: Designing adequate test-beds. In: Goh, D.H., Cao, T., Sølvberg, I., Rasmussen, E. (eds.) ICADL 2007. Proc. 10th International Conference on Asian Digital Libraries. LNCS, Springer, Heidelberg (in print, 2007)
8. Ferro, N.: Digital annotations: a formal model and its applications. In: Agosti, M. (ed.) Information Access through Search Engines and Digital Libraries, pp. 113–146. Springer, Heidelberg (in print, 2008)

Evaluation and Requirements Elicitation of a DL Annotation System for Collaborative Information Sharing

Preben Hansen[1], Annelise Mark Pejtersen[2], and Hanne Albrechtsen[3]

[1] Swedish Institute of Computer Science, Sweden
preben@sics.se
[2] Center of Cognitive Systems Engineering, Denmark
ampcse@mail.dk
[3] Institute of Knowledge Sharing, Denmark
hanne.albrechtsen@knowshare.dk

Abstract. We describe an expert evaluation for user requirement elicitation of an annotation system - The Digital Library Annotation Service, DiLAS, that facilitates collaborative information access and sharing. An analytical evaluation was conducted as a Participatory Group Evaluation, which involved presentation beyond the written papers of the objectives and rationale behind the development of the prototype. The empirical evaluation of DiLAS consisted of two experiments. The first evaluation experiment was a bottom up evaluation of the usability of the interface using a qualitative approach. The second stage of our evaluation moved towards a broader work context with a User and Work Centred Evaluation involving an entire, collaborative task situation, which required knowledge sharing on a common real life work task. This paper describes a first evaluation stage in an iterative evaluation process, and the preliminary result is a set of requirements that will inform the next stage of the DiLAS.

Keywords: Collaborative Knowledge Sharing, Evaluation, Work Task, Annotation, Design, Usability, Requirement Elicitation.

1 Introduction

Most contemporary digital libraries are repositories of information items whose contents can be searched or browsed by the user. However, when the users' activity is part of a larger problem solving or work process, searching and browsing of repositories is often not sufficient, since complex problem solving tasks often requires collaboration and sharing of knowledge with other users. Accordingly, a digital library should actively support activities such as collaboration and communication among users through implementing particular facilities and services to improve collaborative knowledge creation and sharing during work.

A digital library can support problem solving and work tasks in many different ways and one such facility for an active support of collaboration, communication and knowledge sharing in digital libraries is the availability of annotation functions. An

C. Thanos, F. Borri, and L. Candela (Eds.): Digital Libraries: R&D, LNCS 4877, pp. 177–186, 2007.

annotation functions may allow the users to collaborate naturally without loosing support from the digital library. Furthermore, it may also provide the users with the option of managing annotations across different digital libraries, i.e. independently of a particular digital library.

A more in-depth understanding of different user and task-related aspects such as domain and task knowledge and user-related experience and preferences of the use of the annotation system for collaborative information sharing through empirical investigation is needed. User requirement elicitation is usually performed prior to the main design phase, or at least in the beginning stages if the design of a prototype version of a system or a system component. An empirical user requirement elicitation and evaluation of DiLAS prototypes with user and with work-tasks studies in focus, will therefore inform the design as an ongoing, *iterative process*, concurrently with the development of the next prototypes in response to the users' evaluations of each new design. The DiLAS prototype will be developed as an iterative process using a *participatory design and evaluation process* with the participation of users, developers, designers and evaluators.

This paper describes a first evaluation stage in a iterative evaluation process, and the results should be considered as preliminary and as a first part that will be concluded by a future end-user evaluation The result is a set of requirements that will inform the next stage of the DiLAS.

2 Digital Libraries and Annotations

2.1 Annotations

Annotations [e.g. 1, 2, 3, 4, 5 and 6] may be considered as a more or less structured interactive user input to a document or a set of documents. This input could be in different forms and is considered as new content of the digital library. In a Digital Library, this annotation may be done by the author of the content or by any other person using the digital library, driven by a number of different motivations. Annotations gives explanations, comments and even personal remarks to a certain document or specific section or sentence and word. Annotation work can also be more or less structured user information on a research topic for which documents are searched and annotations are made. Constructing or answering annotations are not an isolated task; on the contrary, it is embedded in the work task and therefore the construction of an annotation not be separated from the actual task at hand.

Two examples of systems that have developed annotation functionality are: *Collate*, a Collaboratory for Annotation, Indexing and Retrieval of Digitized Historical Archive Material[1], that has a collaborative annotation function similar to DiLAS. The model for knowledge sharing of annotation content has been adopted from linguistic discourse theories [7, 8 and 9]. The second example is taken from empirical analysis of the role of annotations within a large worldwide software company. The project was about studying collaborative aspects of a combined recommendation and annotation tool. The goal was to enhance a business system with a tool for more effective collaboration and cooperation within a specific work-group

---

[1] www.collate.de

such as assigning and searching for experts and knowledgeable people. The purpose was to collect data on: potential expert users: characteristics and needs; different tasks: goals, workflows, current practices, etc. [10 and 11].

2.2 Collaborations and Information Sharing

In order to establish and implement a networked and distributed collaborative annotation system, it is necessary to investigate how the interaction of sharing knowledge on documents and knowledge on work tasks can be facilitated. The sharing of information and collaboration between users is performed in a distributed environment with users that have different domain and task knowledge and different experiences and preferences as well as different social and cultural backgrounds. A more in-depth understanding of these user and task-related aspects of the annotation system for collaborative information sharing are needed through empirical studies. Furthermore, one prevailing assumption is that information access activities are viewed as an *individual activity* and that people are acting in *isolation*. Sharing and handling information in digital libraries can actually lead to social activities [12] is described and [13] discusses sharing information and sharing search results within group situations at four levels: sharing results with other members of a team; self-initiated broadcasting of interesting information; acting as a consultant and handling search requests made by others; and archiving potentially useful information into group repositories. A set of data collection methods used in a real life work setting investigating the information seeking and retrieval processes performed by patent engineers is described in [11]. Some results were that the patent engineers were involved in activities such as collaboration related to internal or external activities and related to individual or group related activities. The importance of providing support for people when searching information systems is reported in [14]. Two case studies were conducted involving engineers and the authors found that people searched for documents to find people and searched for people to obtain documents. Furthermore, they interacted socially to acquire information without engaging in any explicit search activity. It is necessary to consider that there is a need to consult people with specific competencies and experiences. These findings provide further knowledge on that people do engage in collaborative information seeking and retrieval activities.

2.3 DL Systems and Evaluation

In a model of a DL that includes annotation facilities, the system is not only used as a information retrieval and storage device, but can more be described as a collaborative and sharing environment, which is intended to support a more dynamic usage of digital assets by providing annotation functionality. In general, there are 2 types of evaluation approaches that may be applied in a design process: the *formative* and the *summative* evaluation approach. The former evaluation approach involves a close cooperation with the design process in order e.g. to check that the ideas applied are still working with focus on usability and usefulness during the design process. The summative approach is generally product-oriented and is applied in the end of a project when a product has been developed. The evaluation of the DiLAS annotation system will be performed as a formative user-centered evaluation. By definition, user-centered design techniques focus on potential users and their characteristics, their tasks, and their environment whose work is to be supported by an application. This means that functional requirements will be developed based on the user's viewpoint and are referred as user requirements.

Heuristic evaluation [15] enables the evaluators to detect usability problems in an interface based on screen mock-ups or a running system. Heuristic evaluation recommends that a small group of evaluators inspect the system. In addition, Nielsen has found that the effectiveness of heuristic evaluation can be substantially improved by having usability specialists as evaluators. *Cognitive Walkthrough* [16] usually involves the simulation of a user's problem-solving process in a human-computer dialog. Cognitive Walkthrough belongs to a group of *usability inspection methods*, and is more oriented towards evaluation of an interface, but may also highlight larger issues such as how to support user tasks on the *functionality* level [17]. The goal is to detect problems early in the design process so that they may be attended to in good time. Cognitive Walkthrough is a structured and systematic usability inspection method in contrast to for example to heuristic evaluation methods. Walkthroughs of software code follow a standard procedure with a sequence of actions for checking up on particular characteristics and conventions for the code. One important aspect of a Cognitive Walkthrough is the development of a scenario [17] description. Such a scenario may be divided into a sequence of subtasks and actions to be followed. In this way, Cognitive Walkthrough is usually scenario-driven and is ultimately aimed to answer questions about utility and usability of the functionality and design components. *Participatory design* originated in Scandinavia in the 1970s as an approach to involving users directly into the design of information systems [18 and 19]. Participatory Design differs from the related approach of user-centered design in that Participatory Design is design *by* users, whereas user-centered design is *for* users [20]. Participatory Evaluation emphasises the relationship and mutual understanding between the actors in the design process, i.e. between the designers and the prospective users, as well as the designers' and users' individual and inter-subjective reflections about the design process. The evaluators' role is to some degree an instrumental one: to understand the users' needs (through field studies and field experiments) and the developers' ideas and constraints for design. Pejtersen & Rasmussen's work-based evaluation framework [21] attaches primary importance to evaluation of the match between what the system provides and what users need.

In conclusion, it is important to be aware that it is rare for an evaluation or design process to adopt only one method. It is usually a combination of several different methods and evaluation techniques. This is also what is reported in this study.

3   Digital Library Annotations System - DiLAS

The overall goal of DELOS project is to contribute to the development of services for social infrastructures in digital libraries, in terms of services for users' knowledge creation, knowledge sharing and interactive communication. The DiLAS Annotation Service has been integrated into *DAFFODIL*[2] and *MADCOW* [22]. The DiLAS

---

[2] www.daffodil.de/

prototype1 is developed as an add-on facility to the agent-based Daffodil front-end and the MADCOW interface. *Daffodil* (Distributed Agents for User-Friendly Access of Digital Libraries [4] is targeted at the support of the digital library life cycle. Besides publications, users can access and manage relevant conferences, journals and also persons and can be extended with new functionality and services. MADCOW (Multimedia Annotation of Digital Content Over the Web) is the only system that has the functionality of searching annotations, and this function that is accessible in DiLAS. As the design of MADCOW separates platform-independent from platform specific components, it can be implemented as an integration of different browsers (on the client side) and different web servers (on the server side).

In the first stage The DiLAS prototype 1 will serve individual and collaborative work in the Computer Science and Information Science area. For example, the following work tasks may be supported by an annotation functionality: a) writing a thesis and organize relevant literature (summaries and comments); b) collaboratively prepare a submission of a project proposal; and c) reviewing articles. The annotation system of the digital library becomes an open and dynamic work environment. The users are free to choose their own communicative discourse during knowledge sharing activities within the digital library.

DiLAS is designed as a new functionality embedded in the Daffodil system's services. The following gives a short description of the interface actions that the user can perform:

- a) Creating and Viewing Annotations;
- b)   Save annotations in folders;
- c) Browse annotations;
- d) Make relationships among annotations;
- e) List annotations;
- f) Modify and delete annotations; and
- g) Search annotations.

4 Evaluation Methodology

The DiLAS evaluation will investigate how well the prototype can encourage the users' collaboration through annotation as well as their individual and joint contributions to the content of a digital library. It will also guide the implementation of modifications to the interface and annotation functions of the DiLAS Prototype 1 and will investigate:

- i)   the annotation facilities and how users can get access to these facilities;
- ii)   how well the users can understand the interface of the prototype;
- iii)   requirements for modification, based on the results from the evaluation experiments.

The evaluation builds on a formative work and user-centered evaluation and a general conceptual framework for the user-centered design process will guide the work: (figure 1):

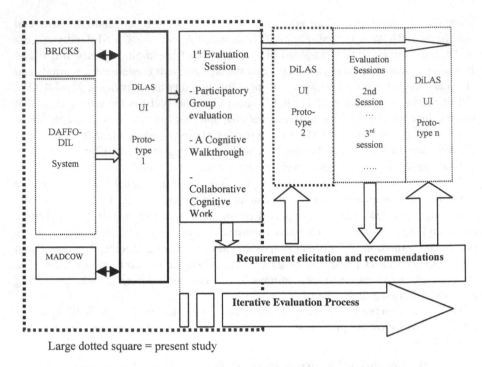

Large dotted square = present study

Fig. 1. General conceptual framework of design stages for DiLAS

4.1   Three Evaluation Experiments with DiLAS

For this purpose, three different methods are applied in three distinct experiments:

- *A Cognitive Walkthrough*
- *A Participatory Group Evaluation,*
- *An evaluation of DiLAS annotations in collaborative work*

The first experiment was a bottom up evaluation that began at the elementary level with an evaluation of the readability of the interface to test if the interface information was understandable. It moved on to a top down evaluation of the overall DiLAS design objectives and their implementation in the DiLAS prototype 1 and the developers' plans for the development of a richer functionality in the forthcoming DiLAS prototypes. Finally, the evaluation moved towards the broader work context with an evaluation involving an entire, collaborative task situation.

Experiment 1: Cognitive Walkthrough of DILAS 1
The Cognitive Walkthrough of the prototype was without any formal evaluation format, it was documented by use of a free form of writing down observations as the task progressed. The focus of the Cognitive Walk Through was on the sequence of actions that the user interface required the user to perform in order to accomplish the user's task. The user did not have a description of the DiLAS prototype, since an actual complete description of the interface of the prototype does not exist yet. The user went through the steps of actions to take and encountered problems and made

observations that were written down. Some examples of sequences of action and observations are described below.

Experiment 2: Participatory Group Evaluation of DiLAS
The second evaluation experiment was to learn what DiLAS was really about and to be informed about the developers' design rationale concerning functionality and interface displays by the expert system developer. There were four participants in this evaluation. The participatory group evaluation took place during the first day of the collaborative evaluation workshop that took place in Copenhagen in May 2006. The developer presented slides, which was followed by a demonstration of a running DiLAS prototype along with a discussion with the evaluators.

Experiment 3: Evaluation of DiLAS Annotations in collaborative work
The evaluation was based on a *realistic work situation* for the collaborating evaluators. There was no discussion of planning of search or tactics and strategies, and after conducting the searches and creating annotations, the group gathered to share their experiences with use of the annotation function of DiLAS, to discuss their different proposals for new requirements and finally reach a consensus. The common work task that the expert evaluators chose to work with together was their own work on the evaluation of DiLAS prototype 1.

The task used in this experiment was to search for literature on annotation tools in a collaborative way, since it was necessary to have a chapter in the final report on related work. The evaluators used three strategies:

- Evaluator #1: defining the research and development context of the DiLAS Annotation.
- Evaluator #2 decided to perform a *subject search on creation of annotations*
- Evaluator #3 chose to *search only on the subject term of annotation*

All three evaluators used paper to record their searches and the process of annotations. They also recorded the problems they encountered during their use of DiLAS. The problems they identified were often followed by ideas for new requirements to the next DiLAS prototype.

5   Results

The *1st experiment* using a Cognitive Walkthrough was applied to determine the possibilities and problems that a users may encounter when using the DiLAS prototype. Together with *experiment number two* (A Participatory Group Evaluation), which involved presentation of the design rationale and reflections behind the development of the prototype, the experiments revealed some comprehensive insight into The DiLAS Prototype:

- *Create Annotations.* It becomes particularly important to make sure that different users easily and successfully could create annotations in an easy way.

- *Create a specific category of annotation.* It will be necessary to investigate whether the present categories corresponds to the users' cognitive activities and their way of thinking about their annotations.
- *New perspectives on annotations.* Annotations can have new, unpredicted functions. As the annotations can be applied as the users' own representation of the document contents, they can also function as another kind of representations of documents, which can support the user's subject access to information

The *third experiment* resulted in a set of requirements. The requirements mainly deal with the users' tasks and extended functionality or new functions that address the need for a more comprehensive support of the collaborative function and the integrated nature of the information retrieval task, the annotation task and the real life work task in which the annotation tasks are undertaken as part of an ongoing collaborative process. The short-term requirements that are listed below are those changes that the evaluators proposed to be implemented before the final and upcoming end user evaluation.

The list of all short-term requirements were grouped according the following main functions: 1) Search and retrieve annotations; 2) Create annotations; 3) Modify and delete annotations; 4) List annotations; and 5) Browse Annotations. The following example of short-term requirements relates to collaborative work:

Access levels. In more complex and distributed environment, it may be necessary to have different access levels. Depending on the role you have in a group, you may be able to access a specific set of information. The different levels may be related to: a) Global level; b) Organisational level; c) Group level; and d) Individual level

Access to the create annotation function. Create new annotation button should be visible, accessible and active all the time. The CREATE function should support: a) Create an annotation (present); b) Creating a folder for set of people working and having access to that folder (authority functionality); c) Create a communication channel such as opening an e-mail or chat programme; and d) Create a working document for which a person can keep track on the annotations made

On-line/Off-line Collaboration. The assumption of DiLAS prototype 1 is that the group work is taking place *off-line* and that it is asynchronous, which means that when a person has a need for information, the person will search DiLAS to find a known item and/or using free text for a subject matter search, and then make an annotation when it is felt to be suitable. However, the task performance of our group showed that the assumptions about collaboration behind DiLAS are too limited, when it comes to online, *synchronous* group work where the *simultaneous* and *dynamic* creation and sharing of the new knowledge is a must. It is necessary for a group working together to create a common workspace. The workspace needs to have different authority levels and access mechanisms depending on the status of the collaborators. There should be functionalities supporting people within a group to create: a) Documents (object) to work on; b) Creating new material (support for knowledge creation); and c) Ways of sharing information and knowledge. It should be possible to notify collaborating users about an annotation *that is related to a common task.* This is relevant for all kinds of annotations, including those that are authored by other users, and which are found to be relevant for the common task.

6 Conclusion

The main topic of this paper is the initial evaluation and (re)design requirements to the first DiLAS prototype. The result was an extensive list of short-term requirements and as well as a long-term requirements (not reported here). In this paper we presented and discussed the short-term list. Short-term requirements are absolutely necessary to implement before the end user evaluation within a minimum of functions. A new design of a DiLAS prototype 2 based on the short-term requirements are already in place together with a planning of a larger evaluation experiment with non-expert end users. DiLAS is, in its present phase, focused on textual annotations made by users. However, it is the future goal to offer access for users to *annotate several types of digital objects* managed by Daffodil/MADCOW besides the current possibility for annotation of documents. It is also the future plan for DiLAS to distinguish between levels of access to annotations, in terms of public, shared and private annotations. Presently, all annotations are public. Likewise, the developers of DiLAS plan to create support for discussions between users through shared and nested annotations.

Acknowledgement

This work was funded in part by the DELOS Network of Excellence on Digital Libraries project (www.delos.info/) sponsored by the European Commission as part of the Information Society Technologies (IST) programme under EC grant number IST-FP6-507618.

References

1. Pejtersen, A.M., Hansen, P., Albrechtsen, H.: A Work Centered Approach to Evaluation of a DL Annotation System for Knowledge Sharing in Collaborative Work. In: ICDL. Proceedings of the International Conference on Digital Libraries, December 5-8, 2006, vol. I, pp. 78–90. TERI, New Delhi (2006)
2. Agosti, M., Ferro, N.: Annotations as Context for Searching Documents. In: Crestani, F., Ruthven, I. (eds.) CoLIS 2005. LNCS, vol. 3507, pp. 155–170. Springer, Heidelberg (2005)
3. Marshall, C., Brush, A.J.: Exploring the relationship between personal and public annotations. In: Proceedings of the 4th ACM/IEEE-CS joint conference on Digital libraries, Tucson, AZ, USA, pp. 349–357. ACM Press, New York (2004)
4. Klas, C.-P., Fuhr, N., Schaefer, A.: Evaluating Strategic Support for Information Access in the DAFFODIL System. In: Heery, R., Lyon, L. (eds.) ECDL 2004. LNCS, vol. 3232, pp. 476–487. Springer, Heidelberg (2004)
5. Shipman, F., Hsieh, H., Moore, M., Zacchi, A.: Supporting personal collections across digital libraries in spatial hypertext. In: Proceedings of the 4th ACM/IEEE-CS joint conference on Digital libraries, Tucson, AZ, USA, pp. 358–367. ACM Press, Tucson (2004)

6. Golovchinsky, G., Price, M.N., Schilit, B.: From reading to retrieval: freeform ink annotations as queries. In: Proceedings of the 22nd annual international ACM SIGIR conference on Research and development in information retrieval, Berkeley, California, United States, pp. 19 – 25 (1999)
7. Cleal, B.R., Andersen, H.H.K., Albrechtsen, H.: Collaboration, communication and categorical complexity: A case study in collaboratory evaluation. J. Digital Inf. Manag. 2(1), 13–20 (2004)
8. Frommholz, I., Brocks, H., Thiel, U., Neuhold, E., Iannone, L., Semeraro, G., Berardi, M., Ceci, M.: Document-Centered Collaboration for Scholars in the Humanities - The COLLATE System. In: Koch, T., Sølvberg, I.T. (eds.) ECDL 2003. LNCS, vol. 2769, pp. 434–445. Springer, Heidelberg (2003)
9. Pejtersen, A.M., Albrechtsen, H., Cleal, B., Hansen, C.B., Hertzum, M.: A Web-based Multimedia Collaboratory. Empirical Work Studies in Film Archives. Roskilde: Risø National Laboratory (2001)
10. Hansen, P., Järvelin, K.: Collaborative Information Searching in an Information-Intensive Work Domain: Preliminary Results. Journal of Digital Information Management 2(1), 26–30 (2004)
11. Hansen, P., Järvelin, K.: Collaborative Information Retrieval in an information-intensive domain. Information Processing & Management 41(5), 1101–1119 (2005)
12. Marshall, C., Bly, S.: Sharing encountered information: digital libraries get a social life. In: Proceedings of the 4th ACM/IEEE- joint conference on Digital libraries, Tuscon, AZ, USA, pp. 218–227. ACM Press, New York (2004)
13. O'Day, V., Jeffries, R.: Information artisans: Patterns of Result Sharing by Information Searchers. In: COOCS 1993. Proceedings of the ACM Conference on Organizational Computing Systems, November 1-4, 1993, pp. 98–107. ACM Press, Milpitas, CA, New York (1993)
14. Hertzum, M.: People as Carriers of Experience and Sources of Commitment: Information Seeking in a Software Design Project. New Review of Information Behaviour Research 1, 135–149 (2000)
15. Nielsen, J., Mack, R.: Usability Inspection Methods. Wiley, New York (1994)
16. Lewis, Wharton: Cognitive walkthroughs: a method for theory-based evaluation of user interfaces. Journal of Man-Machine Studies 36(5), 741–773 (1997)   ´
17. Carroll, J.M.: Scenario-based Design. In: Envisioning Work and Technology in System Development, Wiley, New York (1995)
18. Greebaum, J., Kyng, M.: Design at Work: Cooperative Design of Computer Systems. Lawrence Erlbaum Associates, Hillsdale, N.J (1991)
19. Spinuzzi, C.: The Methodology of Participatory Design. Technical Communication 52(2), 163–174 (2005)
20. Winograd, T.: Bringing Design to Software. Addison-Wesley, Reading (1996)
21. Rasmussen, J., Pejtersen, A.M., Goodstein, L.P.: Cognitive Systems Engineering. John Wiley & Sons, New York (1994)
22. Bottoni, P., Civica, R., Levialdi, S., Orso, L., Panizzi, E., Trinchese, R.: MADCOW: a Multimedia Digital Annotation System. In: AVI 2004. Proc. Working Conference on Advanced Visual Interfaces, pp. 55–62. ACM Press, New York (2004)

INEX 2002 - 2006: Understanding XML Retrieval Evaluation

Mounia Lalmas and Anastasios Tombros

Queen Mary University of London,
Mile End Road, London, UK
{mounia,tassos}@dcs.qmul.ac.uk

Abstract. Evaluating the effectiveness of XML retrieval requires building test collections where the evaluation paradigms are provided according to criteria that take into account structural aspects. The INitiative for the Evaluation of XML retrieval (INEX) was set up in 2002, and aimed to establish an infrastructure and to provide means, in the form of large test collections and appropriate scoring methods, for evaluating the effectiveness of content-oriented XML retrieval. This paper describes the evaluation methodology developed in INEX, with particular focus on how evaluation metrics and the notion of relevance are treated.

1 Introduction

The continuous growth in XML information repositories has been matched by increasing efforts in the development of XML retrieval systems, in large part aiming at supporting content-oriented XML retrieval. These systems exploit the available structural information in documents, as marked up in XML, in order to implement a more *focussed* retrieval strategy and return document components – the so-called *XML elements* – instead of complete documents in response to a user query. This focussed retrieval approach is of particular benefit for information repositories containing long documents, or documents covering a wide variety of topics (e.g. books, user manuals, legal documents), where users' effort to locate relevant content can be reduced by directing them to the most relevant parts of these documents. As the number of XML retrieval systems increases, so does the need to evaluate their effectiveness.

The predominant approach to evaluate system retrieval effectiveness is with the use of test collections constructed specifically for that purpose. A test collection usually consists of a set of documents, user requests usually referred to as topics, and relevance assessments which specify the set of "right answers" for the user requests. Traditional IR test collections and methodology, however, cannot directly be applied to the evaluation of content-oriented XML retrieval as they do not consider structure. This is because they focus mainly on the evaluation of IR systems that treat documents as independent and well-distinguishable separate units of approximately equal size. Since content-oriented XML retrieval allows for document components to be retrieved, multiple elements from the same document can hardly be viewed as independent units. When allowing for the retrieval of arbitrary elements, we must also consider the overlap of elements; e.g. retrieving a complete section consisting of several paragraphs as

C. Thanos, F. Borri, and L. Candela (Eds.): Digital Libraries: R&D, LNCS 4877, pp. 187–196, 2007.
© Springer-Verlag Berlin Heidelberg 2007

one element and then a paragraph within the section as a second element. This means that retrieved elements cannot always be regarded as separate units. Finally, the size of the retrieved elements should be considered, especially due to the task definition; e.g. retrieve minimum or maximum units answering the query, retrieve a component from which we can access, or browse to, a maximum number of units answering the query.

The evaluation of XML retrieval systems thus makes it necessary to build test collections where the evaluation paradigms are provided according to criteria that take into account the imposed structural aspects. The INitiative for the Evaluation of XML retrieval (INEX)[1], which was set up in 2002, established an infrastructure and provided means, in the form of large test collections and appropriate scoring methods, for evaluating how effective content-oriented XML search systems are. This paper provides a detailed overview of the evaluation methodology developed in INEX, with particular focus on the treatment of the notion of relevance and on metrics for the evaluation of retrieval effectiveness.

2   The INEX Test-Beds

In traditional IR test collections, documents are considered as units of unstructured text, queries are generally treated as bags of terms or phrases, and relevance assessments provide judgments whether a document as a whole is relevant to a query or not. Although a test collection for XML IR consists of the same parts, each component is rather different from its traditional IR counterpart. XML documents organise their content into smaller, nested structural elements. Each of these elements in the document's hierarchy, along with the document itself (the root of the hierarchy), represent a retrievable unit. In addition, with the use of XML query languages, users of an XML IR system can express their information need as a combination of content and structural conditions. Consequently, relevance assessments for an XML collection must also consider the structural nature of the documents and provide assessments at different levels of the document hierarchy.

2.1   Document Collections

Up to 2004, the collection consisted of 12,107 articles, marked-up in XML, from 12 magazines and 6 transactions of the IEEE Computer Society's publications, covering the period of 1995-2002, totalling 494 MB in size and 8 million in number of elements. On average, an article contains 1,532 XML nodes, where the average depth of the node is 6.9. In 2005, the collection was extended with further publications from the IEEE. A total of 4,712 new articles from the period of 2002-2004 were added, giving a total of 16,819 articles, and totalling 764MB in size and 11 million in number of elements.

INEX 2006 uses a different document collection, made from English documents from Wikipedia[2] [2]. The collection consists of the full-texts, marked-up in XML, of 659,388 articles of the Wikipedia project, and totaling more than 60 GB (4.6 GB without

---

[1] http://inex.is.informatik.uni-duisburg.de/
[2] http://en.wikipedia.org

images) and 52 million in number of elements. The collection has a structure similar to the IEEE collection. On average, an article contains 161.35 XML nodes, where the average depth of an element is 6.72.

2.2 Topics

Querying XML documents can be with respect to content and structure. Taking this into account, INEX identified two types of topics:

- *Content-only (CO)* topics are requests that ignore the document structure and are, in a sense, the traditional topics used in IR test collections. In XML retrieval, the retrieval results to such topics can be elements of various complexity, e.g. at different levels of the XML documents' structure.
- *Content-and-structure (CAS)* topics are requests that contain conditions referring both to content and structure of the sought elements. These conditions may refer to the content of specific elements (e.g. the elements to be returned must contain a section about a particular topic), or may specify the type of the requested answer elements (e.g. sections should be retrieved).

CO and CAS topics reflect two types of users with varying levels of knowledge about the structure of the searched collection. The first type simulates users who either do not have any knowledge of the document structure or who choose not to use such knowledge. This profile is likely to fit most users searching XML repositories. The second type of users aims to make use of any insight about the document structure that they may possess. CAS topics simulate users who do have some knowledge of the structure of the searched collection. They may then use this knowledge as a precision enhancing device in trying to make the information need more concrete. This user type is more likely to fit, e.g., librarians.

As in TREC, an INEX topic consists of the standard title, description and narrative fields. For CO topics, the title is a sequence of terms. For CAS topics, the title is expressed using the NEXI query language, which is a variant of XPATH defined for content-oriented XML retrieval evaluation - it is more focussed on querying content than many of the XML query languages [9].

In 2005, in an effort to investigate the usefulness of structural constraints, variants of the CO and CAS topics were developed. CO topics were extended into Content-Only + Structure (CO+S) topics. The aim was to enable the performance comparison of an XML system across two retrieval scenarios on the same topic, one when structural constraints are taken into account (+S) and the other when these are ignored (CO). The CO+S topics included an optional field called CAS title (<castitle>), which was a representation of the same information need contained in the <title> field of a CO topic but including additional knowledge in the form of structural constraint. CAS titles were expressed in the NEXI query language.

How to interpret the structural constraints (whether as part of CAS or CO+S topics) evolved over the years, since each structural constraint could be considered as a strict (must be matched exactly) or vague (does not need to be matched exactly) criterion. In the latter case, structural constraints were to be viewed as hints as to where to look for relevant information. In 2002, the structural constraints of CAS topics were strictly interpreted. In 2003, both interpretations, strict and vague, were followed, whereas since 2004 only the latter was followed. As of today, INEX has a total of 401 topics.

2.3 Retrieval Tasks

The main INEX activity is the ad-hoc retrieval task. In IR literature, ad-hoc retrieval is described as a simulation of how a library might be used and involves the searching of a static set of documents using a new set of topics. Here, the collection consists of XML documents, composed of different granularity of nested XML elements, each of which represents a possible unit of retrieval. The user's query may also contain structural constraints, or hints, in addition to the content conditions.

A major departure from traditional IR is that XML retrieval systems need not only score elements with respect to their relevance to a query, but also determine the appropriate level of element granularity to return to users. In INEX, a relevant element is defined to be at the *right level of granularity* if it discusses all the topics requested in the user query – it is *exhaustive* to the query – *and* does not discuss other topics – it is *specific* to that query.

Up to 2004, ad-hoc retrieval was defined as the *general* task of returning, instead of whole documents, those XML elements that are most specific and exhaustive to the user's query. In other words, systems should return components that contain as much relevant information and as little irrelevant information as possible. Within this general task, several sub-tasks were defined, where the main difference was the treatment of the structural constraints.

The *CO sub-task* makes use of the CO topics, where an effective system is one that retrieves the most specific elements, and only those which are relevant to the topic of request. The *CAS sub-task* makes use of CAS topics, where an effective system is one that retrieves the most specific document components, which are relevant to the topic of request and match, either strictly or vaguely, the structural constraints specified in the query. In 2002, a strict interpretation of the CAS structural constraints was adopted, whereas in 2003, both, a strict and a vague interpretation was followed, leading to the *SCAS sub-task* (strict content-and-structure), defined as for the INEX 2002 CAS sub-task, and the *VCAS sub-task* (vague content-and-structure). In that last sub-task, the goal of an XML retrieval system was to return relevant elements that may not exactly conform to the structural conditions expressed within the user's query, but where the path specifications should be considered hints as to where to look. In 2004, the two sub-tasks investigated were the CO sub-task, and the VCAS sub-task. The SCAS sub-task was felt to be an unrealistic task because specifying an information need is not an easy task, in particular for semi-structured data with a wide variety of tag names.

However, within this general task, the actual relationship between retrieved elements was not considered, and many systems returned overlapping elements (e.g. nested elements). Indeed, the top 10 ranked systems for the CO sub-task in INEX 2004 contained between 70% to 80% overlapping elements. This had very strong implications with respect to measuring effectiveness (Section 3), where approaches that attempted to implement a more focussed approach (e.g., between two nested relevant elements, return the one most specific to the query) performed poorly. As a result, the *focussed sub-task* was defined in 2005, intended for approaches aiming at targeting the appropriate level of granularity of relevant content that should be returned to the user for a given topic. The aim was for systems to find the most exhaustive and specific element on a path within a given document containing relevant information and return to the user only this most appropriate unit of retrieval. Returning overlapping elements was not permitted. The INEX ad-hoc general task, as carried out by most systems up to 2004, was renamed in 2005 as the *thorough sub-task*.

Within all the above sub-tasks, the output of XML retrieval systems was assumed to be a ranked list of XML elements, ordered by their presumed relevance to the query, whether overlapping elements were allowed or not. However, user studies [8] suggested that users were expecting to be returned elements grouped per document, and to have access to the overall context of an element. The *fetch & browse task* was introduced in 2005 for this reason. The aim was to first identify relevant documents (the fetching phase), and then to identify the most exhaustive and specific elements within the fetched documents (the browsing phase). In the fetching phase, documents had to be ranked according to how exhaustive and specific they were. In the browsing phase, ranking had to be done according to how exhaustive and specific the relevant elements in the document were, compared to other elements in the same document.

In 2006, the same task, renamed the *relevant in context sub-task*, required systems to return for each article an unranked set of non-overlapping elements, covering the relevant material in the document. In addition, a new task was introduced in 2006, the *best in context sub-task*, where the aim was to find the best-entry-point, here a single element, for starting to read articles with relevant information. This sub-task can be viewed as the extreme case of the fetch & browse approach, where only one element is returned per article.

2.4 Relevance

Most dictionaries define relevance as "pertinence to the matter at hand". In terms of IR, it is usually understood as the connection between a retrieved item and the user's query. In XML retrieval, the relationship between a retrieved item and the user's query is further complicated by the need to consider the structure in the documents. Since retrieved elements can be at any level of granularity, an element and one of its child elements can both be relevant to a given query, but the child element may be more focussed on the topic of the query than its parent element, which may contain additional irrelevant content. In this case, the child element is a better element to retrieve than its parent element, because not only it is relevant to the query, but it is also specific to the query. To accommodate the specificity aspect, INEX defined relevance along two dimensions:

- **Exhaustivity**, which measures how exhaustively an element discusses the topic of the user's request.
- **Specificity**, which measures the extent to which an element focuses on the topic of request (and not on other, irrelevant topics).

A multiple degree relevance scale was necessary to allow the explicit representation of how exhaustively a topic is discussed within an element with respect to its child elements. For example, a section containing two paragraphs may be regarded more relevant than either of its paragraphs by themselves. Binary values of relevance cannot reflect this difference. INEX therefore adopted a four-point relevance scale [4]:

- Not exhaustive: The element does not contain any information about the topic.
- Marginally exhaustive: The element mentions the topic, but only in passing.
- Fairly exhaustive: The element discusses the topic, but not exhaustively.
- Highly exhaustive: The element discusses the topic exhaustively.

As for exhaustivity, a multiple degree scale was also necessary for the specificity dimension. This is to allow to reward retrieval systems that are able to retrieve the appropriate ("exact") sized elements. For example, a retrieval system that is able to locate the only relevant section in a book is more effective than one that returns a whole chapter. A four-point relevance scale was adopted:

- Not specific: the topic is not a theme discussed in the element.
- Marginally specific: the topic is a minor theme discussed in the element.
- Fairly specific: the topic is a major theme discussed in the element.
- Highly specific: the topic is the only theme discussed in the element.

Based on the combination of exhaustivity and specificity, it becomes possible to identify those relevant elements which are both exhaustive and specific to the topic of request and hence represent the most appropriate unit to return to the user. In the evaluation we can then reward systems that are able to retrieve these elements.

Obtaining relevance assessments is a very tedious and costly task [6]. An observation made in [1] was that the assessment process could be simplified if first, relevant passages of text were identified by highlighting, and then the elements within these passages were assessed. As a consequence, at INEX 2005, the assessment method was changed, leading to the redefinition of the scales for specificity. The procedure was a two-phase process. In the first phase, assessors highlighted text fragments containing only relevant information. The specificity dimension was then automatically measured on a continuous scale [0,1], by calculating the ratio of the relevant content of an XML element: a completely highlighted element had a specificity value of 1, whereas a non-highlighted element had a specificity value of 0. For all other elements, the specificity value was defined as the ratio (in characters) of the highlighted text (i.e. relevant information) to the element size. For example, an element with specificity of 0.72 has 72% of its content highlighted.

In the second phase, for all elements within highlighted passages (and parent elements of those), assessors were asked to assess their exhaustivity. Following the outcomes of extensive statistical analysis of the INEX 2004 results [5] - which showed that in terms of comparing retrieval effectiveness the same conclusions could be drawn using a smaller number of grades for the exhaustivity dimension[3] - INEX 2005 adopted the following $3 + 1$ exhaustivity values:

---

[3] The same observation was reached for the specificity dimension, but as the assessment procedure was changed in INEX 2005, the new highlighting process allowed for a continuous scale of specificity to be calculated automatically.

- Highly exhaustive (2): the element discussed most, or all, aspects of the topic.
- Partly exhaustive (1): the element discussed only few aspects of the topic.
- Not exhaustive (0): the element did not discuss the topic.
- Too Small (?): the element contains relevant material but is too small to be relevant on it own.

The category of "too small" was introduced to allow assessors to label elements which, although contained relevant information, were too small to be able to sensibly reason about their level of exhaustivity. An extensive statistical analysis was performed on the INEX 2005 results [5], which showed that in terms of comparing retrieval performance, not using the exhaustivity dimension led to similar results. As a result, INEX 2006 dropped the exhaustivity dimension, and relevance was defined only along the specificity dimension.

3 Metrics

Measures of XML retrieval effectiveness must consider the dependency between elements. Unlike traditional IR, users in XML retrieval have access to other, structurally related elements from returned result elements. They may hence locate additional relevant information by browsing or scrolling. This motivates the need to consider so-called *near-misses*, which are elements from where users can access relevant content, within the evaluation. In this section, we restrict ourselves to the metrics used to evaluate the thorough and focussed sub-tasks, as the evaluation of the other sub-tasks is still an on-going research issue.

The effectiveness of most ad-hoc retrieval tasks is measured by the established and widely used precision and recall metrics, or their variants. When using this family of measures, if we consider near-misses when evaluating retrieval effectiveness, then systems that return *overlapping* elements (e.g. both a paragraph and its enclosing section) will be evaluated as more effective than those that do not return overlapping elements (e.g. either the paragraph or its enclosing section). If both the paragraph and its enclosing section are relevant, then this family of effectiveness measures will count both these nested elements as separate relevant components that increase the count of relevant and retrieved elements. Therefore, despite not retrieving entirely new relevant information, systems that favour the retrieval of overlapping components would receive higher effectiveness scores. To address this problem, INEX used the XCG measures, which are an extension of the Cumulative Gain (CG) based measures [3]. These measures are not based on a counting mechanisms, but on cumulative gains associated with returned results.

For each returned element, a gain value $xG[.]$ is calculated, which is a value in the interval $[0, 1]$. A value of 0 reflects no gain, 1 is the highest gain value, and values between 0 and 1 represent various gain levels. The gain value depends on the element's exhaustivity and specificity. Given that INEX employs two relevance dimensions, the gain value is calculated as a combination of these dimensions, thus reflecting the worth of a retrieved element. INEX uses *quantisation functions* to provide a relative ordering of the various combinations of exhaustivity and specificity values and a mapping of these to a single relevance scale in $[0, 1]$. Various quantisation functions have been used over the years as a means to model assumptions regarding the worth of retrieved elements to users or scenarios. For example, INEX 2003 used the quantisations defined below, where e and s stand, respectively, for exhaustivity and specificity.

$$quant_{strict}(e, s) := \begin{cases} 1 & \text{if } e = 3 \text{ and } s = 3, \\ 0 & \text{otherwise.} \end{cases} \tag{1}$$

The strict function is used to evaluate XML retrieval methods with respect to their capability of retrieving highly exhaustive and highly specific components.

$$quant_{gen}(e, s) := \begin{cases} 1 & \text{if } (e, s) = (3, 3), \\ 0.75 & \text{if } (e, s) \in \{(2, 3), (3, \{2, 1\})\}, \\ 0.5 & \text{if } (e, s) \in \{(1, 3), (2, \{2, 1\})\}, \\ 0.25 & \text{if } (e, s) \in \{(1, 2), (1, 1)\}, \\ 0 & \text{if } (e, s) = (0, 0). \end{cases} \tag{2}$$

The generalised function allows the reward of fairly and marginally relevant elements in the results. Other quantisations were introduced in subsequent years of INEX, emphasising specificity or exhaustivity. In [5], however, it is shown that, although quantisation functions express different user preferences, many of them behave similarly when ranking systems. As a consequence, one form of strict and one form of general quantisation functions have been used since 2005, and were modified to adapt to the new scale used in INEX 2005. In INEX 2006, as the exhaustivity dimension was dropped, the quantisation function simply maps an element to its specificity value.

Given a ranked list of elements e_j, each with their calculated gain value $xC[e_j] = quant(e_j)$ where $quant$ is a chosen quantisation function, the cumulative gain at rank i, denoted as $xCG[i]$, is computed as the sum of the relevance scores up to that rank:

$$xCG[i] := \sum_{j=1}^{i} xC(e_j)) \tag{3}$$

For each query, an ideal gain vector, xCI, is derived by filling the rank positions with $xG(c'_j))$ in decreasing order for all assessed elements c'_j. A retrieval run's xCG vector is compared to this ideal ranking by plotting both the actual and ideal cumulative gain functions against the rank position. Normalised xCG ($nxCG$) is:

$$nxCG[i] := \frac{xCG[i]}{xCI[i]} \tag{4}$$

For a given rank i, $nxCG[i]$ reflects the relative gain the user has accumulated up to that rank, compared to the gain he/she could have attained if the system would have produced the optimum best ranking, where 1 represents ideal performance.

XCG also defines effort-precision/gain-recall ($MAep$). The effort-precision ep at a given gain-recall value gr is defined as the number of visited ranks required to reach a given level of gain relative to the total gain that can be obtained, and is defined as:

$$ep[r] := \frac{i_{ideal}}{i_{run}} \tag{5}$$

where i_{ideal} is the rank position at which the cumulative gain of r is reached by the ideal curve and i_{run} is the rank position at which the cumulative gain of r is reached by the system run. A score of 1 reflects ideal performance, i.e. when the user needs to spend the minimum necessary effort to reach a given level of gain. The gain-recall gr is calculated as:

$$gr[i] := \frac{xCG[i]}{xCI[n]} = \frac{\sum_{j=1}^{i} xG[j]}{\sum_{j=1}^{n} xI[j]} \qquad (6)$$

where n is the number of elements c where $xC[c] > 0$. This method follows the same viewpoint as standard precision/recall, where recall is the control variable and precision the dependent variable. Here, the gain-recall is the control variable and effort-precision is the dependent variable. As with precision/recall, interpolation techniques are used to estimate effort-precision values at non-natural gain-recall points, e.g. when calculating effort-precision at standard recall points of $[0.1, 1]$, denoted as e.g. $ep@0.1$. For this purpose, a simple linear interpolation method is used. Also, the *non-interpolated mean average effort-precision*, denoted as *MAep*, is calculated by averaging the effort-precision values obtained for each rank where a relevant document is returned.

In the case of the thorough sub-task (when overlap is not an issue), the full recall-base is used to derive both the ideal gain vector xCI and the gain vectors, xCG.

For the focussed retrieval task, the elements in the ideal recall-base represent the desired target elements that should be retrieved, while all other elements in the full recall-base may be awarded partial scores. In this case, the ideal gain vector xCI is derived from the ideal recall-base, whereas the gain vectors, xCG, for the retrieval approaches under evaluation are based on the full recall-base to enable the scoring of near-miss elements. As any relevant elements of the full recall-base not included in the ideal recall-base are considered as near-misses, this strategy allows to support the evaluation viewpoint whereby elements in the ideal recall-base *should* be retrieved, whereas the retrieval of near-misses *could* be rewarded as partial success.

The construction of the ideal recall-base requires a preference function among exhaustivity and specificity value pairs. Quantisation functions are used for this purpose as these reflect the worth of retrieved elements. Given a chosen quantisation function, it is possible to quantify the value, or worth, of an element and identify the "best" components within an XML document as those elements with the highest quantised score. Also needed is a methodology for traversing an XML document (its tree structure) and selecting ideal elements based on their relative preference relations to their structurally related elements. The approach adopted in INEX, is to traverse the XML tree of a document bottom-up and to select the element with the highest quantised score. In the case where two elements have an equal score, the one higher in the XML structure is selected.

4   Conclusion

INEX has focused on developing an infrastructure, test collections, and appropriate scoring methods for evaluating the effectiveness of content-oriented XML retrieval. The initiative is now entering its sixth year, with INEX 2007 set to begin in April 2007. The major achievements in XML retrieval evaluation can be summarised as follows:

- A larger and more realistic test collection has been achieved with the addition of the Wikipedia documents. The content of the Wikipedia collection can also appeal to users with backgrounds other than computer science, making the carrying out of user studies with this collection more appropriate.
- A better understanding of information needs and retrieval scenarios. The set of retrieval tasks that were used at INEX 2006 is considered as a good representation of actual retrieval tasks that users of an XML retrieval system may wish to perform.
- A better understanding of how to measure the effectiveness of different retrieval systems by using appropriate metrics. In particular, we now have an understanding of how to deal with near-misses and overlapping elements, and which metrics to use under which retrieval assumptions.

In addition, INEX has been expanding in scope with the addition of a number of additional research tracks that tackle other IR problems related to XML documents. The additional tracks deal with issues such as retrieval of multimedia items, user interaction, retrieval from heterogeneous collections of documents, classification and clustering, etc. As an ongoing effort, empirical data about user behaviour for validating the effectiveness metrics are being considered. The current emphasis in INEX is to identify who the real users of XML retrieval systems are, how they might use retrieval systems and for which realistic tasks. A new research track, the user case studies track, is currently investigating this issue.

Acknowledgments. The authors would like to acknowledge the INEX organisers and participants for their valuable contributions throughout the various INEX campaigns.

References

1. Clarke, C.: Range results in XML retrieval. In: Proceedings of the INEX Workshop on Element Retrieval Methodology (2005)
2. Denoyer, L., Gallinari, P.: The Wikipedia XML Corpus. SIGIR Forum 40(1) (2006)
3. Järvelin, K., Kekäläinen, J.: Cumulated gain-based evaluation of IR techniques. ACM TOIS 20(4), 422–446 (2002)
4. Kekäläinen, J., Järvelin, K.: Using graded relevance assessments in IR evaluation. JASIST 53(13), 1120–1129 (2002)
5. Ogilvie, P., Lalmas, M.: Investigating the exhaustivity dimension in content-oriented XML element retrieval evaluation. In: Proceedings of ACM CIKM, pp. 84–93 (2006)
6. Piwowarski, B., Lalmas, M.: Providing consistent and exhaustive relevance assessments for XML retrieval evaluation. In: Proceedings of ACM CIKM, pp. 361–370 (2004)
7. Kazai, G., Lalmas, M.: eXtended Cumulated Gain Measures for the Evaluation of Content-oriented XML Retrieval. ACM TOIS 24(4), 503–542 (2006)
8. Tombros, A., Malik, S., Larsen, B.: Report on the INEX 2004 interactive track. ACM SIGIR Forum 39(1) (2005)
9. Trotman, A., Sigurbjornsson, B.: Narrowed extended XPATH I (NEXI). In: Proceedings of the INEX Workshop on Element Retrieval Methodology (2004)

Task-Centred Information Management

Tiziana Catarci[1], Alan Dix[2], Akrivi Katifori[3], Giorgios Lepouras[4],
and Antonella Poggi[1]

[1] Dipartimento di Informatica e Sistemistica,
Sapienza Università di Roma,
Via Salaria 113, 00198 Roma, Italy
{poggi,catarci}@dis.uniroma1.it
[2] Computing Department,
Lancaster University,
Lancaster, LA1 4YR, United Kingdom
alan@hcibook.com
[3] Dept. of Informatics and Telecommunications,
University of Athens
Panepistimiopolis, 157 84, Athens, Greece
vivi@mm.di.uoa.gr
[4] Dept. of Computer Science,
University of Peloponnese,
Tripolis, Greece
gl@uop.gr

Abstract. The goal of DELOS Task 4.8 Task-centered Information Management
is to provide the user with a Task-centered Information Management system
(TIM), which automates user's most frequent activities, by exploiting the collection of personal documents. In previous work we have explored the issue of
managing personal data by enriching them with semantics according to a Personal
Ontology, i.e. a user-tailored description of her domain of interest. Moreover, we
have proposed a task specification language and a top-down approach to task inference, where the user specifies main aspects of the tasks using forms of declarative scripting. Recently, we have addressed new challenging issues related to TIM
user's task inference. More precisely, the first main contribution of this paper is
the investigation of task inference theoretical issues. In particular, we show how
the use of the Personal Ontology helps for computing simple task inference. The
second contribution is an architecture for the system that implements simple task
inference. In the current phase we are implementing a prototype for TIM whose
architecture is the one presented in this paper.

1 Introduction

Personal Information Management (PIM) aims at supporting users in the collection,
storage and retrieval of their personal information. It is a crucial challenge nowadays;
indeed, the collection of digital documents stored within the personal repository of each
one of us increases every day, in terms of both size and "personal" relevance. In a
sense, this collection constitutes the Digital Library that is closest to the user and most

C. Thanos, F. Borri, and L. Candela (Eds.): Digital Libraries: R&D, LNCS 4877, pp. 197–206, 2007.

commonly and frequently used. It is often the starting point or reason for wider access to digital resources. Furthermore, the user's personal document collection is daily used to perform routine activities, as booking hotels, and organising meetings. The focus of DELOS Task 4.8 Task-centred Information Management is precisely to provide the user with a Task-centred Information Management system (TIM), which automates these user activities, by exploiting the collection of personal documents considered as a Digital Library.

At the beginning of our investigation, we have faced the issue of providing the user with a system allowing her to access her data through a Personal Ontology (PO), that is unified, integrated and virtual, and reflects the user's view of her own domain of interest [3,10]. The study of such a system is motivated by the need to assign semantics to the user's personal collection of data, in order to help inferring and executing the most frequent user's tasks that either take such data as input or produce it as output. Then, we have focused on defining a task specification language [4], which was appropriate in our context, in the sense that it was both expressive enough to be effectively helpful to the user, and simple enough to allow tasks to be inferred. Moreover, such a language had to be tailored to use the PO to semi-automatically obtain task input and to possibly update the PO after the task execution, according to the task output and semantics. However, having a task specification language allows to semi-automatically execute tasks that the user previously defined. Our further goal is to have the system infer what is the task the user intends to execute next.

This paper addresses the above mentioned issues. Specifically, our main contributions can be summarised as follows:

- First, we cope with task inference in TIM. In particular, we investigate the main task inference theoretical issues. Then we show how to exploit the underlying PO and the features of our task specification language, in order to provide simple task inference in our setting. The main idea here is to suggest appropriate tasks from personal data, based on their semantics.
- Second, we propose a novel architecture for TIM, which implements our solution to the simple task inference issue. More precisely, we propose to integrate into the system an existing web bookmarking tool, called *Snip!t* , whose distinguishing feature is precisely to "intelligently" suggest appropriate actions to perform starting from a Web page content.

The paper is organised as follows. After discussing related work in Section 2, we briefly introduce in Section 3 the previous main task contributions. In Section 4 we discuss task inference related theoretical issues. Then, in Section 5, after introducing *Snip!t* and presenting its distinguishing features, we propose a new architecture for TIM, and show how this provides a simple task inference. Finally, we conclude by presenting future work.

2 Related Work

The issues faced in DELOS Task 4.8 concern several different areas of research. In the following we discuss related work in each of the main areas.

Task management. Recently, research efforts on the problem of managing user's tasks have lead to the prototype Activity-Centered Task Assistant (ACTA), implemented as a Microsoft Outlook add-in [1]. In ACTA, a user's task, named "ACTA activity", is represented as a pre-structured container, that can be created inside the e-mail folder hierarchy. It is a task-specific collection containing structured predefined elements called "components", that embody common resources of the task and appear as activity sub-folders. Thus, for example, by creating an ACTA activity to represent a meeting, and by inserting the component "contacts", the user aims at relating the content of this sub-folder, which will essentially be a list of names, with that particular meeting. More-over, the population of an activity is done semi-automatically, by allowing the user just to drag into the appropriate activity component, the document containing the relevant data, which is afterward automatically extracted and stored. Even though ACTA activities are built relying on user's personal data, their approach is not comparable to ours, since they do not consider tasks as a workflow of actions (e.g. filling and sending the meeting invitation e-mail), which can be inferred and semi-automatically executed.

Task inference. There has been a long history of research into task detection, infer-ence and prediction in human-computer interaction, with a substantial activity in the early 1990s including Alan Cypher's work on Eager [5] and several collections [8]. The line of work has continued (for example [11]), but with less intensity than the early 1990s. Forms of task inference can be found in widely used systems, for example the detection of lists etc. in Microsoft Office or web browsers that auto-fill forms. The first example clearly demonstrates how important it is that the interaction is embedded within an appropriate framework, and how annoying it can be when inference does not do what you want! Some of this work lies under the area of "programming by demon-stration" or "programming by example", where the user is often expected to be aware of the inferences being made and actively modify their actions to aid the system. This is the case of [9] where authors present a learning system, called PLIANT, that helps users anticipating their goal, by learning their preferences and adaptively assisting them in a particular long-running application such as a calendar assistant. Other work falls more under user modelling, intelligent help, automatic adaptation or context-aware in-terfaces where the user may not be explicitly aware that the system is doing any form of inference [2]. Our work lies with the former as we do expect that users will be aware of the inferences being made and work symbiotically with the system in order to create a fluid working environment.

3 Summary of Previous Contributions

In this section we briefly present the DELOS Task 4.8 previous contributions, namely OntoPIM and the task specification language.

OntoPIM. OntoPIM [10] is a module that allows to manage the whole collection of heterogeneous personal data usually maintained in a personal computer (e.g. contacts, documents, e-mails), and to access them through a unified, integrated, virtual and yet user-tailored view of her data. This view is called Personal Ontology (PO), since it re-flects the user's view of her own domain of interest. It is therefore specific to each user.

As for the language to specify the PO, we use the Description Logic called *DL-Lite*$_A$ [13,12], since besides allowing to express the most commonly used modelling constructs, it allows answering expressive queries, i.e. conjunctive queries, in polynomial time with respect to the size of the data. This is clearly a distinguishing and desirable feature of such a language, in a context like ours, since the amount of data is typically huge in one's personal computer. In order to achieve the above mentioned result, OntoPIM proceeds as follows. First it extracts, by means of appropriate wrappers, pieces of relevant data from the actual personal data contained in the personal computer. Then it exploits the so-called Semantic Save module, which *(i)* stores such data in a DBMS, maintaining also its provenance, and *(ii)* stores the relationship existing between the data and the PO, as (implicitly) specified by the user. Note that the latter relationship reflects indeed the data semantics according to the user.

Task Specification. In order to be able to semi-automatically execute user tasks, we defined a task specification language [4] having two main features. First, the language is at the same time expressive enough for actually being helpful to the user, and simple enough for being effectively "usable" and "learnable" by the system. Second, the language allows to specify as a part of the task definition, the input/output data mappings, i.e. the relationships existing between the task and the PO. Specifically, the input data mappings specify the query to be posed over the PO in order to obtain the task input, whereas the output data mapping specify the task output as an update (possibly empty) to be computed over the personal data, according to the semantics of both the task execution and the PO. As we will see, the specification of task input/output data mappings is crucial for task inference/detection/suggestion.

Furthermore, we have explored task inference top-down approaches, where the user specifies aspects of the task using forms of declarative scripting. Our proposal was based on the idea of combining task decomposition and a plan language to describe for each complex task, the execution plan of its sub-tasks. On one hand, a complex task is decomposed into a set of sub-tasks. This allows for a comprehensible view of the task. On the other hand, we have proposed a plan language limited to sequence, alternatives and repetition.

4   Task Inference

In this section, we first address task inference theoretical issues. In particular we focus on bottom-up approaches to simple task inference. Then, we show how the use of a PO can help solving simple task inference in our setting.

As discussed in Section 2, the most successful systems have often been within dedicated applications, where there is a single line of activity and detailed semantic understanding of each action. This was for example the case with EAGER and PLIANT. For more generic systems detection and inference is more difficult, particularly where the user trace data is at a low level either keystroke or click-stream data (which often has to be the case where application support is not assumed). In fact, two particular problems for generic systems are:

– *interleaving*. Users are often performing several tasks simultaneously, perhaps while waiting for something to complete, or because they notice and alert, get a

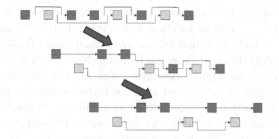

Fig. 1. Untangling interleaved tasks using dependencies

telephone call. Before task inference can begin it is necessary to disentangle these, otherwise each sub-task is littered with the "noise" of the others.

– *generalisation.* Where the user entered data is simply sequences of keystrokes, clicks on locations or basic data types, it is hard to generalise without very large numbers of examples. The use of the PO helps considerably with these problems. Specifically, to face the interleaving problem, we will encourage a drill-down model of interaction where the user either selects previous outputs of actions and then drills forwards (e.g. recent e-mail → sender → Antonella → University → City → Rome → Flights to Rome) or responds to suggested form fills (e.g. from Flight booking form with field 'City' select "Rome because it is the City where Antonella works"). This creates an explicit link either directly between actions or indirectly between them through ontology relationships, which can then be used to separate out interleaved tasks and sub-tasks by tracing lines of dependency, rather like pulling out a string of pearls from a jewellery box (see Figure 1).

Concerning the generalisation problem, because we have a rich typing of task/action input and output data through the PO, we are in a much better position to generalise. If we only know that a form field requires a character string, then given a future character string we may have many possible previous tasks sequences whose initial actions require a string. In contrast, if we know that a character string is in fact a person name or a city name, then faced with a future person name (perhaps from a directory look-up, or an e-mail sender) it is easier to find past tasks requiring as input a person name. In other words, our generalisation is not based on the representation in terms of letters, but in terms of the elements of the ontology.

Let us now focus on simple task inference, where a simple task can include sequences and/or a repetitions of sub-tasks/actions. Thus, here we do not cope with choices. Hence, the job of the inference here is to suggest the most likely single actions and entire task sequences so as to minimise the user's effort in using the system. Intuitively, we intend to build a series of increasingly complex inference mechanisms, both in terms of our development process and in terms of the users' experience. That is, even if we have complex inference mechanisms available, these need to be presented incrementally to the user. In fact, to some extent, even simple type matching can be viewed as a crude form of task inference. However, if this is supplemented by sorting of a few most likely candidate actions/tasks based on past usage, then a form of task sequence comes almost "for free".

For example, suppose that the user has recently (1) taken a phone number, (2) done a reverse directory look-up (in some external web service) to find the person's name, then (3) done an address look-up to find their address and finally (4) taken the address and used a web mapping service to show the location. Now, suppose the user has an e-mail containing a telephone number. The content recogniser finds the number and so suggests a semantic save of the number and also actions using the number. Top of the action list would be likely actions on telephone numbers, and notably the reverse look-up because it was recent. Once this was done, one of the outputs of the reverse look-up would be the person's name and similarly its top option would be the address look-up. So at each stage the previous sequence would be the first option, which means that the task is not totally automated, but little user effort is required. The next step, which likewise requires minimal "intelligence", is simply to offer the entire sequence of actions as one of the options when the telephone number is encountered. This simply requires that all recent/previous task sequences are stored and so recent or frequently performed task sequences starting with the given type are suggested. The user is also given the option of naming a particular sequence of actions. If the user chooses to do this, the task can be used in future interactions. Note too that selection and more so naming is effectively a confirmation by the user that this is a useful task sequence and so will make it far more likely to be presented in future.

More complex tasks including repetitions of sub tasks can similarly be built bottom-up, for example, if the user chooses to perform an action sequence on an instance that is in some visible collection (e.g. selected from a PO concept, or from table of results) and then proceeds to select a second instance in the collection, one of the options would be not only to perform the sequence on the selected item but on all the collection (or selected members of it).

5   *Snip!t* and TIM

In this section, we first present an existing tool, called *Snip!t*, that is a web bookmarking tool, whose distinguishing feature is to suggest appropriate actions to perform starting from a Web page content. Then we propose a novel architecture for TIM, implementing task inference as discussed in Section 4, by integrating *Snip!t* into the system.

Snip!t [6] is a web bookmarking tool, however unlike most web bookmarks, the user can also select a portion (snip) of the page content and then, using a bookmarklet, this selection is sent to the *Snip!t* web application. The snip of the page is stored along with the page url, title etc. and the user can sort the snip into categories or share it with others using RSS feeds. In addition, when the selected text contains a recognised type of data such as a date, post code, person's name, etc., then actions are suggested. For example, if the selected text is recognised as a post code and this leads to suggested actions such as finding the local BBC news for a specific area (see Figure 2).

Snip!t had two contributing origins. In a study of bookmarking organisation some years ago [7] some subjects said that they would sometimes like to bookmark a portion of a page. While the study had different aims this suggestion led to the first version of *Snip!t* in 2003. In addition, this gave an opportunity to use the new platform for data-detector technology originally developed as part of *onCue*, the key product of an

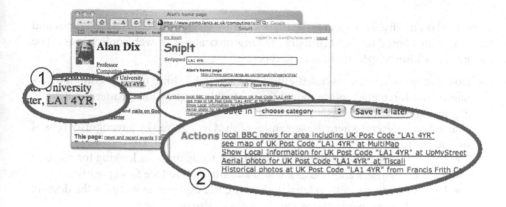

Fig. 2. *Snip!t* in action (actions for a post code)

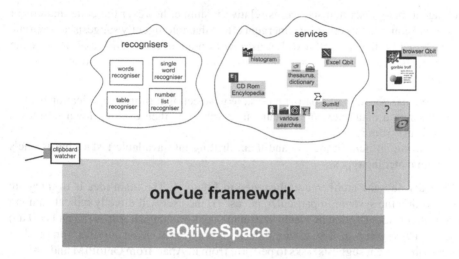

Fig. 3. *onCue* architecture

ex-dot.com company aQtive [6]. So *Snip!t* combines a way of storing and sorting data (portions of web pages) and intelligent suggestion of actions to perform based on the data. Thus it shares some characteristics with the TIM vision.

Internally the bookmarking side of *Snip!t* is fairly straightforward with simple hierarchical categorisation scheme and the ability to assign snips to multiple categories. The snipping of the page contents itself is done using a bookmarklet, that is a small piece of Javascript that is placed as a browser bookmark, usually on the browser toolbar. When the user clicks the bookmarklet the Javascript executes extracts the selected content and then creates a HTTP request to the *Snip!t* server.

The "intelligent" parts of *Snip!t* use an architecture inherited from *onCue*. It consists of two main types of agents: recognisers and services (cf. Figure 3). Recognisers work on plain text and discover various data types whilst services take these data types and suggest actions based on them (usually creating invocations of web applications). The recognisers within *Snip!t* are of several types:

- basic recognisers: can be based either on large table look-up, e.g. common surnames and forenames, place names, or on regular expression / pattern matching, e.g. telephone number, ISBN.
- chained recognisers: where the semantics of data recognised by a recogniser is used by another to:
    - look for a wider data representation, e.g. postcode suggests looking for address; these recognisers are used to allow scalability and reduce false positives;
    - look for a semantically related data, e.g. URL suggests looking for the domain name; these recognisers are used to reduce false negatives;
    - look for inner representation, e.g. from Amazon author URL to author name; these recognisers are also used to allow scalability.

Each agent, recogniser and service, is relatively simple, however the combinations of these small components create an emergent effect that intelligently suggests appropriate actions based on the snipped text. Let us now turn attention to TIM, and the way the user interacts with the system in order to execute a task. The starting point may be of three kinds:

   (i) explicit invocation of a particular task (e.g. selecting it from an application menu),
 (ii) choosing a data value in a document, e-mail etc. then drilling down into tasks possible from it,
(iii) selecting an item in the PO and then, drilling into available tasks (that is one's with matching types).

Consider now the architecture illustrated in Figure 4. The main idea is to integrate *Snip!t* within the system. In particular, in case *(i)* the user will directly indicate among all *Snip!t* services the one he wants to execute next. In contrast, cases *(ii)* and *(iii)* are closer to the typical *Snip!t* scenario. Indeed, in both cases, given a (collection of) data value(s), the system suggests tasks to perform from it. Apart from OntoPIM and *Snip!t*, this new architecture includes the three main TIM modules discussed below.

- **TIM application wrapper:** This module, which is dependent on the particular application enables the user to select any piece of document and send it to *Snip!t* in an appropriate form (cf. snip S). As for a demonstration, we have extended the functionality of Thunderbird mail client, so as to allow the user to select the TIM button while reading a message. A script running on the mail client saves the message, parses the MIME headers filling-in an HTML form which appears in a new browser window. The user can then press the submit button to send the message to *Snip!t*.
- **Personal Ontology Interaction Module (POIM):** Given a collection of data W each with its associated type as returned by *Snip!t* recognisers, this module access the PO and returns a collection of data W' somehow related to W according to the PO. Such data is then used to perform appropriate tasks.
- **Task Inferencer:** This module is responsible for task inference. Intuitively, given a collection of data W' from the POIM and its provenance, the Task Inferencer suggests what is the next task/action to be executed from W.

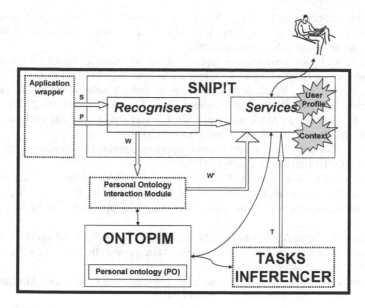

Fig. 4. Integrating *Snip!t* into a personal task-centric system

6   Conclusion and Future Work

In this paper we have investigated new challenges toward a fully equipped TIM system. In particular, we have addressed theoretical task inference issues, and we have proposed a first implementation providing a solution to simple task inference in one's personal computer provided with a PO.

Many other aspects deserve to be further investigated, in particular concerning task inference. Indeed, we have concentrated on simple tasks, possibly including sequences and repetitions of actions, whereas we have not coped with alternatives, i.e. choices. These may arise either where a selection has to be made from a collection (e.g. $1 - m$ relations in the ontology) or where tasks sequences vary slightly depending on aspects of the context or instance (e.g. compress files larger than 100K). Various machine learning techniques can be applied here, which we plan to study in future work.

References

1. Bellotti, V., Thornton, J.: Managing activities with tv-acta: Taskvista and activity-centered task assistant. In: PIM 2006. Proc. of the Second SIGIR Workshop on Personal Information Management (2006)
2. Boone, G.: Concept features in re: Agent, an intelligent email agent. In: Proc. of the Second international Conference on Autonomous Agents, pp. 141–148. ACM Press, New York (1998)
3. Catarci, T., Dong, X., Halevy, A., Poggi, A.: Structure everything. In: Jones, W., Teevan, J. (eds.) Personal Information Management, University of Washington Press (UW Press) (to appear)

4. Catarci, T., Habegger, B., Poggi, A., Dix, A., Ioannidis, Y., Katifori, A., Lepouras, G.: Intelligent user task oriented systems. In: PIM 2006. Proc. of the Second SIGIR Workshop on Personal Information Management (2006)
5. Cypher, A.: Eager: Programming repetitive tasks by example. In: CHI 1991. Proc. of the Conference on Human Factors in Computing Systems, pp. 33–39 (1991)
6. Dix, A., Beale, R., Wood, A.: Architectures to make Simple Visualisations using Simple Systems. In: AVI 2000. Proc. of Advanced Visual Interfaces, pp. 51–60 (2000)
7. Dix, A., Marshall, J.: At the right time: when to sort web history and bookmarks. In: Proc. of HCI International 2003, vol. 1, pp. 758–762 (2003)
8. Finlay, J., Beale, R.: Neural networks and pattern recognition in human-computer interaction. ACM SIGCHI Bulletin 25(2), 25–35 (1993)
9. Gervasio, M.T., Moffitt, M.D., Pollack, M.E., Taylor, J.M., Uribe, T.E.: Active preference learning for personalized calendar scheduling assistance. In: IUI 2005. Proc. of the 10th international conference on Intelligent user interfaces, pp. 90–97. ACM Press, New York (2005)
10. Katifori, V., Poggi, A., Scannapieco, M., Catarci, T., Ioannidis, Y.: OntoPIM: how to rely on a personal ontology for Personal Information Management. In: Proc. of the 1st Workshop on The Semantic Desktop (2005)
11. Lieberman, H.: Your wish is my command: programming by example. Morgan Kaufmann Publishers Inc., San Francisco, CA, USA (2001)
12. Poggi, A.: Structured and Semi-Structured Data Integration. Dipartimento di Informatica e Sistemistica, Università di Roma "La Sapienza" (2006)
13. Poggi, A., Calvanese, D., De Giacomo, G., Lembo, D., Lenzerini, M., Rosati, R.: Linking data to ontologies. Submitted for publication to an international journal (2007)

Viewing Collections as Abstractions

Carlo Meghini[1] and Nicolas Spyratos[2]

[1] Consiglio Nazionale delle Ricerche
Istituto della Scienza e delle Tecnologie della Informazione
Pisa, Italy
meghini@isti.cnr.it
[2] Université Paris-Sud
Laboratoire de Recherche en Informatique
Orsay Cedex, France
spyratos@lri.fr

Abstract. Digital Libraries collections are an abstraction mechanism, endowed with an extension and an intension, similarly to predicates in logic. The extension of a collection is the set of objects that are members of the collection at a given point in time, while the intension is a description of the meaning of the collection, that is the peculiar property that the members of the collection possess and that distinguishes the collection from other collections. This view reconciles the many types of collections found in Digital Library systems, but raises several problems, among which how to automatically derive the intension from a given extension. This problem must be solved *e.g.* for the creation of a collection from a set of documents. We outline basic results on the problem and then show how intensions can be exploited for carrying out basic tasks on collections, establishing a connection between Digital Library management and data integration.

1 Introduction

The notion of collection is central to traditional library information systems, and quite naturally, it also plays a key role in Digital Libraries [9,10,1]. In a Digital Library (DL, for short), a collection is a set of digital resources, which are grouped together in response to some basic need of an actor in the DL environment. As a consequence, there exists several types of collections in the DL literature and in DL management systems, each type being directed towards the needs of some specific actor or task.

- *Physical* collections are holders of the DL resources, strictly mirroring library or museum collections: to be part of a DL means for an object to be part of one (and usually only one) physical collection.
- *Virtual* (or *logical*) collections address the needs of DL users and come in two flavors, named *static* and *dynamic* after the way they evolve.
  - Static collections [11,2] are "places" for storing relevant resources over a long period of time, such as the *book-marks* of a Web browser or the

C. Thanos, F. Borri, and L. Candela (Eds.): Digital Libraries: R&D, LNCS 4877, pp. 207–217, 2007.
© Springer-Verlag Berlin Heidelberg 2007

shelves of a library, and for sharing these resources with a community pursuing a common goal.

- Dynamic collections [4,5,3] represent user information needs that persist beyond a single discovery session. As such they can be understood as user *views* of the underlying DL. As the DL evolves, views evolves of consequence, in an automatic, user-transparent way.

Collections are a central notion of the DL conceptual model, and having many types of collections makes this model harder to understand for users, and complex to manage for the underlying DL management system. We claim that this complexity is unnecessary and stems from lack of proper conceptualization. Indeed, from a computer science science point of view, virtual collections are just abstraction mechanisms of one kind, by which the DL resources *satisfying some homogeneity criterion* become a named whole, thus suppressing the details which differentiate a member of the whole from the other members. In some cases, the homogeneity criterion can be expressed linguistically as a query (dynamic collections). In some other cases the user finds it more convenient to describe the collection ostensibly, that is by pointing out its members (static collections); this, however, does not mean that no homogeneity criterion exists.

This leads to understanding collections as having both an *extension* and an *intension,* very much like predicates in logic, or classes in object-oriented data models. In particular,

- the extension of a collection is the set of objects that are members of the collection at a given point in time;
- the intension of a collection is a description of the meaning of the collection, that is the peculiar property that the members of the collection possess and that distinguishes the collection from other collections.

Treating collections in a purely extensional way, that is by disregarding the intensional aspect, would imply that collections with the same extension are indistinguishable and therefore the same collection, a fact that defeats the definition of collection.

In this paper, we show that understanding collections as abstraction mechanisms endowed of intensions and extensions leads not only to a philosophically well-founded DL model, but also to a more powerful one, which can still be efficiently managed. The proof is carried out in two steps: first, by showing how collection intensions can be (a) defined in a mathematically well-founded way drawing from Formal Concept Analysis (FCA) and (b) automatically computed from a given set of objects. Second, by showing how collection intensions can be exploited for carrying out basic collection management tasks.

2   The Digital Library Model

A DL is characterized by a finite, non-empty set of *documents* which for the purposes of the present work will just be abstract objects making up the set

D. Since the set of documents uniquely determines a DL, we will use D also to denote the underlying DL.

Documents are described by means of *terms*, which may be keywords about the content of documents (such as *nuclear waste disposal* or *database*), or their type (*image*). Terms may also be thought of as attribute values (for instance, *creator*=`carlo` may be thought as a term).

The relation between documents and terms is stored in the *description directory*, which is a relation r from documents to terms, $r \subseteq D \times T$, such that $(d, t) \in r$ means that d is described (or indexed) by term t. From r we define two functions which will turn out very useful in the sequel:

– the *index*, a function $index : D \to \mathcal{P}(T)$, giving the terms which a document is indexed by:

$$\forall d \in D, \ index(d) = \{t \in T \mid (d, t) \in r\}$$

– the *extension*, a function $termext : T \to \mathcal{P}(D)$, giving the documents which a term describes:

$$\forall t \in T, \ termext(t) = \{d \in D \mid (d, t) \in r\}.$$

Terms are used to build *descriptions*. A description is a propositional formula over the alphabet T, built out of the connectives ¬ (negation), ∧ (conjunction) and ∨ (disjunction). We will denote the set of such formulas as $\mathcal{L}_T$, or simply $\mathcal{L}$ when there is no danger of ambiguity.

Descriptions denote sets of documents. This is captured by the *answering* function *ans*, named after the fact that a typical usage of descriptions is for querying a DL. For a given DL with documents D, *ans* is inductively defined as follows, where $t, t' \in T$ and $q, q_1, q_2 \in \mathcal{L}$:

$$ans(t, D) = termext(t)$$
$$ans(\neg q, D) = D \setminus ans(q, D)$$
$$ans(q_1 \wedge q_2, D) = ans(q_1, D) \cap ans(q_2, D)$$
$$ans(q_1 \vee q_2, D) = ans(q_1, D) \cup ans(q_2, D)$$

Let $\alpha, \beta \in \mathcal{L}$ be descriptions. The following definitions will be very useful in the sequel:

– α is *consistent* iff in some DL D, $ans(\alpha, D) \neq \emptyset$. On the contrary, if in all DLs D, $ans(\alpha, D) = \emptyset$, α is *inconsistent*.
– α *is subsumed by* β, $\alpha \sqsubseteq \beta$, iff in all DLs D, $ans(\alpha, D) \subseteq ans(\beta, D)$.

In the course of our study, we will need to consider several sub-languages of $\mathcal{L}$, corresponding to different types of descriptions. The simplest descriptions are conjunctions of terms. We will call these descriptions *simple queries,* and denote their set as $\mathcal{L}_S$. In fact, document descriptions can be regarded as simple queries given by the conjunction of the terms which describe the document.

That is, assuming that the description of a document d is given by $index(\mathsf{d}) = \{\mathsf{t}_1, \mathsf{t}_2, \ldots, \mathsf{t}_n\}$, we may, and in fact will assume that:

$$index(\mathsf{d}) = (\mathsf{t}_1 \wedge \mathsf{t}_2 \wedge \ldots \wedge \mathsf{t}_n) \in \mathcal{L}_S$$

Another relevant class of descriptions is that of conjunctive queries. A *literal* l is either a term $t \in \mathsf{T}$, in which case it is called a *positive* literal, or its negation $\neg t$ (negative literal). A *conjunctive query* is a consistent conjunction of literals:

$$\bigwedge_{1 \leq j \leq n} l_j \quad (n \geq 1).$$

A typical conjunctive query is the *description* of a document $\mathsf{d} \in \mathsf{D}$, $\delta(\mathsf{d})$, given by the conjunction of the terms describing the document with the negation of the terms *not* describing the document:

$$\delta(\mathsf{d}) = \bigwedge\{\mathsf{t} \mid \mathsf{t} \in index(\mathsf{d})\} \wedge \bigwedge\{\neg\mathsf{t}' \mid \mathsf{t}' \notin index(\mathsf{d})\}.$$

Finally, *DNFS queries* are disjunctions of conjunctive queries:

$$\bigvee_{1 \leq i \leq m} D_i \quad (m \geq 1)$$

where for no two distinct disjuncts D_i and D_j, $D_i \sqsubseteq D_j$. It can be shown that subsumption between conjunctive queries can be checked efficiently, thus the set of DNFS queries is efficiently decidable. Let $\mathcal{L}_D$ be such set.

The last component of DL that we need to introduce are *collections*. Collections are abstract objects making up a finite, non-empty set C on which two total functions are defined:

- the collection *extension collext* : $\mathsf{C} \rightarrow \mathcal{P}(\mathsf{D})$, assigning a set of documents to each collection.
- the collection *intension collint* : $\mathsf{C} \rightarrow \mathcal{L}$, assigning a description to each collection.

The question arises how these two notions should be related. An obvious requirement is that the set of documents belonging to the collection must *agree* with the collection intension. This can be expressed by requiring that the collection intension, when used as a query, should retrieve *at least* the documents in the collection extension. Formally:

$$\forall \mathsf{c} \in \mathsf{C}, \ collext(\mathsf{c}) \subseteq ans(collint(\mathsf{c})). \tag{1}$$

For a given collection $\mathsf{c} \in \mathsf{C}$, we define the *precision* of the collection intension, $prec(\mathsf{c})$, the set of documents denoted by $collint(\mathsf{c})$ which are not members of the collection:

$$prec(\mathsf{c}) = ans(collint(\mathsf{c})) \setminus collext(\mathsf{c})$$

If $prec(\mathsf{c}) = \emptyset$ we say that the collection is *precise*, and *imprecise* otherwise. We also say that a description α is precise with respect to a set of documents X just in case $X = ans(\alpha)$.

Table 1. A DL index

Object	Index
1	Harpsichord, Bach, Baroque, MP3
2	Concert, Baroque
3	Harpsichord, Bach, Baroque, Frank
4	Concert, Bach, Baroque, MP3, Frank
5	Harpsichord, Concert, MP3, Frank

3   The Problem

The problem we want to address in this study is the following: given a DL and a subset X of the documents in it, to find a description $\alpha \in \mathcal{L}$ such that $X \subseteq ans(\alpha)$. This problem typically arises when a user has a set of documents and wants to create a collection having those documents as extension.

It should be evident that any set of documents X has a trivial description in $\mathcal{L}_D$, given by the disjunction of the maximal descriptions of documents in X :

$$\bigvee \{\delta(\mathsf{d}) \mid \mathsf{d} \in X, \nexists \mathsf{d}' \in X \text{ such that } \delta(\mathsf{d}) \sqsubseteq \delta(\mathsf{d}')\}$$

This description is as precise as a description of X can be in the DL, but not very interesting: apart from being as large as X itself, it just replicates the index of every document in X, offering no additional information. A more satisfactory formulation of our problem is therefore: given a set of documents X, can we find a description of X which is *better* than the trivial one? In what follows we will outline answers to this question for different languages. For illustration purposes, we will resort to a toy DL consisting of 5 audio objects named from 1 to 5 and described by the following terms:

- *Harpsichord* (abbreviated as H), meaning that the content of the object is music for harpsichord;
- *Concert* (C), meaning that the content of the object is a concert;
- *Baroque* (B), meaning that the content of the object is from the Baroque period;
- *Bach* (JSB), meaning that the content of the object is Bach's music;
- *MP3* (M), meaning that the object is an MP3 file;
- *Frank* (F), meaning that the owner of the digital rights of the object is Frank.

The description directory is illustrated by the index given in Table 1.

4   Solutions

We begin by considering the language of simple queries, which is strictly related to Formal Concept Analysis (FCA) [7,6,8]. To state our result in this language,

Table 2. An augmented DL index

Object	Augmented Index
1	Harpsichord, Bach, Baroque, MP3, ¬Concert, ¬Frank
2	Concert, Baroque, ¬Harpsichord, ¬Bach, ¬MP3, ¬Frank
3	Harpsichord, Bach, Baroque, Frank, ¬Concert, ¬MP3
4	Concert, Bach, Baroque, MP3, Frank, ¬Harpsichord
5	Harpsichord, Concert, MP3, Frank, ¬Bach, ¬Baroque

we need to introduce the functions ψ and φ which denote, respectively, all documents described by a given set of terms and all terms describing a given set of documents:

$$\psi(T) = \bigcap \{termext(\mathsf{t}) \mid \mathsf{t} \in T\} \text{ for all } T \subseteq \mathsf{T}$$

$$\varphi(D) = \bigcap \{index(\mathsf{d}) \mid \mathsf{d} \in D\} \text{ for all } D \subseteq \mathsf{D}$$

Given a set of documents $X \subseteq \mathsf{D}$, it can be proved that $\varphi(X)$ is the most precise description that X has in $\mathcal{L}_S$. If $X = \psi(\varphi(X))$ the description is clearly precise. To exemplify, let us consider the set of documents $\{1, 4\}$. $\varphi(\{1, 4\}) = \{B, JSB, M\}$ is the most precise $\mathcal{L}_S$ description of this set, and it is a precise one, since $\psi(\varphi(\{1, 4\})) = \psi(\{B, JSB, M\}) = \{1, 4\}$. On the contrary, the set $\{1, 2\}$ has no precise description, since $\psi(\varphi(\{1, 2\})) = \psi(\{B\}) = \{1, 2, 3, 4\}$. The precision of the best description, B, is $\{3, 4\}$.

In some cases, the best $\mathcal{L}_S$ description may have an unacceptably large precision. In this case, one possibility is to relax the intension of the collection, by accepting a more expressive description than a simple query. Expressivity can be increased in two ways: by adding negation of single terms, in which case we end in $\mathcal{L}_C$, or by adding disjunction, in which case we end into a subset of $\mathcal{L}_D$, consisting of disjunctions of simple queries.

We will consider conjunctive queries first. Let $\neg$ be a bijection from T to $\mathsf{T}_\neg$, a subset of $\mathcal{T}$ disjoint from T. For simplicity, we will write $\neg\mathsf{t}$ in place of $\neg(\mathsf{t})$ to indicate the negation of any term $\mathsf{t} \in \mathsf{T}$. Moreover, if $T \subseteq \mathsf{T}$ is a set of terms, $\neg(T)$ is the set of the negation of each term in T, i.e. $\neg(T) = \{\neg\mathsf{t} \mid \mathsf{t} \in T\}$.

The *augmentation* of a description directory r, $r_\neg$, is given by

$$r_\neg = r \cup \{(\mathsf{d}, \neg\mathsf{t}) \mid (\mathsf{d}, \mathsf{t}) \notin r\}.$$

As a general rule, we will use $\neg$ as a subscript to indicate that we refer to the augmented directory, e.g. $\varphi_\neg$ is the correspondent of φ in the augmented directory. Table 2 shows the augmented index of our running example.

By applying the same techniques used for $\mathcal{L}_S$, it can be proved that $\varphi_\neg(X)$ is the most precise description that a set of documents $X \subseteq \mathsf{D}$ has in $\mathcal{L}_C$. For example, the set $\{1, 2\}$ has a precise $\mathcal{L}_C$ description, since $\psi_\neg(\varphi_\neg(\{1, 2\})) = \{1, 2\}$. The sought description is given by $\varphi_\neg(\{1, 2\}) = \{B, \neg F\}$ which can be further simplified to $\neg F$. For reasons of space, this simplification process is not described. We also observe that $\mathcal{L}_C$ descriptions can be computed without computing the augmented index. In fact, it can be verified that, for all sets of terms T and sets of documents D :

$$\psi_\neg(T) = \{d \in \mathsf{D} \mid (d,t) \in \mathsf{x} \text{ for all } t \in T \text{ and } (d,t) \notin \mathsf{x} \text{ for all } \neg t \in T\}$$
$$\varphi_\neg(D) = \{t \in \mathsf{T} \mid (d,t) \in \mathsf{x} \text{ for all } d \in D\} \cup \{\neg t \mid (d,t) \notin \mathsf{x} \text{ for all } d \in D\}$$

We now consider disjunction, starting from the language $\mathcal{L}_U$, which is the sub-language of $\mathcal{L}$ consisting of disjunctions of simple queries, or just *disjunctive queries* for brevity.

Disjunctive queries can describe many more sets of documents than simple queries, since disjunction allows to "accumulate" simple queries at will. So, the first question that naturally arises is whether all sets of documents have a precise description in $\mathcal{L}_U$. The answer, perhaps surprisingly, is negative: it can be shown that a set of documents $X \subseteq \mathsf{D}$ has a precise description in $\mathcal{L}_U$ if and only if $\psi(\varphi(\{d\})) \subseteq X$ for all $d \in X$. In order to exemplify this result, let us consider in our running example that $\psi(\varphi(2)) = \{2,4\}$. This is a consequence of the fact that $index(2) \subseteq index(4)$ and implies, in light of the just stated result, that any set of documents containing 2 but not 4 does not have a precise $\mathcal{L}_U$ description. $\{1,2\}$ is one such sets: it has no name in $\mathcal{L}_U$ because 2 and 4 cannot be separated by using only positive terms, even allowing disjunction. Negation is clearly a way of separating documents, and in fact $\{1,2\}$ is precisely described by $\neg F$, as we have already seen.

However, the power of disjunction is not to be underestimated, because while $\mathcal{L}_S$ and $\mathcal{L}_C$ precise descriptions are unique, a set of documents X may have more than one precise $\mathcal{L}_U$ description. In proof, let us consider for instance the set $\{2,3,4,5\}$ in our running example. This set has a precise $\mathcal{L}_U$ description, since it satisfies the above stated condition, namely $\psi(\varphi(2)) \subseteq \{2,3,4,5\}$ and the same holds for 3, 4 and 5. It can be verified that

$$(C \wedge B) \vee (H \wedge JSB \wedge F) \vee (JSB \wedge M \wedge F) \vee (H \wedge M \wedge F)$$

is a precise description of $\{2,3,4,5\}$. However, also $C \vee (H \wedge JSB \wedge F)$ is a precise description of $\{2,3,4,5\}$. This latter description is intuitively preferable over the former, since it denotes the same set but it is much shorter. Indeed, every disjunct of the latter description is a subset of a disjunct of the former description; this means that the former description may have more as well as larger disjuncts (set-theoretically speaking), however both of these can be pruned to obtain an equivalent but shorter description.

In order to capture formally this preference criterion, we define a relation between disjunctive queries. To this end and for the sake of simplicity, we will regard simple queries as sets of terms. Given two disjunctive queries $\alpha = D_1 \vee \ldots \vee D_m$ and $\beta = E_1 \vee \ldots \vee E_n$, α *is preferred over* β, $\alpha \sqsubseteq \beta$, if and only if $ans(\alpha) = ans(\beta)$ and for every disjunct D_i in α there exists a disjunct E_j

Table 3. Computation of the candidate set of $\{2, 3, 4, 5\}$

t	$Y = termext(t) \cap X$	$\varphi(Y)$	candidate set
H	$\{3, 5\}$	$\{H, F\}$	no
C	$\{2, 4, 5\}$	$\{C\}$	yes
B	$\{2, 3, 4\}$	no	
JSB	$\{3, 4\}$	$\{B, JSB, F\}$	no
M	$\{4, 5\}$	$\{M, F\}$	no
F	$\{3, 4, 5\}$	$\{F\}$	yes

in β such that $D_i \subseteq E_j$. It can be proved that $\sqsubseteq$ is reflexive and transitive, thus $(\mathcal{L}_U, \sqsubseteq)$ is a pre-order. A description is said to be *minimal* if it is a minimal element of $(\mathcal{L}_U, \sqsubseteq)$, that is no description is preferred over it. We then set out to find minimal descriptions.

For a given set of documents $X \subseteq \mathsf{D}$, the *candidate sets of X* are given by:

$$\max_{t \in \mathsf{T}} \{Y = (termext(t) \cap X) \mid Y = \psi(\varphi(Y))\} \tag{2}$$

where maximality is with respect to set-containment. Notice that if $X = \psi(\varphi(X))$, X is the only member of this set. Now, it can be proved that a $\mathcal{L}_U$ description is a precise minimal description of X iff it is given by $\varphi(C_1) \vee \varphi(C_2) \vee \ldots \vee \varphi(C_n)$ where $C_1, \ldots, C_n$ are candidate sets of X which form a minimum cover for X. This result sanctions the intractability of computing a minimal $\mathcal{L}_U$ description, since it allows to reduce minimum cover to the problem at hand. However, candidate sets can be computed efficiently, therefore approximations of minimal descriptions can be efficiently obtained.

To see how, let us consider again the set $X = \{2, 3, 4, 5\}$ for which we wish to find a minimal, precise $\mathcal{L}_U$ description in our running example. Table 3 shows the computation of the candidate sets:

- the first column gives the considered term t;
- the second column gives the overlapping Y between the extension of t and X;
- the third column gives $\varphi(Y)$ in case $Y = \psi(\varphi(Y))$, as required by (2);
- finally, the last column tells whether Y is a candidate set.

There turns out to be only 2 candidate sets, out of which only one minimum set cover for X can be constructed, given by $C \vee F$. In this example, the minimum set cover problem has no impact, due to the toy size of the example. In real cases, however, candidate sets can be as many as the terms, and an approximation technique may have to be used in order to avoid long computations. In alternative, an incomplete method may be chosen, returning a non-minimal description.

Table 4. Computing the candidate sets for $\{1, 2, 3\}$

t	$\varepsilon(t) \cap X$	intent	candidate
H	$\{1,3\}$	$\{H, \neg C, B, JSB\}$	yes
C	$\{2\}$	$\{\neg H, C, B, \neg JSB, \neg M, \neg F\}$	no
B	$\{1,2,3\}$	no	
JSB	$\{1,3\}$	already considered	no
M	$\{1\}$	non-maximal	no
F	$\{3\}$	non-maximal	no
$\neg H$	$\{2\}$	already considered	no
$\neg C$	$\{1,3\}$	already considered	no
$\neg B$	$\{\}$	non-maximal	no
$\neg JSB$	$\{2\}$	already considered	no
$\neg M$	$\{2,3\}$	$\{B, \neg M\}$	yes
$\neg F$	$\{1,2\}$	$\{B, \neg F\}$	yes

An imprecise $\mathcal{L}_U$ description might be desirable in case a precise one does not exist or is not satisfactory, for instance because too long. Here the problem is: to find the minimal description amongst the descriptions having minimal imprecision. It can be shown that this problem has as unique solution the simple query $\varphi(X)$.

We conclude by considering DNFS descriptions, that is formulas in $\mathcal{L}_D$. As we have already observed, a set of documents X has always a precise DNFS description, but from the results above we know that there may be more such descriptions. However, since the definition of minimality devised for $\mathcal{L}_U$ descriptions carries over $\mathcal{L}_D$ descriptions, the same technique can be applied. In order to illustrate, let us consider the document set $X = \{1, 2, 3\}$. Table 4 shows the results of computing candidate sets on this set, similarly to Table 3. The 3 candidate sets so identified allow us to construct two minimal, precise $\mathcal{L}_D$ descriptions for the given set of documents, namely:

$$(\bigwedge \{H, \neg C, B, JSB\}) \vee (\bigwedge \{B, \neg M\})$$

$$(\bigwedge \{H, \neg C, B, JSB\}) \vee (\bigwedge \{B, \neg F\})$$

By applying simplification, these reduce to: $\neg C \vee \neg M$ and $\neg C \vee \neg F$. Notice that in either case the collection intension looks very different from the index of the member documents.

5   Conclusion

We have argued that collections are abstraction mechanisms endowed with extension and intension, and outlined the solutions of the problem of finding an intension for a given extension, in the context of a simple, but realistic, DL model.

Collection intensions allow DL users to know the meaning of a collection, in terms of the descriptors used for characterizing the documents in the collection. As such, they are essential to describe the nature of collections. In addition, intensions may be very useful in collection management. To see how, let us consider the following situations:

- A query $q \in \mathcal{L}_U$ and for a certain collection c, $collint(c) \wedge q$ is inconsistent. This means that, whatever the DL, c does not contain any document satisfying q, so it is useless to check the documents in c's extension, because none of these documents belongs to the answer. If, on the other hand, $collint(c)$ is subsumed by q, then the whole collection extension satisfies the query, no matter what the current DL looks like; also in this case searching the collection extension is useless. In sum, the extension of a collection needs to be searched only in case the collection intension is consistent with, but not subsumed by the query.
- A new document d comes in, and the DL system has to determine which collection extensions d "fits in", that is in what collections d might belong without breaking the constraint (1). Suppose that for a certain collection c, $index(d)$ is subsumed by $collint(c)$. This means that, whatever the DL, if $collext(c) \subseteq ans(collint(c), D)$ then $collext(c) \cup \{d\} \subseteq ans(collint(c), D)$. In other words, adding d to the extension of c does not break the constraint (1).
- A new user comes in, whose profile is given by a description $\alpha \in \mathcal{L}_U$, and the DL system has to determine which collections are relevant to this user, that is which collections contain documents which the user may be interested in. Suppose that for a certain collection c, $\alpha \wedge collint(c)$ is consistent. This means that there may be some DL, perhaps the current one, in which c has some documents denoted by α, thus c is relevant to the user in the above sense. Or, we might want a stricter notion of relevance, one in which all the collection extension must satisfy the user profile. In this latter case, we would require that $collint(c)$ is subsumed by α.

In all these situations, the underlying assumption is that the relevant subsumption and consistency decision problems can be efficiently solved. This is in fact the case for the DL model in this paper.

More generally, by putting descriptions at the heart of the Digital Library model, a connection is established between Digital Libraries and other important fields of information systems, notably knowledge management. This should not come as a surprise, since the very purpose of a Digital Library is the sharing of knowledge. Quite to the contrary, it is in fact surprising that the development of DL technology has largely ignored knowledge technology, and this may be one of the reasons why the establishment of DL technology is so slow.

References

1. Bergmark, D.: Collection Synthesis. In: Proceeding of the second ACM/IEEE-CS Joint Conference on Digital Libraries, pp. 253–262. ACM Press, New York (2002)
2. Blair, D.C.: The challenge of commercial document retrieval, Part II: a strategy for document searching based on identifiable document partitions. Information Processing and Management 38, 293–304 (2002)
3. Candela, L.: Virtual Digital Libraries. PhD thesis, Information Engineering Department, University of Pisa (2006)
4. Candela, L., Castelli, D., Pagano, P.: A Service for Supporting Virtual Views of Large Heterogeneous Digital Libraries. In: Koch, T., Sølvberg, I.T. (eds.) ECDL 2003. LNCS, vol. 2769, pp. 362–373. Springer, Heidelberg (2003)
5. Candela, L., Straccia, U.: The Personalized, Collaborative Digital Library Environment CYCLADES and its Collections Management. In: Callan, J., Crestani, F., Sanderson, M. (eds.) Distributed Multimedia Information Retrieval. LNCS, vol. 2924, pp. 156–172. Springer, Heidelberg (2004)
6. Davey, B.A., Priestley, H.A.: Introduction to lattices and order, 2nd edn, ch. 3. Cambridge, second edition (2002)
7. Ganter, B., Wille, R.: Applied lattice theory: Formal concept analysis., http://www.math.tu.dresden.de/$\sim$ganter/psfiles/concept.ps
8. Ganter, B., Wille, R.: Formal Concept Analysis: Mathematical Foundations, 1st edn. Springer, Heidelberg (1999)
9. Geisler, G., Giersch, S., McArthur, D., McClelland, M.: Creating Virtual Collections in Digital Libraries: Benefits and Implementation Issues. In: Proceedings of the second ACM/IEEE-CS Joint Conference on Digital Libraries, pp. 210–218. ACM Press, New York (2002)
10. Lagoze, C., Fielding, D.: Defining Collections in Distributed Digital Libraries. D-Lib Magazine (November 1998)
11. Witten, I.H., Bainbridge, D., Boddie, S.J.: Power to the People: End-user Building of Digital Library Collections. In: Proceedings of the first ACM/IEEE-CS joint conference on Digital libraries, pp. 94–103. ACM Press, New York (2001)

Adding Multilingual Information Access to the European Library

Martin Braschler[1] and Nicola Ferro[2]

[1] Zurich University of Applied Sciences - Switzerland
martin.braschler@zhaw.ch
[2] University of Padova - Italy
nicola.ferro@unipd.it

Abstract. A feasibility study was conducted within the confines of the DELOS Network of Excellence with the aim of investigating possible approaches to extend The European Library (TEL) with multilingual information access, i.e. the ability to use queries in one language to retrieve items in different languages. TEL uses a loose coupling of different search systems, and deals with very short information items. We address these two characteristics with two different approaches: the "isolated query translation" approach, and the "pseudo-translated expanded records" approach. The former approach has been studied together with its implications on the user interface, while the latter approach has been evaluated using a test collection of over 150,000 records from the TEL central index. We find that both approaches address the specific characteristics of TEL well, and that there is considerable potential for a combination of the two alternatives.

1 Introduction

This paper reports on a feasibility study ([1], [6], [12]) conducted in collaboration between DELOS, the European Network of Excellence on Digital Libraries, and The European Library (TEL). TEL is a service fully funded by the participant members (national libraries) of the Conference of European National Librarians (CENL). It aims at providing a co-operative framework for integrated access to the major collections of the European national libraries. The study intends to provide a solid basis for the integration of multilingual information access into TEL.

By multilingual information access (MLIA) we denote search on collections of information items (in the context of this paper, bibliographic records) that are potentially stored in multiple languages. The aim is to allow the user to query the collection across languages, i.e. retrieving information items not formulated in the query language. The term "cross-language information retrieval" (CLIR) is often used to describe this definition of MLIA, distinguishing it from monolingual access to information in multiple languages (which is already implemented in TEL).

Today, mainstream research on CLIR in Europe is carried out within the confines of the *Cross-Language Evaluation Forum* (CLEF) campaign [14]. Most of the experiments in CLEF concentrate on retrieval of lengthy, unstructured full-text

C. Thanos, F. Borri, and L. Candela (Eds.): Digital Libraries: R&D, LNCS 4877, pp. 218–227, 2007.
© Springer-Verlag Berlin Heidelberg 2007

documents using a general vocabulary. An overview of the recent achievements in CLIR can be found in [5], [10], and [11]. Generally, there is a growing sense among the academic community that the CLIR problem as applied to such lengthy, unstructured full-text documents from a general domain is fairly well understood from an academic standpoint [3], [4]. Unfortunately, the situation in the TEL system is substantially different from the ideal "mainstream setting" for CLIR. TEL employs only a loose coupling of systems, i.e. each query is forwarded to the individual libraries. In such cases, translation and retrieval cannot be tightly integrated. We address this problem with the "isolated query translation approach" (Section 3). Furthermore, the large majority of information items are very short. Similarly, the expressions of information needs by the users, i.e. the queries, tend to be very short as well (average length is 2.2 words). These contradictions to the general CLIR setting are addressed by our "pseudo-translation on expanded records" approach (Section 4).

2   TEL Architecture and Functioning

Figure 1 shows the architecture of the TEL system. The TEL system allows easy integration of national libraries [15] by extensively using the *Search/Retrieve via URL* (SRU)[1] protocol. In this way, the user client can be a simple web browser, which exploits SRU as a means for uniformly accessing national libraries.

With this objective in mind, TEL is constituted by three components: (1) a Web server which provides users with the TEL portal and provides integrated access to the national libaries via SRU; (2) a "central index" which harvests catalogue records from national libraries which support the *Open Archives Initiative Protocol for Metadata Harvesting* (OAI-PMH)[2] ; (3) a gateway between SRU and Z39.50[3] which allows national libraries that support only Z39.50 to be accessible via SRU.

This setup directly influences how MLIA/CLIR can be integrated into TEL. Indeed, the TEL system has no control on queries sent to the national libraries, as interaction with national library systems is via SRU. Consequently, introducing MLIA functionalities into the TEL system would have no effect on unmodified national library systems. Modification of these systems, however, is an unviable option due to the effort required and the "low barrier of entry" criteria adopted when designing the TEL system.

Therefore, while still offering some MLIA functionalities, we have investigated the possibility of adding an "isolated query translation" step. Additionally, the TEL "central index" harvests catalogue records from national libraries, containing catalogue metadata and other information useful for applying MLIA techniques, such as an abstract. We show how to extend the functionality of this central index to MLIA by adding a component that pseudo-translates the catalogue records ("pseudo-translation of expanded records"). This addresses the brevity of the information items involved, and is substantially different from approaches on the ideal "mainstream setting" for CLIR.

---

[1] http://www.loc.gov/standards/sru/
[2] http://www.openarchives.org/OAI/openarchivesprotocol.html
[3] http://www.loc.gov/z3950/agency/

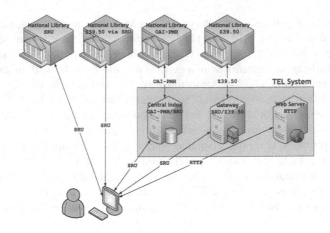

Fig. 1. Present architecture of the TEL system

3 Isolated Query Translation

"Isolated Query Translation" addresses the problems for MLIA generated by the loose coupling of the systems of the individual national libraries. The new component can be directly accessed by the client browser using the SRU protocol. It can be considered as a sort of pre-processing step where the translation problem is treated as completely separate from retrieval.

The approach works as follows: (1) before actually submitting the query, the user asks the browser to translate it; (2) the browser sends the query via SRU to the "isolated query translation" component, which takes care of translating it and, if necessary, applies query expansion techniques to reduce the problem of missing translations; (3) at this point, the user can interactively select the translation which best matches his needs or can change some query term to refine the translation. In this latter case, the translation process may be iterated. (4) Once the desired translation of the query has been obtained, the retrieval process is initiated, using both the translated query and the original one.

This solution is easy to implement and complies with the "low barrier of entry" approach. The national library systems do not require any modification and this new functionality can be transparently applied when querying them. Some user interaction is required, because multiple translations of the same term may need to be disambiguated or the original query may need to be modified.

The main drawback of this approach the separation of the translation from the retrieval process. Relevant documents may be missing in the result set and thus the performance can be low. Moreover, huge linguistic resources, such as dictionaries, are needed since the vocabulary used in queries is expected to be very large; this has to be repeated for each pair of source/target language the system is going to support. Finally, the query expansion mechanism has to be generic and cannot be tailored on the collections queried, since the "isolated query translation" component does not interact with the national library systems.

3.1 Modifications to the TEL System User Interface

In our discussion on how to modify the current user interface of the TEL system for the "isolated query translation" feature we focus our attention on the simple search functionality. First, the interface is extended with an additional link to the "Isolated Query Translation" feature. When the user clicks on the "suggest query in other languages" link (Figure 2), a box with the supported target languages for the translation appears below the search input box. The user can now check the languages for which he wants a translation of the query.

Fig. 2. Selection of the source and target languages in the simple search

Moreover, on the left of the search input box, a list with the possible source languages of the query is now shown, so that the user can specify the language of his original query. Note that the set of languages for the user interace may differ from the languages available for translation.

As shown in Figure 3, for each target language selected by the user, a new text input box appears below the search input box containing the translation of the query in that language. There are different possibilities for managing the user interaction when the translation of the query is shown. A first possibility would be to add a button "Suggest" so that the user presses it and the input boxes with the translation of the query appear (explicit request by user). Another possibility would be a more *Asynchronous JavaScript Technology and XML* (AJAX) style of interaction where the input box with the translation appears as soon as the user selects the target language. In any case, both ways of interaction comply with the current approach of the TEL system in developing the user interface, which already exploits AJAX.

Once the translations have been obtained, we want to allow the user to modify or refine the translations. Since the users of the simple search probably prefer an easy and intuitive way of interacting with the system, the translation refinement step should also be as simple as possible, even if some precision or some expressive power is lost. For this purpose, we can assist the user as follows:

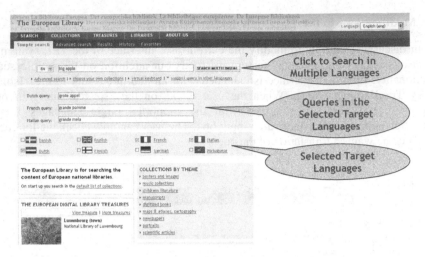

Fig. 3. Query suggestions in other languages in the simple search

1. The user could directly edit each text input box. This means that the user can delete or add words to the translation. If the user has no knowledge of a target language, he will have to use the query suggested by the system without modifications.
2. Some attention has to be paid when multiple translations are possible because they all have to be listed in the input box and thus some visual clue should be provided to help the user in distinguishing between multiple alternatives.
3. If the translation greatly differs from users expectations, there is the possibility of modifying the source query by adding or deleting words to it, thus obtaining a new translation in the target languages.

Once the various translations of the query have been approved, the user can click the "Search Multilingual" button to perform a search in both the original and the selected target languages.

4 Pseudo-Translation of Expanded Records

Today, the large majority of all records available through the search facility in TEL contain bibliographical metadata only (no abstracts or full text). Only short segments of text are thus available for free-text search by the user (such as the "title" field).

While potentially a problem in monolingual search as well, the brevity of the available text exacerbates the problems usually encountered in multilingual information access situations.

4.1 Expansion Techniques and Pseudo-Translation

The solution that was chosen for overcoming the lack of textual content in the information items is automatic expansion of the content fields. The approach used is derived from techniques used in classical information retrieval for query expansion, such as relevance feedback [13]. These techniques extract new statistically related search terms from items that are ranked highly in initial searches. While often used interactively, involving a user picking relevant items from a result set, these techniques can also be applied in an automated fashion. In such cases, the system assumes that the top items returned in response to user requests are relevant. Such a technique is called "blind feedback", and has proven to be beneficial in many CLIR settings [2].

It is possible to use the same techniques independently of specific information needs, by expanding the information item itself instead of the query. While usually not applicable to retrieval on lengthy documents, we expected potential for such an approach in the case of the very short records present in the TEL collection. By using expansion techniques, we intended to address both problems of vocabulary coverage and word sense ambiguity, as usually experienced during translation. Additional terms added during expansion tend to be from a more general vocabulary, as term frequency influences term selection. The new, longer representation of the record also makes it less likely that none of the terms can be translated.

In this proposed solution, we cross the language boundary by translating the "document", i.e. the complete record. Document translation has been found to be very competitive [7] in some general cross-language retrieval settings, although query translation is more prevalent. The main reason for the scarce adoption of the document translation techniques can be attributed to problems of scalability. This problem is much less pronounced in the case of TEL, where the brevity of the records should make document translation applicable even to large numbers of records, e.g. in the order of multiple millions of records. The approach is mainly suitable for integration with the TEL central index. However, the same approach could also be deployed in additional search systems of the national libraries that are accessed remotely via TEL.

Using the translated records for matching with queries only, and not for presentation, means that we can use "pseudo-translations", i.e. to potentially leave terms untranslated or translate them into multiple different terms in the target language. The translation will remain hidden to the end user. This approach of using "rough" translations for retrieval is both cheaper to implement and often more effective for retrieval, as multiple translation alternatives can be retained during the process.

4.2 Outline of Approach, Experiment Setup and Retrieval

The outline of this approach, called in the following "pseudo-translation of expanded records", or "pseudo-translation" for short, is thus: (1) the unstructured content fields of the record are expanded by additional terms that are statistically similar to the original terms in those fields; (2) these additional terms are derived by searching for records that are similar in content to the record that is to be expanded, and then extracting from these additional records the best terms according to well-known blind feedback techniques; (3) the expanded records are translated in their entirety using a simple translation resource; and (4) retrieval takes place on the expanded, (pseudo-) translated records.

With retrieval experiments on test collections, we have aimed to demonstrate how expanded records could be represented, how they would look in their pseudo-translated state and to analyze whether they could be expected to be usable for implementing CLIR in the TEL system.

A full evaluation on a sample of 151,700 bibliographical records in English from the British library (part of the TEL central index) was carried out. We used 99 queries in English derived from three months of logfiles to represent typical information needs. Queries are a mix of one-word statements and longer formulations. The queries were manually translated into German for later cross-language retrieval experiments.

The experiments follow the so-called Cranfield paradigm [9] for retrieval tests. The retrieval system used was Terrier[4], an open-source information retrieval system developed by the University of Glasgow. Note that much of the procedures described would be implemented off-line in an operational system. Translation of the records was done using the PROMT[5] off-the-shelf machine translation system. Again, a variety of different translation resources could be used in support for the chosen CLIR approach.

We expanded the 151,700 records by using each record in turn as a query and running it against the whole collection to determine the set of most similar records. The 10 best-ranked items were used to produce a maximum of 5 expansion terms leading to the most promising results. For some records, no new statistically associated terms can be found, and the records remain unexpanded. In all, approximately 29% of records were not expanded. This ratio should drop if more records were added to the "document" base.

We pseudo-translated all expanded records from English to German using PROMT. The translation suffered from aggressive compound formation by the PROMT software. Since we did not have a German compound splitter available for the Terrier system, retrieval effectiveness may have been negatively affected (For the effect of "decompounding" on retrieval effectiveness, see e.g. [8]).

The following is an example of a pseudo-translated record from our test collection: English record, original:

```
<srw_dc:dc><recordPosition>103899</recordPosition>
<title>Private power : Multinational corporations for the
survival our planet.</title></srw_dc:dc>
```
German record, pseudo-translated, expanded.
```
<srw_dc:dc><recordPosition>103899</recordPosition>
<title>Private Macht : Multinationale Vereinigungen für das
Überleben unser Planet.</title>
<extendedTerms>Entwicklung, Welt, </extendedTerms></srw_dc:dc>
```

The resulting 151,700 pseudo-translated records were loaded into the Terrier system for retrieval.

The 99 queries were hand-translated into German and used to retrieve the top 10 records for each query from the pseudo-translated German records. This constitutes a cross-language retrieval experiment, as each pseudo-translated record can clearly be matched with the original English version it represents in the search index. As a

---

[4] Terrier is available under the Mozillla Public License.
[5] http://www.e-promt.com/

baseline for comparison, we ran the same 99 queries in their original English version against the original English records.

4.3 Analysis of Results

To evaluate retrieval effectiveness, usually recall and precision figures are calculated. Clearly, it was not feasible to do extensive manual relevance assessments for all 99 queries in our study (resulting in 151,700 * 99 assessments). We used so-called "overlap analysis" as a viable alternative. The monolingual English baseline, representing the same information need as the cross-language case, acts as a "gold standard", by assuming that the results from that retrieval experiment have sufficient quality. Any retrieval result sufficiently similar to the monolingual result is then considered to be acceptable. We analyzed the top 10 ranked records to determine the similarity between the monolingual and the cross-language experiment. In all, 30 of the 99 queries had sufficiently similar results, and thus the cross-language results were considered to match the monolingual baseline. These queries were excluded from further analysis.

The remaining 69 queries have results that significantly differ from the monolingual baseline. This, however, does not necessarily indicate that these queries have poor performance. For further analysis, four cases need to be distinguished: (1) good monolingual result; good, but different, cross-language result; (2) good monolingual result; bad cross-language result; (3) bad monolingual result; good cross-language result; (4) bad monolingual result; bad, but different, cross-language result. We supplement this with the previous case: (0) monolingual and cross-language result similar; assumed to be good.

We attempted to classify the remaining 70 queries (one query was accidentially duplicated at this stage) to cases 1-4 based on relevance assessments of the top 10 records for both the monolingual and cross-language experiments. In combination with the actual analysis of the results, it was not possible to process all remaining queries. A total of 18 queries had to be excluded from further processing due to lack of resources. We thus analyzed a grand total of 52 queries, giving a categorization for 82 queries.

We argue that case 0, 1, and 3 provide evidence for good retrieval results, whereas case 4 at least indicates that the cross-language result is not necessarily worse than the monolingual result. In all, using this methodology we found that 55% of queries analyzed showed evidence of good retrieval results, and 83% of queries showed evidence that they did not suffer significantly from the cross-language setup when compared to the monolingual baseline (note that for some of these queries there simply will be no relevant records in the collection!). The latter number is encouraging, being in line with what has been reported as state-of-the-art for CLIR in the CLEF campaign for lengthy documents [4]. Please note, however, that the number has to be treated with care, owing to the limitations described above. The approach should actually benefit in terms of effectiveness when scaling up to larger collections.

Table 1. Summary of evaluation of queries

Case	0	1	2	3	4	not eval.
# queries	30	13	14	2	23	18

5 Conclusions

We have described the results and the findings of a feasibility study carried out to determine how multilingual information access functionalities could be added to the TEL system. We have proposed two different approaches for introducing MLIA functionalities in the TEL system: the first one, called "isolated query translation", performs a pre-processing step to translate the query and then routes the translated query to the national library systems. The second one, called "pseudo-translation", involves only queries sent to the TEL central index but merges the translation process with the retrieval one in order to offer more effective MLIA functionalities. Please note that the two approaches are independent, and we expect considerable potential for combination.

On the whole, we can envision the following evolutionary scenario for implementing MLIA in TEL:

- short-term: the "isolated query translation" solution is a first step for adding MLIA functionalities to TEL and represents a quick way to give TEL users and partners a multilingual experience.
- mid-term: the implementation and deployment of a "pseudo-translation" solution is a second step which better exploit the information directly managed by the TEL central index;
- long-term: the adoption of an inter-lingua approach, where all the translations are made to and from this pivot language, will allow for scaling up the system, when new partners will join TEL. This can be facilitated by combining the two approaches described in this paper.

The work for defining an actual roadmap for introducing MLIA functionalities into TEL is currently ongoing and some initial results in this direction are reported in [1].

Acknowledgments

We thank Marco Dussin for his work on TEL user interface. Many thanks are also due to Bill Oldroyd of the British Library for his assistance in obtaining the set of records used for the experiments on pseudo-translated, expanded records. Thanks also go to Eric van der Meulen and Julie Verleyen of the TEL office for their help with the current TEL architecture. Thomas Arni helped with running the pseudo-translation experiments, and Carol Peters provided corrections to the paper.

The work reported in this paper has been partially supported by the DELOS Network of Excellence on Digital Libraries, as part of the Information Society Technologies (IST) Program of the European Commission (Contract G038-507618).

References

[1] Agosti, M., Braschler, M., Ferro, N., Peters, C., Siebinga, S.: Roadmap for MultiLingual Information Access in The European Library. In: ECDL 2007. Proc. 11th European Conference on Research and Advanced Technology for Digital Libraries. LNCS, vol. 4675, pp. 136–147. Springer, Heidelberg (2007)

[2] Ballesteros, L., Croft, W.B.: Phrasal translation and query expansion techniques for cross-language information retrieval. In: Proc. 20th Annual International ACM SIGIR Conference, pp. 84–91. ACM Press, New York (1997)

[3] Braschler, M., Peters, C.: Cross-Language Evaluation Forum: Objectives, Results, Achievements. Information Retrieval 7(1/2), 7–31 (2004)

[4] Braschler, M.: Robust Multilingual Information Retrieval Dissertation. Institut Interfacultaire d'Informatique, Université de Neuchâtel (2004)

[5] Braschler, M., Di Nunzio, G.M., Ferro, N., Peters, C.: CLEF 2004: Ad Hoc Track Overview and Results Analysis. In: Peters, C., Clough, P.D., Gonzalo, J., Jones, G.J.F., Kluck, M., Magnini, B. (eds.) CLEF 2004. LNCS, vol. 3491, pp. 10–26. Springer, Heidelberg (2005)

[6] Braschler, M., Ferro, N., Verleyen, J.: Implementing MLIA in an existing DL system. In: MLIA 2006. Proc. International Workshop on New Directions in Multilingual Information Access, pp. 73–76 (2006)

[7] Braschler, M.: Combination Approaches for Multilingual Text Retrieval. Information Retrieval 7(1/2), 183–204 (2004)

[8] Braschler, M., Ripplinger, B.: How Effective is Stemming and Decompounding for German Text Retrieval? Information Retrieval 7(3/4), 291–306 (2004)

[9] Cleverdon, C.W.: The Cranfield tests on index language devices. Aslib Proceedings 19, 173–192 (1967), Reprinted in (Sparck Jones and Willett, 1997)

[10] Di Nunzio, G.M., Ferro, N., Jones, G.J.F., Peters, C.: CLEF 2005: Ad Hoc Track Overview. In: Peters, C., Gey, F.C., Gonzalo, J., Müller, H., Jones, G.J.F., Kluck, M., Magnini, B., de Rijke, M., Giampiccolo, D. (eds.) CLEF 2005. LNCS, vol. 4022, pp. 11–36. Springer, Heidelberg (2006)

[11] Di Nunzio, G.M., Ferro, N., Mandl, T., Peters, C.: CLEF 2006: Ad Hoc Track Overview. In: CLEF 2006. Accessing Multilingual Information Repositories: Sixth Workshop of the Cross-Language Evaluation Forum. LNCS, vol. 4730, pp. 21–34. Springer, Heidelberg (2007)

[12] Ferro, N., Braschler, M., Arni, T., Peters, C.: Deliverable D8.3.1 – Feasibility study on Multilinguality. DELOS, A Network of Excellence on Digital Libraries – IST-2002-2.3.1.12, Technology-enhanced Learning and Access to Cultural Heritage (2006)

[13] Frakes, W.B., Baeza-Yates, R.: Information Retrieval. In: Data Structures & Algorithms, Prentice-Hall, Englewood Cliffs (1992)

[14] Peters, C., Braschler, M.: European Research Letter: Cross-language system evaluation. The CLEF campaigns, Journal of the American Society for Information Science and Technology 52(12), 1067–1072 (2001)

[15] van Veen, T., Oldroyd, B.: Search and Retrieval in The European Library. A New Approach. D-Lib Magazine 10(2) (2004)

The OntoNL Framework for Natural Language Interface Generation and a Domain-Specific Application

Anastasia Karanastasi, Alexandros Zotos, and Stavros Christodoulakis

Laboratory of Distributed Multimedia Information Systems / Technical University of Crete
(MUSIC/TUC) University Campus, Kounoupidiana, Chania, Greece
{allegra,azotos,stavros}@ced.tuc.gr

Abstract. We present in this paper the design and implementation of the OntoNL Framework, a natural language interface generator for knowledge repositories, as well as a natural language system for interactions with multimedia repositories which was built using the OntoNL Framework. The system allows the users to specify natural language requests about the multimedia content with rich semantics that result to digital content delivery. We propose and evaluate a semantic relatedness measure for OWL domain ontologies that concludes to the semantic ranking of ontological, grammatically-related structures. This procedure is used to disambiguate in a particular domain of context and represent in an ontology query language, natural language expressions. The ontology query language that we use is the SPARQL. The construction of the queries is automated and also dependent on the semantic relatedness measurement of ontology concepts. We also present the results of experimentation with the system.

Keywords: Natural language interfaces, ontologies, semantic relatedness, query representation.

1 Introduction

We present in this paper the OntoNL Framework for building natural language interfaces to semantic repositories, as well as a natural language interaction interface for semantic multimedia repositories which was build using the OntoNL Framework.

A well known problem with natural language interfaces is that they are notoriously expensive to build. To this end, the OntoNL Framework implements a software platform that automates to a large degree the construction of natural language interfaces for knowledge repositories. To achieve the applicability and reusability of the OntoNL Framework in many different applications and domains, the supporting software is independent on the domain ontologies.

Knowing the context in which an ambiguity occurs is crucial for resolving it. This observation leads us to try to exploit domain ontologies that describe the domain of use of the natural language interface. The methodology that we have developed is reusable, domain independent and works with input only the OWL ontology that was used as a reference schema for constructing a knowledge repository. The methodology depends on a semantic relatedness measure that we have developed for

C. Thanos, F. Borri, and L. Candela (Eds.): Digital Libraries: R&D, LNCS 4877, pp. 228–237, 2007.

domain ontologies that concludes to semantic ranking. The semantic ranking is a methodology for ranking related concepts based on their commonality, related senses, conceptual distance, specificity and semantic relations. This procedure concludes to the natural language representation for information retrieval using an ontology query language, the SPARQL. The SPARQL queries are ranked based on the semantic relatedness measure value that is also used for the automatic construction of the queries.

The software components of the OntoNL Framework address uniformly a range of problems in sentence analysis each of which traditionally had required a separate mechanism. A single architecture handles both syntactic and semantic analysis, handles ambiguities at both the general and the domain specific environment.

The natural language interface to semantic multimedia repositories was built on top of a digital library system that manages multimedia data structures using the MPEG-7 standard and utilizes domain ontologies. The application of the OntoNL Framework addresses a semantic multimedia repository with digital audiovisual content of soccer events and metadata concerning soccer in general, has been developed and demonstrated in the 2nd and 3rd Annual Review of the DELOS II EU Network of Excellence (IST 507618) (http://www.delos.info/). We also present the results of experimentation with the system.

2   The OntoNL Framework

The overall structure of the Framework is shown in **Fig. 1**. It consists of the Linguistic Analyzer component that recognizes the English sentence elements and structures; the Semantic Disambiguator that uses Domain Ontologies to remove as much as possible ambiguities and a Query Formulator that produces the final form of queries that will be submitted to the Application Repository. The Semantic Disambiguator requires that the Domain Ontologies are preprocessed so that clusters of concepts are identified and this is done offline by the Ontologies Processor.

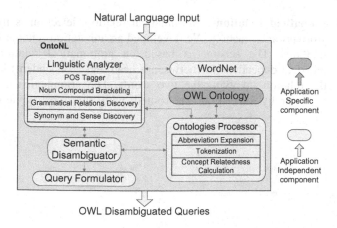

Fig. 1. Framework Architecture

The communication is done through APIs. Note that different domain ontologies may be just imported in the system, provided that they are expressed in the same knowledge representation language (OWL). The Framework is therefore reusable with different domain ontologies.

In the following sub-sections we describe in more detail the functionality of the components of the Framework.

2.1 Linguistic Analyzer

In the application natural language interfaces of the OntoNL system the user inputs requests. Requests do not contain the actual information to address the knowledge repository in the subject of the sentence, but in one or more dependent clauses that complement the independent clause to a complex sentence. We identify what the user asks the system and the additional restrictions that (s)he gives for this 'subject'. The analysis consists of the following parts:

Part-Of-Speech (POS) Tagging. The POS tagging is the first attempt to disambiguate the sense of every word that constitutes the user's request. In our system we used the Stanford Log-Linear POS Tagger (http:// nlp.stanford.edu/ software/ tagger.shtml).

Noun Compound Analysis. The OntoNL deals with noun compounds, firstly, by using a method to expand n-grams into all morphological forms. We have used the dependency model for syntactically analyzing noun compounds, based on its successful performance in previous applications, with training corpus the set of the ontologies that describe each different domain. This may lead to the conclusion that the training corpus is very limited in comparison to a linguistic corpus, but it is more accurate to a specific domain and application. By combining the use of domain ontologies as the training corpus and the WordNet by taking advantage of the hyponyms and synonyms, we maintain the needed information. The procedure of the noun compound bracketing helps in determining correctly the grammatical relationships.

Locating Grammatical Relations. Grammatical relation detection is the semantic basis for the information extraction. We developed an annotation scheme for locating grammatical relations. The scheme is based on grammatical relations that are composed of bilexical dependencies (between a head and a dependent) labeled with the name of the relation involving the two words. The grammatical relations are arranged in a hierarchy (see Fig. 2), rooted with the most generic relation, dep(dependent).

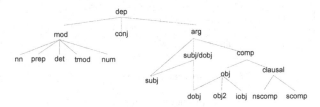

Fig. 2. The grammatical relation hierarchy

For each grammatical relation, we defined one or more patterns over the phrase structure parse tree, produced by the tagger. Conceptually, each pattern is matched against every tree node, and the matching pattern with the most specific grammatical relation is taken as the type of the dependency.

Language Model. To ensure the performance of the semantic disambiguation procedure, the system uses WordNet [2] to obtain all the possible senses and synonyms of words in the user input. The linguistic analysis procedure concludes to a language model described in Fig. 3. In this model diagram there are classes representing the grammatical relations that are connected with associations.

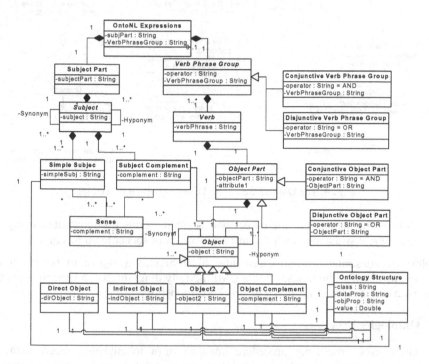

Fig. 3. The language model

2.2 Semantic Disambiguator

The purpose of semantic disambiguation in natural language processing, based on a particular domain is to eliminate the possible senses that can be assigned to a word in the discourse and associate a sense which is distinguishable from other meanings. In particular, the types of ambiguity encountered in the OntoNL system are:

1. The query contains generally keywords that can be resolved by using only the ontology (ontological structures and semantics) (ex.1 "... players of soccer team Milan").
2. One of the subject or object part of the language model cannot be disambiguated by using the ontology (ex.2 "...players of Barcelona").

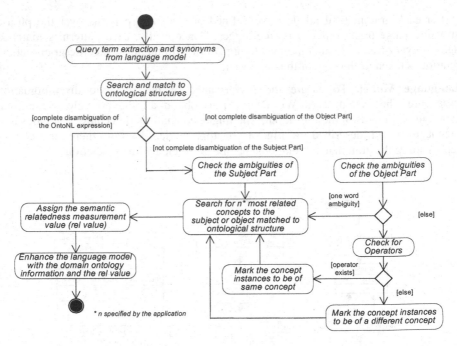

Fig. 4. The OntoNL Semantic Disambiguation procedure

3. Neither the subject nor the object part contains terms disambiguated using the ontological structures (ex.3 "… information about soccer team Milan")

Next, we describe the entire semantic disambiguation algorithm based on the different levels of ambiguities, using a UML activity diagram. It is a general approach where the disambiguation is based on an OWL repository.

2.3 Ontologies Processor

The Ontologies Processing procedure consists of a tokenization mechanism, an abbreviation expansion mechanism and a semantic relatedness measure calculation between the concepts of the ontology-ies. We propose a method that can be used for computing semantic relatedness between concepts that belong to an OWL domain ontology by using structural information and semantics, but also information from WordNet.

The measure is based on the **commonality**, the **related senses**, the **conceptual distance**, the **specificity**, the **specialization** and the **semantic relations**.

The calculation of the semantic relatedness is done once and not in run time. The results are stored and reused when needed. The OntoNL Semantic Relatedness Measure is fully described in.

2.4 Query Formulator

We choose SPARQL (http://www.w3.org/TR/rdf-sparql-query/) as the query language to represent the natural language queries after the syntactic and semantic disambiguation since SPARQL is defined in terms of the W3C's RDF data model and works for any data source that can be mapped into RDF.

To provide an automatic construction of SPARQL queries we need at any point to define the path in the ontological structures that leads from the subject part to the object part of the natural language expression, by taking into account the constraints that are declared from the keywords and the relatedness value between the related classes of the ontology.

The path connecting the classes through OWL ObjectProperties and not IS-A relations, directed from the user expression is given by an algorithm solving the problem of the single-source shortest path: finding a path between two vertices such that the sum of the weights of its constituent edges is minimized. The differentiation here is that the edges linking the classes of the ontology graph are the OWL:ObjectProperties and the weight values are specified by the relatedness measure calculation described earlier in this chapter. So, we need the sum of the weights of its constituent edges to be maximized.

The procedure we follow is summarized by two steps: for each pair of subject-intended object find the optimized directed path through ObjectProperties and form the SPARQL query.

3 Overview of the NL2DL System

The NL2DL System is an application of the OntoNL Framework that addresses a semantic multimedia repository with digital audiovisual content of soccer events and metadata concerning soccer in general. The overall architecture is shown in Fig. 5. The reference ontologies we used is an application of the DS-MIRF ontological infrastructure [3] and the WordNet for the syntactic analysis. The repository for accessing the instances is the DS-MIRF Metadata Repository [4].

The OntoNL Component provides the NL Ontology API and the NL Query API for communication. The NL Query API contains functions to input a natural language query and after the disambiguation outputs a number of weighted SPARQL queries, based on the structures of the ontologies used for the disambiguation. It implements functions for the data transfer between the Framework and the repository. The NL Ontology API consists of the total of functions used for manipulating the ontologies that interfere with the system.

The DS-MIRF OntoNL Manager provides the OntoNL component with the ontologies for the disambiguation and the natural language expression for disambiguation. It is also responsible for retrieving the user request, communicate with the repository, manage the results, rank them based on any existing User Profile information and presented them to the front end the user uses for interactions.

After the natural language expression disambiguation process, the DS-MIRF OntoNL Manager parses the request coming from the OntoNL disambiguation process (SPARQL query) using mappings from domain ontology concepts to internal structures/data model in order to exploit its query/access mechanisms and retrieve the required information.

The retrieval and filtering support in the DS-MIRF Metadata Repository is based on the semantic queries specified by the DS-MIRF OntoNL Manager. The semantic queries may have implicit or explicit boolean operators. The DS-MIRF follows a specific schema for queries. This Schema allows the specification of queries that refer to: (a) multimedia content that satisfies specific criteria; (b) semantic entities that satisfy specific criteria and can be used for the semantic descriptions of multimedia content; and (c) constructs of domain ontologies expressed using MPEG-7 syntax.

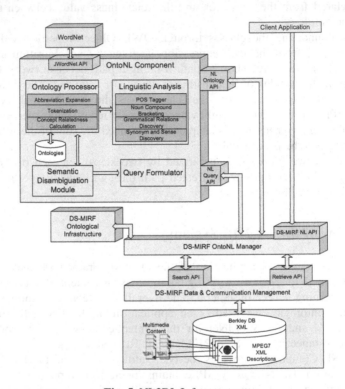

Fig. 5. NL2DL Infrastructure

4   Experimental Results

A screenshot of the NL2DL system for retrieving audio visual content in the domain of the FIFA World Cup 2006 can be seen in Fig. 6. The application also includes the option of inserting the request using speech, but this is not one of the concerns of this work. The result view presents a list with the labels of the XML descriptions that comprise the requested information. The user can choose to see the audiovisual content of the results.

A complete evaluation Framework has been designed for the OntoNL Framework that takes into account a large number of parameters regarding the characteristics of the ontologies involved, the types of users, and different types of performance metrics in order to assess the impact of various algorithms on the overall performance of the system. The results that we obtained are satisfactory and show that the automation in the building of natural language interfaces to semantic multimedia repositories is feasible.

In this paper we are going to present a part of the evaluation results that concern the effective performance of the NL2DL system in the domain of audiovisual content concerning the domain of soccer.

The experiments tested if the language model's components where successfully mapped to ontological structures (Fig. 7) and if the semantic relatedness measure resulted in satisfactory matches (Fig. 8). Also, we were concerned about the overall satisfaction of users of the effectiveness of the results against a keyword-based search (Fig. 9). The performance was measured by users that worked with the ontology and the system developers.

Fig. 6. The multimedia object retrieved

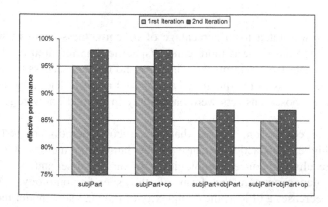

Fig. 7. The effectiveness of ontology mappings (DS-MIRF ontologies for the domain of soccer) to user input

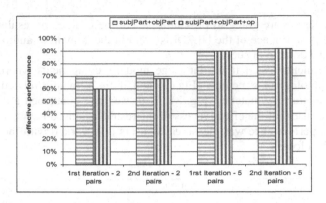

Fig. 8. The effectiveness of the semantic relatedness measure in the DS-MIRF ontologies for the domain of soccer

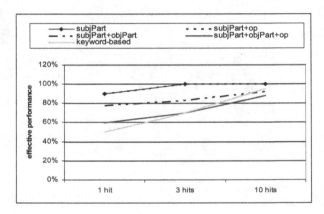

Fig. 9. The effectiveness of the NL2DL in the domain of soccer against a keyword-based search

Each answer was rated for a percentage of its correctness (if there was missing information, or the answer was more general/specific than required by the question, etc.); the effectiveness of performance. The users did not have access to any reference answers in order to assess the quality of a proposed answer. The judgements for the validity of the proposed answers were based only in general knowledge and human opinion.

As a general conclusion, we see that in a second iteration of tests the users expressed a higher satisfaction because of the familiarity increment of using the system. The results that concern ontological structures and semantics (Fig. 7 and 8) are strongly dependent on the form of the specific ontology. Overall, the performance decreases a little as the complexity of the language model increases, but as shown in Fig. 8, we get the correct results sooner and faster against a keyword-based search.

5 Conclusions

We have presented the OntoNL software engineering Framework for the generation of natural language user interfaces to knowledge repositories. The framework contains syntactic and semantic analysis components which are supported by a language model. The semantic analyzer utilizes domain ontologies described in OWL to try to disambiguate or rank the possible user queries.

The motivation of this work came from the absence of a general, domain-independent semantic relatedness measure apart from the WordNet. The measure was successfully used for natural language disambiguation and semantic ranking in the OntoNL Framework. The disambiguation process depends on the domain ontologies and when necessary, the OntoNL Semantic Relatedness Measure is used to rank ontological, grammatically-related concepts.

We have developed an evaluation framework for the OntoNL Natural Language Interface Generator. For the OntoNL Semantic Relatedness Measure evaluation, the framework takes into account a number of parameters regarding the characteristics of the ontologies involved and the types of users. We have observed that when ontologies are used directly from their source (web) a major factor in the performance of the natural language interaction system is the names that are used to describe the ontologies. This may imply that for ontologies that do not utilize "natural language" names for their concepts and relationships we have to provide a mapping to more natural language expressed ontologies.).

Overall, we found that the semantic relatedness measure that is used for the ontology-based semantic ranking of concepts for natural language disambiguation is quite complete and shows very good results. For future improvements, we may need to investigate the influence of more complex structures of OWL vocabulary to the performance.

After this step we continued with an application-based evaluation of the OntoNL measure. We chose to use for the application, the OWL Ontology for the domain of soccer (http://lamia.ced.tuc.gr/ontologies/AV_MDS03/soccer), because it is a big and very specific ontology. Also, the context of the ontology is familiar with the users. The results show that the implementation of semantic natural language interactions with semantic repositories is feasible and inexpensive for a large number of applications domains and domain ontologies.

References

1. Karanastasi, A., Christodoulakis, S.: Ontology-Driven Semantic Ranking for Natural Language Disambiguation in the OntoNL Framework. In: ESWC 2007. LNCS, vol. 4519, pp. 443–457. Springer, Heidelberg (2007)
2. Miller, G., Beckwith, R., Fellbaum, C., Gross, D., Miller, K.J.: Introduction to WordNet: an on-line lexical database. Int. Jrnl of Lexicography 3(4), 235–244 (1990)
3. Tsinaraki, C., Polydoros, P., Christodoulakis, S.: Integration of OWL ontologies in MPEG-7 and TVAnytime compliant Semantic Indexing. In: Persson, A., Stirna, J. (eds.) CAiSE 2004. LNCS, vol. 3084, Springer, Heidelberg (2004)
4. Tsinaraki, C., Christodoulakis, S.: A User Preference Model and a Query Language that allow Semantic Retrieval and Filtering of Multimedia Content. In: Proc. of SMAP 2006 (2006)

Evaluating Preservation Strategies
for Electronic Theses and Dissertations

Stephan Strodl[1], Christoph Becker[1], Robert Neumayer[1], Andreas Rauber[1],
Eleonora Nicchiarelli Bettelli[2], Max Kaiser[2], Hans Hofman[3], Heike Neuroth[4],
Stefan Strathmann[4], Franca Debole[5], and Giuseppe Amato[5]

[1] Vienna University of Technology, Vienna, Austria
[2] Austrian National Library, Vienna, Austria
[3] Nationaal Archief, The Hague, The Netherlands
[4] State and University Library Goettingen, Goettingen, Germany
[5] Italian National Research Council (CNR), Pisa, Italy

Abstract. Digital preservation has turned into a pressing challenge for
institutions having the obligation to preserve digital objects over years. A
range of tools exist today to support the variety of preservation strategies
such as migration or emulation. Heterogeneous content, complex preservation requirements and goals, and untested tools make the selection
of a preservation strategy very difficult. The Austrian National Library
will have to preserve electronic theses and dissertations provided as PDF
files and are thus investigating potential preservation solutions. The DE-
LOS Digital Preservation Testbed is used to evaluate various alternatives
with respect to specific requirements. It provides an approach to make
informed and accountable decisions on which solution to implement in
order to preserve digital objects for a given purpose. We analyse the
performance of various preservation strategies with respect to the specified requirements for the preservation of master theses and present the
results.

Categories and Subject Descriptors: H.3 Information Storage and
Retrieval: H.3.7 Digital Libraries.

General Terms: Digital Library, Digital Preservation, Long Term
Access.

Keywords: Preservation Planning, Migration, Emulation, Case Study.

1 Introduction

An increasing number of organisations throughout the world face national as well
as institutional obligations to collect and preserve digital objects over years.
To fulfil these obligations the institutions are facing the challenge to decide
which digital preservation strategies to follow. This selection of a preservation
strategy and tools is the most difficult part in digital preservation endeavours.
The decision depends on the institutional needs and goals for given settings.

C. Thanos, F. Borri, and L. Candela (Eds.): Digital Libraries: R&D, LNCS 4877, pp. 238–247, 2007.

Technical as well as process and financial aspects of a preservation strategy form the basis for the decision on which preservation strategy to adopt.

A number of strategies have been devised over the last years. An overview is provided by the companion document to the UNESCO charter for the preservation of the digital heritage [1]. All of the proposed strategies have their advantages and disadvantages, and may be suitable in different settings. The most common strategy at the moment is migration, where the object is converted into a more current or more easily preservable file format such as the recently adopted PDF/A standard [2], which implements a subset of PDF optimised for long-term preservation. A report about different kinds of risks for a migration project is done by the Council of Library and Information Resources (CLIR) [3]. Another important strategy is emulation, which aims to provide programmes that mimic a certain environment, e.g. a certain processor or the features of a certain operating system. Jeff Rothenberg [4] envisions a framework of an ideal preservation surrounding. PANIC [5] addresses the challenges of integrating and leveraging existing tools and services and assisting organisations to dynamically discover the optimum preservation strategy.

The Austrian National Library (ONB) will have the future obligation to collect and preserve electronic theses and dissertations from Austrian universities. To fulfil this obligation, the ONB needed a first evaluation of possible preservation strategies for these documents according to their specific requirements.

The DELOS DP Testbed allows the assessment of all kinds of preservation actions against individual requirements and the selection of the most suitable solution. It enforces the explicit definition of preservation requirements and supports the appropriate documentation and evaluation by assisting in the process of running preservation experiments. Thus it was used for assessing potential strategies. The approach presented in this paper basically focuses on the elicitation and documentation of the requirements (objectives). File format repositories such as PRONOM [6] may be used to identify specific technical characteristics of the digital objects at hand. In this paper we describe the workflow for evaluating and selecting DP solutions following the principles of the DELOS DP Testbed. We present the results of the case study involving the Austrian National Library, and demonstrate the benefits of the proposed approach. The case study is also reported in [7].

The remainder of this paper is organised as follows: Following an overview of the principles of the DELOS DP Testbed in Section 2, a description of the workflow is presented in Section 3. We report on the case study on the preservation of electronic theses in PDF format in Section 4. An overview of other case studies is given in Section 5. The closing Section 6 provides conclusions, lessons learned as well as an outlook on future work.

2   The DELOS DP Testbed

The DELOS DP Testbed of the DELOS Digital Preservation Cluster combines the Utility Analysis approach [8] with the testbed designed by the Dutch

National Archive. Figure 1 provides an overview of the workflow of the DELOS DP Testbed, which was described in [8] and recently revised and described in detail in [9]. The 3-phase process, consisting of 14 steps, starts with defining the scenario, setting the boundaries, defining and describing the requirements to be fulfilled by the possible alternatives of preservation actions. The second part of the process identifies and evaluates potential alternatives. The alternatives' characteristics and technical details are specified; then the resources for the experiments are selected, the required tools set up, and a set of experiments is performed. Based on the requirements defined in the beginning, every experiment is evaluated. In the third part of the workflow the results of the experiments are aggregated to make them comparable, the importance factors are set, and the alternatives are ranked. The stability of the final ranking is analysed with respect to minor changes in the weighting and performance of the individual objectives using Sensitivity Analysis. The results are finally evaluated by taking non-measurable influences on the decision into account. After this analysis a clear and well argumented accountable, recommendation for one of the alternatives can be made.

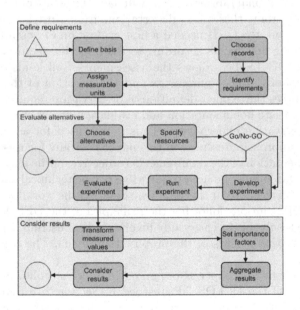

Fig. 1. Overview of DELOS Digital Preservation Testbed's workflow

To simplify the process, to guide users and to automate the structured documentation, a software tool is introduced[1]. It implements the workflow of the DELOS DP Testbed, supporting the documentation of the various steps performed. Results may be stored centrally on a server or exported to an XML file.

---

[1] http://ifs.tuwien.ac.at/dp

3   Testbed Workflow

The detailed workflow consists of fourteen steps as shown in Figure 1, which are described below.

1. **Define Basis**

   The basis of the DELOS Digital Preservation Testbed is a semi-structured description including the required types of records to be considered, a description of the environment in which the testbed process takes place, and information on the amount of files or records.

2. **Choose Records**

   This step selects sample records representing the variety of document characteristics of the considered collection. These samples are later used for evaluating the preservation alternatives.

3. **Define Requirements**

   The goal of this decisive step is to clearly define the requirements and goals for a preservation solution in a given application domain. In the so-called objective tree, high-level goals and detailed requirements are collected and organised in a tree structure.

   While the resulting trees usually differ through changing preservation settings, some general principles can be observed. At the top level, the objectives can usually be organised into four main categories:

   - *File characteristics* describe the visual and contextual experience a user has by dealing with a digital record. Subdivisions may be "Appearance", "Content", "Structure" and "Behaviour", with lowest level objectives being e.g. colour depth, image resolution, forms of interactivity, macro support, or embedded metadata.
   - *Record characteristics* describe the technical foundations of a digital record, the context, the storage medium, interrelationships and metadata.
   - *Process characteristics* describe the preservation process. These include usability, complexity or scalability.
   - *Costs* have a significant influence on the choice of a preservation solution. Usually, they may be divided in technical and personnel costs.

   The objective tree is usually created in a workshop setting with experts from different domains contributing to the requirements gathering process. The tree documents the individual preservation requirements of an institution for a given partially homogeneous collection of objects. Examples include scientific papers and dissertations in PDF format, historic audio recordings, or video holdings from ethnographic studies. Typical trees may contain between 50 to several hundred objectives, usually organised in 4-6 hierarchy levels.

4. **Assign Measurable Units**

   Measurable effects are assigned to the objectives that have been defined in the previous step. Wherever possible, these effects should be objectively measurable (e.g. € per year, frames per second). In some cases, (semi-)

subjective scales will need to be employed (e.g. degrees of openness and stability, support of a standard, degree of file format adoption, etc.).

5. **Choose Alternatives**
   Different preservation solutions, such as different migration tools or emulators, are described. An extensive description of the preservation process ensures a clear understanding of each alternative.

6. **Specify Resources**
   For each alternative defined in the previous step, a project and work description plan is developed, where the amount of work, time and money required for testing the alternative are estimated.

7. **Go/No-Go**
   This step considers the definition of resources and requirements to determine if the proposed alternatives are feasible. The result is a decision for continuing the evaluation process or a justification of the abandonment of certain alternatives.

8. **Develop Experiment**
   In order to run repeatable tests, a documented setting is necessary. This stage produces a specific development plan for each experiment, which includes the workflow of the experiment, software and hardware system of the experiment environment, and the mechanism to capture the results.

9. **Run Experiment**
   An experiment will test one or more aspects of applying a specific preservation alternative to the previously defined sample records.

10. **Evaluate Experiments**
    The results of the experiments are evaluated to determine the degree to which the requirements defined in the objective tree were met.

11. **Transform Measured Values**
    The measurements taken in the experiments might follow different scales. In order to make these comparable, they are transformed to a uniform scale using transformation tables. The resulting scale might e. g. range from 0 to 5. A value of 0 would in this case denote an unacceptable result and thus serve as a drop-out criterion for the whole preservation alternative.

12. **Set Importance Factors**
    Not all of the objectives of the tree are equally important. This step assigns importance factors to each objective depending on specific preferences and requirements of the project.

13. **Aggregate Results**
    With the input of the importance factors and the transformed numbers, a single final value of each alternative is calculated.

14. **Perform Sensitivity Analysis and Consider Results**
    Finally the alternatives are ranked. The software implementation supports varying weights form different users. These are further used for the Sensitivity Analysis of the evaluation, which analyses, e. g., the stability of the ranking with respect to minor changes in weighting of the individual objectives. Additionally, side effects may be considered that are not included in

the numerical evaluation, like the relationship with a supplier or expertise in a certain alternative.

4   Preserving Austrian Theses and Dissertations

The Austrian National Library will have the future obligation to collect and preserve master theses from Austrian Universities. The theses will be provided to the library in a PDF format. The Austrian National Library provides guidelines for creating preservable PDFs [10], but at the moment the ONB is not able to legally enforce these guidelines. This case study gives a starting point to identify the requirements and goals for the digital preservation of master theses. It furthermore allows a first evaluation of the various preservation actions being considered.

This application domain is interesting and highly relevant for digital preservation practice for a number of reasons:

1. PDF is a wide-spread file format and very common in libraries and archives.
2. Although PDF is a single file format, there exist different versions of the standard.
3. Different embedded objects are captured in this case study, such as video and audio content.

In a brainstorming workshop the requirements for this specific application area were collected. The profound knowledge about digital preservation and documents of the workshop participants eases the creation of the objective tree. The required document behaviour and the process characteristics were intensely discussed. The participants agreed on blocking of scripts, deactivation of security mechanism (such as password protected printing) and detailed requirements for the process documentation. The resulting objective tree shows also a strong focus on the structure, content and appearance of the objects; especially layout and structure of the documents need to be preserved.

Characteristics concerning object structure include among others

- Document structure (chapters, sections),
- Reference tables (table of content, list of figures)
- Line and page breaks,
- Headers and footers,
- Footnotes,
- Equations (size, position, structure, caption),
- Figures (size, position, structure, caption), and
- Tables (size, position, structure, caption).

The next step was to assign measurable effects for each leaf of the tree. Most of them are simple yes/no decisions, for example whether the fontsize of text changed or not, or whether table structures have been kept intact.

The weighting of the tree reflects the primary focus on content; at the top level the object characteristics as well as process characteristics and costs have a strong influence on the choice of a preservation strategy.

Table 1. Overall scores of the alternatives

Nr	Alternative	Total score
1	PDF/A (Adobe Acrobat 7 prof.)	4.52
2	TIFF (Document Converter 4.1)	4.26
3	EPS (Adobe Acrobat 7 prof.)	4.22
4	JPEG 2000 (Adobe Acrobat 7 prof.)	4.17
5	RTF (Adobe Acrobat 7 prof.)	3.43
6	RTF (ConvertDoc 4.1)	3.38
7	TXT (Adobe Acrobat 7 prof.)	3.28

Several migration solutions were evaluated using the DELOS DP Testbed:

1. Conversion to plain-text format using Adobe Acrobat 7 Professional.
2. Conversion to Rich Text Format (RTF) using SoftInterface ConvertDoc 3.82.
3. Conversion to RTF using Adobe Acrobat 7 Professional.
4. Conversion to Multipage TIFF using Universal Document Converter 4.1.
5. Conversion to PDF/A using Adobe Acrobat 7 Professional.
   (The generated PDF/A is not completely consistent with PDF/A-ISO-Standard. [2])
6. Conversion to lossless JPEG2000 using Adobe Acrobat 7 Professional.
7. Conversion to Encapsulated PostScript (EPS) using Adobe Acrobat 7 Professional.

All experiments were executed on Windows XP professional on a sample set of five master theses from the Vienna University of Technology. The results as provided in Table 1 show that the migration to PDF/A using Adobe Acrobat 7 Professional ranks on top, followed by migration to TIFF, EPS and JPEG2000; far behind are RTF and plain text. The alternative PDF/A basically preserves all core document characteristics in a wide-spread file format, while showing good migration process performance.

The alternatives TIFF, EPS and JPEG show very good appearance, but have weaknesses regarding criteria such as 'content machine readable'. Furthermore, the migration to JPEG and EPS produces one output file for each page, the object coherence is not as well preserved as in a PDF/A document.

Both RTF solutions exhibit major weaknesses in appearance and structure of the documents, specifically with respect to tables and equations as well as character encoding and line breaks. Object characteristics show a clear advantage for ConvertDoc, which was able to preserve the layout of headers and footers as opposed to Adobe Acrobat. Still, costs and the technical advantages of the Acrobat tool, such as macro support and customization, compensate for this difference and lead to an equal score.

The loss of essential characteristics means that the plain text format fails to fulfil a number of minimum requirements regarding the preservation of important artifacts like tables and figures as well as appearance characteristics like font types and sizes.

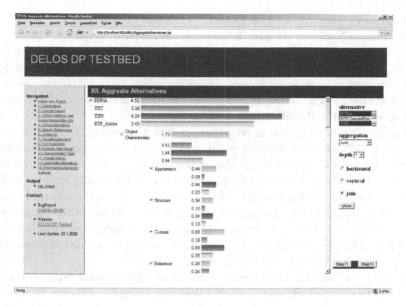

Fig. 2. Screenshot: comparison of results

Figure 2 shows an extract of the results of the software tool. The software supports the comparison of alternatives to highlight strengths and weaknesses of each alternative.

Multimedia content proved to be a difficult task: None of the tested alternatives was able to preserve embedded audio and video content. This issue could be solved in two ways: (1) Use a tool for automated extraction of multimedia content from PDF. (2) Solve the problem on an organisational level by issuing a submission policy which states that multimedia objects have to be provided separately. In both cases, a separate preservation strategy for the multimedia content has to be devised.

Depending on whether preserving multimedia content is a primary goal to be fulfilled, our final recommendation resulting from the evaluation of the experiments is to (1) use migration to PDF/A with Adobe Acrobat 7 Professional or (2) combine the alternative PDF/A with a multimedia extraction tool or a submission policy.

The presented case study presents a relative simple preservation problem. The considered collection consists of homogenous file types and objects are incoherent and not compounded. Complexity in preservation planning is raised by heterogeneous content, complex preservation requirements and goals, and untested tools.

5   Further Case Studies

This paper presents the evaluation of different preservation strategies for master theses, further case studies were conducted within DELOS during the last years including the following.

- **Document records of the Dutch National Archive**
  The Dutch National Archive is responsible for storing all documents generated by the Dutch government, ministries and official bodies. The case study tried to define the objectives for the preservation of different kinds of documents, such as video and audio, focusing particularly on the record characteristics. The resulting objective tree contained around 450 objectives.
- **Migration of a database to XML**
  This case study was done in cooperation with the Italian National Research Council (CNR). The starting point was a legacy database containing descriptive meta data of a small library, consisting of books, registered users, information about lending, order of books, content (field, review) and the budget for new books. The data of the database was to be converted in XML for archiving and further application using e.g. a native XML database. In this case study we tried to reduce the number of objectives, focusing on the critical characteristics. The resulting objective tree contained approximately 70 nodes with a maximum depth of 6 layers.
- **Preserving annual electronic journal of differential equations**
  Within the project of supra-regional literature supply in Germany the State and University Library Goetting holds the collection of "Electronic Journal of Differential Equations". The SUB is committed to preserver the collection of the journals and providing access to them. In a first workshop the requirements and goals for the collection were specified. The specific challenges of this collection are the hierarchical structure of the considered object and the different formats of the sub-objects.

6   Conclusions

The DELOS DP Testbed provides a means to make well-documented, accountable decisions on which preservation solution to implement. It enforces the explicit definition of preservation requirements in the form of specific objectives. It allows evaluating various preservation solutions in a consistent manner, enabling informed and well-documented decisions. Thus, it helps to establish and maintain a trusted preservation environment.

The case study of the Austrian National Library evaluates various migration strategies for PDF. The migration to PDF/A by Adobe Acrobat 7 Professional reaches the highest score and provides a feasible solution for the long term storage of theses and dissertations. Migration to TIFF, EPS and JPEG perform very good at appearance objectives, but have some substantial technical weaknesses. The preservation alternatives RTF and plain text are not able to migrate essential parts of the object and should not be considered further. None of the evaluated alternatives is able to handle multimedia content, this issue has to be solved on another appropriate level - either by extracting the multimedia content or by issuing a submission policy. Further work will evaluate different tools for converting PDF to PDF/A with a focus on process objectives such as duration, capacity, and automation support.

While many of the processing steps of the DELOS DP Testbed are automated, a significant amount of work is still involved in acquiring the measurements of the experiment outcomes. Ongoing work on preservation plan decision support within the European Union PLANETS project (http://www.planets-project.eu) is based on the DELOS Digital Preservation Testbed. It will integrate tools for preservation action and object characterisation to further reduce the workload.

Acknowledgements

Part of this work was supported by the European Union in the 6. Framework Program, IST, through the DELOS DPC Cluster (WP6) of the DELOS NoE on Digital Libraries, contract 507618, and the PLANETS project, contract 033789.

References

1. UNESCO, Information Society Division: Guidelines for the preservation of digital heritage (October 2003)
2. ISO: Document management - Electronic document file format for long-term preservation - Part 1: Use of PDF 1.4 (PDF/A) (ISO/CD 19005-1). International Organization for Standardization (2004)
3. Lawrence, G., Kehoe, W., Rieger, O., Walters, W., Kenney, A.: Risk management of digital information: A file format investigation. In: Technical report, Council on Library and Information Resources (2000)
4. Rothenberg, J.: Avoiding technological quicksand: Finding a viable technical foundation for digital preservation. In: Technical report, Council on Library and Information Resources (1999)
5. Hunter, J., Choudhury, S.: PANIC - An integrated approach to the preservation of composite digital objects using semantic web services. In: IWAW 2005. Proceedings of the 5th International Web Archiving Workshop, Vienna, Austria (September 2005)
6. Brown, A.: Automating preservation: New developments in the pronom service. RGL DigiNews 9(2) The National Archives (April 2007),
   http://www.rlg.org/en/page.php?Page_ID=20571
7. Becker, C., Strodl, S., Neumayer, R., Rauber, A., Bettelli, E.N., Kaiser, M.: Long-term preservation of electronic theses and dissertations: A case study in preservation planning. In: RCDL 2007. Proceedings of the 9th Russian National Research Conference on Digital Libraries, Pereslavl, Russia (2007)
8. Rauch, C., Rauber, A.: Preserving digital media: Towards a preservation solution evaluation metric. In: Chen, Z., Chen, H., Miao, Q., Fu, Y., Fox, E., Lim, E.-p. (eds.) ICADL 2004. LNCS, vol. 3334, Springer, Heidelberg (2004)
9. Strodl, S., Rauber, A., Rauch, C., Hofman, H., Debole, F., Amoato, G.: The DE-LOS testbed for choosing a digital preservation strategy. In: Sugimoto, S., Hunter, J., Rauber, A., Morishima, A. (eds.) ICADL 2006. LNCS, vol. 4312, pp. 323–332. Springer, Heidelberg (2006)
10. Horvath, M.: Empfehlungen zum Erzeugen archivierbarer Dateien im Format PDF. Technical report, Austrian National Library (in German) (2005),
    http://www.onb.ac.at/about/lza/pdf/ONB_PDF-Empfehlungen_1-4.pdf

Searching for Ground Truth: A Stepping Stone in Automating Genre Classification

Yunhyong Kim and Seamus Ross

Digital Curation Centre (DCC)
&
Humanities Adavanced Technology Information Institute (HATII)
University of Glasgow
Glasgow, UK
{y.kim,s.ross}@hatii.arts.gla.ac.uk

Abstract. This paper examines genre classification of documents and its role in enabling the effective automated management of digital documents by digital libraries and other repositories. We have previously presented genre classification as a valuable step toward achieving automated extraction of descriptive metadata for digital material. Here, we present results from experiments using human labellers, conducted to assist in genre characterisation and the prediction of obstacles which need to be overcome by an automated system, and to contribute to the process of creating a solid testbed corpus for extending automated genre classification and testing metadata extraction tools across genres. We also describe the performance of two classifiers based on image and stylistic modeling features in labelling the data resulting from the agreement of three human labellers across fifteen genre classes.

Keywords: information extraction, genre classification, automated metadata extraction, metadata, digital library, data management.

1 Introduction

As digital resources become increasingly common as a form of information in our everyday life, the task of storing, managing, and utilising this information becomes increasingly important. Managing digital objects not only involves storage, efficient search, and retrieval of objects - tasks already expected by traditional libraries - but also involves ensuring the continuation of technological requirements, tracking of versions, linking and networking of independently produced objects, and selecting objects and resources for retention from a deluge of objects being created and distributed. Knowledge representation, embodying the core information about an object, e.g. metadata summarising the technical requirements, function, source, and content of data, play a crucial role in the efficient and effective management and use of digital materials (cf. [22]), making it easier to tame the resources within. It has been noted that the manual collection of such information is costly and labour-intensive and that a

C. Thanos, F. Borri, and L. Candela (Eds.): Digital Libraries: R&D, LNCS 4877, pp. 248–261, 2007.

collaborative effort to automate the extraction or creation of such information would be undoubtedly necessary[1].

There have been several efforts (e.g. [11], [12], [23], DC-dot metadata editor[2], [3] and [14]) to automatically extract relevant metadata from selected genres (e.g. scientific articles, webpages and emails). These often play heavily on the structure of the document, which characterises the genre to which the document belongs. It seems, therefore, reasonable to employ automated genre classification to bind these genre-dependent tools. However, there is a distinct lack of consolidated corpora on which automated genre classification and the transferability or integrability of tools across genres can be tested. One of the reasons such corpora have not yet been constructed relates to the elusive nature of genre classification, which seems to take on a different guise in independent researches. Biber's analysis ([5]) tried to capture five genre dimensions (information, narration, elaboration, persuasion, abstraction) of text, while others ([13], [6]) examined popularly recognised genre classes such as FAQ, Job Description, Editorial or Reportage. Genre has been used to describe stylistic aspects (objectivity, intended level of audience, positive or negative opinion, whether it is a narrative) of a document ([10], [15]), or even to describe selected journal and brochure titles ([1]). Others ([21], [2]) have clustered documents into similar feature groups, without attempting to label the samples with genre facets or classes.

The difficulty of defining genre is already emphasised in the literature, and many proposals have been reasonably suggested. However, very little active search for ground truth in human agreement over genre classification has been conducted to scope for a useful genre schema and corpus. To shed some light on the situation, we have undertaken experiments to analyse human agreement over genre classification: the agreement analysis will establish the degree of agreement that can be reached by several human labellers in genre classification, isolate the conditions that give meaning to genre classification, and provide a statistically well understood corpus. The corpus will also function as a testbed for examining transferability of tools tailored to work in a small number of genres to other genres, and constructing metadata extraction tools which integrate tools developed independently for different genres. In addition, a study of human performance in genre classification provides a means of scoping new emerging genres, and helps us to grasp the history of genre development. To this end, we have constructed a schema of seventy genres (Section 2) and present results in document collection and categorisation by human labellers in Section 3.

Genre classification, in its most general understanding, is the categorisation of documents according to their structural (e.g. the existence of a title page, chapter, section) and functional (e.g. to record, to inform) properties. The two are, however, not divorced from each other: the structure evolves to optimise the functional requirements of the document within the environment (e.g. the target

---

[1] Issues addressed in The Cedars Project at the University of Leeds:
http:// www.leeds.ac.uk/cedars/guideto/collmanagemnet/guidetocolman.pdf
[2] dc-dot, UKOLN Dublin Core Metadata Editor,
http://www.ukoln.ac.uk/ metadata/dcdot/

community, publisher and creator), just as the structure of organisms evolves to meet their survival functions within the natural environment. And, just as the functional aspect of an organism is central to its survival, the functional properties of a digital object is the crucial driving force of document genre. The functional aspect of the document, however, is a high level concept which is inferred from selected structural aspects of the document, and, in turn, the structural aspects are defined by lower level features which constitute genes in the DNA of the document. Unlike organisms, we have not even come close to identifying the DNA sequence of a digital document, let alone parsing the sequence into genes to understand how they are expressed to create semantic information (e.g. genre or subject). Accordingly, automated classification has traditionally taken to examining a large pot of related and unrelated features, to be refined by selection or creation algorithms to distinguish between a small number of predefined classes. This method might result in three immediately noticeable problems:

- The reason for specific selections and creations of features remains opaque.
- Features will be selected to conform to the unavoidable bias in the training data.
- The performance of the tool on a new set of classes is unpredictable, and most likely, the tool will have to be reconstructed by re-running feature selection over new data.

To address these points, we propose grouping features according to similar type (e.g. those which come together to describe a well-defined aspect of document structure) in analogy to genes. This makes it easier to identify the reasons behind errors and see if success is an artefact of unrepresentative data. We also propose that a study of a wider variety of genre classes may be necessary. A classifier which performs well to distinguish three classes can be expected to perform well to distinguish two of the three classes; whereas the behaviour of a classifier which recognises two classes in distinguishing three classes is less predictable. The amount of information the class of a document encompasses is in direct relationship to the number of other classes to which it could belong. By building a system which can detect selected genre classes from a vast range of classes, we are building a better informed system.

We have previously identified ([16]) five feature types: image features (e.g white space analysis; cf. [1]), stylistic features (e.g. word, sentence, block statistics; cf. [21]), language modelling features (e.g. Bag-of-Words and N-gram models), semantic features (e.g. number of subjective noun phrases) and source or domain knowledge features (e.g. file name, journal name, web address, technical format structures, institutional affiliations, other works by the author). We reported preliminary results of classifiers built on two or more of the first three feature types on a privately labelled corpus ([16], [18],[19]). In this paper, we look at the performance of a classifier modeled on the first two types of features on new data labelled by three human labellers, as further study of the correlation between genres and feature types.

2   Genre Schema

In this paper we are working with seventy genres which have been organised into ten groups (Table 1). The schema was constructed from an examination of PDF documents gathered from the internet using a list of random search words. The schema captures a wide range of commonly used genres. The aim is to initially vie for a coverage of as many genres as possible rather than to employ a well established structure. In response, certain distinctions may seem at first inconsistent or ambiguous: for instance, Legal Proceedings versus Legal Order, or Technical Manual versus Manual. However, the hope is that when you view the entire path as genres, e.g. Evidential Document - Legal Proceedings versus Other Functional Document Legal Order, the distinction will become clearer. The schema will form a fundamental field to be harvested for further refinement. It will be adjusted to exclude ill-defined genres depending on emerging results of the human labelling experiments described in Section 3.

Table 1. Genre schema (numbers in parentheses are assigned database IDs)

Book		
Academic Monograph (2)	Book of Poetry (4)	Other Book (6)
Book of Fiction (3)	Handbook (5)	
Article		
Abstract (8)	Other Research (10)	News Report (12)
Scientific Article (9)	Magazine Article (11)	
Short Composition		
Fictional Piece (14)	Dramatic Script (16)	Short Biographical Sketch (18)
Poems (15)	Essay (17)	Review (19)
Serial		
Periodicals (News, Mag) (21)	Conference Proceeding (23)	
Journals (22)	Newsletter (24)	
Correspondence		
Email (26)	Memo (29)	
Letter (27)	Telegram (30)	
Treatise		
Thesis (32)	Technical Report (34)	Technical Manual (36)
Business/Operational Rept (33)	Miscellaneous Report (35)	
Information Structure		
List (38)	Table (41)	Programme (44)
Catalogue (39)	Menu (42)	Questionnaire (45)
Raw Data (40)	Form (43)	FAQ (46)
Evidential Document		
Minutes (48)	Financial Record (50)	Slip (52)
Legal Proceedings (49)	Receipt (51)	Contract (53)
Visual Document		
Artwork (55)	Graph (58)	Poster (61)
Card (56)	Diagram (59)	Comics (62)
Chart (57)	Sheet Music (60)	
Other Functional Document		
Guideline (64)	Product Description (70)	Forum Discussion (76)
Regulations (65)	Advertisement (71)	Interview (77)
Manual (66)	Announcement (72)	Notice (78)
Grant/Project Proposal (67)	Appeal/Propaganda (73)	Resume/ CV (79)
Legal Proposal/Order (68)	Exam or Worksheet (74)	Slides (80)
Job/Course/Project Desc. (69)	Factsheet (75)	Speech Transcript (81)

3   Human Labelling Experiment

We have undertaken two human document genre classification experiments in this research. First we had students retrieve sample documents of the seventy genres in Table 1 (Document Retrieval Exercise), and subsequently had them re-assigned with genres from the same schema (Reclassification) to validate, quantify, or examine agreement over its membership to any one genre.

Document Retrieval Exercise: In this experiment, university students were assigned genres and asked to retrieve 100 samples of PDF files belonging to their assigned genre written in English. They were also asked to give reasons for including the particular sample in the set and asked not to retrieve more than one document from each source. They were not introduced to pre-defined notions of the genre before retrieval.

Reclassification: Two people from a secretarial background were employed to reclassify the retrieved documents. They were not allowed to confer, and the documents, without their original label, were presented in a random order from the database to each labeller. The secretaries were not given descriptions of genres. They were expected to use their own training in record-keeping to classify the documents. The number of items which have been stored in the database is described in Table 2.

At first, it may seem odd not to provide definitions for the genres in the schema. However, note that it is not true that every genre class requires the same amount of detail in its definition to achieve the same level of precision. In fact, as we will see, the level of agreement on some genres is high regardless of the lack of definition.

Table 2. Database composition (left) and Agreement of Labellers (right)

Total	with three labels	with two labels	damaged
5485	5373	103	9

Labellers	Agreed
student & secretary A	2745
student & secretary B	2974
secretary A & B	2422
all labellers	2008

Some of the collected data can not be considered to be examples of the genre. For instance, some students introduced articles about email into the database as samples of the genre Email. Others submitted empty receipt forms as samples of the genre Receipt. The genre Card was also heavily populated with forms (e.g. unfilled identity cards). While the first set of errors are due to a misunderstanding of the instructions and stems from the fact that emails are hard to find in PDF format, the latter sets of errors are due to differing opinions of the genre definition. These items were not removed from the database because:

- this would introduce the bias of the remover into the database; and,
- documents which have been included erroneously will be automatically filtered out of the collection once reclassification labels and agreement data are acquired.

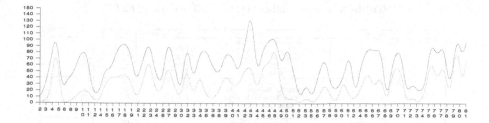

Fig. 1. Two labeller agreement (top graph) versus three labeller agreement (bottom graph)

Full analysis of these errors will be carried out before the release of the corpus, at which time, the rationale presented by students to justify the inclusion of particular items will also be analysed for elements that might characterise genres. In Figure 1, we have presented the numbers of documents in each of the seventy genres on which labellers have agreed. The graph exhibiting higher numbers presents the number of documents on which at least two labellers have assigned the same label, and the lower level graph displays the number of documents on which all three labellers have assigned the same label. The genre classes are indicated as numbers (to save space) along the bottom of the graph, indicating the assigned genre IDs given in Table 1. Note that there is a large discrepancy between the agreement with respect to the genre Form (43), but that selected genres such as Handbook (5), Minutes (48) and Resume/CV(79) show little difference between the two labeller agreement and the three labeller agreement, suggesting the latter genres as less context-dependent genres.

4   Case Study

In this section we will look at the student performance on documents for which secretaries have given the same label. There are 2422 items on which the decision of the secretaries concurred. The figures in Table 2 show the number of documents on which different groups of labellers have agreed. The statistics in Table 2 show that there is more agreement between the student and either of the secretaries than between the two secretaries. A possible explanation for the discrepancy could be that secretaries are trained to identify strictly defined properties of a limited number of genres, while students detect broadly defined properties of a vast range of genres. Further labellers and studies will be required to make any decisive conclusions.

4.1   Precision Versus Recall

In this section we present the recall and precision of student classification on the data which was given the same label by the secretaries. The results are shown in Table 3. Compared to some other classification tasks (e.g. classification of

Table 3. Human Labelling: Overall accuracy: 82.9%

Genre group	Genre	no. of items	Recall(%)	Precision(%)
Book	Academic Monograph	3	0	0
	Book of Fiction	8	37	100
	Book of Poetry	12	67	23
	Handbook	105	88	100
	Other Book	0	0	0
Article	Abstract	1	100	8
	Scientific Research Article	15	47	32
	Other Research Article	36	50	69
	Magazine Article	40	50	61
	News Report	9	89	89
Short Composition	Fictional Piece	1	100	33
	Poems	37	78	91
	Dramatic Script	43	98	100
	Essay	59	68	89
	Short Biographical Sketch	46	100	98
	Review	46	85	83
Serial	Periodicals (Newspaper, Magazine)	21	29	100
	Journals	34	91	86
	Conference Proceedings	76	96	99
	Newsletter	28	71	80
Correspondence	Email	21	90	70
	Letter	67	93	100
	Memo	29	93	71
	Telegram	7	100	78
Treatise	Thesis	66	89	98
	Business/Operational Report	12	75	36
	Technical Report	52	88	94
	Miscellaneous Report	38	34	81
	Technical Manual	7	86	27
Information Structure	List	26	73	86
	Catalogue	51	90	90
	Raw Data	40	73	91
	Table Calendar	30	93	68
	Menu	52	100	96
	Form	114	53	100
	Programme	29	66	100
	Questionnaire	61	98	91
	FAQ	71	90	98
Evidential Document	Minutes	94	97	100
	Legal Proceedings	36	50	58
	Financial Record	7	86	75
	Receipt	8	100	21
	Slips	0	0	0
	Contract	10	90	82
Visual Document	Artwork	2	100	13
	Card	9	100	35
	Chart	39	82	74
	Graph	14	71	48
	Diagram	6	33	18
	Sheet Music	37	100	100
	Poster	23	48	85
	Comics	7	100	27
Other Functional Document	Guideline	48	58	93
	Regulations	53	94	91
	Manual	43	60	96
	Grantor Project Proposal	45	98	81
	Legal Appeal/Proposal/Order	0	0	0
	Job/Course/Project Description	62	89	96
	Product/Application Description	56	100	89
	Advertisement	6	33	25
	Announcement	12	83	56
	Appeal/Propaganda	1	100	25
	Exam/Worksheet	22	81	90
	Factsheet	80	86	93
	Forum Discussion	38	97	79
	Interview	64	98	97
	Notice	9	89	89
	Resume/CV	100	98	100
	Slides	27	85	92
	Speech Transcript	71	97	96

pronouns in [17]), the overall accuracy of 82.9% is a low percentage. However, as genre classification is a task involving high level conceptual analysis, this seems a reasonable ageement level. Having said this, the agreement within Scientific Research Article is unexpectedly low. There could be at least two reasons for such discord between the labellers. For example, there might have been a misunderstanding which caused poor quality in the initial document retrieval exercise, or certain genres might inherently be dependent on experience or training and are not clearly recognisable by members of other communities. Upon examination of the documents, it seems to be that both reasons are in play. For instance, numerous forms were labelled as receipts by students, under the impression that receipts which have not been filled are still receipts. Those with a secretarial background did not share this notion. Likewise, some articles on the subject of email were retrieved as samples of the class Email by the students. On the other hand, there was only a single example out of one hundred abstracts collected by students which the secretaries, who are not necessarily academically inclined, agreed as being an abstract. Nevertheless, the results are encouraging in that an 82.9% overall agreement along with the high precision rate of many genres suggest that, even without giving extensive definitions of each genre class, a reasonable agreement is already achieved with common genre terms. It should be mentioned, however, that each secretary's overall accuracy on the agreement data of the other two labellers was also examined and found to be lower at 73.2% and 67.5%.

4.2   Disagreement Analysis

The groups in Table 4 represent cluster of genres for which frequent cross labelling was observed. The groups in Table 4 are not exclusive of other confusion. The table is meant to convey the clusters of the most confused genre classes. It should also be noted that two genres may be included in the same cluster, but the frequency at which one is labelled as the other may not be comparable in both directions. For instance, Manual was often given the label Technical Manual but not vice versa. The confusion between Receipt and Form is due to perceiving a receipt form prior to its completion as a sample of Receipt. The groups in Table 4 suggest that most of the confusion arises within the genre groups (cf. Table 1), which seems to add partial value to our genre schema.

Table 4. Genre cross-labelling cluster groups

Group	Genres
Group A	Book of Fiction, Poetry Book, Fictional Piece, Poems
Group B	Magazine Article, Scientific Research Article, Other Research Article
Group C	Technical Report, Business/Operational Report, Miscellaneous Report
Group D	Posters, Artwork, Advertisement
Group E	Diagram, Graph, Chart
Group F	Form, Receipt
Group G	Handbook, Technical Manual, Manual
Group H	List, Catalogue, Raw Data, Table
Group I	Legal Proceedings, Legal Appeal/Proposal/Order

4.3   Improving the Corpus

Acquiring a representative corpus is difficult ([4]). Part of the reason for this is because representativeness is meaningful only within the context of the task to be performed. For example, a well known part-of-speech tagger ([9]), trained on the well-designed Penn Treebank Wall Street Journal corpus ([20]), fails to tag instances of He (Helium) in Astronomy articles correctly ([17]) because the training data failed to be representative of astronomy articles - the task domain. As purposes and domains change, we propose that a well-designed corpus should not emphasise representativeness but be based on the level of annotation, qualifications, and consolidation. Most existing corpora are designed to hold a number of selected categories populated by samples from well-defined sources, upon the agreement of expert knowledge of the categories. Here we would like to propose the construction of a different type of corpus. We set forth the following principles:

- every member of the database must be accompanied by a vector of dimension N (the size of the final genre schema) indicating the number of times each genre was assigned to the item by human labellers, and,
- labellers from a selected number of characterising groups should be employed to label the data, and each instance of a genre assignment should be qualified by the group of the labeller.

The selection of labellers determines the classification standard or the policy one wishes to represent in an automated classification. If the objective is to model genre classification based on common sense, a large number of labellers from a diverse set of backgrounds should be represented. But, if the objective is to design a classifier for specialists of a selected domain, this corpus is likely to prove inadequate for representing the domain population. A corpus built on the above principles would provide us with greater scope for analysis, for achieving representativeness of different populations, and for fine tuning an automated system, by making transparent:

- the confidence level of each item's membership in each genre class,
- the labeller's possible bias by indicating the labeller background, and,
- the fact that classification is not a binary decision (deciding whether or not an item is a sample of a class) but a selection of several probable options.

5   Experiments

5.1   Data

The dataset used in this sections's experiments consists of the data on which all labellers have agreed in the human labelling experiment described in Section 3. The experiment was conducted over only sixteen of the seventy genres presented in Table 1. The range of genres was limited to be more easily comparable to earlier experiments in [16], [18], [19]. The results of experiments on the full range of genres will be available after further analysis of the human experiments have been carried out.

5.2   Classifiers

In [16], we reported results on using the Nave Bayes model to detect instances of Periodicals, Scientific Research Article, Thesis, Business Report, and Forms from a pool of documents belonging to nineteen genres. In this paper we have abandoned the Nave Bayes Model. The Nave Bayes Model was only chosen as a preliminary testing ground as it is one of the most basic probabilistic models available. In reality, Nave Bayes is well known to have problems when dealing with features which are not independent and, in the current context, we want to identify features of one genetic feature type, i.e. features which are dependent on each other, which makes Nave Bayes an inappropriate choice. In its place we have chosen the Random Forest method ([7]), which has been presented as being effective when dealing with imbalanced data ([8]). We have examined two classifiers in this paper:

Image classifier: The first page of the document was sectioned into a sixty-two by sixty-two grid. Each region on the grid is examined for non-white pixels, where non-white pixel is defined to be those of a value less than 245. All regions with non-white pixels are labelled 1, while those which are completely white are labelled 0. The choice of sixty-two to define the size of the grid reflects the fact that the level of granularity seemed to be the coarsest level at which some of the documents were recognisable as belonging to specific genres even by the human eye. The resulting vector was then probabilistically modeled via the Random Forrest Decision method, with nineteen trees using the Weka Machine Learning Toolkit([24]). The motivation for this classifier comes from the recognition that certain genres have more (or less) white space in the first page (e.g. the title page of the book), and that the page is often more strictly formatted (e.g. slides for a conference presentation) to catch the attention of the reader (e.g. the reverse colouring on a magazine cover) and introduce them to the type of document at hand without detailed examination of the content. Note that another advantage of white space analysis is that it is easily applicable to documents of any language and does not depend heavily on character encoding and the accessibility of content.

Style classifier: From a previously collected data set, the union of all words found in the first page, of half or more of the files in each genre, was retrieved and compiled into a list. For each document a vector is constructed using the frequency of each word in the compiled list. The collection of vectors is modeled again via the Random Forrest Decision method with nineteen trees using the Weka toolkit([24]). The feature are different from the classifiers in [16] and [17] which also incorporated the number of words, font sizes and variations. This classifier is intended to capture frequency of words common to all genres as well as words which only appear in some genres. The contention of this paper is that even words which appear in a wide variety of genres may be a significant metric, when the frequency is also taken into consideration. A typical example of its weight is embodied in the fact that forms are less likely to contain as many definite or indefinite articles as theses. The two classifiers were used to predict

Table 5. Image classifier: overall accuracy 38.37%

Group	Genre	no. of items	Recall (%)	Precision(%)
Article	Magazine Article	20	5	17
	Scientific Research Article	7	0	0
	Other Research Article	18	67	50
Book	Book of Fiction	3	25	18
Information Structure	Form	60	50	40
	List	19	0	0
Serial	Periodicals (Newspaper,Magazine)	6	14	33
	Newsletter	20	6	13
Treatise	Technical report	46	11	19
	Business/Operational Report	9	0	0
	Thesis	59	84	56
Evidential Document	Minutes	91	77	47
Other Functional Document	Slides	23	73	94
	Product/Application Description	56	10	14
	Guideline	28	0	0
	Factsheet	69	33	25

Table 6. Style classifier: overall accuracy 69.96%

Group	Genre	no. of items	Recall (%)	Precision (%)
Article	Magazine Article	20	47	82
	Scientific Research Article	7	0	0
	Other Research Article	18	39	56
Book	Book of Fiction	3	0	0
Information Structure	Form	60	88	69
	List	10	47	57
Serial	Periodicals (Newspaper, Magazine)	6	0	0
	Newsletter	20	18	100
Treatise	Technical Report	46	73	74
	Business/OperationalReport	9	25	67
	Thesis	59	86	72
Evidential Document	Minutes	91	99	99
Other Functional Document	Slides	23	27	40
	Product/Application Description	56	80	62
	Guideline	28	25	35
	Factsheet	69	62	67

the genres of documents spanning over sixteen genres. The genres that were examined and the results are given in Section 6.

6   Results

The results of the image classifier in Table 5 do not show the same level of accuracy level as the results previously given in [19]. However, the results in our previous work was of binary classification. As distinctions between larger number of genres have to be made in the current context, it is more likely that any single class resembles another without sharing its identity.

The style classifier (cf. Table 6) shows a surprisingly high level of accuracy on the new data, suggesting that the frequency of words may be a key feature in detecting genres. The prediction of Minutes is particularly noticeable. Parallel to the results in [16] and [19], Periodicals are better recognised by the image classifier than the style classifier. Slides also seem to show the same tendency. As might be expected, genres which depend heavily on the content such as Technical

Report fare much better with the word frequency model. Another observation to be made from the results of Tables 5 and 6 is that the image classifier seems to fare better on a small amount of data (e.g. periodicals, book of fiction).

7 Error Analysis

For a thorough error analysis, a well-designed experimental corpus is required. Until the human labelling experiment in Section 3 is taken forward to include sufficient data and labels from more labellers for in-depth analysis, we can not claim to have the necessary corpus. Nevertheless, many of the errors can already seen to be due to a lack of data (e.g. Book of Fiction), while others seem inexorably linked to the fact that semantic content plays a heavier role than surface styles and structure (e.g. Guideline). An immediately recognisable flaw in the image representation of the document is that it is too strictly dependent on the exact location of non-white space. Ideally, we would like to detect the topology of the image representation such as the existence of lines, closed loops and other shapes. The location is only loosely relevant. The current representation is too rigid and should be modified to represent the general topology, rather than point-fixed pixel values. Also, more sophisticated linguistic pattern analysis is envisioned to be necessary for the next stage of the stylistic word frequency model.

8 Conclusions

The results in this paper can be summarised by the following:

- Genre classification as an abstract task is ill-defined: there is much disagreement even between human labellers and a detailed study of further human experiments are required to determine conditions which make the task meaningful.
- A fair amount of automated genre classification can be achieved by examining the frequency of genre words.
- The image of the first page alone seems to perform better classification than style, when only a small amount of training data is availabble.
- The performance of the image classifier appears to complement the performance of the style classifier.

It is evident that research in this area is still in its infancy. There is much to do. As we have noted elsewhere, the other classifiers based on language modeling, semantic analysis and domain knowledge should be tested for further comparison. Furthermore, proper error analysis and further gathering of documents and human labelling analysis is required to establish a well designed corpus. To maximise sustainability in an environment where technology changes at a rapid rate, the technical format information (e.g. PDF specification, or metadata extracted by pdfinfo) should only be included in the extraction tool algorithm at the last stage of improvement. The classification of documents into a small number of types has its limits. To be able to utilise these classifiers constructed under different conditions in the larger context of information management, we need to be able to construct systems that can group classifiers into clusters of similar tasks, or more specifically, into clusters of co-dependent classifiers.

Acknowledgments

This research is collaborative. DELOS: Network of Excellence on Digital Libraries (G038-507618)[3] funded under the European Commissions IST 6th Framework Programme provides a key framework and support, as does the UK's Digital Curation Centre. The DCC[4] is supported by a grant from the Joint Information Systems Committee (JISC)[5] and the e-Science Core Programme of the Engineering and Physical Sciences Research Council (EPSRC)[6]. The EPSRC supports (GR/T07374/01) the DCCs research programme. We would also like to thank Andrew McHugh, Adam Rusbridge, and Laura Brouard, who organised the web support and supervised the administrative process for the human labelling experiments.

References

1. Bagdanov, A., Worring, M.: Fine-grained document genre classification using first order random graphs. In: Proceedings 6th International Conference on Document Analysis and Recognition, pp. 79–83 (2001) ISBN 0-7695-1263-1
2. Barbu, E., Heroux, P., Adam, S., Turpin, E.: Clustering document images using a bag of symbols representation. In: Proceedings 8th International Conference on Document Analysis and Recognition, pp. 1216-1220 (2005) ISBN ISSN 1520-5263
3. Bekkerman, R., McCallum, A., Huang, G.: Automatic categorization of email into folders. benchmark experiments on enron and sri corpora. In: Bekkerman, R., McCallum, A., Huang, G. (eds.) Technical Report IR-418, Centre for Intelligent Information Retrieval, UMASS (2004)
4. Biber, D.: Representativeness in Corpus Design. Literary and Linguistic Computing 8(4), 243–257 (1993)
5. Biber, D.: Dimensions of Register Variation:a Cross-Linguistic Comparison. Cambridge University Press, New York (1995)
6. Boese, E.S.: Stereotyping the web: genre classification of web documents. Master's thesis, Colorado State University (2005)
7. Breiman, L.: Random forests. Machine Learning 45, 5–32 (2001)
8. Chao, C., Liaw, A., Breiman, L.: Using random forest to learn imbalanced data (2004), http://www.stat.berkeley.edu/~breiman/RandomForests/
9. Curran, J., Clark, S.: Investigating GIS and Smoothing for Maximum Entropy Taggers. In: Proceedings Aunnual Meeting European Chapter of the Assoc. of Computational Linguistics, pp. 91–98 (2003)

---

[3] http://www.delos.info
[4] http://www.dcc.ac.uk
[5] http://www.jisc.ac.uk
[6] http://www.epsrc.ac.uk

10. Finn, A., Kushmerick, N.: Learning to classify documents according to genre. Journal of American Society for Information Science and Technology 57(11), 1506–1518 (2006)
11. Giuffrida, G., Shek, E., Yang, J.: Knowledge-based metadata extraction from postscript file. In: Proceedings 5th ACM Intl. Conf. Digital Libraries, pp. 77–84. ACM Press, New York (2000)
12. Han, H., Giles, L., Manavoglu, E., Zha, H., Zhang, Z., Fox, E.A.: Automatic document metadata extraction using support vector machines. In: 3rd ACM/IEEECS Conf. Digital Libraries, pp. 37–48 (2003)
13. Karlgren, J., Cutting, D.: Recognizing text genres with simple metric using discriminant analysis. Proceedings 15th Conf. Comp. Ling. 2, 1071–1075 (1994)
14. Ke, S.W., Bowerman, C.: Perc: A personal email classifier. In: Lalmas, M., MacFarlane, A., Rüger, S., Tombros, A., Tsikrika, T., Yavlinsky, A. (eds.) ECIR 2006. LNCS, vol. 3936, pp. 460–463. Springer, Heidelberg (2006)
15. Kessler, G., Nunberg, B., Schuetze, H.: Automatic detection of text genre. In: Proceedings 35th Ann., pp. 32–38 (1997)
16. Kim, Y., Ross, S.: Genre classification in automated ingest and appraisal metadata. In: Gonzalo, J., Thanos, C., Verdejo, M.F., Carrasco, R.C. (eds.) ECDL 2006. LNCS, vol. 4172, pp. 63–74. Springer, Heidelberg (2006)
17. Kim, Y., Webber, B.: Implicit reference to citations: A study of astronomy papers. Presentation at the 20th CODATA international Conference, Beijing, China. (2006), http://eprints.erpanet.org/paperid115
18. Kim, Y., Ross, S.: Detecting family resemblance: Automated genre classification. Data Science 6, S172–S183 (2007), http://www.jstage.jst.go.jp/article/dsj/6/0/s172/_pdf
19. Kim, Y., Ross, S.: The Naming of Cats: Automated genre classification. International Journal for Digital Curation 2(1) (2007), http://www.ijdc.net/./ijdc/article/view/24
20. Marcus, M.P., Santorini, B., Mareinkiewicz, M.A.: Building a large annotated corpus of English: the Penn Treebank. Computational Linguistics 19(2), 313–330 (1994)
21. Rauber, A., Müller-Kögler, A.: Integrating automatic genre analysis into digital libraries. In: Proceedings ACM/IEEE Joint Conf. Digital Libraries, Roanoke, VA, pp. 1–10 (2001)
22. Ross, S., Hedstrom, M.: Preservation research and sustainable digital libraries. International Journal of Digital Libraries, (2005) DOI: 10.1007/s00799-004-0099-3
23. Thoma, G.: Automating the production of bibliographic records. Technical report, Lister Hill National Center for Biomedical Communication, US National Library of Medicine (2001)
24. Witten, H.I., Frank, E.: Data mining: Practical machine learning tools and techniques. Morgan Kaufmann, San Francisco (2005)

Video Transcoding and Streaming for Mobile Applications

Giovanni Gualdi, Andrea Prati, and Rita Cucchiara

University of Modena and Reggio Emilia
{giovanni.gualdi,andrea.prati,rita.cucchiara}@unimore.it

Abstract. The present work shows a system for compressing and streaming of live videos over networks with low bandwidths (radio mobile networks), with the objective to design an effective solution for mobile video access. We present a mobile ready-to-use streaming system, that encodes video using h264 codec (offering good quality and frame rate at very low bit-rates) and streams it over the network using UDP protocol. A dynamic frame rate control has been implemented in order to obtain the best trade off between playback fluency and latency.

1 Introduction

Mobile video browsing has been a very hot topic in the multimedia community in the past years. The increase of computational power has made also possible to perform in real time also the other end of the video stream, that is the grabbing, encoding and network streaming. On top of this it is possible to build mobile live video encoding and streaming; this is quite a challenging target, that presents many technological issues, that can be summarized in the following points:

1. Ubiquitous networks. Given the high grade of mobility required on the application, a network with an (almost) ubiquitous territorial coverage is necessary; therefore, WiFi or UMTS can not be currently used due to their limited coverage; GPRS network has been selected as transportation layer; GPRS is based on the GSM infrastructure, that is covering very high percentage of the territory. In particular, the GPRS-EDGE (Enhanced Data rates for GSM Evolution), also known as EGPRS, version has been used, given that it has the same coverage of GPRS but with a higher available bandwidth. Let's consider that in case that the encoding side is mobile, the video communication will use the wireless network communication in uplink. This is a further constraint since the GPRS/EGPRS and other wireless communications are often asymmetric, favoring the downlink.
2. Live video. The system requires live video encoding and decoding. The encoding must be efficient, so that video can be effectively transmitted on low bandwidth. It's important noting that in on-line video compression, off-line (multi-pass) encoding are not possible.
3. Good perceived video quality; we want the system to offer good understanding of the scene, requiring the streamed live video to offer: single images quality, fluency, no image skipping.

C. Thanos, F. Borri, and L. Candela (Eds.): Digital Libraries: R&D, LNCS 4877, pp. 262–267, 2007.
© Springer-Verlag Berlin Heidelberg 2007

4. Low latency is a very important point, that makes the difference between live video streaming for entertainment of for interaction purposes. In entertainment scenarios, latencies of several seconds might not be considered as a problem; on the contrary, interaction, that requires quick reaction from end to end, must offer low latency.

Commercial or off-the-shelf streaming solutions, are not sufficient to meet our requirements. We considered Windows Media Suite [1], Darwin Streaming Server [2] and Helix Streaming Server [3].

These tools offer excellent streaming solutions for entertainment video streaming and intensive broadcasts. But are not optimized for unicast low latency video streaming. Moreover there are constraints on the choice of the codec, often just proprietary codecs are allowed, or on the network management (poor flexibility in the protocols or the communication ports).

VideoLan (VLC) [4] is a very good open source video streaming solution, flexible and effective. It implements many codecs, including H264 [5] (for both encoding and decoding), but is still show a few blocking limitations:

- Constrains on protocols: for live video streaming on UDP, the video must be encapsulated with MPEG-TS, that is shown to be a waste in bandwidth by [6]
- Latency is not satisfactory, as shown in the experimental results.
- High rate of packets loss; in order to obtain lowest latency, all the buffers (encoding side and decoding side) have been minimized. But this makes the system pretty sensible to any network unsteadiness.

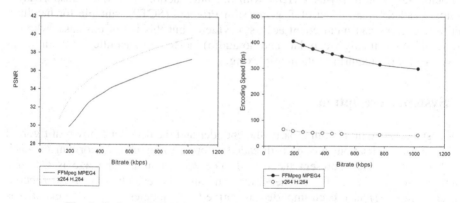

Fig. 1. (1-A and 1-B) H264 vs MPEG4, PSNR and computational load

For all the above reasons, we decided to develop our own live video streaming system, based on H.264/AVC and UDP as transportation layer protocol. Regarding the protocol, our choice of H264 on other codecs is pretty straightforward from a video quality point of view; see the comparison between H264 and MPEG4 on PSNR in figure 1-A.

The drawback of H264 is encoding and decoding complexity (as shown in Figure 1-B). Since the bandwidth is limited, the frame size of the encoded video is pretty small (maximum is CIF), making it possible to perform real time encoding on regular laptop PCs. The decoding can be performed on modest x86 PCs but also on high performance PDAs (tested on 520Mhz xScale).

The decision of using UDP rather than TCP is straightforward, since we are streaming real time data. UDP has a prioritized dispatch over TCP, and this makes it even more suitable for our target application. Moreover the evaluation paragraph will show that it is also very reliable.

2 Related Works

We couldn't find specific works addressing all the 4 aforementioned bottom line points for our mobile application. A very nice application for live video streaming between moving vehicles has been proposed by Guo et al. in [7]. However, their system is based on 802.11 WiFi networks and thus it is not suitable to our case.

Some previous works have proposed systems for video streaming over low-capacity networks, such as GPRS. For instance, Lim et al. in [8] introduced a PDA-based live video streaming system on GPRS network. The system is based on MPEG-4 compression / decompression on PDA. Their system works at 2-3 fps when transmission is over GPRS, that is not compliant with our requirements. This limitation is basically due to the limitation of the video codec. Moreover, no information on the latency of the system is provided.

H.264/AVC [1] opens to new possibilities in video streaming. In fact, the primary goals of this standard are improved video coding and improved network adaptation. Antonios Argyriou in [9] uses H264 with the introduction of a new transport layer protocol called Stream Control Transmission Protocol (SCTP), suitable for handling multiple streams and multi-client access to videos: but this is not our case, where a single video (with only video data and no audio) has to be transmitted to a single receiver, hence not requiring data multiplexing.

3 System Description

Our system can be divided in 2 parts, the encoder and the decoder (shown in figure 2 and 3). Both applications are multi-threaded in order to increase performances; each block of the schema represent the thread. The programming language is C#.NET where possible, for ease of implementation. The intensive calculations blocks (encoding and decoding) have been imported as native C++ modules. The video encoder is build upon the free open source version of X264 [10]. The original X.264 has been modified in the source code in order to load not only videos from file system, but also from a generic circular buffer, that allows higher flexibility, since it can be easily fed with any kind of source (file system, video device, video server, etc.). In our case the video source is obtained through a video file system or a USB camera: the dedicated video grabbing thread provides the YUV frames to the circular buffer. On the other side, the encoder thread asynchronously extracts them from the buffer. If the grabbing rate is higher than the encoding rate for short time, no video data will be lost. As drawback, the buffer introduces some latency; for this reason it is important to keep the buffer at low occupancy.

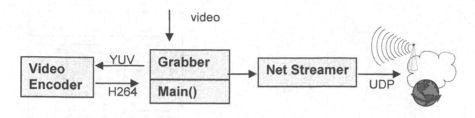

Fig. 2. The encoder side

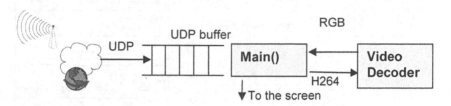

Fig. 3. The decoder side

The raw H.264 encoded stream is then sent over the network, splitting it in UDP datagrams of fixed byte size.

The decoder has been built upon the FFMPEG H264 [11] engine. Depending on the processing load on the encoder (that might be variable for many reasons, like the different motion conditions of the video to encode), on the decoder or on the network, the packet generation rate P.G.R. (encoder side) and the packet extraction rate P.E.R. (decoder side) might differ from time to time. Therefore, the UDP network buffer at the receiver side plays an essential role in order to reduce the effects of these discrepancies. If the P.G.R. remains higher than the P.E.R., the buffer might fill up and, when completely filled the new incoming datagrams will be lost. For this reason we implemented a simple adaptive algorithm to increase or decrease the buffer size dynamically: in practice, the algorithm either doubles the buffer size every time that it gets filled up beyond 80%, or halves it when its level decreases under 20%. These threshold values are computed empirically and depend on the network's conditions.

Since the latency is directly related to the occupancy of the buffer, it's important to keep it as low as possible; this it could be done setting a playback frame rate higher than the encoding frame rate. But this will generate an intermittent playback, since its fluency would be interrupted every time that the buffer gets emptied and the decoder needs to wait for the next incoming datagram to be received. For this reason we implemented a dynamic adaptation of the frame-rate. As shown in figure 4, we define an optimal occupancy gap of the buffer (empirically defined around 5 to 30%), and we modify the playback frame rate according to some multipliers α, β, γ, that are defined as functions of $\Delta(occ\%)$, the derivative of the occupancy of the buffer. The graphs of α, β, γ are shown in figure 4.

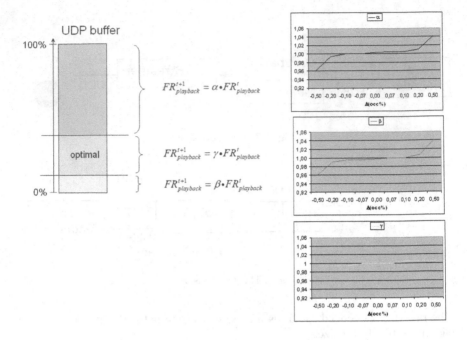

Fig. 4. Dynamic frame rate adaptation

4   Experimental Results

We tested the system with the encoder working on a laptop, connected with EGPRS or GPRS, mounted on a car, that was moving at variable speed (up to 110km/h), for more than 100 minutes of transmission. The decoder was performed on a standard x86 platform, or on a xScale PDA device running Windows Mobile 5.

Less than 0,1% of datagrams have been lost, and none of them was out of order. The measured latency can be seen in table 1. Introducing the adaptation on the playback frame rate, in short time (less than 60 seconds, depending on the functions of α,β,γ) the system removes the interruption of playback.

Some measurements on PSNR have given an average of 34.49db on a CIF sequence of 2500 frames, 10fps, at 120kbps.

Table 1. Latency

System / Setup	Mean (s)	Variance (s)
Windows Media, lowest encoding / playback buffering	4.15	**0.026**
VideoLan, lowest encoding / playback buffering	4.07	2.19
Our System (same x264 encoding parameters used in VLC)	**1.73**	0.042

Acknowledgments

This work is supported by the DELOS NoE on Digital Libraries, as part of the IST Program of the European Commission (Contract G038-507618).

References

1. http://www.microsoft.com/windows/windowsmedia/
2. http://developer.apple.com/opensource/server/streaming/index.html
3. http://www.realnetworks.com/products/mediadelivery.html
4. http://www.videolan.org/vlc/
5. Advanced video coding for generic audiovisual services. Technical report, ITU Rec. H624/ISO IEC 14996-10 AVC (2003)
6. MacAulay, A., Felts, B., Fisher, Y.: WHITEPAPER IP streaming of MPEG-4: Native RTP vs MPEG-2 transport stream. Technical report, Envivio, Inc. (October 2005)
7. Guo, M., Ammar, M., Zegura, E.: V3: a vehicle-to-vehicle live video streaming architecture. In: Proc. of IEEE Intl Conf. on Pervasive Computing and Communications, pp. 171–180 (2005)
8. Lim, K., Wu, D., Wu, S., Susanto, R., Lin, X., Jiang, L., Yu, R., Pan, F., Li, Z., Yao, S., Feng, G., Ko, C.: Video streaming on embedded devices through GPRS network. In: Proc. Of IEEE Intl. Conference on Multimedia and Expo, vol. 2, pp. 169–172 (2003)
9. Argyriou, A., Madisetti, V.: treaming h.264/avc video over the internet. In: Proc. of 1st IEEE Consumer Communications and Networking Conference, pp. 169–174 (2004)
10. http://developers.videolan.org/x264.html
11. http://sourceforge.net/projects/ffmpeg

Prototypes Selection with Context Based Intra-class Clustering for Video Annotation with Mpeg7 Features

Costantino Grana, Roberto Vezzani, and Rita Cucchiara

Department of Information Engineering, University of Modena and Reggio Emilia, Italy
{costantino.grana,roberto.vezzani,rita.cucchiara}@unimore.it

Abstract. In this work, we analyze the effectiveness of perceptual features to automatically annotate video clips in domain-specific video digital libraries. Typically, automatic annotation is provided by computing clip similarity with respect to given examples, which constitute the knowledgebase, in accordance with a given ontology or a classification scheme. Since the amount of training clips is normally very large, we propose to automatically extract some prototypes, or visual concepts, for each class instead of using the whole knowledge base. The prototypes are generated after a Complete Link clustering based on perceptual features with an automatic selection of the number of clusters. Context based information are used in an intra-class clustering framework to provide selection of more discriminative clips. Reducing the number of samples makes the matching process faster and lessens the storage requirements. Clips are annotated following the MPEG-7 directives to provide easier portability. Results are provided on videos taken from sports and news digital libraries.

1 Introduction

In the last decade, a significant increase of the availability of devices able to acquire and store digital videos and the introduction of broadband connections has given a strong impulse to the study and development of video digital libraries management systems. In particular, a growing need is the ability to search for videos basing on their content instead of relying on manually provided metadata. The diffusion of such systems has been strongly limited by the difficulty to generalize results of visual and aural automated processing techniques obtained on tuned test data sets. On the other hand, general internet users are very inexperienced in search, so the media search technologies for the mass have to be very simple, intuitive, and easy to use [1].

From the technical point of view, another question is whether we should go for domain-dependent features or for more general ones, defined at perceptual level only. This last choice could be probably less effective than ad-hoc defined features, but is potentially applicable to wider scenarios. Moreover, the required level of detail goes often beyond the video granularity, in the sense that the user is looking for smaller subsequences, i.e. clips which could be shots or even finer temporal segments.

Examples of automatic semantic annotation systems have been presented recently, most of them in the application domain of news and sports video. Most of the proposals deal with a specific context making use of ad-hoc features. In the work by Bertini et al. [2], the playfield area, the number and the placement of players on the play

C. Thanos, F. Borri, and L. Candela (Eds.): Digital Libraries: R&D, LNCS 4877, pp. 268–277, 2007.

field, and motion cues are used to distinguish soccer highlights into subclasses. Differently, a first approach trying to apply general features is described by Chang et al. [3]. Employing color, texture, motion, and shape, visual queries by sketches are provided, supporting automatic object based indexing and spatiotemporal queries.

In this paper, we propose a general framework which allows to automatically annotating video clips by comparing their similarity to a domain specific set of prototypes. In particular, we focus on providing a flexible system directly applicable to different contexts and a standardized output by means of the MPEG-7 tools. To this aim, the clip characterizing features, the final video annotation, and the storage of the reference video objects and classes are realized using this standard. Starting from a large set of manually annotated clips, according with a classification scheme, the system exploits the potential perceptual regularity and generates a set of prototypes, or visual concepts, by means of a intra-class clustering procedure. Then, only the prototypes are stored as suitable specialization concepts of the defined classes. The adoption of the limited set of prototypes instead of the whole set of examples reduces the required storage space and allows the generation and the sharing of a context classifier on the Web. Thanks to the massive use of the MPEG-7 standard, a remote system could then perform its own annotation of videos using these context classifiers.

As most of the papers, we refer to already subdivided clips. The automatic subdivision of videos into clips is a widely faced problem, and several solutions are available. Our system uses the approach described in [4], followed by a fuzzy c-means frame clustering to provide clips at sub-shot granularity.

The paper is organized as follows: in Section 2 a similarity measure between clips based on standard low level features is described. Based on it, a nearest neighbor automatic annotation is presented in Section 3 together with some details about the use of MPEG-7. Section 4 depicts the prototype creation algorithm, the proposed index for automatic level selection, and a context based dissimilarity measure. Results over sports and news videos are reported in Section 5.

2 Similarity of Video Clips

Clip similarity can be seen as a generalization of a image similarity task: as for images, each clip may be described by a set of visual features, such as color, shape and motion. These are grouped in a feature vector:

$$\mathbf{V}_i = \left[F_i^1, F_i^2, \ldots, F_i^N \right] \tag{1}$$

where i is the frame number, N is number of features and F_i^j is the j-th feature computed at frame i. However, extracting a feature vector at each frame can lead to some problems during the similarity computation between clips, since they may have different lengths; at the same time keeping a single feature vector for the whole clip cannot be representative enough, because it does not take into account the features temporal variability. Here, a fixed number M of feature vectors is used for each clip, computed on M frames sampled at uniform intervals within the clip. In our experiments, a good tradeoff between efficacy and computational load suggests the use of $M = 5$ for clips of averaging 100 frames. To provide a general purpose system, we avoid to select context dependent features, relaying on broad range properties of the clips. To allow easier interoperability and feature reuse, we tried to select features which comply with the MPEG-7 standard [6]. In particular the following three features are employed: Scalable color (a color histogram, with 16 values in H and 4 values in each S and V, 256 bins in total), Color layout (to account for the spatial distribution of the colors, an 8x8 grid is superimposed to the picture and the average YCbCr values are computed for each area) and Parametric motion (making use of the MPEG motion vectors, the translational motion of each quarter of frame is estimated).

Thus, the distance between two clips S_u and S_v is defined as

$$d\left(S_u, S_v\right) = \frac{1}{M} \sum_{i=1}^{M} \left\| \mathbf{k}^{\mathrm{T}} \left(\mathbf{V}_{u_i} - \mathbf{V}_{v_i}\right) \right\| = \frac{1}{M} \sum_{i=1}^{M} \sum_{j=1}^{N} k_j \left\| F_{u_i}^j - F_{v_i}^j \right\|, \tag{2}$$

where, $\mathbf{k} = \left(k_1, \ldots, k_N\right)$ is a weight vector and u_i and v_i are the frame numbers of the i-th subsampled frames of S_u and S_v respectively. The weights $k_j \in [0,1]$ provide dimensional coherence among the different features and at the same time they allow to change their relative significance.

3 Automatic Annotation

Given a domain-specific video digital library, we assume that it is possible to partition the clips of videos of that context into a set of L classes $\mathbf{C} = \left(C_1, \ldots, C_L\right)$, which describe different contents or camera views .Given a large set of training clips, we implemented an interactive user-friendly interface [5] to quickly assign each of them to a specific class C_k and then employ it for automatic annotation purposes.

A screenshot of the developed annotation tool is shown in Fig. 1. An unknown clip can be classified using a nearest neighbor approach and the similarity measure defined above. The weights k_i of Eq. 2 may be tuned to optimize the classification results on a training video, by searching the set which provides the maximum number of correct class assignments. This process is done once for all during the context classifier design, so the optimization phase is not time constrained and an exhaustive search can be employed. Since the MPEG-7 standard can naturally include pictorial elements such as objects, key-frames, clips and visual descriptors, we used it to store the classification data by means of the double description provided by the *Classification-SchemeDescriptionType* Descriptor Schema (DS) combined with a *ModelDescriptionType* DS which includes a *Collection ModelType* DS.

The classification scheme allows the definition of a taxonomy or thesaurus of terms which can be organized by means of simple term relations. The collection model is instead an *AnalyticModel,* and therefore it describes the association of labels or semantics with collections of multimedia content. The collection model contains a *Content CollectionType* DS with a set of visual elements which refer to the model being described. In particular, we linked the selected clips and a representation of their features by means of the *ScalableColor* Descriptor (D), *ColorLayout* D and the

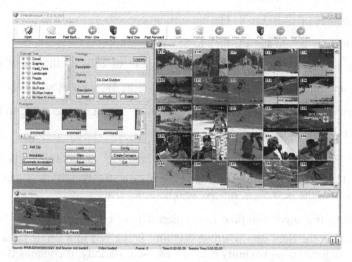

Fig. 1. Screenshot of the annotation framework with a ski video opened. On the right, the automatically detected shots, on the lower part a sub-shots windows reports a finer granularity division, and on the left the classification scheme and the selected prototypes are drawn.

ParametricMotion D. An advantage of adopting a MPEG-7 framework is that other systems may employ the same data enabling interoperability and easier integration.

4 Prototypes Creation

As stated above, we adopt a nearest neighbor approach to classify each clip of the test sequences. Increasing the number of training clips the classification performance consequently improves, since a finer partitioning of the feature space is obtained. Unfortunately, in such a manner the space required to store the data, the corresponding transmission time -if needed-, and the computational cost for nearest neighbor selection increase.

4.1 Intra-class Clustering

Since not all the clips are equally important to obtain the final classification due to perceptual redundancy in specific domains, we employ a hierarchical clustering method, based on *Complete Link* [7], to reduce the number of clip of each class, keeping only some representative prototypes, which capture the most significant aspects of a set of clips. This technique guarantees that each clip must be similar to every other in the cluster and any other clip outside the cluster has dissimilarity greater than the maximum distance between cluster elements.

For this clustering method a dissimilarity measure between two clusters W_i and W_j is defined as

$$D(W_i, W_j) = \max_{S_x \in W_i, S_y \in W_j} d\left(S_x, S_y\right). \tag{3}$$

where d is computed as in Eq. 2. The algorithm proceeds as follows:

1. For each class C_k do steps from 2 to 5:
2. Initially each cluster contains a single clip. Let us call E_n the set of clusters at level n, and initialize it to $E_{P_k} = \{\{S_1\}, \{S_2\}, ..., \{S_{P_k}\}\}$, with $P_k = card(C_k)$.
3. The least dissimilar pair of clusters, $W_i, W_j \in E_n$, is found according to Eq. 3., i.e.
   $$D(W_i, W_j) \leq D(A, B) \ \forall A, B \in E_n.$$
4. W_i and W_j are merged into the same cluster and E_{n+1} is accordingly updated.
5. If everything is merged into a single cluster or a stop condition is met, the algorithm goes to the next class, otherwise it resumes from step 2.

For each class, this algorithm produces a hierarchy of clips partitions with P_k levels, where level 1 is the final step where everything is merged in a single cluster. To implement the algorithm, a proximity matrix was used: initially, it contains the distances between each pair of clips. At each step, the matrix is updated by deleting rows and columns corresponding to the selected clusters and adding a new row and column corresponding to the merged cluster. The values in the new row/column are the maximum of the values in the previous ones.

4.2 Automatic Clustering Level Selection

Instead of a manual selection of the desired clustering level, or a threshold guided one, an automatic selection strategy is proposed. Such a rule has to be based on cluster topology concerns, being a trade-of between data representation and small number of clusters, and it is not possible to choose the *right* one. In literature different proposals are presented, such as the Dunn's Separation Index [8], but the corresponding results on our data sets were not satisfactory. Better results (in terms of a subjective evaluation) have been obtained with the following approach. Let us define the cluster diameter and the cluster distance as

$$\Delta(W_i) = D(W_i, W_i) \tag{4}$$

$$\delta(W_i, W_j) = \min_{S_x \in W_i, S_y \in W_j} d(S_x, S_y) \tag{5}$$

The *Clustering Score* at level n is defined as

$$CS_n = \min(\Delta_1 - \Delta_n, \delta_n) \tag{6}$$

Where

$$\Delta_n = \max_{W_i \in E_n} \Delta(W_i) \quad \delta_n = \min_{W_i, W_j \in E_n, i \neq j} \delta(W_i, W_j) \tag{7}$$

The selected level is the one which minimizes CS_n. It is possible to observe that Δ_n and δ_n are both monotonically increasing with n, thus CS_n has a unique global

Table 1. Results of Self Annotation on three different videos

Video	# Frames	# Clips	Correct
Ski	178.181	1212	90%
Bob	50.835	1422	92%
F1	215.638	2339	82%

minimum. Therefore, the clustering algorithm can be stopped when CS_n start to increase without computing the remaining levels. A single prototype can be generated from each cluster, by computing the M average feature vectors. The clip which minimizes the distance from the prototype features is associated to it, in order to provide a representative of the visual concept. An example of some F1 classes and visual concepts is provided in Fig. 3. The automatic selection of prototypes allows a remarkable reduction of examples. We tested in many different contexts, such as the Olympic Winter Games, soccer matches, Formula 1 races, news, and the automatic clustering selects about 10% to 30% only of the provided clips as visual concepts (see Table 1).

4.3 Intra-class Clustering with Context Data

In section 4.1 an intra-class clustering has been presented in order to generate a set of significant prototypes for each class. The choice is guided by how similar the original clips are in the feature space, without considering the elements belonging to the other classes (*context data*). This may lead to a prototype selection which is indeed representative of the class but lacks the properties useful for discrimination purposes. To better understand this concept, an example is reported in Fig. 2, in which 150 random samples are extracted from three different Gaussian distributions. Two of them (blue color) belong to the same class, while the third distribution (purple color) is a different one. With the clustering technique described in the previous section, the generation of the prototypes for the first class does not take into account the second distribution; the automatic index selection could merge the two distributions leading to a single prototype. To cope with this problem, a context based similarity measure is provided as follows. We define an *isolation coefficient* for each clip as:

$$\gamma(S_u) = \sum_{i=1, i \neq j}^{L} \sum_{S_v \in C_i} \frac{1}{d(S_u, S_v)}, S_u \in C_j. \tag{8}$$

Then we can introduce a class based *dissimilarity measure* between two clips as:

$$\bar{d}(S_u, S_v) = d(S_u, S_v) \cdot \gamma(S_u) \cdot \gamma(S_v). \tag{9}$$

The *intra-class complete link* clustering is thus enhanced with context data by substituting the clips distance in Eq. 3 and Eq. 5 with this dissimilarity measure.

In Fig. 2 four samples of the blue class have been selected. Even if the central points (B,C) are closer each other than the corresponding colored ones (A and D respectively), the interposed purple distribution largely increases their dissimilarity measure, preventing their merge in a single cluster.

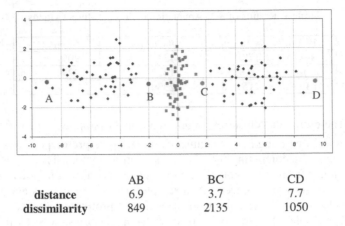

	AB	BC	CD
distance	6.9	3.7	7.7
dissimilarity	849	2135	1050

Fig. 2. Example of the effect of the context on the dissimilarity measure

5   Experimental Results

The knowledge representation by means of textual and pictorial concepts is particularly suitable for summarization and fast video access. The described system has been tested on video of different contexts: here we provide experiments to test the effectiveness of these prototypes and we propose a semiautomatic annotation framework, to speedup a metadata creation task.

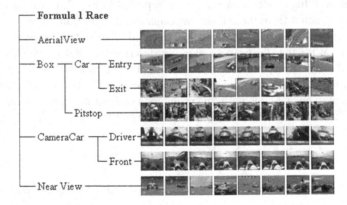

Fig. 3. Example of a few prototypes for the F1 race context. Of the 21 classes available, only 7 classes and 8 prototypes per class are shown.

5.1   Automatic Annotation

As a first test a self-annotation task was performed, i.e. we automatically classify the clips of a video using a leave-one-out cross validation (i.e., each clip is classified exploiting all the other clips of the same video). Since this corresponds to counting how many clips belong to the same class of their nearest neighbor, we can check how separable the defined classes are in the selected feature space. For the second test, we checked the generalizing properties of the context classifier by using two different sets for the training and test phases. In Table 1 the results of the first test on three different videos are reported, confirming that the selected feature space is quite effective in the considered contexts. In particular, the ski context presents an higher degree of repetitiveness, so the visual classification performs better than in the F1 one.

To create training sets for different contexts, we used a first part of each video and the rest was used as test. The results of this test are reported in Table 2. All the training clips have been reduced by the prototype creation algorithm and the number of the generated prototypes is about a third of the initial samples. Other experiments on larger training sets have shown higher reduction rates, which also depend on the number of sample per class. The results obtained on the training set show that the clustering process is able to keep the original structure of the data. On the test set, it is possible to see that the use of this approach reach a classification rate around 70% on average, depending on the context. In Table 3 the confusion matrix of the F1 experiment is reported. It is possible to see that the classification provides good results with specific and well constrained classes (e.g. InCarCamera); for more generic classes (e.g. AerialView-FarView), the training data could not be sufficient to describe all the possible samples, so the correspondent results are worse.

5.2 Semi-automatic Annotation Framework

From previous experiments, it is clear that without context specific features it is not feasible to reach very high automatic classification rates. We believe that 70% correct classification with a generic feature set is a realistic figure. A possible approach to the distribution of annotated videos over internet may be the use of this kind of generic tools followed by manual correction of errors, as it is common for example with every day use of OCR software. To this aim we tested on some winter Olympic Games of Torino 2006 the speedup obtained using our automatic classifier followed by a manual error correction instead of a completely manual annotation. In Fig. 4 the results over a sample video are shown. The score of the automatic classification of the non annotated clips grows with the rise of the manually annotated ones; even though, it is not convenient to annotate to much clips since the increase in correct annotations does not compensate the increased time requirements. In our experiments, the best compromise is reached around 10%.

Table 2. Confusion matrix of the first experiment of Table 2

	1	2	3	4	5	6	7	8	9	10	11
1. AerialView	53							47			
2. Box.Car.Entry		78	10	8	3						
3. Box.Car.Exit		9	81	6	4						
4. Box.PitStop	3	6	17	57	6				6	6	
5. Box.Staff.Waiting			12	41	18				12	18	
6. InCarCam.Front.Bottom						100					
7. InCarCam.Front.Top			1				97		1		
8. FarView		2	2					47	49		
9. NearView			12					12	76		
10. People	10	3	7	10			3		14	41	10
11. Advertising	1		1			1		1			96

Table 3. Results of Test 2. NN: Nearest Neighbor classification with the originally selected training clips, CL: classification after prototype creation with classic Complete Link clustering, CBCL: classification after prototype creation with Context-Based Complete Link clustering.

		Ski	Bob	F1
#Training set		300	300	500
#Test set		912	1122	1839
# of Visual Concepts	NN	300	300	500
	CL	84	126	191
	CBCL	78	122	203
Results on training set	NN	300 (100%)	300 (100%)	500 (100%)
	CL	299 (99.7%)	292 (97.3%)	478 (95.6%)
	CBCL	300 (100%)	285 (95%)	492 (98.4%)
Results on test set	NN	660 (72.4%)	854 (75.8%)	1181 (64.2%)
	CL	654 (71.7%)	846 (75.1%)	1159 (63.0%)
	CBCL	657 (72%)	852 (75.7%)	1209 (65.7%)

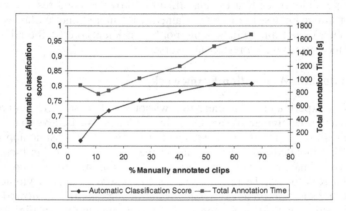

Fig. 4. Manually annotating all the clips is slower than correcting the errors of automatic tools

6 Conclusions

We presented a general purpose system for the automatic annotation of video clips, by means of standardized low level features. A process for reducing space and computational requirements by the creation of prototypes with context based intra-class clustering was described. The classifier data are stored in MPEG-7 compliant format to improve the interoperability and integration of different systems.

The annotation has shown satisfactory results without specific feature development. This approach allows a system to behave differently by simply providing a different context, thus expanding its applicability to mixed sources digital libraries.

Acknowledgments

This work is supported by the DELOS NoE on Digital Libraries, as part of the IST Program of the European Commission (Contract G038-507618).

References

1. Jaimes, A., Christel, M., Gilles, S., Sarukkai, R., Ma, W.: Multimedia information retrieval: what is it, and why isn't anyone using it? In: MIR 2005. Proc. of the 7th ACM SIGMM Int'l Workshop on Multimedia Information Retrieval, pp. 3–8. ACM Press, New York (2005)
2. Bertini, M., Cucchiara, R., Del Bimbo, A., Torniai, C.: Video Annotation with Pictorially Enriched Ontologies. In: Proceedings of IEEE International Conference on Multimedia and Expo, Amsterdam, The Netherlands, pp. 1428–1431. IEEE Computer Society Press, Los Alamitos (2005)
3. Chang, S., Chen, W., Meng, H.J., Sundaram, H., Zhong, D.: A Fully Automated Content-Based Video Search Engine Supporting Spatiotemporal Queries. IEEE Transactions on Circuits and System for Video Technology 8(5), 602–615 (1998)
4. Grana, C., Tardini, G., Cucchiara, R.: MPEG-7 Compliant Shot Detection in Sport Videos. In: ISM 2005. Proc. of the IEEE Int'l Symposium on Multimedia, pp. 395–402 (2005)
5. Grana, C., Vezzani, R., Bulgarelli, D., Barbieri, F., Cucchiara, R., Bertini, M., Torniai, C., Del Bimbo, A.: PEANO: Pictorial Enriched ANnotation of VideO. In: Proceedings of the 14th ACM international Conference on Multimedia, pp. 793–794 (2006)
6. ISO/IEC Std. 15 938-3: Information technology - Multimedia content description interface - Part 3: Visual (2003)
7. Jain, A.K., Dubes, R.C.: Algorithms for clustering data. Prentice-Hall, Englewood Cliffs, NJ (1988)
8. Dunn, J.C.: A fuzzy relative of the ISODATA process and its use in detecting compact well-separated clusters. Journal of Cybernetics 3(3), 32–57 (1973)

Automatic, Context-of-Capture-Based Categorization, Structure Detection and Segmentation of News Telecasts

Arne Jacobs[1], George T. Ioannidis[1], Stavros Christodoulakis[2],
Nektarios Moumoutzis[2], Stratos Georgoulakis[2], and Yiannis Papachristoudis[2]

[1] Center for Computing Technologies (TZI), University of Bremen, Germany
{jarne,george.ioannidis}@tzi.de
[2] Laboratory of Distributed Multimedia Information Systems and Applications, Technical University of Crete (TUC/MUSIC), 73100 Chania, Greece
{stavros,nektar,stratos,ipapachr}@ced.tuc.gr

Abstract. The objective of the work reported here is to provide an automatic, context-of-capture categorization, structure detection and segmentation of news broadcasts employing a multimodal semantic based approach. We assume that news broadcasts can be described with context-free grammars that specify their structural characteristics. We propose a system consisting of two main types of interoperating units: The recognizer unit consisting of several modules and a parser unit. The recognizer modules (audio, video and semantic recognizer) analyze the telecast and each one identifies hypothesized instances of features in the audiovisual input. A probabilistic parser analyzes the identifications provided by the recognizers. The grammar represents the possible structures a news telecast may have, so the parser can identify the exact structure of the analyzed telecast.

Keywords: News, Segmentation, Classification, Audio Analysis, Video Analysis, Semantic Analysis, Probabilistic Grammars.

1 Introduction

News programs are a valuable information source for what is happening in the world. The coverage of news programs is very comprehensive, and it is likely that individual viewers are interested in only a few stories out of the complete news broadcast. Automatic story segmentation and indexing techniques provide a convenient way to store, browse and retrieve news stories based on the user preferences.

News segmentation in broadcast videos is an emerging research problem, and many researchers from various areas, such as multimedia, information retrieval and video processing, are interested in it. To address this problem, low-level features (referring to the audio and/or the visual signal of the video) could be extracted and then higher level features (such as the identification of news story boundaries and their classification) can be inferred. The problem of relating low-level features with higher-level ones that correspond to the human-like understanding of video content is the well-known problem of bridging the 'semantic gap' and a solution to it is necessary for effective retrieval performance.

C. Thanos, F. Borri, and L. Candela (Eds.): Digital Libraries: R&D, LNCS 4877, pp. 278–287, 2007.
© Springer-Verlag Berlin Heidelberg 2007

A first key observation to help bridge the semantic gap in the news video domain is that semantic concepts in news videos are conventionalized in many ways and this fact can be exploited. E.g., different news stories are usually separated by anchor shots containing the presentation of the story that follows. We assume that these news format models can be described with context-free grammars. Such a grammar can effectively support a multimodal segmentation process by removing ambiguities in classification, or by associating certain audiovisual cues with segment classes (e.g., news story, weather report, etc.). It models all interesting constraints in visual, audio and semantic features that are partly due to the way news programs are produced and partly to the habits and ways of work of the journalists and other agents related to news production. Combining these features of different modalities through an appropriate grammar we achieve a multimodal analysis of the news telecasts.

For parsing of a news video following a corresponding model, we propose a system consisting of two main types of interoperating units: The recognizer unit consisting of several modules and a parser unit. The recognizer modules analyze the telecast and each one identifies hypothesized instances of features in the audiovisual input. Such features could range from upper-level concepts like a specific person appearing in a shot (e.g., the anchor), the appearance of a certain series of frames (e.g., the introduction sequence, which many news broadcasts have in their beginning), to low-level, e.g., the similarity of two frames. A probabilistic parser using a probabilistic grammar analyzes the identifications provided by the recognizers. In essence, the recognizers provide the parser with actual lexical tokens such as a lexical analyzer would provide to a programming language parser. The grammar represents the possible structures the news telecast may have, so the parser can identify the exact structure of this telecast.

In the rest of this paper we first present related work in the area of news segmentation and classification and justify the suitability of our grammar-based approach (section 2). Section 3 presents the overall design adopted. Section 4 presents the main components of the architecture in more detail and section 5 concludes.

2   Related Work and Suitability of Our Approach

The typical way of integrating multimodal features in order to achieve news segmentation and classification (i.e. extracting and classifying news stories from news videos) is through statistical methods such as Hidden Markov Models [1, 2, 5, 6, 7, 10]. In these approaches, the basic hypothesis is that the multimodal (low-level) features observed can be considered Markovian in some feature space and that efficient training data exists to automatically learn a suitable model to characterize data.

However, in other similar domains such as recognition of visual activities and interactions in videos (e.g. surveillance videos, gesture videos, etc.) another complementary approach based on various parsing strategies has been used [11, 13, 15]. In these approaches the goal is to recognize structurally defined relationships of features where purely statistical approaches to recognition are less than ideal. These situations can be characterized following [11] by one or more of the following conditions:

- *Insufficient data:* Complete data sets are not always available, but component examples are easily found.
- *Semantic ambiguity:* Semantically equivalent processes possess radically different statistical properties.
- *Temporal ambiguity:* Competing hypotheses can absorb different lengths of the input stream, raising the need for naturally supported temporal segmentation.
- *Known structure:* Structure of the process is difficult to learn but is explicit and a priori known.

When these conditions arise, it seems natural to divide the problem in two:

1. Recognition of low-level features (primitives) and
2. Recognition of structure.

The goal then becomes to combine statistical detection of primitives with a structural interpretation method that organizes the data. The news segmentation domain satisfies the above conditions and thus, an approach for automatic segmentation that distinguishes between the recognition of low-level features and structure is viable.

In this work we adopt the method of [11] that combines mainly statistical techniques used to detect low-level features (primitives) of a more complex process structure. We combine results of the lower level feature recognizers into a consistent interpretation with the maximum likelihood using a Probabilistic Context-Free Grammar (PCFG) parser. The grammar provides a convenient means for encoding the external knowledge about the problem domain, expressing the expected structure of the high-level process.

3   Overall Architecture

The architecture adopted is depicted in Fig. 1. The central components of the architecture are the two main interoperating modules: the recognizers and the parser.

The recognizers analyze the telecast and each one identifies hypothesized instances of features in the audiovisual input:

- The visual recognizer identifies visual features on the news stream, such as a face appearing at an expected position in the video.
- The audio recognizer, in turn, identifies audio features such as the presence of speech or music, e.g., a signature tune, and clustering of speakers.
- The semantic recognizer identifies the semantics involved in the telecast. This includes topic detection, high-level event detection, discourse cues etc. The semantic recognizer has access to the Upper Ontologies as well as domain specific ontologies created for news. The concepts acquired from these ontologies will define those detectable semantics that can be identified in the telecast.

The Probabilistic Context-Free Grammar Parser interoperates with the recognizers. It uses a probabilistic grammar in order to analyze the identifications provided by the recognizers. The parser computes and passes to the recognizer token probabilities, which are used by the recognizer to aid in the recognition of lexical tokens, closing the feedback loop between the recognizer and the parser. When the parsing is complete and all the structural elements of the input have been analyzed, the Segmentation Description Creator Module uses that information to provide an MPEG7 compliant XML document with the description of identified news story segments with semantic topics and semantic events.

The grammar for each broadcast station, even for different news programs of the same station, is distinct. This is because the grammar captures the directing elements of the broadcast, and no two different programs have exactly the same directional structure. Therefore, an initial context-free grammar (without probabilities) has to be produced manually for each program of interest, a task on which the system relies heavily, if processing is to be robust. For the grammar to be probabilistic, it is necessary to complete a training process in order to assign probabilities to each production rule in the grammar. This training is carried out by the Probabilities Computation Module that uses a set of correctly labeled broadcast scenarios (created manually or through a semi-automatic annotation tool for ease of use).

The Environment Initialization Module provides a basic system initialization, according to the "working environment", a concept that encapsulates specific parameters of the system's functionality according to the input that will be analyzed.

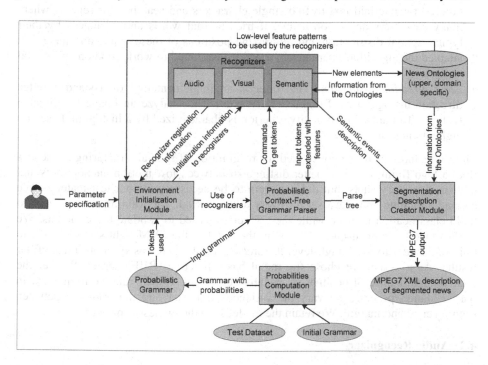

Fig. 1. Overall architecture of the system for automatic, context-of-capture-based categorization, structure detection and segmentation of news telecasts

4 Main Components of the Architecture

4.1 Visual Recognizer

The visual recognizer incorporates an image feature classifier that uses every 20th frame of an input video to do its calculations. Within these calculations filters are used to calculate a probability for every high level feature/ structural token. The following visual features are computed on every considered frame, followed by an SVM-based classification to get a visual token:

- *Color correlogram:* This filter is an implementation of a standard color correlogram filter [9]. A color correlogram (henceforth correlogram) expresses how the spatial correlation of pairs of colors changes with distance. We used the correlogram for the high-level features Charts, Desert, Explosion/Fire, and Maps.
- *Color histogram filter:* The color histogram filter reduces the amount of colors by removing a parameterizable number of bits inside every RGB color channel. We use color histograms with sizes of 4 or 8 bins per dimension (R, G, and B), for a total of 64 or 512 bins, respectively. These histograms are used either with or without the ROI filter (see above).
- *Text detection filter:* The text detection filter is based on an algorithm developed in a Diploma thesis at the University of Bremen [19]. It uses an edge detection filter tailored for overlaid text to find single characters and searches for regions where many characters appear on a line. It tries to find words and sentences by their typical spatial distribution and returns the positions of these inside an image. We adapted the algorithm's parameters to values we found to work good on an internal test set.
- *Edge direction histogram:* This filter is an implementation of a standard edge direction histogram by Tamura [18]. We use it to analyze an image for directed textures. Tamura's directionality criterion is characterized by a histogram based on eight orientations.

Motion features could be considered for recognition of special structuring sequences (like a logo flying in) or to better distinguish between low-motion anchor shots and high-motion story shots, but did not seem to be necessary for our test material. We created a training and a test set for every token to find. The training set was used to build classification models, while the test set was used to validate these models. We use a support vector machine (SVM) in the form of the SVM-light software [12] to train one model for each high-level feature/structural token, based on our image filter results. As a kernel we chose the radial basis function (RBF) kernel. We set the relative significance of positive vs. negative examples to their relative frequency. In our validation process, we vary the variance parameter and the trade-off between training error and margin. We retain the model with the highest F-measure.

4.2 Audio Recognizer

The audio recognizer incorporates a classifier that searches the audio tracks of the input videos for a number of previously learned sounds. The classifier is built up of two stages. In the first stage we extract spectral features from the audio tracks. In the second step we use a supervised learning algorithm for training and prediction. Our approach is based on the algorithm proposed by [8] but it differs in classifying. While [8] suggest a decision tree classifier, we chose to use a support vector machine (SVM) in the classifier stage, in the form of the Libsvm library [4].

The first step of the sound feature extraction module is to create an abstract feature representation of the audio signal using an FFT on a temporally shifted window of the audio track. From the spectral representation, a set of 63 descriptive features is computed [8] to serve as input to the classifier. The size of the window is dependent of the type of sound that should be detected. The longer the sound, the bigger the window. We use windows ranging from 800 milliseconds to 1200 milliseconds. When applying the final classifiers to the test set, the window is shifted in steps of 100 milliseconds. For training, we manually cut a set of training sounds for each type of sound to be detected.

Regarding the classification using a support vector machine (SVM) we chose to manually create a training set for the sound we wanted to detect. We cut a small number of short example sounds between 0.5 and 2.5 seconds, including all the disturbing sounds that might be in the background. The manual searching and cutting of sample sounds takes a long time, but is in the end the only way to ensure that the system learns the right type of sounds. It turned out that the selection type and also the number of training sounds has a great effect on the prediction quality of the SVM. During the testing of the system for various videos, the prediction sometimes returned very few or no results, even if the news contained plenty of the regarded sound events. The reason for this was probably that the analyzed sounds were too different from the training examples. However, finding good training examples that cover the whole variance of sounds is hard to manage, and it is very hard to cut the sounds from the test material. Our solution to this problem was to lower the threshold on the prediction values yielded by the SVM classifier, such that not only positive predictions are counted, but also negative results down to -0.4 or lower. That way, we reached a much bigger number of positives.

4.3 Semantic Recognizer

The semantic recognizer component is responsible for all semantic-related recognition and classification involved in the system. In a first simplified approach, the semantic recognizer is based on the format of the TRECVID'03 collection transcripts, and incorporates mechanisms for a 3-staged transcript and words in transcript processing.

At the first stage the Semantic Recognizer parses the transcript in order to extract and internally store the transcript words and other information. The second stage of transcript processing concerns the tagging of the words previously found into the transcript. For this task a part-of-speech (POS)-tagger is involved (http:// nlp. stanford.edu/software/tagger.shtml). The POS-tagger is responsible for the tag-ing of the words given to it in sentences. An important issue at this point was how to bind together words in sentences for which no information is available about what their relation is. A proper sentence-grouping is very important in order to achieve the most accurate tagging. For this reason a pre-tagging is made in order to locate subjects, verbs and objects. The third and last stage of the processing of words in transcripts, targets on topic detection. The idea is to use lexical chains [16] and lexical similarity upon the nouns into the transcript. In order to implement this it is necessary to define the window length for the lexical chaining and the measure of calculating the similarity of the words in each window. Test results until now give us 5 to 7 words as a satisfactory window length spotting the expected limits of topics in the test data set. Similarity between the words in each window is currently calculated using WordNet [14].

In the next version of the semantic recognizer, actual ontologies will be used to facilitate better performance in the identification of semantic features as well as to perform semantic event extraction from news stories identified.

4.4 Probabilistic Parsing

As already stated, the temporal structure characteristic for a news broadcast format may be modeled as a probabilistic context free grammar (PCFG) with probabilities associated with production rules. This is a probabilistic extension of a Context-Free Grammar where a probability measure p is attached to every production rule:

$$A \rightarrow L \ [p]$$

This probability is a conditional probability of the production being chosen, given that non-terminal A is up for expansion (in generative terms).

In order to integrate story segmentation and classification information, the scenario PCFG is based on the news segmentation model that contains all the different parts of a news story and news broadcast such as: INTRO, START-OF-PREVIEW, PREVIEW, END-OF-PREVIEW, START-OF-STORY, PRESENTATION, REPORT, END-OF-STORY, COMMERCIAL, OUTRO etc. These structural components may be inferred by the PCFG parser from tokens coming from the recognizer modules using appropriate grammar rules.

The implementation of the PCFG parsing process distinguishes between three necessary modules: (1) the PCFG parser component; (2) the Environment Initialization Module and (3) the Probabilities Computation Module which are described next.

The PCFG parser

The PCFG parser uses the probabilistic extension of the Earley parsing algorithm [17]. Earley parser is a combined top/down bottom/up parsing algorithm that spans the parse tree on both directions. It uses the concept of a chart, where every edge represents a production rule. The algorithm proceeds in three steps:

- *Prediction:* The prediction step is used to hypothesize the possible continuation of the input based on the current position in the parse. Prediction essentially expands one branch of the grammar down to the set of its leftmost leaf nodes to predict the next possible input terminals. At this step, any edge corresponding to predicted production rules is added to the chart as a pending (or active) edge.
- *Scanning:* Scanning step simply reads an input symbol and matches it against all pending states for the next iteration. When a pending state is matched, a terminal rule is added to the chart, and the pending state becomes inactive.
- *Completion:* The completion step updates pending derivations. When a production rule has finished, it converts the corresponding edge to a completed one.

When the parsing is finished, the algorithm walks through the chart and exports the parsing tree from the production rules that have been completed.

The probabilistic extension of the Earley parsing algorithm uses a PCFG, i.e. a context-free grammar with probabilities attached to each production rule. During parsing, the algorithm computes two kinds of probability metrics:

- A forward probability, which represents the probability of the whole parse tree.
- An inner probability, which represents the probability for every individual parse step.

The forward probability can be used to choose the most probable parse among many completed parses and the inner probability is used for clever pruning, where we can define probability thresholds and reduce the size of the parse tree accordingly.

The ambiguity of the input tokens due to the probabilistic nature of the recognizers affects computed probabilities at the scanning step of the algorithm. In this way, the values of inner and forward probabilities weight competing derivations not only by the typicality of corresponding production rules, but also by the certainty about the input symbol recognized at each step.

We have introduced some modifications to the parsing algorithm described above. One major change is the ability to add many candidate input tokens to the chart at every scanning step in order to address the need to use an arbitrary number of recognizers working in synch and each producing a series of tokens along with their likelihood. Another important modification is the use of the prediction step of the algorithm so as to guide the recognizers. This step gives the parser the opportunity to have an overall control of the recognizers, by giving them information of the predicted forthcoming tokens. Finally we have extended the parsing algorithm to accommodate time constraints in order to discard productions that correspond to erroneous recognitions of tokens taking into account the minimum and maximum durations of certain types of segments identified.

For the implementation of the parser we have used Javachart parser (http://nlpfarm.sourceforge.net/javachart/) that implements a bottom-up chart parsing algorithm and uses features for every edge in the chart. In our implementation we modified the main parsing algorithm to function as a probabilistic Earley parser along with the extensions we have introduced.

Environment Initialization Module

The Environment Initialization Module will provide system initialization according to specific parameters related to the audio-visual input. This module will initialize the recognizers and give appropriate information to the parser about which recognizers are available for every telecast analysis. It can also "map" tokens between a grammar and the recognizers. For advanced functionality, the module must use News ontologies that describe specific low level features. (e.g., the sample images or voice patterns of the possible newscasters in a news telecast) in order to pass this information to the recognizers for appropriate feature extraction from the audiovisual signal.

Probabilities Computation Module - Training the Probabilistic Grammar

The training of the grammar will be performed by parsing "perfect" tokenizations of a set of news telecasts. As in traditional feature grammar training methods, the higher the number of times each production rule is expanded the higher its final probability measure. The algorithm that will be employed is described in [11]. The "perfect" token representations of a telecast can either be created manually or with the assistance of a semi-automated annotation tool, where the user can correct the series of automatically recognized tokens.

4.5 Segmentation Description Creator Module

The Segmentation Description Creator Module (SDCM) will create the final output of the system, an MPEG7 compliant XML document with segmentation and semantic metadata. In order to produce this XML document, the most probable parse tree of the parsing phase will be used along with the information of the detected semantic events from the semantic recognizer. The News Ontologies will also be used in order to find additional information regarding the semantic content of the detected segments (i.e. news stories).

5 Conclusions

The current implementation of the system described here consists of separate recognizer modules along with the basic modules for parsing and is still work in progress.

An application of the visual and audio recognizers has been done in TRECVID 2006, with focus on the detection of so-called high-level features instead of structural tokens [3].

The current parser demonstrator provides a fully operational PCFG parser that uses manually created probabilistic grammars describing specific classes of news telecasts available in the TRECVID'03 collection. Simulated streams of tokens, as they will be provided by the system's recognizers, are used as input to the PCFG parser for parsing. After parsing this simulated input, the parser returns with a set of parse trees along with their probabilities. The parse trees contain all the required information (in their inner nodes representing the non-terminals of each probabilistic grammar) for the segmentation of the news telecasts.

The integration of the actual recognizers in this demonstrator requires the transformation of their current output format into token-like form as well as the provision of their functionality using a well defined web-services interface. This is currently under implementation. In the final implementation a full version of the Semantic Recognizer along with the fully developed News Ontologies and the Semantic Description Creator Module will be used to provide the final MPEG7 compliant XML description of the segmented and semantically analyzed news telecasts.

Acknowledgments. The work presented in this paper is partially funded by the DELOS II Network of Excellence on Digital Libraries (IST – Project 507618).

References

1. Boreczky, J.S., Wilcox, L.D.: A Hidden Markov Model Framework for Video Segmentation Using Audio and Image Features. In: proc. IEEE ICASSP, Seattle (USA) (1998)
2. Brand, M., Kettnaker, V.: Discovery and Segmentation of Activities in Video. IEEE Trans. Pattern Anal. Mach. Intel 22(8), 844–851 (2000)
3. Bruckmann, A., Lerbs, B., Gao, D., Eidtmann, J., Mozogovenko, L., Buczilowski, M., Jughardt, T., Xu, Y., Jacobs, A., Lüdtke, A.: Trecvid 2006 high level feature extraction. In: TRECVID 2006 Workshop Notebook Papers (2006)
4. Chang, C.C., Lin, C.J.: LIBSVM: a library for support vector machines (2001), Software available at http://www.csie.ntu.edu.tw/~cjlin/libsvm
5. Dimitrova, N., Agnihotri, L., Wei, G.: Video classification based on HMM using text and faces. In: European Signal Processing Conference. Tampere (Finland) (2000)
6. Eickeler, S., Muller, S.: Content-based video indexing of TV broadcast news using hidden markov models. In: IEEE International Conference on Acoustics, Speech, and Signal Processing, Phoenix (USA), pp. 2997–3000. IEEE Computer Society Press, Los Alamitos (1999)
7. Greiff, W., Morgan, A., Fish, R., Richards, M., Kundu, A.: Fine-Grained Hidden Markov Modeling for Broadcast-News Story Segmentation. In: Proceedings of the first international conference on Human language technology research, San Diego (USA), pp. 1–5 (2001)
8. Hoiem, D., Ke, Y., Sukthankar, R.: Solar: Sound object localization and retrieval in complex audio environments. In: Proc. of the IEEE International Conference on Acoustics, Speech and Signal (2005)
9. Huang, J., Kumar, R., Mitra, M., Zhu, W.J., Zabih, R.: Image indexing using color correlograms. In: CVPR 1997. Proceedings of the 1997 Conference on Computer Vision and Pattern Recognition (1997)
10. Huang, J., Liu, Z., Wang, Y., Chen, Y., Wong, E.K.: Integration of multimodal features for video scene classification based on HMM. In: IEEE Workshop on Multimedia Signal Processing, Copenhagen (Denmark) (1999)
11. Ivanov, Y., Bobick, A.F.: Recognition of Visual Activities and Interactions by Stochastic Parsing. IEEE Transactions on Pattern Analysis and Machine Intelligence 22(8) (2000)
12. Joachims, T.: Making large-Scale SVM Learning Practical. MIT Press, Cambridge (1999)
13. Johnston, M.: Deixis and Conjunction in Multimodal Systems. In: Proceedings of the 18th conference on Computational linguistics, vol. 1, pp. 362–368 (2000)
14. Miller, G., Beckwith, R., Fellbaum, C., Gross, D., Miller, K.J.: Introduction to WordNet: an on-line lexical database. International Journal of Lexicography 3(4), 235–244 (1990)
15. Moore, D., Essa, I.: Recognizing multitasked activities using stochastic context-free grammar. In: Proceedings of Workshop on Models vs Exemplars in Computer Vision (2001)
16. Stokes, N., Carthy, J., Smeaton, A.F.: SeLeCT: A lexical Cohesion Based News Story Segmentation System. Journal of AI Communications 17(1), 3–12 (2004)
17. Stolcke, A.: An efficient Probabilistic Context-Free Parsing Algorithm That Computes Prefix Probabilities. Computational Linguistics 21(2), 165–201 (1995)
18. Tamura, H., Mori, S., Yamawaki, T.: Textural feratures corresponding to visual perception. IEEE Trans. Syst., Man, Cyb. 8(6), 460–473 (1978)
19. Wilkens, N.: Detektion von Videoframes mit Texteinblendungen in Echtzeit. Diploma thesis. Universität Bremen (2003)

Description, Matching and Retrieval by Content of 3D Objects

S. Berretti, A. Del Bimbo, and P. Pala*

Dipartimento di Sistemi e Informatica
University of Firenze
via S.Marta 3, 50139 Firenze, Italy

Abstract. In this work, we report on three research results achieved during the first three years of activities carried out under the task 3.8 of the DELOS Network of Excellence.

First, two approaches for 3D objects description and matching for the purpose of 3D objects retrieval have been defined. An approach based on *curvature correlograms* is used to globally represent and compare 3D objects according to the local similarity of their surface curvature. Differently, a view based approach using *spin image signatures* is used to capture local and global information of 3D models by using a large number of views of the object which are then grouped according to their similarities. These approaches have been integrated in task prototypes and are now under integration into the DELOS DLMS.

To open the way to 3D objects retrieval based on similarity of object parts, a method for the automatic decomposition of 3D objects has been defined. This approach exploits Reeb-graphs in order to capture topological information identifying the main protrusions of a 3D object.

1 Introduction

Beside image and video databases, archives of 3D models have recently gained increasing attention for a number of reasons: advancements in 3D hardware and software technologies, their ever increasing availability at affordable costs, and the establishment of open standards for 3D data interchange (e.g., VRML, X3D).

Three-dimensional acquisition of a real-world object, capturing both object geometry and its visual features (surface color and texture), can be achieved through many different techniques, including CAD, 3D laser scanners, structured light systems and photogrammetry. Thanks to the availability of these technologies, 3D models are being created and employed in a wide range of application domains, including medicine, computer aided design and engineering, and cultural heritage. In this framework the development of techniques to enable retrieval by content of 3D models assumes an ever increasing relevance. This is particularly the case in the fields of cultural heritage and historical relics, where

---

* This work is partially supported by the Information Society Technologies (IST) Program of the European Commission as part of the DELOS Network of Excellence on Digital Libraries (Contract G038-507618).

C. Thanos, F. Borri, and L. Candela (Eds.): Digital Libraries: R&D, LNCS 4877, pp. 288–297, 2007.

there is a growing interest in solutions enabling preservation of relevant artworks (e.g., vases, sculptures, and handicrafts) as well as cataloging and retrieval by content. In these fields, retrieval by content can be employed to detect commonalities between 3D objects (e.g., the "signature" of the artist) or to monitor the temporal evolution of a defect (e.g., the amount of bending for wooden tables).

Based on this, the main objective of the DELOS task 3.8 is the definition of new techniques supporting retrieval by content of 3D objects. In the first three years of the task, a set of relevant research and application results have been obtained at the Media Integration and Communication Center of the University of Firenze. First, two approaches for 3D objects description and matching for the purposes of 3D objects retrieval have been defined. An approach based on curvature correlograms is used to globally represent and compare 3D objects according to the local similarity of their surface curvature. Differently, a view based approach using spin image signatures is used to capture local and global information of 3D models by using a large number of views of the object. These views are then grouped in a set of clusters according to their similarity. At the end, the centers of the clusters are used to as representative (salient) views of the object. These approaches have been integrated in task prototypes and are now under integration into the DELOS DLMS. To open the way to 3D retrieval based on the similarity of object parts, a method for the automatic decomposition of 3D objects has been defined. This approach exploits Reeb-graphs in order to capture topological information identifying the main protrusions of a 3D object.

The paper is organized in two Sections and Conclusions. In Sect.2, approaches developed for 3D objects description and matching for retrieval purposes are described. These solutions are extended in Sect.3, by addressing an approach for automatic decomposition of 3D objects. This aims to partition a 3D objects according to its main protrusions thus enabling the description and matching of individual object parts. In Sect.4, we shortly present the current and future research activities.

2   3D Objects Retrieval

Two original solutions for 3D objects retrieval have been defined. Curvature correlograms have been proposed to provide global representations of 3D objects based on curvature information of the object surface. Spin image signatures, have been defined in order to capture local and global information of 3D objects based on multiple views.

2.1   Curvature Correlograms

In [1], histograms of surface curvature have been used to support description and retrieval of 3D objects. However, since histograms do not include any spatial information, the system is liable to false positives. To overcome such problem, we used curvature correlograms as a model for representation and retrieval of 3D objects [2], [3]. Correlograms have been previously and successfully used for retrieval of images based on color content [4]. In particular, with respect to description based on histograms of local features, correlograms enable the encoding of information about the relative position of local features.

Correlograms are used to encode information about curvature values and their localization on the object surface. For this peculiarity, description of 3D objects based on correlograms of curvature proves to be very effective for the purpose of content based retrieval of 3D objects.

High resolution 3D models obtained through scanning of real world objects are often affected by high frequency noise, due to either the scanning device or the subsequent registration process. Therefore, smoothing is required in order to extract their salient features. This is especially the case if salient features are related to differential properties of mesh surface (e.g., surface curvature). Selection of a smoothing filter is a critical step, in that the application of some filters entails changes in the shape of the models. In the proposed solution, we adopted the filter first proposed by Taubin [5].

Let $\mathcal{M}$ be a mesh, and E, V and F, the sets of *edges*, *vertices* and *faces* of the mesh. With N_V, N_E and N_F, we denote the cardinality of sets V, E and F. Given a vertex $v \in \mathcal{M}$, the principal curvatures of $\mathcal{M}$ at vertex v are indicated as $k_1(v)$ and $k_2(v)$. The mean curvature $\bar{k}_v$ is related to the principal curvature $k_1(v)$ and $k_2(v)$ by the equation: $\bar{k}_v = \frac{k_1(v)+k_2(v)}{2}$. Details about computation of the principal and mean curvatures for a mesh can be found in [6].

Values of the mean curvature are quantized into $2N + 1$ classes of discrete values. For this purpose, a quantization module processes the mean curvature value through a stair-step function so that many neighboring values are mapped to one output value:

$$\mathcal{Q}(\bar{k}) = \begin{cases} N\Delta & \text{if } \bar{k} \geq N\Delta \\ i\Delta & \text{if } \bar{k} \in [i\Delta, (i+1)\Delta) \\ -i\Delta & \text{if } \bar{k} \in [-(i+1)\Delta, -i\Delta) \\ -N\Delta & \text{if } \bar{k} \leq -N\Delta \end{cases} \tag{1}$$

with $i \in \{0, \ldots, N-1\}$ and Δ a suitable quantization parameter (in the experiments reported in the following, $N = 100$ and $\Delta = 0.15$). Function $\mathcal{Q}(\cdot)$ quantizes values of $\bar{k}$ into $2N + 1$ distinct classes $\{c_i\}_{i=-N}^{N}$. To simplify the notation, $v \in \mathcal{M}_i$ is synonymous with $v \in \mathcal{M}$ and $\mathcal{Q}(\bar{k}_v) = c_i$.

The correlogram of curvature is defined with respect to a predefined distance value δ. In particular, the curvature correlogram $\gamma_{c_i c_j}^{(\delta)}$ of a mesh $\mathcal{M}$ is defined as:

$$\gamma_{c_i,c_j}^{(\delta)}(\mathcal{M}) = \Pr_{v_1,v_2 \in \mathcal{M}} [(v_1 \in \mathcal{M}_{c_i}, v_2 \in \mathcal{M}_{c_j}) \mid \|v_1 - v_2\| = \delta]$$

In this way, $\gamma_{c_i,c_j}^{(\delta)}(\mathcal{M})$ is the probability that two vertices that are δ far away from each other have curvature belonging to class c_i and c_j, respectively.

Ideally, $\|v_1 - v_2\|$ should be the geodesic distance between vertices v_1 and v_2. However, this can be approximated with the $k-$ring distance if the mesh $\mathcal{M}$ is regular and triangulated [7]. In particular, given a generic vertex $v_i \in \mathcal{M}$, the *neighborhood* or *1-ring* of v_i is the set: $V^{v_i} = \{v_j \in \mathcal{M} : \exists e_{ij} \in E\}$ being E the set of all mesh edges (if $e_{ij} \in E$ there is an edge that links vertices v_i and v_j).

The set V^{v_i} can be easily computed using the morphological operator *dilate*: $V^{v_i} = dilate(v_i)$. Through the dilate operator, the concept of *1-ring* can be used to define, recursively, generic k^{th} order neighborhood: $ring_k = dilate^k \cap dilate^{k-1}$. Definition of kth order neighborhood enables definition of a true metric between vertices of a mesh.

This metric can be used for the purpose of computing curvature correlograms as an approximation of the usual geodesic distance (that is computationally much more demanding). According to this, we define the $k-$ring distance between two mesh vertices as $d_{ring}(v_1, v_2) = k$ if $v_2 \in ring_k(v_1)$. Function $d_{ring}(v_1, v_2) = k$ is a true metric. Based on the $d_{ring}(\cdot)$ distance, the correlogram of curvature can be redefined as follows:

$$\gamma_{c_i,c_j}^{(k)}(\mathcal{M}) = \Pr_{v_1,v_2 \in \mathcal{M}}[(v_1 \in \mathcal{M}_{c_i}, v_2 \in \mathcal{M}_{c_j}) | d_{ring}(v_1, v_2) = k]$$

Figs.1(a)-(b) show the correlograms of three models derived from two different model categories, *statue* and *dinosaur*, respectively.

Several distance measures have been proposed to compute the dissimilarity of distribution functions. In order to compute the similarity between curvature correlograms of two distinct meshes $\gamma_{c_i,c_j}^{(k)}(\mathcal{M}_1)$ and $\gamma_{c_i,c_j}^{(k)}(\mathcal{M}_2)$ we experimented the following distance measures: *Minkowsky-form distance, Histogram intersection, χ^2-statistics, Kullback-Leibler divergence*.

Using a ground-truth database, the above distance measures have been compared in terms of precision and recall figures. Results of this analysis (not reported in this paper for lack of space) suggest that the best performance is achieved by using χ^2-statistics to measure the distance between curvature correlograms:

$$d_{\chi^2} = \sum_{i,j=-N}^{N} \frac{\left(\gamma_{c_i,c_j}^{(k)}(\mathcal{M}_1) - \gamma_{c_i,c_j}^{(k)}(\mathcal{M}_2)\right)^2}{2\left(\gamma_{c_i,c_j}^{(k)}(\mathcal{M}_1) + \gamma_{c_i,c_j}^{(k)}(\mathcal{M}_2)\right)}$$

(a)

(b)

Fig. 1. In (a) and (b) correlograms of three models, taken from two distinct categories, namely statue and dinosaur, are shown

2.2   Spin Image Signatures

Many 3D retrieval solutions proposed so far, rely on the extraction of content descriptors capturing global properties of 3D object surface: moments, distributions of vertex distances, surface curvature or angles between faces. Alternatively, surface properties can be described in transformed domains, like the wavelets and the spherical harmonics.

During the second year of the DELOS task 3.8, we defined a new solution combining the advantages of view-based and structural-based approaches to description and matching of 3D objects. The new solution relies on spin image signatures and clustering to achieve an effective, yet efficient representation of 3D object content [8].

For each mesh vertex V, a spin image is built mapping any other mesh vertex x onto a two-dimensional space (see the left of Fig.2). The grey-level spin images are derived by considering the density of mesh vertices that map on the same point of the spin image, and evaluating the influence of each vertex over the neighboring pixels of its projection, according to a bilinear interpolation scheme. On the right of Fig.2 a sample model of a teapot is shown with spin images computed from four different vertices of the model. Spin images are then partitioned into sectors of circular crowns for the upper $(\beta > 0)$ and lower $(\beta < 0)$ half-planes and circular sectors centered in the origin. For each of them, the number of vertex projections that fall in the region have been considered. Experimentally a number of 6 circular crowns for the upper and lower half planes and for the circular sectors has been found to be a satisfactory trade-off between representation compactness and selectivity. This leads to compress the spin image informative content into a 18-dimensional vector.

Description vectors have been clustered using fuzzy clustering so as to take the centers of the clusters as signatures of the spin image representation. The optimal number of clusters is derived considering two functions that express a measure of under- and over-partitioning, respectively. The optimal number of clusters is the number that minimizes the sum of the two functions representing the trade-off between under- and over-partitioning. Finally, similarity between spin image signatures of 3D objects is obtained considering the permutation that minimizes the sum of distances between the corresponding cluster centers.

In order to validate the retrieval performance of the proposed approach, a compound 3D repository of VRML models has been constructed by gathering 3D models featuring different characteristics mainly in terms of resolution and complexity. In particular, the 3D repository includes 3D models collected from the Web, from the 3D Princeton Shape Benchmark Archive [9] and from the De Espona Encyclopedia [10].

All models of the compound 3D repository have been processed in order to extract the Spin Image signature and signatures of four other approaches for 3D objects representation and retrieval that we used for comparison purposes. A variety of dissimilarity measures to compare content descriptors have been also considered. In addition, models of the compound 3D repository have been manually annotated so as to represent semantic information about their content.

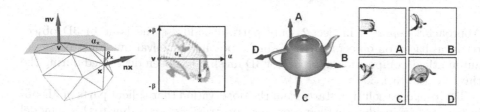

Fig. 2. A spin image computed on the vertex of a 3D model is shown on the left. On the right, spin images for the same object computed along the four normals A, B, C, D to the object surface, are shown.

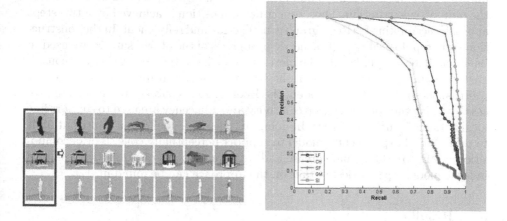

Fig. 3. On the left, retrieval results are reported for three query models. Average precision/recall results are reported on the right comparing Spin Images (SI) against four different approaches for 3D object retrieval, namely, Light Field (LI), Curvature Histogram (CH), Shape Functions (SF) and Curvature Moments (CM).

Annotations are used to automatically extract precision and recall curves. These have been used to provide a representative comparison of the performance of prototype retrieval engines. Retrieval performance based on Spin Image signatures has been compared against the performance of four other prototype retrieval engines, using Light Field (LI) [11], Curvature Histogram (CH) [1], Shape Functions (SF) [9] and Curvature Moments (CM). Comparison has been carried out in terms of figures of precision and recall. Comparison suggests that retrieval based on Spin Image signatures outperforms the other prototype retrieval engines for medium- and high-resolution 3D models. In particular, on the right of Figure 9 the average precision/recall curves are reported for the five methods under investigation. This has been obtained by using objects from every model category of the Princeton shape benchmark database as query model.

3   Automatic Decomposition of 3D Objects

Approaches reported in Sect.2, only partially address the issue of 3D object retrieval based on objects parts. To make possible retrieval by object parts, an automatic decomposition approach of 3D meshes has been developed during the third year of task 3.8.

The proposed solution starts from the observation that salient parts of 3D objects usually coincide with their prominent protrusions. According to this, a model for perceptually consistent decomposition of 3D objects based on Reeb-graphs is proposed. Our approach is motivated by the need to overcome limitations of solutions which only use curvature information to perform mesh decomposition. In particular, we propose the use of Reeb-graphs to extract structural and topological information of a mesh surface and to drive the decomposition process. Curvature information is used to refine boundaries between object parts, in accordance to the minima rule criterion. Thus, object decomposition is achieved by a two steps approach accounting for Reeb-graph construction and refinement. In the construction step, topological as well as metric properties of the object surface are used to build the Reeb-graph. Due to the metric properties of the object that are considered for building the Reeb-graph, the structure of this graph reflects the object protrusions. In the refinement step, the Reeb-graph is subject to an editing process by which the notions of deep concavity and adjacency are used to support fine localization of part boundaries. In doing so, the main goal of our contribution is to provide and experiment a model to support perceptually consistent decomposition of 3D objects to enable reuse and retrieval of parts of 3D models archived in large model repositories. Details on the approach can be found in [12].

3.1   Results

To demonstrate the effectiveness of the proposed solution, a comparison with two alternative approaches to object decomposition is proposed. Furthermore, in order to estimate the extent to which object decomposition matches perceptually salient object parts, a test is carried out using a ground-truth archive of manually partitioned objects. In the following, a summary of the *subjective* and *objective* evaluation of the segmentation approach is reported.

The *subjective* evaluation is accomplished by presenting decomposition results on a set of reference 3D models covering a variety of objects with different structural complexity and resolution. We refer to this evaluation as subjective because we do not provide objective measures of the performance of the decomposition models under analysis. Rather, performance of each approach is evaluated subjectively by comparing decomposition results on the set of reference 3D models. Differently, the *objective* evaluation is accomplished by defining a measure of the perceptual saliency of decompositions. For this purpose, a ground-truth set of annotated 3D objects has been constructed through a user based experiment. In the experiment, some people were asked to identify relevant parts of 3D models representing real objects of different structural complexity. Answers were used to assess the degree by which decomposition provided by the approaches under comparison matched relevant parts identified by users.

The proposed solution for 3D objects decomposition based on Reeb graphs (RG) has been compared against the approach for decomposition based on *pulse-coupled oscillator networks* (PON) [13], and the approach for decomposition based on *curvature clustering* (CC) [14]. Selection of these approaches is motivated by the fact that they exploit different characteristics of the object surface with respect to RG, in that both PON and CC basically use the sole curvature information to produce object decomposition.

Decomposition of Sample 3D Objects. Fig.4 presents decomposition results for two reference models using RG (leftmost column), PON (central column) and CC (rightmost column) approaches.

Reference models are selected so as to test decomposition approaches on models characterized by different structural complexity in terms of local surface variations and presence of large object protrusions.

The RG approach produces satisfactory results for both the reference models. The decompositions of the human body shown in Fig.4(a), clearly evidence the differences between RG and the other two solutions. In fact, the geodesic distance analysis which characterizes the RG approach, provides this method with the capability to identify salient protrusions: legs, harms and the head are correctly separated from the body. PON and RG, relying on the sole curvature information, produce an over-decomposition of the model that does not match perceptually relevant parts. Similar results occur for the models in Fig.4(b).

Perceptual Saliency of Decomposed Objects. In order to quantitatively measure the saliency of 3D object decompositions, a test has been carried out aiming to compare results of manual versus automatic objects decomposition. The comparison has been carried out on a ground-truth archive composed of 10 reference 3D models which represent real objects of different structural complexity. In particular, models belong to three categories: surfaces of revolution (SOR), vases and complex objects. An agreement value between manual segmentations, provided by a set of users for the reference models, and the automatic segmentations is used to measure the goodness of segmentations. Fig. 5 shows ranges of the agreement for the three approaches (RG, PON and CC) on the three categories of objects included in the ground-truth archive.

Results show different behaviors for the three categories, the RG approach featuring the best performance on average. For the category, on the average, the three approaches score the best results in terms of average values (68.4%, 75.77% and 75.48%, for PON, CC and RG, respectively). As expected, a curvature based approach like CC performs well in this case, but it is relevant that also the RG solution is capable to score almost the same results as CC. For the vases category, the agreement for CC consistently decreases (decreasing to 60.86%), while the mean value of the agreement for PON and RG keeps almost constant (70.37% and 76.08% for PON and RG, respectively) with respect to the results scored for the SOR category. Finally, as expected, for the category including complex

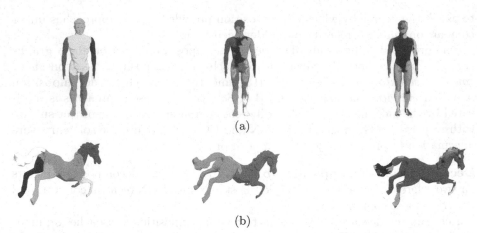

(a)

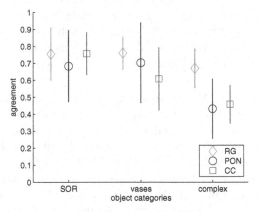

(b)

Fig. 4. Decomposition of sample objects of different resolution using the proposed approach (RG, leftmost column), the oscillator network (PON, central column) and the curvature clustering (CC, rightmost column). Different colors are used to evidence the regions identified by the automatic partitioning. Model (a) has 23280 vertices and (b) 9207.

Fig. 5. Mean and variance spread of the agreement for the RG, PON and CC approaches on the three categories of objects included in the ground-truth archive

objects the agreement is much lower especially for PON and CC (43.21% and 45.84%, respectively), while RG outperforms the other two approaches by over twenty percentage points (67.06%). More details and results on this 3D objects decomposition approach can be found in [15].

4   Conclusions

In this paper, we have summarized the main results obtained in the researches conducted during the past three years of the task 3.8 of the DELOS network of excellence. In particular, two approaches for 3D objects retrieval have been proposed based on object surface curvature and object views, respectively. A method for 3D objects decomposition has been also developed in order to allow 3D objects retrieval based on object parts. Current and future work are mainly focused on methods for representing and comparing 3D face models for the purpose of recognition.

References

1. Hetzel, G., Leibe, B., Levi, P., Schiele, B.: 3rd object recognition from range images using local feature histograms. In: Proc. International Conference on Computer Vision and Pattern Recognition, Kauai Marriott, Hawaii (2001)
2. Antini, G., Berretti, S., Del Bimbo, A., Pala, P.: Retrieval of 3d objects using curvature correlograms. In: Proc. IEEE International Conference on Multimedia & Expo, Amsterdam, The Netherlands, pp. 735–738 (2005)
3. Antini, G., Berretti, S., Del Bimbo, A., Pala, P.: Curvature correlograms for content based retrieval of 3d objects. In: Roli, F., Vitulano, S. (eds.) ICIAP 2005. LNCS, vol. 3617, pp. 859–866. Springer, Heidelberg (2005)
4. Huang, J., Kumar, R., Mitra, M., Zhu, W.J., Zabih, R.: Spatial color indexing and application. International Journal of Computer Vision 35, 245–268 (1999)
5. Taubin, G.: Estimating the tensor of curvature of a surface from a polyhedral approximation. In: Proc. International Conference on Computer Vision, Boston, MA, vol. 1, pp. 902–907 (1995)
6. Berretti, S.: A signal processing approach to fair surface design. Computer Graphics 29, 351–358 (1995)
7. Desbrun, M., Meyer, M., Schroder, P., Barr, A.H.: Discrete differential-geometry operators in nd (2000)
8. Assfalg, J., Bertini, M., Del Bimbo, A., Pala, P.: Content based retrieval of 3d objects using spin image signatures. IEEE Transactions on Multimedia 9, 589–599 (2007)
9. Shilane, P., Min, P., Kazhdan, M., Funkhouser, T.: The princeton shape benchmark. In: Proc. Shape Modeling International Conference, Genova, Italy (2004)
10. Online: The de espona enciclopedya, http://www.deespona.com
11. Chen, D.Y., Tian, X.P., Shen, Y.T., Ouhyoung, M.: On visual similarity based 3d model retrieval. In: Proc. EUROGRAPHICS 2003 (2003)
12. Berretti, S., Del Bimbo, A., Pala, P.: Segmentation of 3d models using reeb graphs. In: Proc. International Conference on Pattern Recognition, Hong-Kong, China, vol. 1, pp. 19–22 (2006)
13. Ceccarelli, E., Del Bimbo, A., Pala, P.: Segmentation of 3d objects using pulse-coupled oscillator networks. In: Proc. International Conference on Multimedia & Expo, Amsterdam, The Netherlands, pp. 153–156 (2005)
14. Lavoué, G., Dupont, F., Baskurt, A.: A new cad mesh segmentation method, based on curvature tensor analysis. Computer Aided Design 37, 975–987 (2005)
15. Berretti, S., Del Bimbo, A., Pala, P.: 3d mesh decomposition using reeb graphs. Submitted to Image and Vision Computing (2006)

3D-Mesh Models: View-Based Indexing and Structural Analysis

Mohamed Daoudi, Tarik Filali Ansary,
Julien Tierny, and Jean-Philippe Vandeborre

TELECOM Lille 1 / LIFL / USTL (France)
mohamed.daoudi@lifl.fr, tarik.filali@lifl.fr,
julien.tierny@lifl.fr, jean-philippe.vandeborre@lifl.fr

Abstract. 3D-mesh models are widely used to represent real objects in synthesized scenes for multimedia or cultural heritage applications, medical or military simulations, video games and so on. Indexing and analyzing these 3D data is a key issue to enable an effective usage of 3D-mesh model for designers and even for final users.

The researches of our group mainly focus on these problems. In this paper, we present the work of our group for the DELOS NoE during the year 2006. We have worked on two approaches for 3D-model indexing and analyzing: view-based approach and structural approach. View-based approaches for 3D-model indexing are a very intuitive way to retrieve 3D-models among wide collections by using 2D natural views (as a human uses to represent 3D-objects). Structural analysis of a 3D-mesh model gives a structural decomposition of the object from a raw boundary representation of it, then this decomposition can be used to segment or index 3D-models.

Keywords: 3D-model, 3D-mesh, indexing, view based approach, Bayesian indexing, topological analysis, Reeb graph.

1 Introduction

Exploiting the information contents of digital collections poses several problems. In order to create added-value out of these collections, users need to find information that match certain expectations – a notoriously hard problem due to the inherent difficulties of describing visual information content.

In recent years, as a solution to these problems, many systems have been proposed that enable effective information retrieval from digital collections of images and videos. However, solutions proposed so far to support retrieval of images and videos – which are intrinsically bidimensional – are not always effective in application contexts where the information is intrinsically three-dimensional.

To satisfy this need, a variety of retrieval methods have been proposed that enable the efficient querying of model repositories for a desired 3D shape, many of which use a 3D-model as a query and attempt to retrieve models with matching shape from the database.

C. Thanos, F. Borri, and L. Candela (Eds.): Digital Libraries: R&D, LNCS 4877, pp. 298–307, 2007.

In our group, we have worked on two approaches: view based approach and structural approach. This paper presents, in the next two sections, these approaches, achieved work of our group for the DELOS NoE during the year 2006.

2 View-Based Approach

The human visual system has an uncanny ability to recognize objects from single views, even when presented monocularly under a fixed viewing condition. The issue of whether 3D-object recognition should rely on internal representations that are inherently three-dimensional or on collections of two-dimensional views has been explored by Risenhuber and Poggio [1]. They show that, in a human vision system, a 3D-object is represented by a set of 2D-views.

The process of comparing two 3D-objects using their views can be separated into two main steps: 3D-model indexing (also known as the off-line step) and 3D-model retrieval (the on-line step). In the 3D-model indexing step, each 3D-object is characterized by a set of 2D views. For each view, a 2D descriptor is calculated. In the 3D-model retrieval step, the same descriptor is applied to the 2D request views. A matching process is then started to match the request 2D views to the views from the 3D-objects of the database.

2.1 Characteristic View Selection

The main idea of view-based similarity methods is that two 3D-models are similar, if they look similar from all viewing angles. This paradigm leads to the implementation of query interfaces based on defining a query by one or more views, sketches, photos showing the query from different points of view.

A point which will have an impact on the effectiveness and the speed of the view based methods is the number and the position of views used to describe a 3D-object. This number is directly related to the performances of the system. It is necessary to decrease to the number of views to have a fast method, all in preserving the descriptive capacity of the views. Two approaches can be used to choose the number of characteristic views: using a fixed and restricted number of views; or using a dynamic number of views, that correspond the number of views to the geometrical complexity of views.

In the Adaptive Views Clustering (AVC) method, presented by our group [2], we use an initial set of 320 views to select positions for the views, which must be equally spaced, we use a two-unit icosahedron centered on the origin. We subdivide the icosahedron twice by using the Loop-subdivision schema to obtain a 320 faceted polyhedron. To generate the initial set of views, we place the camera on each of the face-centers of the polyhedron looking at the coordinate origin. To represent each of these 2D views, we use 49 coefficients of Zernike moment descriptor [3]. Finally, the initial set of views has to be reduced as we want from the method to adapt the number of characteristic views to the geometrical complexity of the 3D-model.

As every 2D view is represented by 49 Zernike moment coefficients, choosing a set of characteristic views that best characterise the 3D-models (320 views) is equivalent to choose a subset of points that represent a set of 320 points in a 49-dimension space. Choosing X characteristic views which best represent a set of $N = 320$ views is well known as a *clustering problem*.

This kind of problem is generally solved by using *K-means* algorithm [4]. Its attractiveness lies in its simplicity and in its local-minimum convergence properties. However, it has one main shortcoming: the number of clusters K, no *a priori* known in our problem, has to be supplied by the user. To avoid this problem, we adapted a method derived from K-means – called X-means [5] –, and we also used a *Bayesian Information Criteria* (BIC) [6], which scores how likely the representation model fits the data. More details about this process can be found in [2].

2.2 Probabilistic Approach for 3D-Model Indexing

The main idea of our probabilistic approach is that *not* all views of a 3D-model have the same importance. There are views which represent the 3D-model better than others. On the other hand, simple objects (e.g. cube, sphere) can be at the root of more complex objects, so they have a higher probability to be relevant. In this section, we present a probabilistic approach that takes into account that views do not have the same importance, and that simple objects have higher probability to appear than more complex one.

According to the previous step (characteristic view selection), each 3D-model of the collection is represented by a set of characteristic views $V = \{V_1, V_2, \ldots, V_C\}$, with C the number of characteristic views. Moreover, to each characteristic view corresponds a set of represented views called V_r.

We want to find the 3D-models that corresponds to one or more request photos – which could also be the characteristic views of a 3D-model given as a query. We assume that in a query $Q = \{I_1, I_2, \ldots, I_K\}$ all K images represent the same object.

Considering a query Q, we wish to find the 3D-model M_i from the collection which is the closest to the query Q. This model is the one that has the highest probability $P(M_i|Q)$. A query is composed of one or more images, then this probability can be written:

$$P(M_i|Q) = \sum_{k=1}^{K} \frac{1}{K} P(M_i|I_k),$$

with K the number of images in the query Q.

The Bayesian retrieval framework we developed, takes into account the number of characteristic views of the 3D-models and the importance (amount of information) of their views. More details about our probabilistic approach can be found in [2] for a general explanation of our Bayesian framework, and [7] especially for 3D-model retrieval system with photo-oriented queries.

2.3 Experimental Results

In this section, we present the experimental process and the results we obtained. The algorithms we described in the previous sections have been implemented using C++ and the TGS Open-Inventor libraries. The system consists of an off-line characteristic view extraction algorithm and an on-line retrieval process.

To experiment our algorithms, we also developed an on-line 3D search engine[1]. Our search engine can be reached from any device having compatible web browser (PC, PDA, SmartPhone, etc.). Depending on the web access device he/she is using, the user face two different kind of web interfaces : a rich web interface for full-featured web browsers, and a simpler interface for PDA web browsers. In both cases, the results returned by the 3D search engine are the same. The only difference lies in the design of the results presentation. Figure 1 shows three screenshots of our 3D retrieval system in its rich web interface version. Request could be expressed as a 3D-model, a 2D-sketch or one or more photos.

To evaluate our method, we used the *Princeton Shape Benchmark database*[2] (known as PSB), a standard shape benchmark widely used in shape retrieval community. PSB appeared in 2004 and is one of the most exhaustive benchmarks for 3D shape retrieval. It contains a database of 1814 classified 3D-models collected from 293 different Web domains. There are many classifications given to the objects in the database. During our experiments we used the finest granularity classification, composed of 161 classes. Most classes contain objects with a particular function (e.g cars). Yet, there are also cases where objects with the same function are partitioned in different classes based on their shapes (e.g, round tables versus rectangular tables). The mean number of views for the PSB is 23 views per model. The mean size for a 3D-model descriptor is 1,113 bytes.

Our method provides more accurate results with the use of Bayesian probabilistic indexing. The experiment shows that our method Adaptive Views Clustering (AVC) gives better performance than 3D harmonics, Radialized Spherical Extent Function, and Gaussian Euclidean Distance Transform on the *Princeton 3D Shape Benchmark database*. Light Field Descriptor gives better results than our method but uses 100 views, does not adapt the number of views to the geometrical complexity, and uses two descriptors for each view (Zernike moments and Fourier descriptor), which makes it a slower and more memory consuming compared to the method we have presented.

Overall, we conclude that AVC gives a good compromise between quality (relevance) and cost (memory and on-line comparison time) for the 3D-models of the *Princeton 3D Shape Benchmark*.

To evaluate the algorithms in the case of 3D retrieval by a set of photos, we have selected 50 images from the Internet. The images correspond to 10 classes of the *Princeton Shape Benchmark* (five images per class): Airplanes, Bicycles, Chairs, Dogs, Guns, Hammers, Humans arms out, Helicopters, Pots and Swords. The images are composed of six sketches, six synthesized images and 38 real photos of different sizes.

Figure 1 shows the results of a query using (from left to right) one, two and three images of a bicycle. The left side of the figures represent the queries and the

---

[1] http://www-rech.telecom-lille1.eu/3dretrieval/

[2] http://shape.cs.princeton.edu/benchmark/

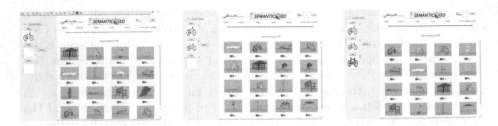

Fig. 1. 3D retrieval results using (from left to right) one, two and three photos

right side represent the 16 top retrieved 3D-models. From the seven 3D-models representing a bicycle in the database, three are in the fifteen top retrieved 3D-models when using only one photo. This number raises to four out of seven when two photos are used. Using three images, we retrieved five out of seven in the top sixteen retrieved 3D-models. The recall/precision curves obtained in [7], show that two or three photos makes a good compromise between time-effort and accuracy.

To extend his/her search, the user can click on a 3D-model from the result window. This 3D-model is then sent to the search engine and used as a query. In this case, the whole set of characteristic views of the 3D-model is considered as the set of query photos. So, the retrieval principle is exactly the same as the one described in the previous section.

At last, to give an idea of our framework performance, in the off-line process, the characteristic view selection takes about 18 seconds per model on a PC with a Pentium IV 2.4 GHZ CPU. In the on-line process, the comparison takes less than 1 second for 1814 3D-models from the PSB.

3   Structural Approaches

Structural indexing of 3D shapes is an interesting direction of research. It enables to retrieve similar 3D shapes that have different postures [8] and provides a promising framework for partial shape retrieval [9]. Our group focuses on the development of 3D mesh structural description algorithms based on topological skeletons [10].

These approaches study the properties of real valued functions computed over triangulated surfaces. Most of the time, those functions are provided by the application context, such as scientific data analysis. When dealing with topological skeletons, it is necessary to define an invariant and visually interesting mapping function, which remains an open issue [10]. Moreover, traditional topological graph construction algorithms assume that all the information brought by the mapping function is pertinent, while in practice, this can lead to large graphs, encoding noisy details.

Finally, topological approaches cannot discriminate visually interesting subparts of identified connected components, like the phalanxes of a finger. This is detrimental to certain applications, such as mesh deformation.

Our group proposed a novel and unified method which addresses the above issues [11,12].

3.1   Method Overview

Given a connected triangulated surface T, we propose a unified method to decompose T into visually meaningful sub-parts, connected components, considering the topological and geometrical characteristics of *discrete contours*.

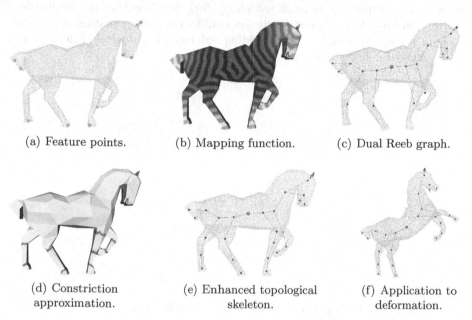

(a) Feature points. (b) Mapping function. (c) Dual Reeb graph.

(d) Constriction   (e) Enhanced topological   (f) Application to
approximation.   skeleton.   deformation.

Fig. 2. Main steps of the decomposition on a standard model

The algorithm proceeds in three stages. Firstly, mesh feature points are extracted (fig. 2(a)) in order to compute an invariant and visually interesting mapping function (fig. 2(b)), denoted f_m in the rest of the paper, revealing the most relevant parts of the mesh. Secondly, for each vertex in the mesh, we compute its *discrete contour*, a closed curve traversing it which is carried by the edges of T, and approximating f_m continuous contour. Thirdly, as the set of *discrete contours* recovers the entire mesh, it is possible to analyze each contour characteristics, either to detect topological changes (enabling a pertinent Reeb graph construction, fig. 2(c)) or to detect geometrical transitions (enabling an approximation of constrictions, fig. 2(d)). The constriction approximation enables the refinement of Reeb graphs into enhanced topological skeletons (fig. 2(e)). The enhanced topological skeleton could then be used in different ways: 3D-mesh deformation (fig. 2(f)), indexing, etc.

Detailed methods and algorithm as well as extended results can be found in [11,12].

3.2 Results

Our scientific contribution resides in three points. *(i)* We propose an original and straightforward algorithm for feature point extraction. It can resolve extraction on constant curvature areas – such as spheres – and it is robust against variations in mesh sampling and model pose. *(ii)* We show that a *discrete contour* formulation enables, without re-meshing and without any input parameter, a pertinent Reeb graph construction providing visually meaningful graphs, affine-invariant and robust to variations in mesh sampling. *(iii)* We show that the geometrical information brought by *discrete contours* enables the approximation of constrictions on prominent components providing enhanced topological skeletons, and consequently Reeb graph refinement.

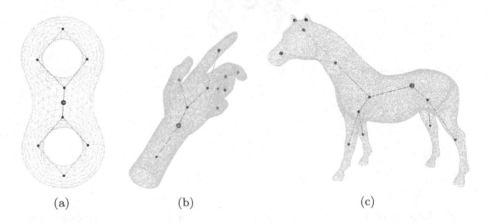

(a)   (b)   (c)

Fig. 3. Dual Reeb graphs of primitive and complex shapes (f_m function)

Figure 3 shows several dual Reeb graphs obtained with the very first steps of our method, without any refinement, with regard to f_m. Connected components are represented by the nodes located at their barycenter. Figure 4 shows several enhanced topological skeleton thanks to the constriction detection process. The enhanced topological skeleton is refined compared to classical Reeb graphs and shows more details in sub-parts.

A video demonstration of this work is available in `http://www.telecom-lille1.eu/people/tierny/stuff/videos/tierny_pacific06.avi`

3.3 Applications of Enhanced Topological Skeletons

Each node of the extracted skeleton references a surface patch on the mesh. This link between the surface and the skeleton enables applications like hierarchical semantic-oriented segmentation [13] or shape retrieval by part [14]. This is the next step of our work we are currently investigating.

Based on our previous work [11], we address the semantic-oriented 3D-mesh hierarchical segmentation problem using enhanced topological skeletons [13].

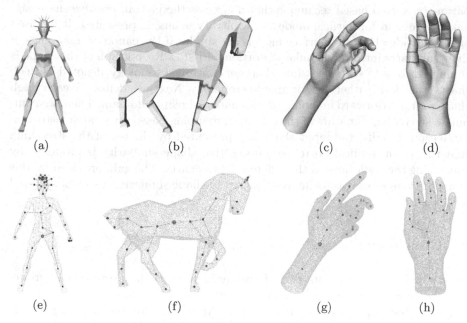

Fig. 4. Constriction approximations and enhanced topological skeletons of standard models

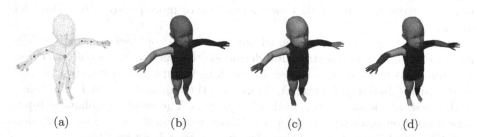

Fig. 5. Hierachical mesh segmentation based on skeleton extraction

This high level information drives both the feature boundary computation as well as the feature hierarchy definition. Proposed hierarchical scheme is based on the key idea that the topology of a feature is a more important decomposition criterion than its geometry. First, the enhanced topological skeleton of the input triangulated surface is constructed. Then it is used to delimit the core of the object and to identify junction areas. This second step results in a fine segmentation of the object. Finally, a fine to coarse strategy enables a semantic-oriented hierarchical composition of features, subdividing human limbs into arms and hands for example. An example of such a multi-level segmentation is shown in figure 5.

Reeb graph based segmentation can also be employed for the problem of arbitrary genus surface comparison [14]. In this work, a novel surface parameterization based technique that addresses the pose insensitive shape signature problem for surface models of arbitrary genus, is presented. It is based on the key idea that two surface models are similar if the canonical mappings of their sub-parts introduce similar distortions. First, a Reeb graph of the shape is computed so as to segment it into charts of controlled topology, denoted as Reeb charts, that have either disk or annulus topology. Next, we define for each Reeb chart a straightforward mapping to the canonical planar domain. Then, we compute a stretching signature of the canonical mapping based on an area distortion evaluation. Finally, the input shape is represented by the set of the stretching signatures. An application to pose-insensitive shape similarity is proposed by comparing the signatures of the different Reeb charts. The gain provided by this new signature as well as its interest for partial shape similarity are demonstrated in [14].

4   Conclusion

This paper briefly presents two of the main research interests of our group: view-based 3D-model indexing and 3D-mesh structural analysis.

In the first topic, we proposed a entire framework for the indexing of 3D-models: a dynamic characteristic view selection process that adapts the number of characteristic view to the complexity of the 3D-model, and a Bayesian approach to 3D-model indexing based on the characteristic views. The framework is capable to manage 2D-view queries (one or more photos) and 3D-model queries.

In the second topic, we presented our method to topologically analyze 3D-mesh model and obtain a structural decomposition named *enhanced topological skeleton*. This method uses a novel approach to feature point extraction as well as mapping function computation. Moreover, the enhancement of Reeb graphs is obtained with a constriction evaluation process. The resulting enhanced topological skeleton is a major tool for our future works on 3D-model segmentation and 3D partial shape retrieval that already give promising results.

References

1. Riesenhuber, M., Poggio, T.: Models of object recognition. Nature neuroscience 3, 50–89 (2000)
2. Ansary, T.F., Daoudi, M., Vandeborre, J.P.: A bayesian search engine using adaptive views clustering. IEEE Transactions on Multimedia 9(1) (2007)
3. Khotanzad, A., Hong, Y.H.: Invariant image recognition by Zernike moments. IEEE Transactions on Pattern Analysis and Machine Intelligence 12(5), 489–497 (1990)
4. Duda, R.O., Hart, P.E.: Pattern classification and scene analysis. John Wiley and Sons, Chichester (1973)
5. Pelleg, D., Moore, A.: X-means: Extending k-means with efficient estimation of the number of clusters. In: International Conference on Machine Learning, pp. 727–734 (2000)

6. Schwarz, G.: Estimating the dimension of a model. The Annals of Statistics 6, 461–464 (1978)
7. Ansary, T.F., Vandeborre, J.-P., Daoudi, M.: On 3D retrieval from photos. In: 3DPVT 2006. 3rd IEEE International Symposium on 3D Data Processing, Visualization and Transmission, Chapel Hill, North Carolina, USA (2006)
8. Hilaga, M., Shinagawa, Y., Kohmura, T., Kunii, T.: Topology matching for fully automatic similarity estimation of 3D shapes. In: ACM SIGGRAPH, pp. 203–212 (2001)
9. Funkhouser, T., Kazhdan, M., Shilane, P., Min, P., Kiefer, W., Tal, A., Rusinkiewicz, S., Dobkin, D.: Modeling by example. ACM Transactions on Graphics 23, 652–663 (2004)
10. Biasotti, S., Marini, S., Mortara, M., Patanè, G.: An overview on properties and efficacy of topological skeletons in shape modelling. In: Shape Modeling International, pp. 245–254 (2003)
11. Tierny, J., Vandeborre, J.-P., Daoudi, M.: 3D mesh skeleton extraction using topological and geometrical analyses. In: Pacific Graphics 2006. 14th Pacific Conference on Computer Graphics and Applications, Taipei, Taiwan, pp. 85–94 (2006)
12. Tierny, J., Vandeborre, J.P., Daoudi, M.: Invariant high-level reeb graphs of 3D polygonal meshes. In: 3DPVT 2006. 3rd IEEE International Symposium on 3D Data Processing, Visualization and Transmission, Chapel Hill, North Carolina, USA (2006)
13. Tierny, J., Vandeborre, J.-P., Daoudi, M.: Topology driven 3D mesh hierarchical segmentation. In: Shape Modeling International 2007. IEEE International Conference on Shape Modeling and Applications, Lyon, France (2007) (short paper)
14. Tierny, J., Vandeborre, J.-P., Daoudi, M.: Reeb chart unfolding based 3D shape signatures. In: Eurographics, Prague, Czech Republic (2007) (short paper)

Similarity-Based Retrieval with MPEG-7 3D Descriptors: Performance Evaluation on the Princeton Shape Benchmark

Costantino Grana, Matteo Davolio, and Rita Cucchiara

Dipartimento di Ingegneria dell'Informazione, Università degli Studi di Modena e Reggio Emilia, Via Vignolese 905/b, 41100 Modena, Italy
{costantino.grana,davolio.matteo.77,rita.cucchiara}@unimore.it

Abstract. In this work, we describe in detail the new MPEG-7 Perceptual 3D Shape Descriptor and provide a set of tests with different 3D objects databases, mainly with the Princeton Shape Benchmark. With this purpose we created a function library called Retrieval-3D and fixed some bugs of the MPEG-7 eXperimentation Model (XM). We explain how to match the Attributed Relational Graph (ARG) of every 3D model with the modified nested Earth Mover's Distance (mnEMD). Finally we compare our results with the best found in literature, including the first MPEG-7 3D descriptor, i.e. the Shape Spectrum Descriptor.

1 Introduction

In last years a large amount of audiovisual information is becoming available in digital form on the World Wide Web, and this number intends to grow in the future. The value of information often depends on how easy it can be retrieved; a clarifying metaphor may be a library with a lot of books but without a coherent order: obviously it is not so useful and forces people to lose time in a search task. The question of identifying and managing multimedia content is not just restricted to database retrieval applications such as digital libraries, but extends to areas like broadcast channel selection, multimedia editing, and multimedia directory services. MPEG-7 [1], formally named "Multimedia Content Description Interface", intends to be the answer to this need. MPEG-7 is an ISO/IEC standard developed by the Moving Picture Experts Group, which provides a rich set of standardized tools to describe multimedia content. In this paper, we will examine only the part inherent 3D models descriptions.

In this work, we describe in detail the recently proposed MPEG-7 Perceptual 3D Shape Descriptor, how to decompose a mesh to create an Attributed Relational Graph and the use of the modified nested Earth Mover's Distance to compare two of them. To support our tests, we created a 3D object analysis application called Retrieval-3D and in the process we fixed some bugs of the MPEG-7 eXperimentation Model (XM). Finally we compare its results on the Princeton Shape Benchmark with related work, including the first MPEG-7 3D descriptor, i.e. the Shape Spectrum Descriptor.

C. Thanos, F. Borri, and L. Candela (Eds.): Digital Libraries: R&D, LNCS 4877, pp. 308–317, 2007.
© Springer-Verlag Berlin Heidelberg 2007

Fig. 1. Gear wheel and it's perceptual descriptor

2 Perceptual 3D Shape Descriptor

The Perceptual 3D Shape descriptor P3DS [2] has been recently proposed and adopted as an MPEG-7 standard. P3DS is based on the part-based representation of a given object. The part-based representation is expressed by means of an attributed relational graph (ARG) which can be easily converted into the P3DS descriptor. More specifically, the P3DS descriptor is designed to represent and identify 3-D objects based on the part-based simplified representation using ellipsoidal blobs. Unfortunately the authors recommended using manifold mesh objects with no holes for faster processing and better result. As expected, if the encoder does not produce the part-based representation properly, the retrieval performance would not be good.

Unlike the conventional descriptors, the P3DS descriptor supports the functionalities like Query by Sketch and Query by Editing which are very useful in real retrieval system. We now introduced P3DS with a gear wheel 3D model sample: we show it's image, the relative ellipsoidal blobs and the formal syntax of description according to MPEG-7 standard.

2.1 Part Subdivision

In order to extract P3DS a decomposition of a given shape is performed, and this matches with that based on human insight. To resolve this problem Kim, Yun and Lee proposed a new shape decomposition method [3]. It is based on a scheme that stands on two psychological rationales: human being recognizes skills and definition of nearly convex shapes. That scheme recursively performs constrained morphological decomposition (CMD) based on the opening operation with ball-shaped structuring elements (SE's) and weighted convexity. Note that the parts to be decomposed are rendered convex or nearly convex by using the ball-shaped SE, since it is convex itself and rotation-invariant. Then, a merging criterion employing the weighted convexity difference, which determines whether adjacent parts are merged or not, is adopted for the sake of providing a compact representation. The proposed scheme consists of three stages, the initial decomposition stage (IDS), the recursive decomposition stage (RDS), and the iterative merging stage (IMS). The aim of all this operation is to provide a representation of the 3D model, that can be easily inserted in an Attributed Relational Graph composed of a few nodes and edges.

2.2 Descriptor Extraction

There two equivalent ways to represent a model with the P3DS: with the standard syntax of MPEG-7, like the previous code, or with an Attributed Relational Graph (ARG). An ARG is composed of a few nodes and edges. A node represents a meaningful part of the object with unary attributes, while an edge implies binary relations between nodes. In the descriptor, there are 4 *unary* attributes and 3 *binary* relations which are derived from the geometric relation between the principal axes of the connected nodes. In detail, a *node* is represented by an ellipsoid parameterized by *volume v* , *convexity c*, and two *eccentricity* values e_1 and e_2. More specifically, the convexity is defined as the ratio of the volume in a node to that in its convex hull, and the eccentricity is composed of two coefficients:

$$c = \frac{v_n}{v_{ch}} \quad e_1 = \sqrt{1 - c^2 / a^2} \quad e_2 = \sqrt{1 - c^2 / b^2} \tag{1}$$

Where a, b, and c (a $\geq$ b $\geq$ c) are the maximum ranges along 1st, 2nd, and 3rd principal axes, respectively. *Edge* features are extracted from the geometric relation between two ellipsoids. They are: *Binary relations* between two nodes, the *distance between centers* of connected ellipsoids and two *angles*. The first angle is between first principal axes of connected ellipsoids and the second one is between second principal axes of them.

Instead the P3DS descriptor contains three *node* attributes, such as *Volume*, *Variance*, and *Convexity*. Next, it contains two *edge* attributes, such as *Center* and *Transform*. Note that Volume, Center, Variance and Convexity are normalized in the interval [0,1], while Transform is normalized in the interval [-1,1]. Then all are quantizated to 2 rise to the BitsPerAttribute power.

2.3 Modified Nested Earth Mover's Distance

It's not an easy work define a valid distance between two group of ellipsoids that often don't have the same number of elements. Kim, Yun and Lee at this aim present the modified nested Earth Mover's Distance (mnEMD) [3]. However, the ARG matching can be considered as a 2-step procedure: forming a distance matrix with combinatorial differences between each pair of nodes, then the correspondence between nodes in the two ARG's is established based on that matrix by using an appropriate algorithm. So they propose a modified version of nested Earth Mover's Distance algorithm for the ARG matching. This implementation can deal with partially-connected ARG's in an efficient manner and reduce the computational complexity by adopting the notion of imaginary point. The EMD can be introduced intuitively with this example: given two distributions, one can be seen as piles of earth in feature space, the other as a collection of holes in that same space. EMD measures the least amount of work needed to fill the holes with earth. Here, a unit of work corresponds to transporting a unit of earth by a unit of ground distance. Actually, the mnEMD algorithm has two kinds of EMD's: inner and outer, which correspond to the first step and the second step in the 2-step procedure, respectively. Then, in order to

```xml
<?xml version='1.0' encoding='ISO-8859-1' ?>
<Mpeg7 xmlns = "http://www.mpeg7.org/2001/MPEG-7_Schema" xmlns:xsi =
"http://www.w3.org/2000/10/XMLSchema-instance">
  <DescriptionUnit xsi:type = "DescriptorCollectionType">
    <Descriptor xsi:type = "Perceptual3DShape">
    <numberOfNodes>1</numberOfNodes>
    <BitsPerAttribute>6</BitsPerAttribute>
    <IsAdjacent>
      1 1 1 1 1 1 1 1 1 1 1 1 1 1 1 1 1 1    0 0 0 0 0 0 0 0 0 0 0 0 0 0 0 0 0
      0 0 0 0 0 0 0 0 0 0 0 0 0 0 0 0    0 0 0 0 0 0 0 0 0 0 0 0 0 0 0 0
      0 0 0 0 0 0 0 0 0 0 0 0 0 0    0 0 0 0 0 0 0 0 0 0 0 0 0
      0 0 0 0 0 0 0 0 0 0 0 0    0 0 0 0 0 0 0 0 0 0 0 0
      0 0 0 0 0 0 0 0 0    0 0 0 0 0 0 0 0 0 0
      0 0 0 0 0 0 0    0 0 0 0 0 0 0
      0 0 0 0 0    0 0 0 0 0
      0 0 0 0    0 0 0
      0 0    0
    </IsAdjacent>
    <Volume>46 0 1 0 0 0 1 0 1 0 0 0 1 1 1 0 0 1 0 </Volume>
    <Center_X>31 2 3 5 6 12 13 20 22 30 32 40 42 48 50 55 57 59 59 </Center_X>
    <Center_Y>31 27 37 17 46 9 54 4 58 2 59 3 58 8 52 15 44 25 35 </Center_Y>
    <Center_Z>31 31 31 31 31 31 31 31 31 31 31 31 31 31 31 31 31 31 31 </Center_Z>
    <Transform_1>32 58 63 28 55 54 15 42 11 32 32 27 47 17 54 9 58 62 59 </Transform_1>
    <Transform_2>63 50 26 31 9 54 59 57 56 32 63 63 60 60 54 54 49 22 48 </Transform_2>
    <Transform_3>32 33 32 63 32 32 31 48 31 63 32 32 30 30 32 32 35 32 32 </Transform_3>
    <Transform_4>63 30 31 62 31 32 32 25 32 32 32 31 33 32 31 29 32 32 </Transform_4>
    <Transform_5>31 31 32 41 31 31 32 16 32 63 32 32 33 33 31 31 28 32 32 </Transform_5>
    <Transform_6>32 63 63 35 63 63 63 59 63 32 63 63 63 63 63 63 63 63 63 </Transform_6>
    <Variance_X>25 4 4 3 4 3 4 5 5 3 3 4 4 4 4 4 4 4 4 </Variance_X>
    <Variance_Y>25 3 3 4 3 3 4 3 2 3 3 3 3 3 3 3 3 3 3 </Variance_Y>
    <Variance_Z>3 3 3 3 3 3 3 3 4 2 2 3 3 3 3 3 3 3 3 </Variance_Z>
    <Convexity>62 61 55 53 55 59 54 59 55 63 63 54 53 57 61 53 56 57 63 </Convexity>
    </Descriptor>
  </DescriptionUnit>
</Mpeg7>
```

compute both inner and outer EMD's, the weight is identically provided for all nodes as reciprocal of the max number of cluster in the two ARG.

2.4 Other Descriptors

In previous work, we studied two different implementations of the MPEG-7 3D Shape Spectrum Descriptor (SSD), based on the Shape Index introduced by J.J. Koenderink [4]. One was developed by us [5] and calculates the Principal Curvatures, necessary to know Shape Index, employing the normal at the vertex of the mesh, looking upon the area of the neighboring faces. The other one instead takes the normal at the face, and was suggest by T. Zaharia and F. Prêteux [6] and implemented in MPEG-7 XM.

In literature D. V. Vranić tested a large number of 3D descriptors with the Princeton Shape Benchmark and other databases. He found that no single descriptor is perfect for every task, but obtained a good mix of performance and precision with an Hybrid Descriptor [7], obtained by crossbreeding three complementary descriptors: Depth Buffer, Silhouette and Ray-Based Descriptor.

MPEG-7 description tools are implemented in the part 6 of the standard, reference software, and the latest version of this implementation can be obtained as described in [8]. The reference software, known as the eXperimentation Model (XM), in theory gives the tools to extract the two MPEG-7 3D descriptor from WRL 3D model and to compute the distance between the related features. A few bugs, like memory deallocation and fixed size structures have to be fixed, but the library is overall quite

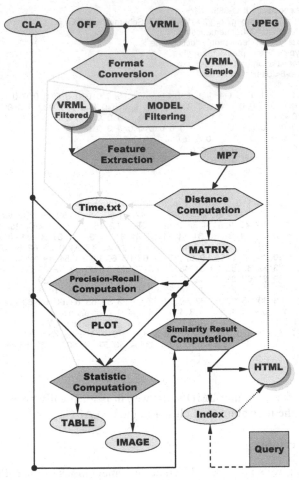

Fig. 2. Retrivial-3D scheme

good. In particular most problems may be solved by filtering the mesh to remove duplicated triangles or flat surfaces.

3   A New 3D Function Library: Retrieval-3D

The developed library allows for mesh filtering removing coincident faces or faces with coincident vertexes; translation of OFF models and non standard WRL models in a WRL file formatted as required by XM. Our WIN32 application provides an integrated environment to execute console applications with the appropriate parameters, obviously making their use simpler, intuitive and fast. Retrieval-3D can execute, other than XM applications, the Princeton Shape Benchmark statistical tools over a set of distance matrices and a classification file, with obviously reduction of the time needed to set all the parameters.

Fig. 4 shows the functions and how they work on a generic classified database. With the color orange the software suggest by MPEG-7 eXperimentation Model (XM) is shown, while in violet we have the Princeton console application for statistic purposes. With green color we show the functions supported directly by Retrieval3D, finally with yellow we indicate the file that stored the time necessary for the different process.

4 Experimental Results

Two series of tests have been conducted. In the first one the input files were extracted from an example VRML database comprising different objects and statues. For each object, different variations were present, constructed by means of geometric transformations and deformations. The database was provided by the Visual Information Processing Lab of the University of Florence. The second test was performed on the Princeton Shape Benchmark [9], a free resource made by Princeton University. This database was created to benchmark different algorithms with the same large number of objects, all classified, by consistent statistic applications. The database is separated in two parts of 907 models each, collected from the web, to allow training of the software on one half, and then verify the result of the best settings on the second part. The polygonal surface geometry of each 3D model is described in an Object File Format (.off) file.

An important note on the P3DS is that the size of the voxel grid is strongly related with the computational complexity and consequently the time required for each object analysis. The evaluation is done by means of the following descriptors: best matches (a web page for each model displaying images of its best matches in rank order. The associated rank and distance value appears below each image, and images of models in the query model's class (hits) are highlighted with a thickened frame), precision-recall plot (a plot describing the relationship between precision and recall in a ranked list of matches. For each query model in class C and any number K of top matches, "recall" (the horizontal axis) represents the ratio of models in class C returned within the top K matches, while "precision" (the vertical axis) indicates the ratio of the top K matches that are members of class C), distance image and tier image (the first is an image of the distance matrix where the lightness of each pixel (i,j) is proportional to the magnitude of the distance between models i and j. Models are grouped by class along each axis, and lines are added to separate classes, which makes it easy to evaluate patterns in the match results qualitatively, i.e. the optimal result is a set of dark class-sized blocks of pixels along the diagonal indicating that every model matches the models within its class better than ones in other classes. Tier is an image visualizing nearest neighbour, first tier, and second tier matches. This image is often more useful than the distance image because the best matches are clearly shown for every model. The optimal result is a set of black/red, class-sized blocks of pixels along the diagonal indicating that every model matches the models within its class better than ones in other classes).

A table that includes different statistic evaluations is also provided with the following information:

- Nearest neighbour: the percentage of the closest matches that belong to the same class as the query.
- First-tier and Second-tier: the percentage of models in the query's class that appear within the top K
- matches, where K depends on the size of the query's class.
- E-Measure: a composite measure of the precision and recall for a fixed number of retrieved results. The intuition is that a user of a search engine is more interested in the first page of query results than in later pages.
- Discounted Cumulative Gain (DCG): a statistic that weights correct results near the front of the list more than correct results later in the ranked list under the assumption that a user is less likely to consider elements near the end of the list. Tests have been conducted on a Pentium 4 1.5GHz CPU with 512MB of RAM.

PSB train	Extraction of descriptor		Calculate distance matrix
	days	Seconds	Seconds
SSD	0.170	14703.984	7.682
P3DS 512	0.064	5520.201	233.145
P3DS 1784	0.205	17719.633	577.320
P3DS 4096	1.479	127792.468	920.354
P3DS 9261	6.233	538530.109	8262.000

Fig. 3. Computational time

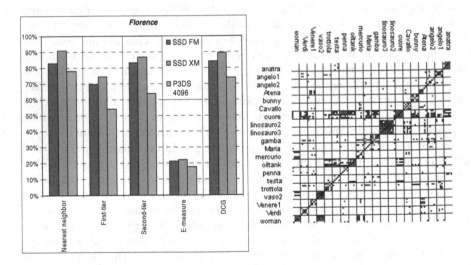

Fig. 4. Table from Florence DB and Tier image for P3DS

All the descriptor have good performance on the Florence small database, which has only 2-manifold models. But the old SSD descriptor is more effective than new P3DS. The XM implementation is better than ours FindMesh.

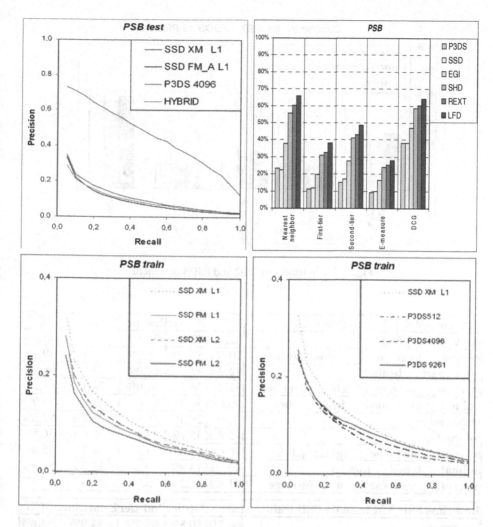

Fig. 5. Performance of Vranic's Hybrid descriptor, SSD, P3DS, and other descriptors. Precision and recall with different distance and different grid dimensions.

From these Precision/Recall Graphs it's possible to infer that performances of P3DS rise with number of point in the grid used to decompose the model. But the best result still inferior to that of SSD. The best performance for the SSD is obtained using the simple L1 distance and XM implementation. But all this descriptors are clearly less performing than Vranic proposal. Many of the descriptors in literature tested by the authors of the Princeton Shape Benchmark are evidently performing better than the choice of MPEG-7. These descriptors are called Extended Gaussian Image EGI, Spherical Harmonic Descriptor SHD, Radialized Spherical Extent Function REXT and Light Field Descriptor LFD. In Fig. 7 it is possible to see that that most of the best result classes are common to both MPEG-7 descriptors, which suggests that the classes in the Princeton benchmark are not equally difficult.

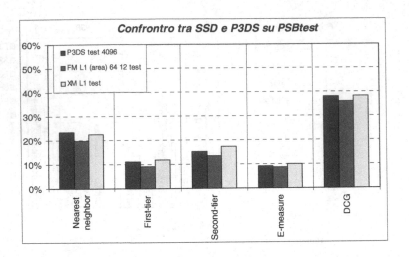

Fig. 6. Performances of SSD and P3DS descriptor

Best class P3DS XM on PSB train	NN	1st-tier	2nd-tier	E-measure	DCG
body_part___face	82,4%	58,8%	76,1%	50,7%	85,3%
animal___quadruped___apatosaurus	50,0%	50,0%	75,0%	17,1%	69,3%
body_part___brain	42,9%	47,6%	69,0%	25,6%	66,8%
aircraft___balloon_vehicle___dirigible	71,4%	26,2%	31,0%	24,1%	63,2%
animal___arthropod___insect___bee	50,0%	50,0%	50,0%	8,6%	59,9%
chess_piece	52,9%	28,3%	39,3%	26,2%	57,3%
microchip	42,9%	35,7%	38,1%	18,0%	56,5%
aircraft___airplane___fighter_jet	28,0%	15,0%	23,2%	14,7%	55,8%
animal___biped___human	40,0%	13,9%	20,4%	13,3%	55,3%
aircraft___airplane___multi_fuselage	71,4%	26,2%	35,7%	18,8%	55,1%

Best class SSD XM train on PSB train	NN	1st-tier	2nd-tier	E-measure	DCG
ice_cream	66,7%	50,8%	68,2%	34,9%	68,8%
body_part___face	88,2%	30,9%	36,8%	24,5%	66,6%
body_part___skeleton	80,0%	45,0%	70,0%	22,2%	65,9%
animal___biped___human	48,0%	27,3%	42,6%	23,8%	65,6%
aircraft___airplane___fighter_jet	58,0%	23,8%	40,6%	22,1%	65,4%
body_part___brain	57,1%	28,6%	31,0%	14,3%	55,7%
animal___biped___human___human_arms_out	23,8%	20,7%	40,5%	26,7%	53,8%
hat___helmet	70,0%	23,3%	28,9%	17,1%	52,7%
furniture___seat___chair___dining_chair	36,4%	22,7%	30,9%	17,7%	49,5%
animal___arthropod___spider	27,3%	22,7%	31,8%	17,7%	48,5%

Fig. 7. Table of best Class retrieval for P3DS and SSD descriptor

5 Conclusions

In this paper, we performed a deep analysis of the MPEG-7 Perceptual 3D Shape Descriptor. As a first conclusion, it is possible to say that XM (ISO/IEC Std. 15938-6) implementation of the P3DS gives results which are even worse then SSD, which uses the implementation provided also in the MPEG-7 eXperimentation Model (XM). Moreover these results do not stand the comparison to other state of the art descriptors.

A second conclusion is that even a bigger grid for the decomposition of the model in part cannot discriminate effectively different P3DS. The use of the new MPEG-7 descriptor seems interesting only for the advantage consisting in the possibility to execute query by sketch due the particular nature of the descriptor. As the authors underline the performance are better for 2-manifold mesh without boundary, but the nature of the 3D model generally found in the web is not like this.

References

1. ISO/IEC Std, 8, MPEG Group, "Information Technology - Multimedia Content Description Interface". ISO/IEC Final Draft International, Sydney, July 2001: ISO/MPEG N4285, Standard 15938-1: IT - MCDI - Part 1 "Systems", ISO/MPEG N4288, S. 15938-2: IT - MCDI - Part 2 "Description Definition Language", ISO/MPEG N4358, S. 15938-3 IT: - MCDI - Part 3 "Visual", ISO/MPEG N4224, S. 15938-4 IT: - MCDI - Part 4 "Audio", ISO/MPEG N4242, S. 15938-5 IT: - MCDI - Part 5 "Multimedia Description Schemes" (1593)
2. Kim, D.H., Yun, I.D., Lee, S.U.: Interactive 3-D shape retrieval system using the attributed relational graph. In: International Workshop on Multimedia Data and Document Engineering, pp. 20–31 (2004)
3. Kim, D.H., Yun, I.D., Lee, S.U.: A new shape decomposition scheme for graph-based representation. Pattern Recognition 38, 673–689 (2005)
4. Koenderink, J.J., van Doorn, A.J.: Surface shape and curvature scales. Image and Vision Computing. 10, 557–565 (1992)
5. Grana, C., Cucchiara, R.: Performance of the MPEG-7 Shape Spectrum Descriptor for 3D objects retrieval. In: 2nd Italian Research Conference on Digital Library Management Systems, Italy (2006)
6. Zaharia, T., Prêteux, F.: 3D Shape-based retrieval within the MPEG-7 framework. In: Sattar, A., Kang, B.-H. (eds.) AI 2006. LNCS (LNAI), vol. 4304, pp. 133–145. Springer, Heidelberg (2006)
7. Vranić, D.V.: 3D Model Retrieval (2004)
8. ISO/IEC Std. 15938-6. MPEG-7 Implementation Studies Group, "Information Technology – Multimedia Content Description Interface - part 6: Reference Software," ISO/IEC FCD 15938-6 / N4006, MPEG-7, Singapore (2001)
9. Shilane, P., Min, P., Kazhdan, M., Funkhouser, T.: The Princeton Shape Benchmark. In: Shape Modeling International, Italy (2004)

Application of the Peer-to-Peer Paradigm in Digital Libraries

Stratis D. Viglas[1], Theodore Dalamagas[2], Vassilis Christophides[3], Timos Sellis[2], and Aggeliki Dimitriou[2]

[1] University of Edinburgh, UK
[2] National Technical University of Athens, Greece
[3] ICS, FORTH, Heraklion, Greece

Abstract. We present the architecture of a largely distributed Digital Library that is based on the Peer-to-Peer computing paradigm. The three goals of the architecture are: (*i*) increased node autonomy, (*ii*) flexible location of data, and (*iii*) efficient query evaluation. To satisfy these goals we propose a solution based on schema mappings and query reformulation. We identify the problems involved in developing a system based on the proposed architecture and present ways of tackling them. A prototype implementation provides encouraging results.

1 Introduction

A Digital Library (DL) can be thought of as an interconnected network of individual library nodes. These nodes can be part of the same physical network (*e.g.*, the library of a single institution), or they can be part of a larger, distributed network (*e.g.*, a common gateway to institutional libraries). In both scenarios the key idea is to provide transparent access to a single virtual network; in other words, we want to *abstract* the network structure so the user of the DL is presented with a single view to the DL's data.

Peer-to-Peer (P2P) systems are distributed systems in which no centralised authority exists and all peers are considered to provide the same functionality. The key premise of a P2P system is to provide a decentralised implementation of a dictionary interface, so that any peer in the system can efficiently locate any other peer responsible for a given data item. The semantics of the data stored in a P2P system are handled by the application, rather than the storage layer.

It seems natural to combine the two into a single framework. In this paper we will present our approach to extending P2P technology and tailoring it to the DL domain: the P2P paradigm will act as the transparent storage layer of a largely distributed DL. Our vision for a P2P DL involves data management in a dynamic network of autonomously managed peers. We aim to address the following objectives:

- **Joining and leaving the library.** Each peer in the system chooses itself when to join and/or leave the library network. The system should gracefully adapt to these joins and departures without any global structural knowledge.
- **Data management.** A peer is responsible for managing its own local data, as well as maintaining information about data residing at other peers.
- **Query processing.** Given a query posed at any peer of the system, the system must first identify the peers capable of answering the query and then optimise and evaluate the query across those peers.

C. Thanos, F. Borri, and L. Candela (Eds.): Digital Libraries: R&D, LNCS 4877, pp. 318–327, 2007.

We propose an architecture based on *schema mappings* and *query reformulation*. The high-level description of such a system is presented in Figure 1. Each peer has a data model its own data conform to. However, it exports a description of its schema, mapped to a *common data model* across all peers of the system; for our purposes, this common data model is XML or RDF (see *e.g.*, [1,5]). We refer to the exported schema as the *local schema* and it is effectively the data that each peer is capable of "serving" to other peers in the system[1].

Once peers have exported their schemas, the next step is combining this information to allow seamless querying across the entire system. This will be achieved through *schema mappings*: ways of maintaining schema correspondences between the various peers of the system. These mappings allow a peer to translate a locally posed query to the schema exported by remote peers, so these peers can contribute to the answer. The key issue here is identifying these mappings in the first place and keeping them up to date as the system evolves. Mappings are not only used to translate queries, but also to identify the peers that can be used to answer a specific query. Therefore, the mappings act as a decentralised index that is used to *route* data retrieval requests to the peers capable of serving them. This identification and translation process is termed *query reformulation* (see *e.g.*, [2,4]).

After a query has been reformulated it needs to be evaluated across the participating peers. The query needs to be optimised so all individual queries posed to the peers are efficiently scheduled and their results appropriately combined. This calls for novel techniques for *distributed query optimization and evaluation* in the context of a decentralised P2P system (see *e.g.*, [3,6,7]). For instance, an important aspect is making sure the number of visits to each participating peers is minimised; at the same time, individual queries need to be scheduled in a way that minimises intermediate result sizes. Another interesting problem stems from the sheer scale of a largely distributed system, leading in a blow-up of the number of evauation plans considered. The additional parameter of discovering the relevant data through mappings and incrementally having to reformulate the results leads to an even greater search space explosion. Furthermore, there may be competitive metrics: for example, one user may be more interested in the quantity of returned results (*i.e.*, taking as many mappings into account as possible) while another may be interested in response time (*i.e.*, receiving an answer fast, without the answer necessarily being of the highest quality, for some metric of quality). These observations give way to modeling query processing as a multi-objective optimisation problem. Clearly, this calls for novel query optimisation and processing techniques.

In light of the proposed architecture of a P2P DL we have identified three main axes to our research:

Logical foundations of query reformulation. We will develop a theory modelling query reformulation in largely distributed systems. We will focus on the logical foundations behind query mappings and how these foundations can be used to declaratively reason about queries posed across multiple sites.

Routing indexes. We will develop primitives for storing and maintaining mappings across the peers of a distributed system, to facilitate efficient access to the information stored at each peer. These indexes will aid in (*i*) identifying

---

[1] An interesting aspect here is having the peers export different schemas to different peers; this presents a way for the peers of the system to implement their own security models.

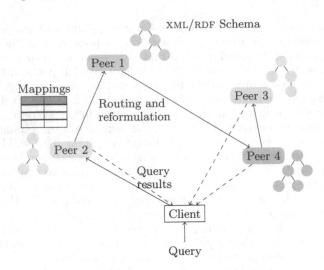

Fig. 1. The architecture of a P2P DL

the peers relevant to a particular query and (*ii*) routing a complicated data retrieval request across the peers of the entire system. Moreover, we will address the problem of maintaining these indexes as the system evolves.

Distributed query optimization and evaluation. We will identify new distributed query processing paradigms that are directly applicable to the P2P setting. We will identify the appropriate metrics that characterise performance in such an environment, and provide ways of employing these metrics in optimising distributed queries. Moreover, we will introduce query evaluation algorithms and techniques for efficiently executing queries across the peers of the system.

2   Logical Foundations of Query Reformulation

The two building blocks of our architecture are: (*i*) local peer schemas exported to a common data model, and (*ii*) mappings across the schemas of the peers. In this section, we will present the first steps towards building a theory over said representations. The goals are (*i*) to develop a declarative way to reason about the queries posed to the system, and (*ii*) to map this declarative framework to a procedural and optimizable one, that will allow us to identify the primitives to be used during query evaluation.

Local and Mapping Schemas. We focus on representing both local schemas and mappings in a common framework that will allow us to reason about queries. Our approach is reminiscent of *nested relational calculus*. As noted in Section 1 all peers in the system export their local schemas to XML or RDF. We will not tie our representation to any of those data models, but instead follow a "least common denominator" approach and treat them both as generalizations of the same model.

The local schema $S_l(n)$ of a peer n is a set of tuples of the form: $(e, \{\!\{a\}\!\}, \{\!\{e'\}\!\})$ where:

- $s \in S_l(n)$ denotes a tuple variable *i.e.*, an iterator over each particular tuple in $S_l(n)$; a particular s is termed a tuple instance.

- e is an entity name and is unique across all tuple instances $s \in S_l$.
- $\{\!\{a\}\!\}$ is a set of attributes associated with e. For a tuple instance $s \in S$, and an attribute a_i, s/a_i is a *path expression* denoting the binding for a_i in s;
- $\{\!\{e'\}\!\}$ is a set of entities that are *reachable* by e.
- $s/e_1/e_2/\ldots/e_{n-1}/e_n/a_j$ denotes a path expression of length n with the semantics that each entity e_i is reachable by entity e_{i-1}. The path expression leads to a_j *i.e.*, the binding for a_j in e_n.

Given this representation, we can pose queries in logic to identify whether a peer contains information about some particular entity. The next step is allowing a way to model correspondences from local entities to remote ones. This is achieved through a *mapping schema*. The mapping schema $S_m(n)$ of a peer n is a set of tuples of the form: $(e_l, a_l, \{\!\{\sigma(n_r, e_r, a_r)\}\!\})$ where:

- $s \in S_m(n)$ is again a tuple variable over all tuples in $S_m(n)$.
- e_l and a_l denote the a_l attribute of local entity e_l.
- $\{\!\{\sigma(n_r, e_r, a_r)\}\!\}$ is a *view definition* of remote data where n_r is a remote peer identifier and e_r and a_r are a remote entity and a remote attribute name, respectively. The semantics is that a local attribute a_l of a local entity e_l is known to a remote peer n_r as a view over its own data (*i.e.*, combinations of remote elements and attributes, e_r and a_r, respectively). By including n_r in the definition, we can define views *across* multiple peers, further increasing the expressive power of our mapping formalism.

The fact that there is a mapping at a peer n's mapping schema $S_m(n)$ from local entity e_l to a remote entity e_r at peer n_r does not necessarily imply that there is a corresponding mapping in $S_m(n_r)$ from e_r to e_l at n. This allows for a *loose coupling* across the peers of the system.

With those two schemas we can identify peers in the system that carry information for particular entities. We can also identify corresponding terms at remote peers and perform the necessary renamings to the entities used in a query that will allow us to evaluate it at remote peers. These form the building blocks of query reformulation.

3 Routing Indexes

To evaluate any query, we first need to identify the relevant data, which will then be further processed to compute the final query result. In all but the trivial of cases (*i.e.*, when a query only needs to access data residing in a single peer) we will have to access all peers capable of satisfying the data retrieval request in the most efficient way. In other words, we need to *route* the request across the participating peers. To address the issue, we propose to employ routing indexes: decentralised data structures that can be thought of as the access methods to the underlying data of a largely distributed system. These routing indexes need to be kept up to date with respect to peers joining and leaving the network, *i.e.*, the index should be evolving through time along with the system.

3.1 Mapping Indexes

In this section we identify ways of efficiently implementing our mapping formalisms in a distributed system. Moreover, this implementation must be helpful

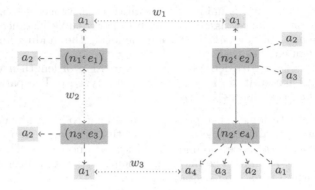

Fig. 2. An example of a mapping index

in mapping discovery, as well as in routing data retrieval requests across the peers of the system. We will first propose a complete structure for the index of the entire system, and then see how this structure can be decentralised across all participating peers.

The system's mapping index is a node-labelled, (possibly) edge-weighted graph, as shown in Figure 2. The weights represent the cost of making a routing step and are set to zero for local steps, or to some non-zero quantity for remote steps. Each node in the graph is either:

- An entity node, labelled with (n_i, e_i), where n_i is a node identifier and e_i is an entity at node n_i.
- An attribute node, labeled with a_i where a_i is an attribute name.

Correspondingly, there are three types of edge in the mapping index:

- A *containment edge*, from an entity node (n_i, e_i) to an attribute node a_i (denoted by a dashed line in Figure 2) means that a_i is contained in entity e_i at peer n_i. Containment edges bear no weight.
- A *reachability edge*, from an entity node (n, e_i) to an entity node (n, e_j) (denoted by a solid line in Figure 2) means that entity e_j is reachable from entity e_i in peer n's local schema. Reachability edges, again, bear no weight.
- A *mapping edge* (denoted by a dotted line in Figure 2) can either be (*i*) from an attribute node a_i to an attribute node a_j representing the mapping between the two attributes, or (*ii*) from an entity node (n_i, e_i) to an entity node (n_j, e_j) meaning that the entire entity e_i at peer n_i is mapped to the entire entity e_j at peer n_j; this is only possible if all attributes across the two entities share a name (thus making the per-attribute mappings obvious). Mapping edges are weighted with the cost of making the transition.

The index is used for routing data requests and reformulating queries. By following paths consisting of reachability and/or containment edges, a peer is capable of retrieving requests over the data it manages itself; by following a mapping edge, a peer knows exactly how to reformulate a query and what cost this reformulation and/or routing step entails. Choosing the cheapest path between multiple such routes forms the basis of efficient routing.

As noted, Figure 2 presents an example of a global mapping index. Naturally, it is impossible to assume that this index is centrally stored, or each peer maintains a copy. We propose that each peer of the system maintain the parts of the index rooted at entity nodes for which it is responsible. Moreover, we allow each peer to autonomously manage that part of the index as the system evolves through time.

Given this modelling, we can define useful properties and operations to support query reformulation; one such example is mapping composition. Since the DL nodes may join and leave the P2P DL network at any time, it is ineffective to keep large numbers of mappings between pairs of nodes in the network. Inferring new mappings from already known ones is thus a critical issue. We will include mapping generation within the query execution task, providing methods to keep the appropriate set of mappings so that we can produce the necessary ones for answering a query.

By following paths in the mapping index, a peer knows exactly how to reformulate a query in order to be evaluated at other peers. However, there might be several paths to follow for such a reformulation. We plan to consider issues of information loss due to mappings.

3.2 System Evolution

An interesting aspect of index maintenance stems from system evolution. As noted, each peer in the system is autonomous in the sense that it joins and/or leaves the network at will. This means that new schemas are introduced to the system while existing schemas cease being available. Moreover, whenever a local schema is introduced, or removed, so do the mappings to/from that schema. The problem now becomes one of *consistency*: should all peers have the same, consistent view of the system, or do we allow for inconsistencies?

A way to have all peers share the same consistent view is to follow a flooding protocol *a la* Gnutella. This results in increased network traffic, which in turn compromises performance. What we would like is an *adaptive* approach, allowing each peer to make decisions on what mappings to store and how often to update them. We propose that the peers of the system implement an update protocol. Each peer *periodically*: (i) contacts other peers from its mapping tables and retrieves parts of their mappings, and (ii) to those peers, it propagates its own mappings. The parameters of the update protocol are:

- *Update frequency* ϕ. This specifies how often a peer of the system runs its update protocol. It can be set, for instance, according to the query workload of the peer, or according to a guarantee of service the peer must adhere to.
- *Retrieval percentage* α. Whenever a peer contacts another peer as part of the update protocol, this is the percentage of the remote mappings retrieved.
- *Propagation percentage* β. Whenever a peer contacts another peer, this is the percentage of local mappings propagated to the remote peer.

Note that α and β can be "throttled" by each individual peer and do not have to be equal. Moreover, these are not system-wide parameters, but, rather, peer-specific. Criteria for changing the values of these parameters include, but are not limited to, the following: the peer's workload (if a peer is overloaded with query processing requests, it can reduce ϕ); coverage guarantees (if a peer must have a high coverage of all mappings present in the system, it may choose to increase α); relative data item importance (if a peer receives many requests for its own data, it may choose to increase β so as to make its data items more "visible" to other peers of the system).

4 Peer-to-Peer Query Processing

Query processing involves two phases: query planning and query evaluation. In our proposal, query planning and evaluation are executed in an interleaved way in order to obtain the first parts of the query answer as fast as possible.

4.1 Query Planning and Evaluation

Query planning generates plans according to the routing information returned by the mapping index. Moreover, it is responsible for estimating the cost of those plans, considering:

- **Data transfer.** An online system must have a high throughput and a low response time. We plan to use the rate at which data is transferred to the requesting peer as a metric. An alternative metric, closer to a traditional view of distributed processing, is the volume of data being moved across the network in order to compute the result; but even in that case, provisions must exist so that data is moved as fast as possible.
- **Number of visits to each peer.** Observe that our mapping framework allows for a single peer to be visited multiple times for a query to be answered. In such cases, the query planner must make sure that the number of visits to each peer is minimised.
- **Precision.** The query planner and executor should ensure that only relevant answers are retrieved. This is directly tied to the evolution and maintenance concepts of the system, as these are what will effectively allow the mapping index to be up-to-date with mapping information.
- **Quality of retrieved answers.** Quality in this context is different than what we previously described as precision. It has to do not so much with the quantity of the answers and whether these are relevant to the query at hand, but with how close to the best possible answer in terms of semantics the retrieved result set is.
- **Coverage.** In a largely decentralised system coverage comes in two flavours: the number of peers actually "touched" to generate the result set , but also the number of possible relevant mappings exploited during reformulation. The two do not necessarily converge to the same value and, hence, depending on the specific coverage type employed, different result sets will be generated.

Those factors are the basis for the so-called *data quality driven processing.*

Query processing starts by considering the query as a whole, but then utilises a fragmentation technique which is applied in an interleaved way with the routing mechanism. This *interleaved query routing and planning* mechanics involves a query fragmentation phase where the query fragmented by taking as input the number of joins are required between the produced fragments in order to evaluate the original query. The output is all possible query fragmentations for that number of joins. At each iteration of interleaved routing and planning, the number of joins is increased by one. The initial round starts from zero joins, meaning that no fragmentation is applied (the query is considered as a whole). In the last round, the query is decomposed to its primitive components (*i.e.*, entities).

The advantage of such a technique lies in that the generated plans after each round can be executed by the involved peers the moment they become available. Thus, we can obtain the first parts of the query result as soon as possible, therefore increasing the response time and throughput of the system. Interleaved execution leads to the creation and execution of multiple query plans that, when unioned, will return the complete answer.

4.2 Data Quality Driven Processing

As the number of peers in a DL network increases and query plans become complex, the number of alternative execution plans becomes huge. As a result, we need to prune the search space by considering quality metrics of the data hosted by each peer. Our approach is based on *ranking* the peers contributing to a plan, and, in consequence, the plans themselves. Ranking is performed according to data quality metrics allowing the optimiser to discard plans producing results of poor quality We consider data quality metrics such as *coverage*, *density* and *completeness* of the view instances published by the peers *w.r.t.* the PDMS schema and its virtual instantiation. More precisely, we address the following issues:

1. Provide closed formulae for estimating the data quality of peer databases and query plans according to the local schema. The *coverage* of a peer database *w.r.t.* a schema fragment is a global quality metric defined as the ratio of the maximum number of fragment instances one expects to obtain through its exported schema to the total number of instances published by all peers having the same exported schema. On the other hand, *density* is a local quality metric, defined as the ratio of the actual number of fragment instances exported by a peer to the maximum number of fragment instances considered previously. Finally, *completeness* of a peer database is a global quality metric defined as the product of the coverage and density of a peer. Specifically, completeness of a peer captures the ratio of the actual cardinality of the fragment instances in a peer to the total cardinality of the schema fragment in all the peers that export it.
2. Enrich existing query planning algorithms with the above data quality metrics. Specifically, we discard plans that are ranked below a specific data-quality threshold. This reduces planning time, while ensures that the chosen plan will be of the highest data quality. A challenge in this context is multi-objective query optimisation, which extends the framework to consider not only the data quality characteristics, but also others such as availability of a data source, timeliness, *etc.*
3. Experimentally illustrate the gains of our approach for pruning the search space and thus improving the overall query processing time *w.r.t.* to a DL network of increasing size and queries of increasing complexity.

5 Current Status

We are currently working on a prototype P2P DL implementing the above framework. We are building our system on top of the JXTA P2P framework[2]. JXTA technology is a set of open protocols that allow any connected device on the network, ranging from cell phones and wireless PDAs to PCs and servers, to communicate and collaborate in a P2P manner. We have exploited JXTA facilities to set up decentralised sharing of data among numerous autonomous DL nodes, employing heterogeneous metadata schemas for describing their data and computational resources.

---

[2] http://www.jxta.org

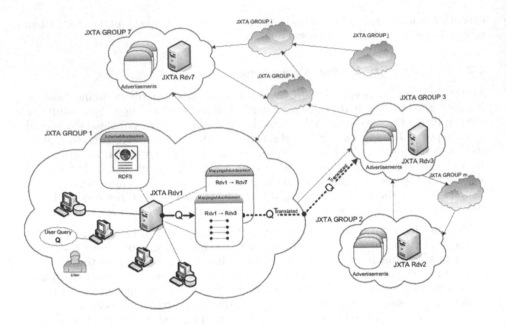

Fig. 3. A P2P DL prototype

Every DL node in our system stores data organized in the RDFS model. However, there are no restrictions on content representation nor any global schema information, *i.e.*, a DL node may use its own RDFS representation.

The network is organised in JXTA *groups*. Each group consists of nodes that store resources, or pose queries conforming to the particular group schema. At least one DL node in each group provides the necessary scope to message propagation. Such a node is a JXTA *rendezvous peer*. Every such DL node maintains two types of JXTA *advertisements*: (*i*) **Single schema advertisement**: an XML document stored in the DL node, which encodes RDFS classes and properties that the DL node exports to the DL network. Schema advertisements are publicly available to any DL node. (*ii*) **Multiple mapping advertisements**: XML documents stored in the DL node, which encode mappings between the DL node and other nodes. At the current stage, we keep simple $1 - 1$ mappings between RDFS properties. Mapping advertisements are available only through explicit requests initiated in the DL network.

Our system implements the following facilities: (*i*) **Setup**: DL nodes are created as rendezvous JXTA peers. After its creation, every new DL node makes its schema advertisement public to any other DL node. (*ii*) **Joining the network**: to join the network, a DL node obtains the list of available DL nodes. Then, the DL node's admininstrator manually selects some of those DL nodes (that will form its *neighborhood*) and determine the mappings between those nodes and the new DL node. Mappings are stored in the mapping advertisements of the new DL node. Mapping definition is assisted through a graphical tool (not shown due to space limitations). (*iii*) **Querying**: queries can be issued at any DL node and propagated to other DL nodes in its neighbourhood (and so on). Query reformulation is assisted by a graphical query wizard (again, not shown due to space limitations). At each DL node, we provide a SESAME RDF query engine[3]. A query formulated using the wizard is transformed to a SESAME RDF query to be executed on the RDF data. A query is reformulated by renaming its RDFS properties according to the mappings defined in the mapping advertisement, so as to match schema information at remote DL nodes. (*iv*) **Leaving the network**: when a DL node is about to leave the network, it sends its mapping advertisement to all other DL nodes that include it in their neighborhood.

The architecture of our prototype P2P DL system is presented in Figure 3. We have implemented the setup task, the joining task and a query processing method that exploits 1 − 1 mappings to reformulate and propagate queries in the DL network. Next, we plan to work on the design and implementation of mapping indexes as well as on supporting system evolution facilities.

6 Conclusions

We have presented an architecture for a Digital Library that is based on Peer-to-Peer principles. In particular, we have focussed on providing primitives for a system employing increased node autonomy in terms of both data management and intermittent network behaviour. The system is based on acquiring and maintaining mappings between the exported schemas of the participating DL nodes. On top of that, a flexible query engine based on query reformulations is implemented. A prototype system employing the aforementioned principles is already in development and the results are encouraging.

Acknowledgements. We would like to thank Yiorgos Giannopoulos for providing assistance with several implementation issues.

References

1. Kaoudi, Z., Dalamagas, T., Sellis, T.K.: RDFSculpt: Managing RDF Schemas Under Set-Like Semantics. In: Gómez-Pérez, A., Euzenat, J. (eds.) ESWC 2005. LNCS, vol. 3532, pp. 123–137. Springer, Heidelberg (2005)
2. Kokkinidis, G., Christophides, V.: Semantic Query Routing and Processing in P2P Database Systems: The ICS-FORTH SQPeer Middleware. In: Lindner, W., Mesiti, M., Türker, C., Tzitzikas, Y., Vakali, A.I. (eds.) EDBT 2004. LNCS, vol. 3268, pp. 486–495. Springer, Heidelberg (2004)
3. Kokkinidis, G., Christophides, V., Dalamagas, T., Viglas, S.D.: Query Processing in P2P Database Management Systems: A State-of-the-Art. Technical report, IST-FP6, DELOS Network of Excellence, NoE G038-507618 (April 2005)
4. Sidirourgos, L., Kokkinidis, G., Dalamagas, T.: Efficient Query Routing in RDF/S schema-based P2P Systems. In: HDMS 2005. 4th Hellenic Data Management Symposium (August 2005)
5. Spyropoulou, E., Dalamagas, T.: SDQNET: a Platform for Semantic Query Processing in Loosely Coupled Data Sources. In: Manolopoulos, Y., Pokorný, J., Sellis, T. (eds.) ADBIS 2006. LNCS, vol. 4152, Springer, Heidelberg (2006)
6. Viglas, S.D.: Pyragrid: Bringing Peer-to-Peer and Grid Architectures Together. In: DELOS Workshop: Digital Library Architectures, pp. 1–12 (2004)
7. Viglas, S.D.: Distributed File Structures in a Peer-to-Peer Environment. In: Proceedings of the International Conference on Data Engineering (2007)

---

[3] http://www.openrdf.org/

Efficient Search and Approximate Information Filtering in a Distributed Peer-to-Peer Environment of Digital Libraries

Christian Zimmer, Christos Tryfonopoulos, and Gerhard Weikum

Department for Databases and Information Systems
Max-Planck-Institute for Informatics, 66123 Saarbrücken, Germany
{czimmer,trifon,weikum}@mpi-inf.mpg.de

Abstract. We present a new architecture for efficient search and approximate information filtering in a distributed Peer-to-Peer (P2P) environment of Digital Libraries. The *MinervaLight* search system uses P2P techniques over a structured overlay network to distribute and maintain a directory of peer statistics. Based on the same directory, the *MAPS* information filtering system provides an approximate publish/subscribe functionality by monitoring the most promising digital libraries for publishing appropriate documents regarding a continuous query. In this paper, we discuss our system architecture that combines searching and information filtering abilities. We show the system components of MinervaLight and explain the different facets of an approximate pub/sub system for subscriptions that is high scalable, efficient, and notifies the subscribers about the most interesting publications in the P2P network of digital libraries. We also compare both approaches in terms of common properties and differences to show an overview of search and pub/sub using the same infrastructure.

1 Introduction

Peer-to-Peer (P2P) has been a hot topic in various research communities over the last few years. Today, the P2P approach allows handling huge amounts of data of digital libraries in a distributed and self-organizing way. These characteristics offer enormous potential benefit for search capabilities powerful in terms of scalability, efficiency, and resilience to failures and dynamics. Additionally, such a search engine can potentially benefit from the intellectual input (e.g., bookmarks, query logs, click streams, etc. [13, 14]) of a large user community. However, recent research on structured P2P architectures [8, 9] is typically limited to exact-match queries on keys. This is insufficient for text queries that consist of a variable number of keywords, and it is absolutely inappropriate for full-fledged Web search where keyword queries should return a ranked result list of the most relevant approximate matches. In the area of distributed data management, many prototypes have been developed [15, 16, 17] including our P2P Web search engine prototype Minerva [2, 18].

In such a dynamic P2P setting, information filtering (IF) [1, 3, 5, 10], also referred to as publish/subscribe or continuous querying or information push, is equally important to one-time querying, since users are able to subscribe to information sources and be

C. Thanos, F. Borri, and L. Candela (Eds.): Digital Libraries: R&D, LNCS 4877, pp. 328–337, 2007.
© Springer-Verlag Berlin Heidelberg 2007

notified when documents of interest are published by any digital library. This need for push technologies is also stressed by the deployment of new tools such as Google Alert or the QSR system. In an information filtering scenario, a user posts a subscription (or profile or continuous query) to the system to receive notifications whenever certain events of interest occur, e.g. a document matching the continuous query is added to a digital library.

In this paper, we present the architecture for efficien search and approximate information filtering in a distributed P2P environment of digital libraries. Our MinervaLight search system uses P2P techniques over a structured overlay network to distribute and maintain a directory of peer statistics. Based on the same directory, the MAPS[1] information filtering system provides approximate pub/sub functionality by monitoring the most promising digital libraries for publishing appropriate documents regarding a continuous query.

The paper is organized as follows: In Section 2, we presen the main search architecture of MinervaLight using one-time queries. The pub/sub functionality of MAPS is explained in Section 3. Section 4 compares MinervaLight and MAPS and stresses the common properties of both systems and shows the main differences, and Section 5 concludes the paper.

2   MinervaLight Search Architecture

In MinervaLight, we view every digital library as autonomous and each digital library refers to a peer in the network. MinervaLight [24] combines different building blocks under one common graphical user interface.

2.1   BINGO!

MinervaLight uses *BINGO!* [19], a focused Web crawler that mimics a human user browsing the Web by only indexing documents that are thematically related to a predefined set of user interests. BINGO! is a multi-language parser, i.e., it can detect the language of documents and restrict the crawl to documents of a language of choice. BINGO! learns the user interest profile by running a feature analysis over the bookmarks that it can import from the user's Web browser. Within the user's interest, the system can further classify the documents it indexes into predefined and automatically trained categories. Alternatively, BINGO! can instantaneously start a high-performing, multi-threaded Web crawl from a set of interactively entered URLs. Crawling is continuously performed in the background, without manual user interaction. BINGO! automatically parses and indexes all applicable content types (currently text, html, and pdf) to build a local search index from these documents. It utilizes stemming and stopword elimination. The search index (in form of inverted index lists) is stored in the embedded Cloudscape/Derby database. Different score values are computed without any user interaction, to support ranked retrieval queries. In order to support more sophisticated document scoring models, BINGO! can compute link-based authority scores (PageRank, HITS) on its local Web graph.

---

[1] Minerva Approximate Publish/Subscribe.

2.2 TopX

TopX [20] is a search engine for ranked retrieval of XML and plain-text data, that supports a probabilistic-IR scoring model for full-text content conditions (including phrases, boolean expressions, negations, and proximity constraints) and tag-term combinations, path conditions for all XPath axes as exact or relaxable constraints, and ontology-based relaxation of terms and tag names as similarity conditions for ranked retrieval. For speeding up top-k queries, various techniques are employed: probabilistic models as efficient score predictors for a variant of the threshold algorithm, judicious scheduling of sequential accesses for scanning index lists and random accesses to compute full scores, incremental merging of index lists for on-demand, self-tuning query expansion, and a suite of specifically designed, precomputed indexes to evaluate structural path conditions.

2.3 Distributed Directory

MinervaLight continuously monitors the local search index and computes compact statistics (called posts) that describe the quality of the index concerning particular terms. These statistics contain information about the local search index, such as the size of the index, the number of distinct terms in the index, the number of documents containing a particular term, and optionally elaborate estimators for score distributions, based on histograms or Poisson mixes. MinervaLight publishes that information into a fully distributed directory, effectively building a term to peer directory, mapping terms to the set of corresponding statistics published by digital libraries from across the network. This directory is significantly smaller than naively distributing a full-fledge term to document index, which eventually makes P2P search feasible [21].

In order to further limit the size of the directory, each peer can determine whether it is a valuable source of information for a particular term, and only publish statistics for terms if it is considered a valuable resource for that term. The publishing process can also be extended beyond individual terms to also account for popular key sets or phrases [6]. The directory implementation is based on Past [22], a freely available implementation of a distributed hash table (DHT). It uses FreePastry's route primitive to support the two hash table functionalities $insert(key, value)$ and $retrieve(key)$. A previous version of the Minerva prototypes used Chord [9], another structured overlay network to build-up the distributed directory. The choice of the underlying DHT is not a serious decision since MinervaLight (as MAPS) is network agnostic.

MinervaLight passes *(term, post)* pairs to the DHT, which transparently stores it at the peer in the network that is currently responsible for the key term. For this purpose, we have extended the DHT with bulk insertion functionality, in order to send batches of statistical synopses instead of sending them individually, greatly reducing the incurred network overhead. Each directory peer maintains a list of all incoming synopses for a randomized subset of keys; this metadata is additionally replicated to ensure availability in the presence of network dynamics.

2.4 P2P Search and Ranking

MinervaLight offers a simple search interface that allows a user to enter query terms, which starts the global query execution using the DHT as follows: for each term appearing in the query, MinervaLight executes retrieve(term) to retrieve all applicable post lists from the directory, which serve as the input to query routing, i.e., selecting a small subset of promising digital libraries that are most likely to provide high-quality results for a particular query. MinervaLight uses the DHT route primitive to send the user query to these selected digital libraries, which evaluate the query using their local TopX engines on top of their local indexes and return their top-matching results to the query initiator. MinervaLight appropriately combines the URLs from these autonomous sources (result merging) and returns the final results to the user.

Lately, the JXP algorithm [23] to efficiently compute PageRank scores in a distributed environment of autonomous peers with overlapping local indexes is integrated into MinervaLight. As PageRank has repeatedly been shown to improve the user perceived result quality, the incorporation of JXP into MinervaLight is expected to increase the result quality beyond what has so far been achieved with other existing approaches solely based on statistics or based on PageRank scores derived from the local partitions of the Web graph at each peer individually. Preliminary experimental results in the paper referenced above support this hypothesis.

3 MAPS Information Filtering Architecture

In this section, we present the main system architecture of MAPS based on the P2P search engine Minerva. Each peer or digital library that participates in MAPS implements three types of services: a publication, a subscription, and a directory service.

A peer implementing the publication service of MAPS has a (thematically focused) web crawler and acts as an information producer. The publication service is used to expose content crawled by the peer's crawler and also content published by the peer's user to the rest of the network. Using the subscription Service users post continuous queries to the network and this service is also responsible for selecting the appropriate peers that will index the user query. Finally, the directory service is used to enable the peer to participate in the P2P network, and is also responsible for acquiring the IR statistics needed by the subscription service to perform the ranking.

3.1 Publishing of Resources

Publications in a peer or digital library p occur when new documents are made available to the rest of the network. Each publication is matched against its local query index using appropriate local filtering algorithms, and triggers notifications to subscriber peers. Notice that only peers with their continuous query indexed in p will be notified about the new publication, since the document is not distributed to any other peer in the network. This makes the placement of a peer's continuous query a crucial decision, since only the peers storing the query can be monitored for new publications, and the publication and notification process does not need any additional communication costs.

3.2 Selecting Appropriate Publishers

When a peer p receives a continuous query q from the user, p has to determine which peers or digital libraries in the network are promising candidates to satisfy the continuous query with similar documents published in the future. To do so, p issues a request to the directory service for each term contained in q, to receive per-peer statistics about each one of the terms. Statistics from the retrieved lists are gathered and a peer score is computed based on a combination of resource selection and peer behavior prediction formulas as shown by the equation below.

$$score(p, q) = (1 - \alpha) \cdot sel(p, q) + \alpha \cdot pred(p, q)$$

The tunable parameter α affects the balance between authorities (digital libraries with high $sel(p, q)$ score) and promising peers (peers with high $pred(p, q)$ score) in the final ranking. Finally, based on the total score calculated for each peer a ranking of peers is determined, and q is forwarded to the first k peers in the list, where k is a user specified parameter. The continuous query is then stored in these peers, and a notification is sent to the user every time one of the peers publishes a document that matches the query.

A continuous query needs to get updated after a specific time period. For this reason, a query contains a time-to-live (ttl) value such that the peer holding the query can remove it after the ttl is expired. The peer initiating the continuous query process requests new statistics from the directory and reselects the updated most promising peers for q.

3.3 Resource Selection

The function $sel(p, q)$ returns a score for a peer or digital library p and a query q, and is calculated using standard resource selection algorithms from the IR literature (such as simple tf-idf, CORI etc. [4,7]). Using $sel(p, q)$ we can identify authorities specialised in a topic, but as we show later this is not enough in a filtering setting. In our experimental evaluation we use a simple but efficient approach based on the peer document frequency (df) as the number of documents in the peer collection containing a term, and the maximum peer term frequency (tf^{max}) as the maximum number of term occurrences in the documents of the digital library.

3.4 Peer Behavior Prediction

Function $pred(p, q)$ returns a score for a peer p and a query q that represents how likely peer p is to publish documents containing terms found in q in the future. This prediction mechanism is based on statistical analysis of appropriate IR metrics such as the document frequency of a term. These statistics are made available through appropriate requests form the directory service, and are treated as time series data. Then an appropriate smoothing technique is used to model peer behavior and predict future publications. In our prototype implementation, we use the evolution of the peer document frequency (df) to predict a number of documents in the next period containing a certain term, and we use the progression of the collection size (cs) to predict the publishing rate. The values for all terms of the multi-term query are again summarized. The publishing of relevant documents is more accented than the dampened publishing rate.

The main idea behind predicting peer behavior or publishing behavior of digital libraries is to view the IR statistics as time series data and use statistical analysis tools to model peer behavior. Time series analysis accounts for the fact that the data points taken over time have some sort of internal structure (e.g., trend, periodicity etc.), and uses this observation to analyse older values and predict future ones. In our context this hypothesis is valid; a digital library currently crawling publishing many documents about soccer is likely to publish documents about soccer also in the future.

There are many different techniques to predict future values: moving average techniques can not cope well with trends in the data values and assign equal weights to past observations. Since both weaknesses are critical in our scenario, we use the second group of techniques, exponential smoothing techniques. We have chosen double exponential smoothing as the most appropriate method to model a peer's behavior and to predict publication activity in the future. Double exponential smoothing considers trends in contrast to single exponential smoothing. For an application with many long-lasting queries, one could use triple exponential smoothing, so that seasonality is taken into account.

3.5 Why Prediction is Necessary

A key component of the peer selection procedure is the prediction mechanism introduced here. Prediction is complementary to resource selection and the following example demonstrates its necessity in a filtering setting:

Assume that a digital library dl_1 is specialised in soccer, and thus it has become an authority in articles about soccer, although it is not publishing new documents any more. Contrary, digital library dl_2 is not specialised in soccer but currently it publishes documents concerning soccer. Now imagine a user subscribing for documents with the continuous query soccer world cup 2010 to be held in four years in South Africa. A ranking function based only on resource selection algorithms would always choose digital library dl_1 to index the user query. To get a high ranking score, and thus get selected for indexing the user profile, digital library dl_2 would have to specialise in soccer, a long procedure that is inapplicable in a filtering setting which is by definition dynamic. The fact that resource selection alone is not sufficient is even more evident when news items are published. News items have a short shelf-life, making them the worst candidate for slow-paced resource selection algorithms. The above shows the need to include better reactions in slow-paced selection algorithms, to cope with dynamics.

3.6 Directory Maintenance

As shown before, accurate per-peer statistics are necessary for the peer ranking and selection process. The MAPS system uses the same directory as Minerva to maintain the IR statistics. A conceptually global but physically distributed directory, which is layered on top of a Chord-style distributed hash table (DHT), manages aggregated information about each digital library in compact form. This way, we use the Chord DHT to partition the term space, such that every peer is responsible for the statistics of a randomized subset of terms within the directory. To maintain the IR statistics up-to-date, each one distributes per-term summaries (*posts*) of its local index along with its contact information to the global directory. The DHT determines a peer currently responsible for this term and this peer maintains a list of all posts for this term.

Notice that our architecture is network-agnostic. The directory service implemented by the peers does not have to use Chord, or any other DHT to provide this information;

our architecture allows for the usage of any type of P2P network (structured or un-structured), given that the necessary information (i.e., the per-peer IR statistics) is made available to the rest of the services. Thus, unstructured networks with gossip-based pro-tocols, hierarchical networks where the super-peers collect this type of information as well as any structured overlay can implement the directory service. Nevertheless, user the same infrastructure as the Minerva search engine enables to save message costs.

3.7 Experimental Results

First experiments with MAPS have shown promising results. We used different pub-lishing scenarios to investigate the system properties in terms of recall as the ratio of received notifications and the number of relevant published documents. We also con-sidered a benefit/cost ratio to investigate the number of filtering messages needed to get one notification. In comparison to existing exact information filtering approaches [11, 12], MAPS enhances the scalability of P2P information filtering. Especially, by exploiting peer specialization, we can achieve high recall even when indexing queries to a small fraction of publishing digital libraries.

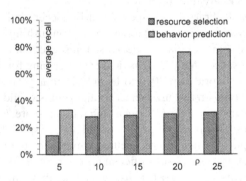

Fig. 1. Experimental Results for MAPS using Resource Selection and Behavior Prediction

Figure 1 shows the results of an experimental evaluation using 1,000 publishers and 30 two-, three- and four-term continuous queries. The peers are specialized in one of the ten categories (e.g., *Sports, Music* etc.). The chart shows the filtering effectiveness in terms of recall (ratio of total number of received notifications to the total number of published documents matching a continuous query) where each peer publishes 30 doc-uments within a specific time period and we investigate the results after ten publishing rounds. We vary the percentage ρ of publisher peers that store the continuous query. Figure 1 illustrates that the use of behavior prediction improves recall over resource selection as it manages to model more accurately the publishing behavior of peers.

4   Architectural Comparison

MinervaLight and MAPS are two different systems dealing with different issues, but both approaches have several properties in common. In this section, we provide a

	MinervaLight	MAPS
Directory	Both use the same infrastructure to store statistical information of peers. This index forms a conceptually global, but physically distributed directory with term-peer statistics layered on top of a DHT.	
Overlay network (DHT)	Past DHT, using FreePastry's routing primitives; other DHT implementations possible.	Chord DHT; other DHT implementations possible (Pastry, CAN, Tapestry…)
Query Character	<ul><li>one-time queries</li><li>multi-term queries</li><li>other queries possible</li></ul>	<ul><li>continuous queries (subscriptions)</li><li>multi-term queries</li><li>other queries possible</li></ul>
Main Problem	**Query Routing:** MinervaLight uses the directory to select the most promising peers to answer a one-time user query.	**Query Assignment:** MAPS uses the peer statistics to select the most promising peers on which a continuous query subscription is placed.
	Peer Selection: In both approaches, the selection of the most promising peers is the most critical system decision at query run-time.	
Peer Selection	MinervaLight uses the current statistics to apply resource selection methods (e.g., CORI, GlOSS, etc.).	MAPS combines resource selection methods with peer behavior prediction based on time-series analyses.
Extensions to improve Peer Selection	MinervaLight uses knowledge about correlated terms, and overlap-awareness to improve the peer selection step. Distributed PageRank improves result quality.	MAPS can be extended to consider term correlations. Other extensions are future work.
Retrieval Measurements	**Relative Recall** as the percentage of top-k results of a centralized search engine.	**Recall** as the ratio of received notifications to the total number of relevant documents published in the network
Scalability	MinervaLight scales well by only sending a query to a set of promising peers.	MAPS improves scalability of P2P information filtering in contrast to exact information filtering system.

Fig. 2. Salient features and Comparison of MinervaLight and MAPS

comparison considering architectural issues. The following table 2 surveys salient system properties of MinervaLight and MAPS in a side-by-side fashion:

5 Conclusion

In this paper, we presented a system architecture for efficient search and approximate information filtering in a distributed P2P environment of digital libraries. P2P techniques are used to build a global directory of peer statistics. This directory is used for peer selection in two scenarios: searching and approximate information filtering. To build-up the directory, the architecture can use different underlying P2P system such as Chord or Pastry.

We compared MinervaLight and MAPS in terms of various system properties: MinervaLight is a distributed P2P system to search one-time queries in a network of digital libraries. The approximate information filtering MAPS system uses the same infrastructure as MinervaLight including the distributed directory with term to peer statistics. In MAPS, peer selection determines the most promising digital library peers to publish documents of interest in the future to satisfy a continuous query. The selection process combines well-known resource selection techniques with new peer behavior prediction approaches.

References

1. Bell, T., Moffat, A.: The Design of a High Performance Information Filtering System. In: SIGIR (1996)
2. Bender, M., Michel, S., Triantafillou, P., Weikum, G., Zimmer, C.: Improving Collection Selection with overlap-awareness. In: SIGIR (2005)
3. Callan, J.: Document Filtering With Inference Networks. In: SIGIR (1996)
4. Callan, J.: Distributed Information Retrieval. Kluwer Academic Publishers, Dordrecht (2000)
5. Hull, D., Pedersen, J., Schuetze, H.: Method Combination for Document Filtering. In: SIGIR (1996)
6. Michel, S., Bender, M., Ntarmos, N., Triantafillou, P., Weikum, G., Zimmer, C.: Discovering and Exploiting Keyword and Attribute-Value Co-Occurrences to Improve P2P Routing Indices. In: CIKM (2006)
7. Nottelmann, H., Fuhr, N.: Evaluating Different Methods of Estimating Retrieval Quality for Resource Selection. In: SIGIR (2003)
8. Ratnasamy, S., Francis, P., Handley, M., Karp, R.M., Shenker, S.: A scalable Content-Addressable Network. In: SIGCOMM (2001)
9. Stoica, I., Morris, R., Karger, D.R., Kaashoek, M.F., Balakrishnan, H.: Chord: A scalable Peer-to-Peer Lookup Service for Internet Applications. In: SIGCOMM (2001)
10. Tang, C., Xu, Z.: pFilter: Global Information Filtering and Dissemination using structured Overlay Networks. In: FTDCS (2003)
11. Tryfonopoulos, C., Idreos, S., Koubarakis, M.: LibraRing: An Architecture for Distributed Digital Libraries Based on DHTs. In: Rauber, A., Christodoulakis, S., Tjoa, A.M. (eds.) ECDL 2005. LNCS, vol. 3652, Springer, Heidelberg (2005)
12. Tryfonopoulos, C., Idreos, S., Koubarakis, M.: Publish/subscribe functionality in IR environments using structured overlay networks. In: SIGIR (2005)
13. Bender, M., Michel, S., Zimmer, C., Weikum, G.: Bookmark-driven query routing in Peer-to-Peer Web Search. In: P2PIR (2004)
14. Luxenburger, J., Weikum, G.: Exploiting community behavior for enhanced link analysis and Web search. In: Zhou, X., Su, S., Papazoglou, M.M.P., Orlowska, M.E., Jeffery, K.G. (eds.) WISE 2004. LNCS, vol. 3306, Springer, Heidelberg (2004)
15. Crespo, A., Garcia-Molina, H.: Routing indices for Peer-to-Peer systems. In: ICDCS (2002)
16. Cuenca-Acuna, F.M., Peery, C., Martin, R.P., Nguyen, T.D.: PlanetP: Using gossiping to build content addressable Peer-to-Peer Information sharing communities. In: HPDC (2003)
17. Huebsch, R., Chun, B.N., Hellerstein, J.M., Loo, B.T., Maniatis, P., Roscoe, T., Shenker, S., Stoica, I., Yumerefendi, A.R.: The architecture of Pier: an internet-scale query processor. In: CIDR (2005)
18. Bender, M., Michel, S., Triantafillou, P., Weikum, G., Zimmer, C.: Minerva: Collaborative P2P Search. In: VLDB (2005)

19. Bookmark-Induced Gathering of Information with Adaptive Classification into Personalized Ontologies. `http://www.mpi-inf.mpg.de/units/ag5/software/bingo/`
20. Theobald, M., Schenkel, R., Weikum, G.: An efficient and versatile query engine for topX search. In: VLDB (2005)
21. Li, J., Loo, B., Hellerstein, J., Kaashoek, M., Karger, D., Morris, R.: On the Feasibility of Peer-to-Peer Web Indexing and Search. In: Kaashoek, M.F., Stoica, I. (eds.) IPTPS 2003. LNCS, vol. 2735, Springer, Heidelberg (2003)
22. Rowstron, A., Druschel, P.: Pastry: Scalable, Decentralized Object Location, and Routing for Large-Scale Peer-to-Peer Systems. In: Guerraoui, R. (ed.) Middleware 2001. LNCS, vol. 2218, Springer, Heidelberg (2001)
23. Parreira, J.X., Donato, D., Michel, S., Weikum, G.: Efficient and decentralized PageRank approximation in a Peer-to-Peer Web search network. In: VLDB (2006)
24. Bender, M., Crecelius, T., Michel, S., Parreira, J.X.: P2P Web Search: Make it Light, Make it Fly (Demo). In: CIDR (2007)

Management of and Access to Virtual Electronic Health Records

M. Springmann[1], L. Bischofs[2], P.M. Fischer[3], H.-J. Schek[4], H. Schuldt[1], U. Steffens[2], and R. Vogl[5]

[1] Database and Information Systems Group, University of Basel, Switzerland
[2] OFFIS Oldenburg, Germany
[3] Institute of Information Systems, ETH Zurich, Switzerland
[4] University of Konstanz, Germany
[5] HITT - health information technologies tirol, Innsbruck, Austria

Abstract. Digital Libraries (DLs) in eHealth are composed of electronic artefacts that are generated and owned by different healthcare providers. A major characteristic of eHealth DLs is that information is under the control of the organisation where data has been produced. The electronic health record (EHR) of patients therefore consists of a set of distributed artefacts and cannot be materialised for organisational reasons. Rather, the EHR is a virtual entity. The virtual integration of an EHR is done by encompassing services provided by specialised application systems into processes. This paper reports, from an application point of view, on national and European attempts to standardise electronic health EHR. From a technical perspective, the paper addresses how services can be made available in a distributed way, how distributed P2P infrastructures for the management of EHRs can be evaluated, and how novel content-based access can be provided for multimedia EHRs.

1   Introduction

eHealth Digital Libraries contain electronic artefacts that are generated by different healthcare providers. An important observation is that this information is not stored at one central instance but under the control of the organization where data has been produced. The electronic health record (EHR) of patients therefore consists of a set of distributed artefacts and cannot be materialized for organizational reasons. Rather, the EHR is a virtual entity and has to be generated by composing the required artefacts each time it is accessed. The virtual integration of an EHR is done by encompassing services provided by specialized application systems into processes. A process to access a virtual EHR encompasses all the services needed to locate the different artefacts, to make data from the different healthcare providers available, to perform the format conversations needed, and to present the result to a user. This requires an infrastructure that is highly dependable and reliable. Physicians must be given the guarantee that the system is always available. Moreover, the infrastructure has to allow for the transparent access to distributed data, to provide a high degree of scalability,

C. Thanos, F. Borri, and L. Candela (Eds.): Digital Libraries: R&D, LNCS 4877, pp. 338–347, 2007.
© Springer-Verlag Berlin Heidelberg 2007

and to efficiently schedule the access to computationally intensive services by applying sophisticated load balancing strategies. Physicians need information immediately in order to make vital decisions. Long response times due to a high system load cannot be tolerated. An example is content-based similarity search across a potentially large set of documents which requires the availability of several building blocks, some of them being highly computationally intensive, which have to be combined to processes.

This paper gives an overview on various aspects of management and access to virtual EHRs and research that have been carried out in this field within the last three years. The paper is organized as follows: Section 2 describes health@net, a novel national Austrian eHealth IT infrastructure which allows the access to health records across collaborating institutions. Section 3 explains how complex processes spanning over several institutions can be modelled and executed and thus, perform all required actions to convert, aggregate, or anonymize data of the virtual EHRs. Section 4 shows how similarity search technology can be used to enhance retrieval of EHRs. Since security and permissions are essential for such sensitive data as health records, Section 5 gives an outlook on how the behaviour of such distributed peer-to-peer can be simulated. Section 6 concludes.

2   Health@net

Establishing EHRs in hospitals has been the central issue for hospital IT management in the past more than ten years. In the industrialized countries, a very good coverage with hospital IT systems for documentation of patient related data and their integration to form a common EHR has now been reached (for the European situation, see the HINE study 2004, as presented in the proceedings of the EU high level conference eHealth2006: Rising to the challenges of eHealth across Europe's regions). Currently, the main issue for the European countries, as called for by the European eHealth action plan of 2004, is the establishment of national EHR systems that allow for the standardized exchange of electronic health data between healthcare providers with the vision of European interoperability. In view of this, the Austrian Ministry of Health (MoH) has initiated the Austrian eHealth Initiative in early 2005 – a stakeholders group which delivered the Austrian eHealth strategy to the Austrian Ministry of Health at the end of 2005. The health@net project [1] did very actively and influentially contribute to the formulation of the strategy and to subsequent consultations with the MoH in the course of 2006, ensuring the elaborate Digital Library ideas for distributed archive systems and high level security mechanisms were maintained in that strategy and implemented in a subsequent feasibility study commissioned by the MoH. The health@net team has developed a reference implementation [2] of its distributed secure architecture (see Figure 1) for shared EHRs with special focus on secure web services with service and user role based access control (RBAC) relying on the SECTET toolkit developed by the project partners at the Institute for Software Engineering at Innsbruck University. Pilot projects utilizing this architecture for topical EHR applications (e. g., online access to health

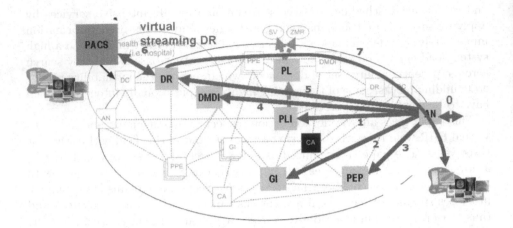

Fig. 1. The health@net Architecture and its Utlization for Access to Multimedia Documents Across Healthcare Organizations. The Functional Components are realized as Web Services (AN: Access Node; DMDI: Distributed Meta Data Index; DR: Document Repository; PL: Ratient Lookup; PLI: Patient Lookup Index; GI: Global Index; PEP: Policy Enforcement Point).

record data between the hospital trusts in Vienna (KAV) and Tirol (TILAK); a haemophilia register for quality insurance and epidemiological studies; an autistic children therapy register; a portal for report access by a group of general practitioners) have been commissioned and are currently in implementation. A certification of the compliance with IHE (integrating the Healthcare Enterprise) has been prepared.

3   XL System

XL [3] is a system which provides an environment for definition, composition, and deployment of Web services on a set of different platforms. XL Web services are expressed by the XL language. XL is specifically designed for processing XML data as the most common data representation within the Web service domain. The XL language uses the XQuery/XSLT 2.0 types throughout the whole system, and further uses XQuery expressions (including XML Updates) for processing XML. XML message passing in XL is based on the XML SOAP (Web Services) standard.

A full implementation of XL has been available since 2002. There is also comprehensive tool support: There is an Eclipse Plug-in for XL which includes syntax-driven editing, debugging, and simple deployment. XL is deployable on any Platform supporting at least Java 1.3, including application servers and gateways to existing systems, personal computers of physicians and scientific personnel as well as patients, and even embedded devices like PDAs and mobile phones.

Virtual EHRs need to deal with distributed artefacts of medical data (from different healthcare providers, health insurances, public authorities and the patients themselves) that cannot be materialized due to organizational reasons or privacy concerns. For this reason, it is necessary to perform tasks as: (1) locate the different artefacts, (2) make data from the different healthcare providers available, (3) perform the format conversions needed, (4) aggregate/anonymize the data, and (5) finally present the result to a user. XL can contribute solutions to those requirements, if the system is realized in the context of web services.

Fig. 2. Screen-shot of the XL system

The strengths of XL are in the areas of high-level format conversions, aggregation/ anonymization and presentation of results. Locating services that provide relevant artifacts is possible using either UDDI or more content-oriented services directories. XL might also be used to make data from the individual providers available as web services, but needs to be complemented by additional software for low-level format conversion and feature extraction. Results can be presented as web pages (HTML / XHTML) on different devices using built-in components. Orchestration and composition of services (e.g., running workflows defined by BPEL) allows for quick and easy development of new services based on open standards.

As a demonstrator for the usage of XL in the context of Virtual EHRs, the rapid development of web service to integrate some medical data will be shown.

The service demonstrated here collects information about the patient age for cases of a given illness from two health providers which make that data available as web services. The data transfer format and the call parameters are different, however. The service retrieves all the necessary information from all the services and transforms it into a common result document that only contains the age information for each cases (presumably for reasons of anonymity).

To keep the demonstrator short and concise, no advanced features of web service interaction and data manipulation are shown here. They can be added to the example easily when required. The development is done using the XL platform and the development environment XLipse, as shown in Figure 2.

To start developing, a new XL Project needs to be created, following the usual Eclipse approach. To this project, a file with the name find_illness.xl is added. The relevant service and operation signature are added. Inside the operation, the variable for the case list is initialized as an XML fragment. The first web service (a hospital) is called; this one supports a parameter to specify the illness. The result is stored in the variable $hospital_1$. The age information for each of the hospitalizations in that variable are now added to the case list. The second provider only allows querying all cases after a given date, so all cases after a date in the past a retrieved into $healthProvider_2$. Since this provider also does not have a strict schema, we retrieve all reports off illnesses (regardless of their position in the document) and keep those that have a diagnosis corresponding to the requested illness. The age information for those cases is then added to the case list. Finally, the case list is returned.

4   Similarity Search for EHRs

Electronic health records have become a very important patient-centred entity in health care management. They represent complex documents that comprise a wide diversity of patient-related information, like basic administrative data (patient's name, address, date of birth, name of physicians, hospitals, etc.), billing details (name of insurance, billing codes, etc.), and a variety of medical information (symptoms, diagnoses, treatment, medication, X-ray images, etc.). Each item is of a dedicated media type, like structured alphanumeric data (e.g., patient name, address, billing information, laboratory values, documentation codes, etc.), semi-structured text (symptoms description, physician's notes, etc.), images (X-ray, CT, MRT, images for documentation in dermatology, etc.), video (endoscopy, sonography, etc.), time series (cardiograms, EEG, respiration, pulse rate, blood pressure, etc.), and possibly others, like DNA sequence data. State-of-the-art medical information systems aggregate massive amounts of data in EHRs. Its exploitation, however, is mainly restricted to accounting and billing purposes, leaving aside most medical information. In particular, similarity search based on complex document matching is out of scope for today's medical information systems.

We believe that efficient and effective matching of patient records forms the rewarding foundation for a large application variety. Data mining applications that rest upon our patient record matching approach will foster clinical research and enhanced therapy, in general. Specifically, our approach allows for effective comparison of similar cases to (1) shorten necessary treatments, (2) improve diagnoses, and (3) ensure the proper medication to improve patients' well-being and reduce cost. This can be achieved, by no longer resting entirely on exact matching, but employing the paradigm of similarity search to the content of EHRs. In particular, health records at present contain a vast number of medical images, stored in electronic form, that captures information about the patients health and progress of treatments. This information is only used indirectly for retrieval in the form of the metadata stored in the DICOM header in PACS system or the diagnosis of a radiologist.

State-of-the-art image retrieval technology can assist the retrieval by using the medical images for search in addition to traditional search approaches. One example of such a retrieval system is ISIS(Interactive SImilarity Search), which is a prototype application for information retrieval in multimedia collections built at ETH Zürich [4] and has been extended at UMIT and the University of Basel. It supports content-based retrieval of images, audio and video content, and the combination of any of these media types with sophisticated text retrieval [5].

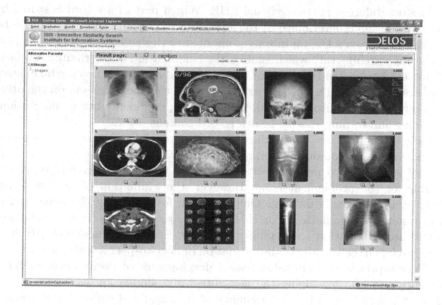

Fig. 3. ISIS Demonstrator

A set with more than 50,000 medical images, which sum up to roughly 4.65 gigabytes of data, has been inserted and indexed with the ISIS system. The files originate from four different collections. All of them have been used for the Medical Image Retrieval Challenge for the Cross Language Evaluation Forum 2005 (ImageCLEFmed 2005, http://ir.ohsu.edu/image/ [6]). The results of our experiments as well as the overall experience described for ImageCLEFmed is that the combined retrieval using visual and textual information improves the retrieval quality compared to queries using only one source of information, either visual or textual.

A variation of this setting is the automatic classification of medical images. This approach is also addressed as a task in ImageCLEF and one goal in this approach in clinical practice is, to be able check the plausibility e.g., of DICOM header information and other kind of automatically or manually entered metadata in order to reduce errors. The recent activities performed at University o

Basel in this area focused on the improvement of the retrieval quality and also the retrieval time for such classification tasks using the ImageCLEF benchmark. As shown in [7], a long running classification task could be speed up by factors in the range of 3.5 to 4.9 using an early termination strategy and by using parallel execution on 8 CPUs even to a total speed up of 37.34.

5   RealPeer Simulation Environment

eHealth Digital Libraries connect a number of different collaborating institutions which store different parts of virtual EHR. Which part of a record is stored by which institution is determined by the institutions' role concerning their patients' medical care. From a Digital Library point of view this calls for a flexible support by a system architecture which enables the combination of distributed artefacts against the background of different organisational and topical contexts, offering simple and fast access to physicians in charge on the one hand and on the other hand guaranteeing autonomy and, in particular, confidentiality to institutions producing and owning specific health record content.

Bischofs and Steffens [8] introduces a new approach for a class of peer-to-peer systems based on combined overlay networks, which are able to map organisational structures to peer-to-peer systems and which are therefore especially suitable for the problem at hand. However, the evaluation of such new, not yet existing systems is difficult. One approach for analysing the behaviour of such systems is simulation. For this purpose, the time discrete, event-based peer-to-peer simulation tool eaSim [9] and the RealPeer Framework [10] have been developed. eaSim allows the evaluation of peer-to-peer search methods and RealPeer supports the simulation-based development of peer-to-peer systems. Currently, we are developing the new integrated simulation environment *RealPeer SE*, which joins the functionality of eaSim and RealPeer. Additionally, RealPeer SE resolves some drawbacks of the eaSim simulation model and allows the simulation-based development of peer-to-peer systems with combined overlays. Unlike other peer-to-peer simulators which primarily focus on concrete systems, RealPeer SE follows a generic approach considering different overlay topologies and search methods.

The graphical user interface of RealPeer SE (see Figure 4) assists the user throughout the simulation process. The overlays of the simulation model are visualized by using the Java Universal Network/Graph Framework (JUNG). Predefined metrics help understanding the dynamic behaviour and efficiency of the simulated peer-to-peer system. These metrics are visualized by using the JFreeChart library. Figure 5 contains an example of a simulation result demonstrating four different metrics concerning a search in a peer-to-peer system with the following combined overlays. The first overlay is based on Chord [11], which builds a ring topology of peers and allows inter-organisational queries. The second overlay contains the relationships within organisational units (e.g., institutions) to allow an intra-organisational breadth-first search. Both overlays are interconnected through the physical network so that messages can be routed

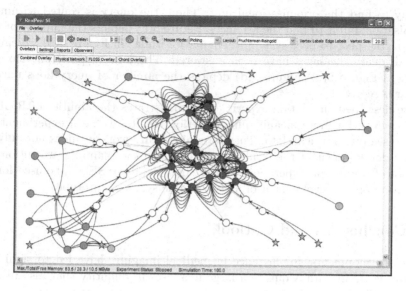

Fig. 4. Graphical user interface of the RealPeer Simulation Environment

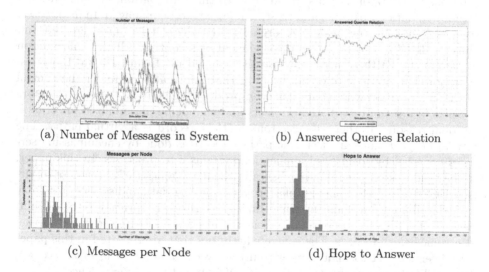

(a) Number of Messages in System   (b) Answered Queries Relation

(c) Messages per Node   (d) Hops to Answer

Fig. 5. Simulation results of an experiment with 100 search queries in a peer-to-peer system with 250 nodes

from one overlay to another. In the simulation experiment described in this paper, 100 search queries have been started from a random node at a random point in time in a peer-to-peer system containing 250 nodes. The queries search for artefacts of type *File* (e.g., EHR) within a specific organisational unit (e.g., an institution). Therefore the query message is first routed within the Chord overlay to find the organisational unit. Then, the query is routed within the organisational unit to find the artefacts. Figure 5(a) depicts the number of messages in the peer-to-peer system at simulation time. In Figure 5(b) we can see that all query messages have been answered. The load of particular nodes is shown in Figure 5(c). Figure 5(d) depicts the number of query hops until an answer is received.

The described simulation experiment demonstrates the abilities of RealPeer SE. However, for more meaningful simulation results, we need experiment settings based on empirical data. Therefore, our future work includes not only the further development of the RealPeer SE but also the planning, execution and analysis of simulation experiments. After that, RealPeer SE can be used for the simulation-based development of an executable system prototype.

6   Conclusions and Outlook

Recent developments, for instance in medical imaging, have led to significant improvements in data acquisition large increases in quantity (but also in quality) of medical data. Similarly, in health monitoring, the proliferation of sensor technology has strongly facilitated the continuous generation of vast amounts of physiological data of patients. In addition to this information, more traditional structured data on patients and treatments needs to be managed. In most cases, data is owned by the healthcare organization where it has been created and thus needs to be stored under the organization's control. All this information is part of the EHRs of a patient, thus is included in eHealth Digital Libraries. A major characteristic of eHealth DLs is that information is under the control of the organization where data has been produced. The EHR patients therefore consists of a set of distributed artefacts and cannot be materialized for organizational reasons. Rather, the electronic patient record is a virtual entity. The virtual integration of an electronic patient record is done by encompassing services provided by specialized application systems into processes. In this paper, we have addressed several major issues in the management of and access to virtual EHRs. First, this includes platforms for making data and services available in a distributed environment while taking security and privacy into account. Second, it addresses support for efficient and effective search in these virtual electronic health records. The concrete activities that are reported in this paper have been subject to joint work within the task *Management of and Access to Virtual Electronic Health Records* of the DELOS network of excellence.

References

1. Schabetsberger, T., Ammenwerth, E., Breu, R., Hoerbst, A., Goebel, G., Penz, R., Schindelwig, K., Toth, H., Vogl, R., Wozak, F.: E-health approach to link-up actors in the health care system of austria. Stud Health Technol. Inform. 124 (2006)
2. Vogl, R., Wozak, F., Breu, M., Penz, R., Schabetsberger, T., Wurz, M.: Architecture for a distributed national electronic health record system in austria. In: Proceedings of EuroPACS 2006, June 15-17, 2006, Trondheim (Norway) (2006)

3. Florescu, D., Grünhagen, A., Kossmann, D.: Xl: a platform for web services. In: CIDR (2003)
4. Mlivoncic, M., Schuler, C., Türker, C.: Hyperdatabase infrastructure for management and search of multimedia collections. In: di Pula, S.M. (ed.) Digital Library Architectures: Peer-to-Peer, Grid, and Service-Orientation, Pre-proceedings of the Sixth Thematic Workshop of the EU Network of Excellence DELOS, June 24-25, 2004, Cagliari,Italy, pp. 25–36 (2004)
5. Springmann, M.: A novel approach for compound document matching. Bulletin of the IEEE Technical Committee on Digital Libraries (TCDL) 2(2) (2006)
6. Clough, P., Müller, H., Deselaers, T., Grubinger, M., Lehmann, T.M., Jensen, J.R., Hersh, W.R.: The clef 2005 cross-language image retrieval track. In: Peters, C., Gey, F.C., Gonzalo, J., Müller, H., Jones, G.J.F., Kluck, M., Magnini, B., de Rijke, M., Giampiccolo, D. (eds.) CLEF 2005. LNCS, vol. 4022, pp. 535–557. Springer, Heidelberg (2006)
7. Springmann, M., Schuldt, H.: Speeding up idm without degradation of retrieval quality. In: Nardi, A., Peters, C. (eds.) Working Notes of the CLEF Workshop 2007 (September 2007)
8. Bischofs, L., Steffens, U.: Organisation-oriented Super-Peer Networks for Digital Libraries. In: Türker, C., Agosti, M., Schek, H.-J. (eds.) Peer-to-Peer, Grid, and Service-Orientation in Digital Library Architectures. LNCS, vol. 3664, pp. 45–62. Springer, Heidelberg (2005)
9. Bischofs, L., Giesecke, S., Gottschalk, M., Hasselbring, W., Warns, T., Willer, S.: Comparative evaluation of dependability characteristics for peer-to-peer architectural styles by simulation. Journal of Systems and Software (February 2006)
10. Hildebrandt, D., Bischofs, L., Hasselbring, W.: Realpeer - a framework for simulation-based development of peer-to-peer systems. In: PDP 2007. Proceedings of the 15th Euromicro International Conference on Parallel, Distributed and Network-based Processing, Naples, Italy, February 7-9, 2007, pp. 490–497. IEEE, Los Alamitos (2007)
11. Stoica, I., Morris, R., Karger, D., Kaashoek, M.F., Balakrishnan, H.: Chord - a scalable peer-to-peer lookup service for internet applications. In: Proceedings of the 2001 Conference on Applications, Technologies, Architectures, and Protocols for Computer Communications, pp. 149–160. ACM Press, San Diego, California, USA (2001)

Author Index

Lecture Notes in Computer Science

Sublibrary 3: Information Systems and Application, incl. Internet/Web and HCI

For information about Vols. 1– 4480
please contact your bookseller or Springer

Vol. 4690: Y. Ioannidis, B. Novikov, B. Rachev (Eds.), Advances in Databases and Information Systems. XIII, 377 pages. 2007.

Vol. 4675: L. Kovács, N. Fuhr, C. Meghini (Eds.), Research and Advanced Technology for Digital Libraries. XVII, 585 pages. 2007.

Vol. 4674: Y. Luo (Ed.), Cooperative Design, Visualization, and Engineering. XIII, 431 pages. 2007.

Vol. 4663: C. Baranauskas, P. Palanque, J. Abascal, S.D.J. Barbosa (Eds.), Human-Computer Interaction – INTERACT 2007, Part II. XXXIII, 735 pages. 2007.

Vol. 4662: C. Baranauskas, P. Palanque, J. Abascal, S.D.J. Barbosa (Eds.), Human-Computer Interaction – INTERACT 2007, Part I. XXXIII, 637 pages. 2007.

Vol. 4658: T. Enokido, L. Barolli, M. Takizawa (Eds.), Network-Based Information Systems. XIII, 544 pages. 2007.

Vol. 4656: M.A. Wimmer, J. Scholl, Å. Grönlund (Eds.), Electronic Government. XIV, 450 pages. 2007.

Vol. 4655: G. Psaila, R. Wagner (Eds.), E-Commerce and Web Technologies. VII, 229 pages. 2007.

Vol. 4654: I.-Y. Song, J. Eder, T.M. Nguyen (Eds.), Data Warehousing and Knowledge Discovery. XVI, 482 pages. 2007.

Vol. 4653: R. Wagner, N. Revell, G. Pernul (Eds.), Database and Expert Systems Applications. XXII, 907 pages. 2007.

Vol. 4636: G. Antoniou, U. Aßmann, C. Baroglio, S. Decker, N. Henze, P.-L. Patranjan, R. Tolksdorf (Eds.), Reasoning Web. IX, 345 pages. 2007.

Vol. 4611: J. Indulska, J. Ma, L.T. Yang, T. Ungerer, J. Cao (Eds.), Ubiquitous Intelligence and Computing. XXIII, 1257 pages. 2007.

Vol. 4607: L. Baresi, P. Fraternali, G.-J. Houben (Eds.), Web Engineering. XVI, 576 pages. 2007.

Vol. 4606: A. Pras, M. van Sinderen (Eds.), Dependable and Adaptable Networks and Services. XIV, 149 pages. 2007.

Vol. 4605: D. Papadias, D. Zhang, G. Kollios (Eds.), Advances in Spatial and Temporal Databases. X, 479 pages. 2007.

Vol. 4602: S. Barker, G.-J. Ahn (Eds.), Data and Applications Security XXI. X, 291 pages. 2007.

Vol. 4601: S. Spaccapietra, P. Atzeni, F. Fages, M.-S. Hacid, M. Kifer, J. Mylopoulos, B. Pernici, P. Shvaiko, J. Trujillo, I. Zaihrayeu (Eds.), Journal on Data Semantics IX. XV, 197 pages. 2007.

Vol. 4592: Z. Kedad, N. Lammari, E. Métais, F. Meziane, Y. Rezgui (Eds.), Natural Language Processing and Information Systems. XIV, 442 pages. 2007.

Vol. 4587: R. Cooper, J. Kennedy (Eds.), Data Management. XIII, 259 pages. 2007.

Vol. 4577: N. Sebe, Y. Liu, Y.-t. Zhuang, T.S. Huang (Eds.), Multimedia Content Analysis and Mining. XIII, 513 pages. 2007.

Vol. 4568: T. Ishida, S. R. Fussell, P. T. J. M. Vossen (Eds.), Intercultural Collaboration. XIII, 395 pages. 2007.

Vol. 4566: M.J. Dainoff (Ed.), Ergonomics and Health Aspects of Work with Computers. XVIII, 390 pages. 2007.

Vol. 4564: D. Schuler (Ed.), Online Communities and Social Computing. XVII, 520 pages. 2007.

Vol. 4563: R. Shumaker (Ed.), Virtual Reality. XXII, 762 pages. 2007.

Vol. 4561: V.G. Duffy (Ed.), Digital Human Modeling. XXIII, 1068 pages. 2007.

Vol. 4560: N. Aykin (Ed.), Usability and Internationalization, Part II. XVIII, 576 pages. 2007.

Vol. 4559: N. Aykin (Ed.), Usability and Internationalization, Part I. XVIII, 661 pages. 2007.

Vol. 4558: M.J. Smith, G. Salvendy (Eds.), Human Interface and the Management of Information, Part II. XXIII, 1162 pages. 2007.

Vol. 4557: M.J. Smith, G. Salvendy (Eds.), Human Interface and the Management of Information, Part I. XXII, 1030 pages. 2007.

Vol. 4541: T. Okadome, T. Yamazaki, M. Makhtari (Eds.), Pervasive Computing for Quality of Life Enhancement. IX, 248 pages. 2007.

Vol. 4537: K.C.-C. Chang, W. Wang, L. Chen, C.A. Ellis, C.-H. Hsu, A.C. Tsoi, H. Wang (Eds.), Advances in Web and Network Technologies, and Information Management. XXIII, 707 pages. 2007.

Vol. 4531: J. Indulska, K. Raymond (Eds.), Distributed Applications and Interoperable Systems. XI, 337 pages. 2007.

Vol. 4526: M. Malek, M. Reitenspieß, A. van Moorsel (Eds.), Service Availability. X, 155 pages. 2007.

Vol. 4524: M. Marchiori, J.Z. Pan, C.d.S. Marie (Eds.), Web Reasoning and Rule Systems. XI, 382 pages. 2007.

Vol. 4519: E. Franconi, M. Kifer, W. May (Eds.), The Semantic Web: Research and Applications. XVIII, 830 pages. 2007.

Vol. 4518: N. Fuhr, M. Lalmas, A. Trotman (Eds.), Comparative Evaluation of XML Information Retrieval Systems. XII, 554 pages. 2007.

Vol. 4508: M.-Y. Kao, X.-Y. Li (Eds.), Algorithmic Aspects in Information and Management. VIII, 428 pages. 2007.

Vol. 4506: D. Zeng, I. Gotham, K. Komatsu, C. Lynch, M. Thurmond, D. Madigan, B. Lober, J. Kvach, H. Chen (Eds.), Intelligence and Security Informatics: Biosurveillance. XI, 234 pages. 2007.

Vol. 4505: G. Dong, X. Lin, W. Wang, Y. Yang, J.X. Yu (Eds.), Advances in Data and Web Management. XXII, 896 pages. 2007.

Vol. 4504: J. Huang, R. Kowalczyk, Z. Maamar, D. Martin, I. Müller, S. Stoutenburg, K.P. Sycara (Eds.), Service-Oriented Computing: Agents, Semantics, and Engineering. X, 175 pages. 2007.

Vol. 4500: N.A. Streitz, A.D. Kameas, I. Mavrommati (Eds.), The Disappearing Computer. XVIII, 304 pages. 2007.

Vol. 4495: J. Krogstie, A. Opdahl, G. Sindre (Eds.), Advanced Information Systems Engineering. XVI, 606 pages. 2007.